Frommer's®

Las Vegas

D1022783

Here's what the critics say about Frommer's:

"The smartest, most complete, most frank guide to Las Vegas that I've seen. I prize it as a reference and lend it to reporters who are planning a Vegas vacation."

—Denver Post

♦

"Amazingly easy to use. Very portable, very complete."

—Booklist

♦

"The only mainstream guide to list specific prices. The Walter Cronkite of guidebooks—with all that implies."

—Travel & Leisure

♦

"Complete, concise, and filled with useful information."

—New York Daily News

♦

"Hotel information is close to encyclopedic."

—Des Moines Sunday Register

Other Great Guides for Your Trip:

Frommer's Portable Las Vegas

Unofficial Guide to Las Vegas

The Complete Idiot's Guide to Las Vegas

Frommer's® 99

Las Vegas

by Mary Herczog

MACMILLAN • USA

ABOUT THE AUTHOR

Mary Herczog lives in Los Angeles and works in the film industry. She is the author of *Frommer's New Orleans,* and contributed to *Frommer's Los Angeles.* She still isn't sure when to hold and when to hit in blackjack.

ACKNOWLEDGMENTS

Very special thanks to Rick Garman.

Thanks to Dan Glover, Robin Ochiba-Campbell, Carolyn McCue, An Dragavon, John Griego, Cheryl Ladd-Campbell, Thomas Lynch, Steve Hochman (for Saltines and Jell-O), Leslie Ransdall, Mr. Wayne Newton, *Scope* magazine, and especially to everyone at Frommer's for their much appreciated patience this past year.

MACMILLAN TRAVEL

A Simon & Schuster Macmillan Company
1633 Broadway
New York, NY 10019

Find us online at **www.frommers.com**

ISBN 0-02-862324-X
ISSN 0899-3262

Editor: Dan Glover
Production Editor: Robyn Burnett
Photo Editor: Richard Fox
Design by Michele Laseau
Digital Cartography by Raffaele DeGenarro, Jim Moore, & John Decamilllis
Page Creation by John Bitter, Toi Davis, & Natalie Evans

SPECIAL SALES

Bulk purchases (10+ copies) of Frommer's and selected Macmillan travel guides are available to corporations, organizations, mail-order catalogs, institutions, and charities at special discounts, and can be customized to suit individual needs. For more information write to Special Sales, Macmillan General Reference, 1633 Broadway, New York, NY 10019.

Manufactured in the United States of America

Contents

List of Maps

AN INVITATION TO THE READER

In researching this book, we discovered many wonderful places—hotels, restaurants, shops, and more. We're sure you'll find others. Please tell us about them, so we can share the information with your fellow travelers in upcoming editions. If you were disappointed with a recommendation, we'd love to know that, too. Please write to:

Frommer's Las Vegas
Macmillan Travel
1633 Broadway
New York, NY 10019

AN ADDITIONAL NOTE

Please be advised that travel information is subject to change at any time—this is especially true of prices. We therefore suggest that you write or call ahead for confirmation when making your travel plans. The authors, editors, and publisher cannot be held responsible for the experiences of readers while traveling. Your safety is important to us, however, so we encourage you to stay alert and be aware of your surroundings. Keep a close eye on cameras, purses, and wallets, all favorite targets of thieves and pickpockets.

WHAT THE SYMBOLS MEAN

✪ Frommer's Favorites

Our favorite places and experiences—outstanding for quality, value, or both.

The following abbreviations are used for credit cards:

AE	American Express	ER	enRoute
CB	Carte Blanche	JCB	Japan Credit Bank
DC	Diners Club	MC	MasterCard
DISC	Discover	V	Visa

FIND FROMMER'S ONLINE

Arthur Frommer's Outspoken Encyclopedia of Travel (www.frommers.com) offers more than 6,000 pages of up-to-the-minute travel information—including the latest bargains and candid, personal articles updated daily by Arthur Frommer himself. No other Web site offers such comprehensive and timely coverage of the world of travel.

Introducing Las Vegas

The point about [Las Vegas], which both its critics and its admirers overlook, is that it's wonderful and awful *simultaneously*. So one loves it and detests it at the same time.
—David Spanier, *Welcome to the Pleasure Dome:*
Inside Las Vegas

As often as you might have seen it on TV or in a movie, there is nothing that prepares you for that first sight of Las Vegas. The skyline is hyperreality, a mélange of the Statue of Liberty, a giant lion, a pyramid and a Sphinx, and preternaturally glittering buildings. At night, it's so bright you can actually get disoriented—and also get a sensory overload that can reduce you to hapless tears or fits of giggles. And that's without setting foot inside a casino, where the shouts from the craps tables, the crash of coins from the slots, and general roar combine into either the greatest adrenaline rush of your life or the eleventh pit of hell.

Las Vegas is a true original; there is nothing like it in America or arguably the world. In other cities, hotels are built near the major attractions. Here, the hotels *are* the major attractions. For that matter, what other city has a skyline made up almost entirely of buildings from other cities' skylines? Instead of historical codes to follow, builders in Vegas have to worry about the height of the roller coaster in their hotel.

The result is that once you go to Vegas, you will want to come back again, if only to make sure you didn't dream it all. It's not just the casinos with their nonstop action and sound; it's not the almost blinding lights; it's not the buildings that seek to replicate some other reality (Rome, New York, ancient Egypt); it's not the mountains of shrimp at the buffets, the wedding chapels that will gladly unite two total strangers in holy wedlock, the promise of free money. It's the whole package. It's the megabucks slots. It's Frank and Dino and Sammy. It's Elvis—the Fat Years. It's volcanoes and white tigers and cocktail waitresses dressed in Roman togas. It's cheesy and sleazy and artificial and wholly, completely unique. It's wonderful. It's awful. It's wonderfully awful and awfully wonderful. Love it, loathe it, or both, no one has ambivalent feelings about Vegas.

Las Vegas can be whatever the visitor wants, and for a few days, the visitor can be whatever he or she wants. Just be prepared to leave all touchstones with reality behind. Just for this time, you will rise at noon and gorge on endless amounts of rich food at 3am. You will watch your money grow or (more probably) shrink. You will watch a volcano explode and pirates fight the British. And after a while, it will all seem pretty normal. This is not a cultural vacation, okay? Save the thoughts of museums and historical sights for the real New York, Egypt, and Rome. Vegas is about fun. Go have some. Go have too much. It won't be hard.

The Vegas of the Rat Pack years, classic old Las Vegas, does not exist anymore. Even as ancient civilizations are replicated, "old" in Vegas terms is anything over a decade. Indeed, by the end of 1998, thanks to teardowns and renovations, there will be nothing original left on the Strip. In a way that is both admirable and ghastly, and also part of what makes Vegas so *Vegas*. What other city can completely shed its skin in such a short amount of time?

But as much as one might mourn the loss of such landmarks as the Sands and regret the upcoming change in the facade of Caesars Palace, one has to admit that time marches on, and Vegas has to keep pace. Nostalgia for the vanished does not mean you can't enjoy what turns up in its place. Even as you might sneer at the sheer gaudy tastelessness of it all, if you stop to think about it, what's out there in plain view is undeniably remarkable.

And when it's all lit up at night—well, even those who have lived here for years agree there is nothing like the sight of the Strip in all its evening glory. "It still takes my breath away, even after all this time," says one longtime resident. Everything is in lights in Vegas: hotels, casinos, 7-Elevens, the airport parking garage. Stand still long enough, and they'll probably cover you in neon.

Oh, the gambling? Yes, there is plenty of that. Which is much like saying there is plenty of sand at the beach. Let's not kid ourselves; that's the main attraction of Vegas. The rest—the buffets, the shows, the cartoonish buildings—is so much window dressing to lure you and your money to the city. But even a nongambler can have a perfectly fine time in Vegas, though the lure of countless slot machines has tempted even the most puritan of souls in their day.

Unfortunately, the days of an inexpensive Las Vegas vacation are gone. Once, the hotels used to undercharge for everything, figuring this made the guest feel more inclined to drop bigger bucks at the tables, and feel better about it. The modern hotels don't seem to care how they get your money, and besides, they have big construction costs to recoup. The cheap buffets and meal deals still exist, as do some cut-rate rooms, but both are likely to prove the old adage about getting what you pay for. If all you are looking for is fuel and a place to catch a quick nap, they'll do just fine. Be prepared to pay if you are looking for glamour and fine dining.

But free drinks are still handed to anyone lurking near a slot, and if show tickets aren't in the budget, you won't lack for entertainment. Free lounge shows abound, and the people-watching opportunities alone never pall. From the Armani-clad high rollers in the baccarat rooms to the polyester-sporting couples at the nickel slots, Vegas contains a cross section of America.

Yes, it's noisy and chaotic. Yes, it's gotten more and more like Disneyland for adults. Yes, it's a shrine to greed and the love of filthy lucre. Yes, there is little ambience and even less "culture." Yes, someone lacking self-discipline can come to great grief.

But in its own way, Vegas is every bit as amazing as the nearby Grand Canyon, and every bit as much a must-see. It's one of the Seven Wonders of the Artificial World. And everyone should experience it at least once—and might find themselves coming back for more.

1 Frommer's Favorite Las Vegas Experiences

- **A Stroll on the Strip After Dark.** You haven't really seen Las Vegas until you've seen it at night. This neon wonderland is the world's greatest sound-and-light show. Begin at the Luxor and work your way down past the incredible new New York New York. If your strength holds out, you will end at Circus Circus, where live acrobat acts take place overhead while you gamble. Make plenty of stops en route to take in the ship battle at Treasure Island, see the Mirage volcano erupt, and enjoy the light, sound, and water show at Bally's.
- **Casino-Hopping on the Strip.** The interior of each lavish new hotel-casino is more outrageous and giggle-inducing than the last. Just when you think they can't possibly top themselves, they do. From Rome to ancient Egypt, from a rain forest to a pirate's lair, from King Arthur's castle to New York City, it is still all, totally, completely, and uniquely Las Vegas. See chapters 5 and 8 for our reviews.
- **The Penny Slots at the Gold Spike.** Where even the most budget-conscious traveler can gamble for hours. See chapter 8.
- **A Creative Adventures Tour.** Char Cruze of **Creative Adventures** (☎ **702/ 361-5565**) provides personalized tours that unlock the mysteries of the desert canyons and make regional history come vibrantly alive. See "Organized Tours" in chapter 7.
- **A Dinner Show at Caesars Magical Empire.** A solid dinner plus hours of entertainment, including your own personal magic show, make this one of the best values in Vegas, and a heck of a good time. See "Las Vegas Attractions" in chapter 7.
- **Buffets.** They may no longer be the very best of bargains, as the cheaper ones do not provide as good food as the more pricey ones, but there is something about the endless mounds of food that just screams "Vegas" to us. We've covered the best in chapter 6.
- **Cirque du Soleil's Mystère.** You haven't really seen Cirque du Soleil until you've seen it at Treasure Island, with a showroom equipped with state-of-the-art sound-and-lighting systems, and a seemingly infinite budget for sets, costumes, and high-tech special effects. It's an enchantment. See chapter 10.
- **An Evening in Glitter Gulch.** Set aside an evening to tour Downtown hotels and take in the overhead light show of the Fremont Street Experience. Unlike the lengthy and exhausting Strip, you can hit 17 casinos in about 5 minutes. See chapters 5 and 7.
- **The Liberace Museum.** It's not the Smithsonian, but then again, the Smithsonian doesn't have rhinestones like these. Nowhere else but here. See "Las Vegas Attractions" in chapter 7.
- **Your Favorite Headliners.** As soon as you arrive in town, pick up a show guide and see who's playing during your stay. For the top showrooms, see chapter 10.
- **Finding the Worst Lounge Shows.** Some feel this is the ultimate Vegas experience and dedicate many an evening to it. Be sure to watch out for Cook E. Jarr and the Crumbs. See chapter 10.

Impressions

There are no innocent bystanders in Las Vegas. Nobody comes to Las Vegas to be innocent.

—Michael Ventura, *The Death of Frank Sinatra*

- **The Shopping Forum at Caesars Palace.** This is an only-in-Vegas shopping experience—an arcade replicating an ancient Roman streetscape, with classical piazzas and opulent fountains. Don't miss the scary Audio-Animatronic statues as they come to glorious, cheesy life. See "Hotel Shopping Arcades" in chapter 9.
- **The Dolphins at the Mirage.** Actually, a most un-Vegas experience. Zone out as you watch these gorgeous mammals frolic in their cool blue pool. If you are really lucky, they will play ball with you. See "Las Vegas Attractions" in chapter 7.

2 The City Today & Tomorrow

Las Vegas is on a roll. A major resort, New York New York, went up in 1997. In 1998, expect the opening of Bellagio, the latest creation from Steve Wynn, owner of the Mirage and Treasure Island, and just down the street, Mandalay Bay. At this writing, another 11,500 rooms in five new megaresorts and additions to existing properties are under construction; that figure will more than double by the turn of the century (see chapter 5 for more details on upcoming hotels). No matter how many rooms the town builds, tourists just keep arriving to fill them up. Las Vegas's room inventory is already the largest of any city in the nation. And at 90%, its room occupancy rate is also one of the highest.

But Las Vegas isn't resting on its laurels. Hoteliers are very aware that if occupancy rates are to keep pace with burgeoning room counts, tourists must be lured to the town. Gone are the days when a hotel could simply offer a casino, a show, and some formula restaurants. Today, each new property has to do something spectacular to garner attention (from rooftop roller coasters to celebrity-chef restaurants), while existing hotels frantically renovate in hopes of competing successfully with sensationalist newcomers.

The phenomenal growth in tourism (the city had about 30 million visitors last year) is paralleled by a population explosion. Las Vegas has had a 26% increase in its population over the last 5 years, and between 4,000 and 6,000 people are relocating into the area monthly. This is the only city in America where the phone book is published twice a year, in order to keep up with all the changes and newcomers. While this has been terrific for the local economy, it has caused many problems, such as congested highways and insufficient schools and services. For tourists, the town's all-too-rapid growth is most evident along the Strip, which is totally inadequate to accommodate us in such huge numbers. While monorails and other traffic solutions are under consideration, Strip traffic remains frustratingly bumper-to-bumper at almost all times.

Snarled traffic notwithstanding, the excitement generated by new hotels, restaurants, and sightseeing options easily outweighs the inconveniences. Every year, the Strip undergoes a major change, gaining an erupting volcano here, a towering Eiffel Tower or Empire State Building there. Downtown Las Vegas is also spiffing up, proud of its new look centered on the Fremont Street Experience. Each time, you think, "They can't possibly top this." And yet, they do. And one thing's for sure—somehow, they always will.

3 A Look at the Past

Dateline
- A.D. 1150 Anasazi leave the area. Nomadic Paiutes

continues

For many centuries the land that would become Nevada was inhabited only by several Native American tribes: the Paiute, Shoshone, and Washoe. It wasn't until 1826 that Europeans set foot in the future state, and not until 1829 that Rafael Rivera, a scout for Mexican traders, entered a verdant valley nurtured by desert springs and called it Las Vegas ("the meadows"). From 1831 to 1848 these springs served as a watering place on the Old Spanish Trail for trading caravans plying the route between Santa Fe and the California coast. Explorer, soldier, and pathfinder Col. John C. Frémont (for whom the main thoroughfare downtown is named) rested near the headwaters of Las Vegas Springs on an overland expedition in 1844. A decade later Congress established a monthly mail route through Las Vegas Springs. And in 1855 Mormon leader Brigham Young sent 30 missionaries to Las Vegas to help expand Mormonism between Salt Lake City and southern California. Just north of what is today Downtown (what would these missionaries think if they could see it now?) the Mormon colony built an adobe fort and dwellings. They raised crops, baptized Paiutes, and mined lead in the nearby mountains. However, none of these ventures proved successful, and the ill-fated settlement was abandoned after just 3 years.

The next influx into the area came as a result of mining fever in the early 1860s, but this soon subsided. However, gold prospector Octavius Decatur Gass stayed behind and, in 1865, built the 640-acre Las Vegas Ranch using structures left by the Mormons as his base. Since Gass controlled the valley's water, he finally found "gold" offering services to travelers passing through. Gass planted crops and fruit orchards, started vineyards, raised cattle, established cordial relations with the Paiutes (he even learned their language), and served as a legislator. This became the first significant settlement in the area. By 1900 the Las Vegas valley had a population of 30.

A TENT CITY IN THE WILDERNESS The city of Las Vegas was officially born in 1905 when the Union Pacific Railroad connecting Los Angeles and Salt Lake City decided to route its trains through this rugged frontier outpost, selected for its ready supply of water and the availability of timber in the surrounding mountains. On a sweltering day in May, 1,200 town-site lots were auctioned off to eager pioneers and real estate speculators who had come from all over the country. The railroad depot was located at the head of Fremont Street (site of today's Amtrak station). Championing the spot was Montana senator

- become the dominant group.
- **1831–48** Artesian spring waters of Las Vegas serve as a watering place on the Old Spanish Trail.
- **1855** Mormon colony of 30 missionaries establishes settlement just north of today's Downtown. Unsuccessful in its aims, the colony disbands in 1858.
- **1864** President Lincoln proclaims Nevada the 36th state of the Union. Las Vegas, however, is still part of the Territory of Arizona.
- **1865** Gold prospector Octavius D. Gass builds Las Vegas Ranch, the first permanent settlement in Las Vegas, on the site of the old Mormon fort.
- **1880s** Due to mining fever, the population of Nevada soars to more than 60,000 in 1880. The Paiutes are forced onto reservations.
- **1895** San Franciscan inventor Charles Fey creates a three-reel gambling device—the first slot machine.
- **1907** Fremont Street, the future "Glitter Gulch," gets electric lights.
- **1909** Gambling is made illegal in Nevada, but Las Vegas pays little heed.
- **1911** William Howard Taft, first American president to pass through Las Vegas, waves at residents from his train.
- **1928** Congress authorizes construction of Hoover Dam 30 miles away, bringing thousands of workers to the area. Later, Las Vegas will capitalize on hundreds of thousands who come to see the engineering marvel.
- **1931** Gambling is legalized once again.
- **1932** The 100-room Apache Hotel opens Downtown.

continues

- **1933** Prohibition is repealed. Las Vegas's numerous speakeasies become legit.
- **1934** The city's first neon sign lights up the Boulder Club Downtown.
- **1941** The luxurious El Rancho Las Vegas becomes the first hotel on the Strip. Downtown, the El Cortez opens.
- **1946** Benjamin "Bugsy" Siegel's Flamingo extends the boundaries of the Strip. Sammy Davis Jr. debuts at the Last Frontier. Downtown (dubbed "Glitter Gulch") gets two new hotels: the Golden Nugget and the Eldorado.
- **1947** United Airlines inaugurates service to Las Vegas.
- **1948** The Thunderbird becomes the fourth hotel on the Strip.
- **1950** The Desert Inn adds country club panache to the Strip.
- **1951** The first of many atom bombs is tested in the desert just 65 miles from Las Vegas. An explosion of another sort takes place when Frank Sinatra debuts at the Desert Inn.
- **1952** The Club Bingo (opened in 1947) becomes the desert-themed Sahara. The Sands's Copa Room enhances the city's image as an entertainment capital.
- **1954** The Showboat pioneers buffet meals and bowling alleys in a new area of Downtown.
- **1955** The Strip gets its first high-rise hotel, the 9-story Riviera, which pays Liberace the unprecedented sum of $50,000 to open its showroom. The Riviera is the ninth hotel on the Strip.

continues

William Clark, who had paid the astronomical sum (for that time) of $55,000 for the nearby Las Vegas Ranch and springs. The coming of a railroad more or less ensured the growth of the town. As construction began, tent settlements, saloons, ramshackle restaurants, boardinghouses, and shops gradually emerged. The early tent hotels charged a dollar to share a double bed with a stranger for 8 hours!

By present-day standards, the new town was not a pleasant place to live. Prospectors' burros roamed the streets braying loudly, generally creating havoc and attracting swarms of flies. There were no screens, no air conditioners, no modern showers or baths (the town's bathhouse had but one tub) to ameliorate the fierce summer heat. The streets were rutted with dust pockets up to a foot deep that rose in great gusts as stage coaches, supply wagons, and 20-animal mule teams careened over them. It was a true pioneer town, complete with saloon brawls and shoot-outs. Discomforts notwithstanding, gaming establishments, hotels, and nightclubs—some of them seedy dives, others rather luxurious—sprang up and prospered in the Nevada wilderness. A red-light district emerged on Second Street between Ogden and Stewart avenues. And gambling, which was legal until 1909, flourished.

THE EIGHTH WONDER OF THE WORLD
For many years after its creation, Las Vegas was a mere whistle-stop town. That all changed in 1928 when Congress authorized the building of nearby Boulder Dam (later renamed Hoover Dam), bringing thousands of workers to the area. In 1931 gambling once again became legal in Nevada, and Fremont Street's gaming emporiums and speakeasies attracted workers from the dam. Upon the dam's completion, the Las Vegas Chamber of Commerce worked hard to lure the hordes of tourists who came to see the engineering marvel (it was called "the Eighth Wonder of the World") to its casinos. Las Vegas was about to make the transition from a sleepy desert town to "a town that never sleeps." But it wasn't until the early years of World War II that visionary entrepreneurs began to plan for its glittering future.

LAS VEGAS GOES SOUTH   Contrary to a popular conception, Bugsy Siegel didn't actually stake a claim in the middle of nowhere—he just built a few blocks south of already existing properties. Development a few miles south of Downtown on Highway 91 (the future Strip) was already underway in the 1930s, with such establishments as the Pair-O-Dice Club and the Last Frontier. And in 1941 El Rancho Vegas, ultraluxurious for its time, was built on the same remote stretch of highway (across the street from where the Sahara now stands). According to legend, Los Angeles hotelier Thomas E. Hull had been driving by the site when his car broke down. Noticing the extent of passing traffic, he decided to build there. Hull invited scores of Hollywood stars to his grand opening, and El Rancho Vegas soon became the hotel of choice for visiting film stars. Beginning a trend that still continues today, each new property tried to outdo existing hotels in luxurious amenities and thematic splendor. In 1943 the Last Frontier (the Strip's second hotel) created an authentic western setting by scouring the Southwest in search of authentic pioneer furnishings for its rooms, hiring Zuni craftsmen to create baskets and wall hangings, and picking up guests at the airport in a horse-drawn stagecoach. Las Vegas was on its way to becoming the entertainment capital of the world.

Las Vegas promoted itself in the 1940s as a town that combined Wild West frontier friendliness with glamour and excitement. As Chamber of Commerce president Maxwell Kelch aptly put it in a 1947 speech, "Las Vegas has the impact of a Wild West show, the friendliness of a country store, and the sophistication of Monte Carlo." Throughout the decade, the city was largely a regional resort—Hollywood's celebrity playground. Clara Bow and Rex Bell (a star of westerns) bought a ranch in Las Vegas where they entertained such luminaries as the Barrymores, Norma Shearer, Clark Gable, and Errol Flynn. The Hollywood connection gave the town glamour in the public's mind. So did the mob connection (something Las Vegas has spent decades trying to live down), which became clear early on when notorious underworld gangster Benjamin "Bugsy" Siegel (with partners Lucky Luciano and Meyer Lansky) built the fabulous Flamingo, a tropical paradise and "a real class joint." In 1947 the Club Bingo opened across the street from El Rancho Vegas, bringing a new game to town.

A steady stream of name entertainers came to Las Vegas. In 1947 Jimmy Durante opened the showroom at the Flamingo. Other headliners of the 1940s included Dean Martin and Jerry Lewis,

A month later, the Dunes becomes the 10th.

- **1956** The Fremont opens Downtown, and the Hacienda becomes the southernmost hotel on the Strip.

- **1957** The Dunes introduces bare-breasted showgirls in its *Minsky Goes to Paris* revue. The most luxurious hotel to date, the Tropicana, opens on the Strip.

- **1958** The 1,065-room Stardust opens as the world's largest resort complex with a spectacular show from France, the *Lido de Paris*.

- **1959** The Las Vegas Convention Center goes up, presaging the city's future as a major convention city. Another French production, the still-extant *Folies Bergère*, opens at the Tropicana.

- **1960** The Rat Pack, led by Chairman of the Board Frank Sinatra, holds a 3-week "Summit Meeting" at the Sands. A championship boxing match, the first of many, takes place at the Convention Center. El Rancho Las Vegas, the Strip's first property, burns to the ground.

- **1963** McCarran International Airport opens. Casinos and showrooms are darkened for a day as Las Vegas mourns the death of President John F. Kennedy.

- **1965** The 26-story Mint alters the Fremont Street skyline. Muhammad Ali defeats Floyd Patterson at the Las Vegas Convention Center.

- **1966** The Aladdin, the first new hotel on the Strip in 9 years, is soon eclipsed by the unparalleled grandeur of Caesars Palace. The Four Queens opens Downtown.

continues

Howard Hughes takes up residence at the Desert Inn. He buys up big chunks of Las Vegas and helps erase the city's gangland stigma.

- **1967** Elvis Presley marries Priscilla Beaulieu at the Aladdin, the city's all-time most celebrated union.
- **1968** Circus Circus gives kids a reason to come to Las Vegas.
- **1969** The Landmark and the International (today the Hilton) open within a day of each other on Paradise Road. Elvis Presley makes a triumphant return headlining at the latter.
- **1973** The ultraglamorous 2,100-room MGM Grand assumes the mantle of "world's largest resort." Superstars of magic, Siegfried and Roy, debut at the Tropicana.
- **1976** Fittingly, pioneer aviator Howard Hughes dies aboard a plane en route to a Houston hospital. Dean Martin and Jerry Lewis make up after a 20-year feud.
- **1978** Leon Spinks dethrones "the Greatest" (Muhammad Ali) at the Las Vegas Hilton. Crime solver Dan Tanna (Robert Urich) makes the streets of Vega$ safer, and better known.
- **1979** A new international arrivals building opens at McCarran International Airport.
- **1980** McCarran International Airport embarks on a 20-year, $785 million expansion program. Las Vegas celebrates its 75th birthday. A devastating fire destroys the MGM Grand, leaving 84 dead and 700 injured. Bally's takes over the property.

continues

tap-dancing legend Bill "Bojangles" Robinson, the Mills Brothers (who first recorded "Bye-Bye Blackbird"), skater Sonja Henie, and Frankie Laine. Future Las Vegas legend Sammy Davis Jr. debuted at El Rancho Vegas in 1945.

While the Strip was expanding, Downtown kept pace with new hotels such as the El Cortez and the Golden Nugget. By the end of the decade, Fremont Street was known as "Glitter Gulch," its profusion of neon signs proclaiming round-the-clock gaming and entertainment.

THE 1950S: BUILDING BOOMS AND A-BOMBS Las Vegas entered the new decade as a city (no longer a frontier town) with a population of about 50,000. Photographs indicate that Las Vegas was more glamorous in the 1950s than it is today. Men donned suits and ties, women floor-length gowns, to attend shows and even for casino gambling. Hotel growth was phenomenal. The Desert Inn, which opened in 1950 with headliners Edgar Bergen and Charlie McCarthy, brought country club elegance (including an 18-hole golf course and tennis courts) to the Strip. In 1951 the Eldorado Club Downtown became Benny Binion's Horseshoe Club, which would gain fame as the home of the annual World Series of Poker. In 1954 the Showboat sailed into a new area east of Downtown. Although people said it could never last in such a remote location, they were wrong. The Showboat not only innovated buffet meals and a bowling alley (106 lanes to date) but offered round-the-clock bingo. In 1955 the Côte d'Azur–themed Riviera became the ninth big hotel to open on the Strip. Breaking the ranch-style mode, it was, at 9 stories, the Strip's first high-rise. Liberace, one of the hottest names in show business, was paid the unprecedented sum of $50,000 a week to dazzle audiences in the Riviera's posh Clover Room. The 15-story Fremont Hotel Downtown became the highest building in Las Vegas, and the Hacienda extended the boundaries of the Strip by opening 2 miles south of the nearest resort. Elvis appeared at the New Frontier in 1956 but wasn't a huge success; his fans were too young to fit the Las Vegas tourist mold. In 1957 the Tropicana joined the Hacienda at the far end of Las Vegas Boulevard. In 1958 the $10 million, 1,065-room Stardust upped the spectacular stakes by importing the famed *Lido de Paris* from the French capital. It became one of the longest-running shows ever to play Las Vegas.

Throughout the 1950s, most of the above-mentioned hotels competed for performers whose followers spent freely in the casinos. The advent of big-name Strip entertainment tolled a death knell for glamorous nightclubs in America; owners simply could not compete with the astronomical salaries paid to Las Vegas headliners. Major '50s stars of the Strip included Rosemary Clooney, Nat King Cole, Peggy Lee, Milton Berle, Judy Garland, Red Skelton, Ernie Kovacs, Abbott and Costello, Fred Astaire and Ginger Rogers, the Andrews Sisters, and Marlene Dietrich. Two performers whose names have ever since been linked to Las Vegas—Frank Sinatra and Wayne Newton—made their debuts there. Mae West not only performed in Las Vegas but cleverly bought up a half mile of desolate Strip frontage between the Dunes and the Tropicana.

Competition for the tourist dollar also brought nationally televised sporting events such as the PGA's Tournament of Champions to the Desert Inn golf course (the winner got a wheelbarrow filled with silver dollars). In the 1950s the wedding industry helped make Las Vegas one of the nation's most popular venues for "goin' to the chapel." Nevada requires no blood test or waiting period. Celebrity weddings of the 1950s that sparked the trend included singer Dick Haymes and Rita Hayworth, Joan Crawford and Pepsi chairman Alfred Steele, Carol Channing and TV exec Charles Lowe, and Paul Newman and Joanne Woodward.

- **1981** Siegfried and Roy begin a record-breaking run in their own show, *Beyond Belief,* at the Frontier.
- **1982** A Las Vegas street is named Wayne Newton Boulevard.
- **1989** Steve Wynn makes headlines with his spectacular Mirage, fronted by an erupting volcano. He signs Siegfried and Roy to a 5-year, $57 million showroom contract (since extended)!
- **1990s** The medieval Arthurian realm of Excalibur opens as the new "world's-largest-resort" title holder with 4,032 rooms, a claim it relinquishes when the MGM Grand's new 5,005-room megaresort/theme park opens in 1994. Other properties to come aboard in the 1990s include the \Luxor Las Vegas, Treasure Island, the Hard Rock, the Monte Carlo, and the Stratosphere.

On a grimmer note, the '50s also heralded the atomic age in Nevada, with nuclear testing taking place just 65 miles northwest of Las Vegas. A chilling 1951 photograph shows a mushroom-shaped cloud from an atomic bomb test visible over the Fremont Street horizon. Throughout the decade, about one bomb a month was detonated in the nearby desert.

THE 1960S: THE RAT PACK AND A PACK RAT The very first month of the new decade made entertainment history when the Sands hosted a 3-week "Summit Meeting" in the Copa Room presided over by "Chairman of the Board" Frank Sinatra with Rat Pack cronies Dean Martin, Sammy Davis Jr., Peter Lawford, and Joey Bishop (all of whom happened to be in town filming *Ocean's Eleven*).

Impressions

They printed a lot of crap about Ben. He just wanted to be somebody. He used to pal around with Clark Gable, Gary Cooper, Cary Grant, and a lot of other big stars. I used to copy a lot of Ben's mannerisms when I played gangsters. Ben and the other tough guys . . . they were like gods to me. Ben had class, he was a real gentleman, and a real pal.

—Movie star George Raft on his pal Benjamin "Bugsy" Siegel

Farewell to Frank

Only a few times in its history have the lights of Vegas been off at night. Twice it happened in the '60s, for President Kennedy (when the casinos themselves actually closed) and for Martin Luther King Jr. And it happened twice in the '90s; the Strip went completely dark for 10 minutes to honor the passing of Sammy Davis Jr. When Dean Martin died in 1996, the Strip dimmed again.

So when Frank Sinatra, the man who practically built this town, died in 1998, we were sure Vegas would do something big to honor the paramount Rat Packer. We were wrong. The Strip went dark, but for 1 lousy minute. (Did we mention Sammy got 10?) And some of the lesser casinos and buildings never shut off at all. Still, some of the hotels put up tributes to Frankie on their signs, while cars drove down the Strip honking their horns, and a few of the hundreds of tourists who lined the boulevard to watch this historic moment burst into applause for The Voice.

It was something. And it's unlikely we will ever see anything like it happen again.

On November 25, 1963, Las Vegas mourned the death of President John F. Kennedy with the rest of the nation. Between 7am and midnight, all the neon lights went off, casinos stood empty, and showrooms were dark.

The building boom of the '50s took a brief respite. The Strip's first property, the El Rancho Vegas, burned down in 1960. And the first new hotel of the decade, the first to be built in 9 years, was the exotic Aladdin in 1966. A year after it opened, the Aladdin hosted the most celebrated Las Vegas wedding of all time when Elvis Presley married Priscilla Beaulieu. In 1966 Las Vegas also hailed Caesar—Caesars Palace, that is—a Lucullan pleasure palace whose grand opening was a million-dollar, 3-day Roman orgy with 1,800 guests.

During the '60s, negative attention focused on mob influence in Las Vegas. Of the 11 major casino hotels that had opened in the previous decade, 10 were believed to have been financed with mob money. Attorney General Robert Kennedy ordered the Department of Justice to begin serious scrutiny of Las Vegas gaming operations. Then, like a knight in shining armor, Howard Hughes rode into town. He was not, however, on a white horse. Ever eccentric, he arrived (for security rather than health reasons) in an ambulance. The reclusive billionaire moved into a Desert Inn penthouse on Thanksgiving Day 1966 and did not set foot outside the hotel for the next 4 years! It became his headquarters for a $300 million hotel- and property-buying spree, which included the Desert Inn itself (in 1967). Hughes was as "bugsy" as Benjamin Siegel any day, but his pristine reputation helped bring respectability to the desert city and lessen its gangland stigma. For a while, it worked.

Las Vegas became a family destination in 1968 when Circus Circus burst on the scene with the world's largest permanent circus and a "junior casino" comprising dozens of carnival midway games on its mezzanine level. In 1969 the Landmark and the dazzling International (today the Hilton) ventured into a new area of town: Paradise Road near the Convention Center. That same year Elvis made a triumphant return to Las Vegas at the International's showroom and went on to become one of the city's all-time legendary performers. His fans had come of age.

Hoping to establish Las Vegas as "the Broadway of the West," the Thunderbird Hotel presented Rodgers and Hammerstein's *Flower Drum Song*. It was a smash hit. Soon the Riviera picked up *Bye, Bye, Birdie*, and, as the decade progressed, *Mame* and *The Odd Couple* played at Caesars Palace. While Broadway played the Strip, production shows such as the Dunes's *Casino de Paris* became ever more lavish, expensive, and technically innovative. Showroom stars of the 1960s included Barbra Streisand, Phyllis Diller, Carol Burnett, Little Richard (who billed himself as "the bronze Liberace"), Louis Armstrong, Bobby Darin, the Supremes, Johnny Carson, Bob Newhart, the Smothers Brothers, and Aretha Franklin. Liza Minnelli filled her mother's shoes, while Nancy Sinatra's boots were made for walking. And Tom Jones wowed 'em at the Flamingo.

THE 1970S: MERV, MIKE, MGM & MAGIC   In 1971 the 500-room Union Plaza opened at the head of Fremont Street on the site of the old Union Pacific Station. It had what was, at the time, the world's largest casino, and its showroom specialized in Broadway productions. The same year, talk-show host Merv Griffin began taping at Caesars Palace, taking advantage of a ready supply of local headliner guests. He helped popularize Las Vegas even more by bringing it into America's living rooms every afternoon. Rival Mike Douglas soon followed suit at the Las Vegas Hilton.

The year 1973 was eventful: The Holiday Inn (today Harrah's) built a Mississippi riverboat complete with towering smokestacks and foghorn whistle, which was immediately dubbed "the ship on the Strip." Dean Martin headlined in the celebrity room of the magnificent new MGM Grand, named for the movie *Grand Hotel.* And over at the Tropicana, illusionists extraordinaire Siegfried and Roy began turning women into tigers and themselves into legends in the *Folies Bergère.*

Two major disasters hit Las Vegas in the 1970s. First, a flash flood devastated the Strip, causing more than $1 million in damage. Hundreds of cars were swept away in the raging waters. Second, gambling was legalized in Atlantic City. Las Vegas's hotel business slumped as fickle tourists decided to check out the new East Coast gambling mecca.

On a happier note, audiences were moved when Frank Sinatra helped to patch up a 20-year feud by introducing Dean Martin as a surprise guest on Jerry Lewis's 1976 *Muscular Dystrophy Telethon* at the Sahara. Martin and Lewis hugged and made up. Who would cross Sinatra?

As the decade drew to a close, Dan Tanna began investigating crime in glamorous *Vega$,* an international arrivals building opened at McCarran International Airport, and dollar slot machines caused a sensation in the casinos. Hot performers of the '70s included Ann-Margret, Tina Turner, Englebert Humperdinck, Bill Cosby,

Favorite Vegas Movies from the Mayor of Las Vegas

Jan Laverty is the mayor of Las Vegas.

- *Ocean's Eleven*
- *Viva Las Vegas*

(10 Other Vegas Movies the Mayor Didn't Pick & Possible Reasons Why)

- *Leaving Las Vegas.* Alcoholics and hookers are not good role models.
- *One from the Heart.* Shot on a soundstage rather than in Las Vegas.
- *Vegas Vacation.* Griswald family *not* typical Vegas tourists.
- *Casino.* Puts the squeeze on heads rather than on wallets.
- *They Came to Rob Las Vegas.* The title says it all.
- *The Electric Horseman.* Robert Redford successfully steals valuable horse from casino.
- *Indecent Proposal.* Robert Redford successfully wins a million dollars from casino.
- *Fear and Loathing in Las Vegas.* Bad Craziness not the kind of image the Tourist Commission wishes to promote.
- *Showgirls.* Need we say more?
- *Honeymoon in Vegas.* Beats us. Who doesn't love Flying Elvii?

Sonny and Cher, Tony Bennett, Mel Tormé, Bobby Darin, Gregory Hines (with his brother and dad), Donny and Marie, The Jackson 5, Gladys Knight and the Pips, and that "wild and crazy guy" Steve Martin. Debbie Reynolds introduced her daughter Carrie with a duet performance before a Desert Inn audience. Shirley MacLaine began an incarnation at the Riviera. And country was now cool; the names Johnny Cash, Bobby Gentry, Charlie Pride, and Roy Clark went up in marquee lights.

THE 1980S: THE CITY ERUPTS   Las Vegas was booming once again. McCarran Airport began a 20-year, $785 million expansion program. On a tragic note, in 1980 a devastating fire swept through the MGM Grand, leaving 84 dead and 700 injured. Shortly thereafter, Bally acquired the property and reopened the MGM Grand.

Siegfried and Roy were no longer just the star segment of various stage spectaculars. Their own show, *Beyond Belief,* ran for 6 years at the Frontier, playing a record-breaking 3,538 performances to sellout audiences every night. It became the most successful attraction in the city's history.

In 1989 Steve Wynn made Las Vegas sit up and take notice. His gleaming white-and-gold Mirage was fronted by 5-story waterfalls, lagoons, and lush tropical foliage—not to mention a 50-foot volcano that dramatically erupted, spewing great gusts of fire another 50 feet into the air every 15 minutes after dark! Wynn gave world-renowned illusionists Siegfried and Roy carte blanche (and more than $30 million) to create the most spellbinding show Las Vegas had ever seen.

Stars of the '80s included Eddie Murphy, Don Rickles, Roseanne Barr, Dionne Warwick, Paul Anka, the Captain and Tennille, Donna Summer, Rich Little,

George Carlin, Barry Manilow, Bernadette Peters, and Diahann Carroll. Country continued to be cool, as evidenced by frequent headliners Willie Nelson, Kenny Rogers, Dolly Parton, Crystal Gale, Merle Haggard, and Barbara Mandrell. Joan Rivers posed her famous question, "Can we talk?" and bug-eyed comic Rodney Dangerfield complained he got "no respect."

THE 1990S: KING ARTHUR MEETS KING TUT   The decade began with a blare of trumpets heralding the rise of a turreted medieval castle fronted by a moated drawbridge and staffed by jousting knights and fair damsels. Excalibur's interior had so many stone castle walls that a Strip comedian quipped, "It looks like a prison for Snow White." Excalibur also reflects the '90s marketing trend to promote Las Vegas as a family vacation destination.

Several sensational megahotels have opened on the Strip since 1993, and they're all running at close to 100% occupancy, as are older properties benefitting from the visitor excitement generated by the megahotels. They include the *new* MGM Grand Hotel, backed by a full theme park (it ended Excalibur's brief reign as the world's largest resort); the Luxor Las Vegas; and Steve Wynn's Treasure Island.

On October 27, 1993, a quarter of a million people crowded onto the Strip to witness the implosion of the 37-year-old Dunes Hotel. Vegas-style, it went out with a bang. Later that year a unique pink-domed, 5-acre indoor amusement park, Grand Slam Canyon, became part of the Circus Circus Hotel. In 1995 the Fremont Street Experience was completed, revitalizing Downtown Las Vegas. Closer to the Strip, rock restaurant magnate Peter Morton opened the Hard Rock Hotel, billed as "the world's first rock 'n' roll hotel and casino." The year 1996 saw the advent of the French Riviera–themed Monte Carlo and the Stratosphere, its 1,149-foot tower the highest building west of the Mississippi. The unbelievable New York New York arrived in 1997. As the millennium approaches, Las Vegas is flourishing as never before, and the ongoing metamorphosis of the Strip continues to thrill visitors who find a dramatic new streetscape every time they visit.

4 Recommended Books

If you believe in "reading more about it," here are a very select few of our favorites you might turn to:

- McCracken, Robert D., *Las Vegas: The Great American Playground* (University of Nevada Press, 1997). A comprehensive history of Las Vegas.
- Spanier, David, *Welcome to the Pleasure Dome: Inside Las Vegas* (University of Nevada Press, 1992). First-person history and analysis of the Las Vegas phenomenon.
- Thompson, Hunter S., *Fear and Loathing in Las Vegas* (Random House, 1971). The gonzo journalist and his Samoan lawyer head to Sin City for the all-time binge. An instant classic, recently a movie starring Johnny Depp.
- Tronnes, Mike, ed., *Literary Las Vegas* (Henry Holt, 1995). A terrific collection of different essays and excerpts from books about Vegas.

2 Planning a Trip to Las Vegas

Before any trip, you need to do a bit of advance planning. When should I go? Should I take a package deal or make my own hotel and airline reservations? Will there be a major convention in town during my visit? We'll answer these and other questions for you in this chapter, but you might want to read through the sightseeing and excursions in chapters 7 and 11 for some ideas on how to spend your time if you tire of gambling.

1 Visitor Information

For advance information call or write the **Las Vegas Convention and Visitors Authority,** 3150 Paradise Rd., Las Vegas, NV 89109 (☎ **800/332-5333** or 702/892-0711). They can send you a comprehensive packet of brochures, a map, a show guide, an events calendar, and an attractions list; help you find a hotel that meets your specifications (and even make reservations); and tell you if a major convention is scheduled during the time you would like to visit Las Vegas. Or stop by when you're in town. They're open Monday to Friday 8am to 6pm and Saturday and Sunday 8am to 5pm.

Another excellent information source is the **Las Vegas Chamber of Commerce,** 711 E. Desert Inn Rd., Las Vegas, NV 89109 (☎ **702/735-1616**). Ask them to send you their *Visitor's Guide,* which contains extensive information about accommodations, attractions, excursions, children's activities, and more. They can answer all your Las Vegas questions, including those about weddings and divorces. They're open Monday to Friday 8am to 5pm.

And for information on all of Nevada, including Las Vegas, contact the **Nevada Commission on Tourism** (☎ **800/638-2328**). They have a comprehensive information packet on Nevada.

If you're surfing the Net, you can get information about Las Vegas from these Web sites:

- **The "Official" Las Vegas Leisure Guide and Resource Directory:** www.pcap.com
- **Las Vegas Hack Attack** is written by area taxi drivers who "know all the inside scoops": www.lasvegastaxi.com
- **Las Vegas Online:** www.lvol.com
- *Scope* **Magazine,** an on-line version of the weekly alternative magazine: vegasnet.com

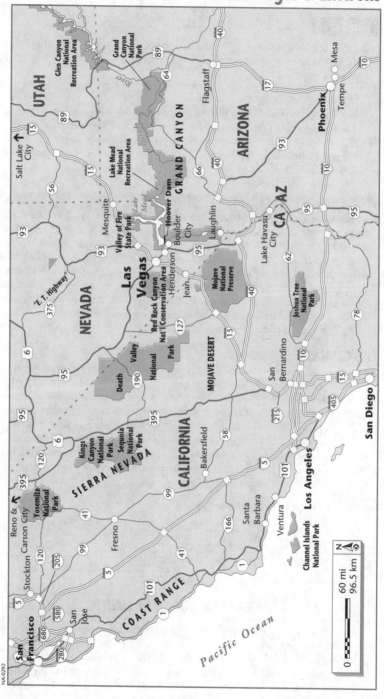

NA-0292

15

Fun Fact

In 1995, Don Harrington entered a satellite event at the World Series of Poker for just $220, won his way into the $10,000 buy for the Championship Event, and went on to win the $1 million prize.

- **Las Vegas Convention and Visitors Authority:** www.lasvegas24hours.com
- *Las Vegas Review Journal* is the largest paper in town: www.lvrj.com
- *What's On* Magazine, the local tourist paper: www.whats-on.com
- **Vegas 4 Visitors** is an opinionated Web site with reviews for tourists: www.vegas4visitors.com

2 When to Go

Since most of a Las Vegas vacation is usually spent indoors, you can have a good time here year-round. The most pleasant seasons are spring and fall, especially if you want to experience the great outdoors. Weekdays are slightly less crowded than weekends. Holidays are always a mob scene and come accompanied by high hotel prices. Hotel prices also skyrocket when big conventions and special events are taking place. The slowest times of year are June and July, the week before Christmas, and the week after New Year's. If a major convention is to be held during your trip, you might want to change your date.

THE CLIMATE

One thing you'll hear again and again is that even though Las Vegas gets very hot, the dry desert heat is not unbearable. This is true. The humidity averages a low 22%, and even on very hot days there's apt to be a breeze. Also, except on the hottest summer days, there's relief at night when temperatures often drop as much as 20°. But it also gets really cold, especially in the winter, when at night it can drop to 30°F and lower. The breeze can also become a cold, biting wind. If you aren't traveling in the height of summer, bring a wrap. Also, remember your sunscreen and hat—even if it's not all that hot, you can burn very easily and fast. (You should see all the lobster-red people in the casinos at night.)

Las Vegas's Average Temperatures (°F)

	Jan	Feb	Mar	Apr	May	June	July	Aug	Sept	Oct	Nov	Dec
Average	44	50	57	66	74	84	91	88	81	67	54	47
Avg. High	55	62	69	79	88	99	105	103	96	82	67	58
Avg. Low	33	39	44	53	60	68	76	74	65	53	41	36

LAS VEGAS CALENDAR OF EVENTS

You may be surprised that Las Vegas does not offer as many annual events as most tourist cities. The reason is Las Vegas's very raison d'être: the gaming industry. This town wants its visitors spending their money in the casinos, not off at Renaissance fairs and parades. When in town, check the local paper and call the **Las Vegas Convention and Visitors Authority** (☎ 800/332-5333 or 702/892-0711), **Las Vegas Events** (☎ 702/731-2115), or the **Chamber of Commerce** (☎ 702/735-1616) to find out about other events scheduled during your visit.

Las Vegas Advisor

Professional gambler and longtime Las Vegas resident Anthony Curtis, author of *Bargain City: Booking, Betting, and Beating the New Las Vegas,* knows all the angles for stretching your hotel, restaurant, and, most important, gaming dollar. His 12-page monthly newsletter, the *Las Vegas Advisor,* is chock-full of insider tips on how to maximize your odds on every game, which slot tournaments to enter, casino promotions that represent money-making opportunities for the bettor, where to obtain the best fun books, which hotel offers a 12-ounce margarita for 99¢ or a steak dinner for $3, what are the best buffet and show values in town, and much, much more. Subscribers get more than $400 worth of coupons for discounts on rooms, meals, show tickets, and car rentals, along with free slot plays, two-for-one bets, and other perks. A subscription is $45 a year, a single issue $5. To subscribe, call ☎ **800/244-2224** or send a check to Las Vegas Advisor, 3687 S. Procyon St., Las Vegas, NV 89103.

January
- **The PBA Classic.** The **Showboat Hotel,** 2800 Fremont St. (☎ **800/ 826-2800**), hosts this major bowling tournament every January.

March
- **The PBA Invitational.** Another major annual bowling tournament, also at the Showboat Hotel.

April
- **The World Series of Poker.** This famed 21-day event takes place at **Binion's Horseshoe Casino,** 128 Fremont St. (☎ **702/382-1600**), in late April and early May, with high-stakes gamblers and show-biz personalities competing for six-figure purses. There are daily events with entry stakes ranging from $125 to $5,000. To enter the World Championship Event (purse $1 million), players must put up $10,000. It costs nothing to go watch the action.
- **TruGreen-ChemLawn Las Vegas Senior Classic.** This 4-day event in mid- to late April or early May takes place at the **Tournament Players Club (TPC),** The Canyons, 9851 Canyon Run Dr., in nearby Summerlin. For details and driving information, call ☎ **702/382-6616.**

June
- **Helldorado.** This Elks-sponsored Western heritage celebration takes place over a several-day period in mid-June. It includes a bull-riding event, a trail ride, a barbecue, and four major Professional Rodeo Cowboys Association (PRCA) rodeos at the Thomas and Mack Center at UNLV. For information call the **Elks Lodge** (☎ **702/870-1221**) or check the local papers. For **tickets** call ☎ **702/ 895-3900.**

September
- **Oktoberfest.** This boisterous autumn holiday is celebrated from mid-September through the end of October at the Mount Charleston Resort (☎ **800/955-1314** or 702/872-5408) with music, folk dancers, sing-alongs around a roaring fire, special decorations, and Bavarian cookouts.

October
- **PGA Tour Las Vegas Invitational.** This 5-day championship event, played on three local courses, is televised by ESPN. For details call ☎ **702/382-6616.**

What Things Cost in Las Vegas	U.S.$
Taxi from airport to the Strip	8.00–12.00
Taxi from airport to Downtown	15.00–18.00
Minibus from airport to the Strip	3.50
Minibus from airport to Downtown	4.75
Double room at the Desert Inn (very expensive)	175.00–185.00
Double room at the MGM Grand (expensive)	69.00–119.00
Double at Circus Circus (inexpensive)	36.00–65.00
Five-course tasting menu at Gatsby's without tax or tip, with wines (very expensive)	65.00–85.00
Three-course dinner at Stage Deli without tax or tip (moderate)	20.00
All-you-can-eat buffet dinner at Caesars Palace	13.95
All-you-can-eat buffet dinner at Circus Circus	4.99
Bottle of beer	2.50
Coca-Cola	1.50
Cup of coffee	1.50
Roll of ASA 100 color film, 36 exposures	4.70
Show ticket for *Legends in Concert* (including two drinks; tax and gratuity extra)	25.00
Show ticket for *Enter the Night* (including two drinks; tax and gratuity extra)	35.00
Show ticket for headliners at Caesars (including tax; drinks extra)	45.00–75.00
Show ticket for *Siegfried and Roy* (including two drinks, tax, souvenir brochure, and gratuity)	89.95

December

- **National Finals Rodeo.** This is the Super Bowl of rodeos, attended by close to 170,000 people each year. The top 15 male rodeo stars compete in six different events: calf roping, steer wrestling, bull riding, team roping, saddle bronco riding, and bareback riding. And the top 15 women compete in barrel racing. An all-around "Cowboy of the Year" is chosen. In connection with this event, hotels book country stars in their showrooms, and there's a cowboy shopping spree— the NFR Cowboy Christmas Gift Show, a trade show for western gear—at Cashman Field.

    The NFR runs for 10 days during the first 2 weeks of December at the 17,000-seat Thomas and Mack Center of UNLV. Order tickets as far in advance as possible (☎ 702/895-3900).

- **Las Vegas Bowl Week.** A championship football event in mid-December pits the winners of the Mid-American Conference against the winners of the Big West Conference. The action takes place at the 32,000-seat Sam Boyd Stadium. Call ☎ 702/895-3900 for ticket information.

- **Western Athletic Conference (WAC) Football Championship.** This collegiate championship event takes place the first week in December. Call ☎ 792/731-5595 for ticket information. Ticket prices range from $15 to $100.

Major Convention Dates for 1999

Listed below are Las Vegas's major annual conventions with projected attendance figures for 1999.

Consumer Electronics Show
 1999: Jan 6–10   100,000

**Western Shoe
 Associates**
 1999: Feb 9–12   25,000

**Men's Apparel Guild in
 California (Magic)**
 1999: Mar 3–4   70,000

Associated Surplus Dealers
 1999: Feb 21–25   50,000

**Snowsports Industries of
 America**
 1999: Mar 9–13   28,000

Networld/Interop
 1999: May 10–14   60,000

**International Council of
 Shopping Centers**
 1999: May 23–27   35,000

**Associated Surplus
 Dealers**
 1999: Aug 15–18   32,000

Softbank Comdex
 1999: Nov 15–19   200,000

• **New Year's Eve.** This is a biggie (reserve your hotel room early). Downtown, Fremont Street is closed to traffic between Third and Main streets, and there's a big block party with two dramatic countdowns to midnight (the first is at 9pm, midnight on the East Coast). Of course, there are fireworks.

3 Tips for Travelers with Special Needs

FOR PEOPLE WITH DISABILITIES   On the one hand, Las Vegas is fairly well equipped for the disabled, with virtually every hotel having handicapped rooms, ramps, and other requirements. On the other, however, the distance between each hotel (particularly on the Strip) makes a vehicle of some sort virtually mandatory for most of the disabled, and it may be extremely strenuous and time-consuming to shift around much. Additionally, the casinos can be quite difficult to maneuver in, particularly for a guest with a wheelchair, since they are crowded, and the machines and tables are often laid out close together, with chairs and such further blocking easy access. Consider also how long a trek it often is through the larger hotels between the outside and the room elevators (or for that matter, anywhere in the hotel), usually through said crowded casino.

While each hotel should be able to give you an idea of how accessible it is, consider also writing or calling the **Independent Living Program,** Nevada Association for the Handicapped, 6200 W. Oakey Blvd., Las Vegas, NV 89102 (☎ **702/ 870-7050**). They can recommend hotels and restaurants that meet your needs, help you find a personal attendant, advise about transportation, and answer all questions.

In addition, the **Nevada Commission on Tourism** (☎ **800/638-2328**) offers a free accommodations guide to Las Vegas hotels that includes access information.

Two helpful travel organizations—**Accessible Journeys** (☎ **800/TINGLES** or 610/521-0339) and **Flying Wheels Travel** (☎ **800/535-6790** or 507/ 451-5005)—offer tours, cruises, and custom vacations worldwide for people with physical disabilities; Accessible Journeys can also provide nurses/companions to

---

New Year's Eve in Las Vegas

Over the last couple of years, more and more people have been choosing Las Vegas as their party destination for New Year's Eve. In fact, some estimates indicate that by the time you read this, there will be more people ringing in the new year in Nevada than in New York City's Time Square.

From experience, we can tell you that there are a lot of people who come here on December 31. We mean a lot of people. It seemed that it may very well have been the entire population of the western United States, but we didn't stop to count. (Neither did anyone else, but here's what we know from last year: Almost *all* the 94,000 hotel rooms were sold out by 201,000 visitors. Nearly 400,000 total jammed the Strip to watch the Hacienda implode. Another 25,000 paid $10 apiece to experience New Year's Eve from the Fremont St. Experience.) Traffic is a nightmare, parking (at least legally) is next to impossible, and there is not one square inch of the place that isn't occupied by a human being. Las Vegas doesn't really need a reason to throw a party, but when an event like this comes along they do it up right.

A major portion of the strip is closed down, sending the masses and their mass quantities of alcohol into the street. Each year's celebration is a little different but usually includes a street-side performance by a major celebrity, confetti, the obligatory countdown, fireworks, and an occasional building implosion (the Hacienda on New Year's '97).

Of course there will always be the die-hard gamblers. New Year's '96 at the Stardust Casino was something like this: From outside you heard the countdown ("Three! Two! One!") and everyone in the casino looked up from their slot machines, their glazed eyes clearing slightly as some portion of their brain registered the fact that something important was happening. A few mumbled "Happy-newyear," and then the coins started dropping again.

We would say that all then returned to normal, but it's hard to apply that phrase to Las Vegas with a straight face.

---

travelers. The **Guided Tour Inc.** (☎ **800/783-5841** or 215/782-1370) has tours for people with physical or mental disabilities, the visually impaired, and the elderly.

Mobility International USA, P.O. Box 10767, Eugene, OR 97440 (☎ **503/343-1284**), offers accessibility and resource information to its members. Membership ($25 a year) includes a quarterly newsletter called *Over the Rainbow.*

There's no charge for help via telephone (accessibility information and more) from the **Travel Information Service,** Moss Rehab Hospital (☎ **215/456-9600**). Another organization, the **Society for the Advancement of Travel for the Handicapped (SATH),** 347 Fifth Ave., Suite 610, New York, NY 10016 (☎ **212/447-7284**), charges $5 for sending requested information.

Recommended books: Twin Peaks Press, Box 129, Vancouver, WA 98666 (☎ **360/694-2462**), specializes in books for people with disabilities. Write for their *Disability Bookshop Catalog,* enclosing $5.

Greyhound (☎ **800/752-4841**) allows a disabled person to travel with a companion for a single fare. Call at least 48 hours in advance to discuss this and other special needs.

Airlines don't offer special fares to the disabled. When making your flight reservations, ask where your wheelchair will be stowed on the plane and if your guide dog may accompany you.

FOR SENIORS   Always carry some form of photo ID that includes your birth date so that you can take advantage of discounts wherever they're offered. And it never hurts to ask.

If you haven't already done so, consider joining the **American Association of Retired Persons** (☎ 800/424-3410 or 202/434-2277). Annual membership costs $8 per person or couple. You must be at least 50 to join. Membership entitles you to many discounts. Write to Purchase Privilege Program, AARP Fulfillment, 601 E St. NW, Washington, DC 20049, to receive their *Purchase Privilege* brochure, a free list of hotels, motels, and car-rental firms nationwide that offer discounts to AARP members.

Elderhostel is a national organization that offers low-priced educational programs for people over 55 (your spouse can be any age; a companion must be at least 50). Programs are generally a week long, and prices average about $355 per person, including room, board, and classes. For information on programs in Nevada call or write Elderhostel Headquarters, 75 Federal St., Boston, MA 02110 (☎ 617/426-7788), and ask for a free catalog.

Greyhound also offers discounted fares for senior citizens. Call your local Greyhound office for details.

FOR FAMILIES   Las Vegas in the '90s is discussed in the "Especially for Kids" suggestions in chapter 7. See the "Family-Friendly" boxes for suggestions for hotels, restaurants, and shows. Here are also a few general suggestions to make traveling with kids easier.

If they're old enough, let the kids write to various tourist offices for information and color brochures. If you're driving, give them a map on which they can outline the route. Let them help decide your sightseeing itinerary.

Although your home may be toddler-proof, hotel accommodations are not. Bring blank plugs to cover outlets and whatever else is necessary.

Carry a few simple games to relieve the tedium of traveling. Packing snacks will also help and save money. If you're using public transportation (airlines, bus), always inquire about discounted fares for children.

Children under 12, and in many cases even older, stay free in their parents' rooms in most hotels. Look for establishments that have pools and other recreational facilities (see "Family-Friendly Hotels" in chapter 5).

FOR GAYS & LESBIANS   For such a licentious, permissive town, Las Vegas has its conservative side, and so it is not the most gay-friendly city there is. This will not manifest itself in any signs of outrage toward open displays of gay affection, but it does mean the local gay community is largely confined to the bar scene. This may be changing, with local gay pride parades and other activities.

The *Las Vegas Bugle,* a monthly magazine serving the gay community, provides information about bars, workshops, local politics, support groups, shops, events, and more. A subscription costs $20 for 12 issues. For details call ☎ 702/369-6260. See also listings for gay bars in chapter 10. If you're on the Internet you can check out **Gay Vegas:** www.gayvegas.com, which has helpful advice on lodging, restaurants, and nightlife.

4 Getting There

BY AIR
THE MAJOR AIRLINES

The following airlines have regularly scheduled flights into Las Vegas (some of these are regional carriers, so they may not all fly from your point of origin): **Air**

Canada (☎ 800/776-3000), **Alaska Airlines** (☎ 800/426-0333), **America West** (☎ 800/235-9292), **American/American Eagle** (☎ 800/433-7300), **American Trans Air** (☎ 800/543-3708), **Canadian International** (☎ 800/426-7000), **Condor** (☎ 800/524-6975), **Continental** (☎ 800/525-0280), **Delta/Skywest** (☎ 800/221-1212), **Frontier** (☎ 800/432-1359), **Hawaiian** (☎ 800/367-5320), **Kiwi** (☎ 800/538-5494), **Midway** (☎ 888/226-4392), **Midwest Express** (☎ 800/452-2022), **Northwest** (☎ 800/225-2525), **Reno Air** (☎ 800/736-6247), **Southwest** (☎ 800/435-9792), **Sun Country** (☎ 800/359-6786), **TWA** (☎ 800/221-2000), **United** (☎ 800/241-6522), **US Airways** (☎ 800/428-4322), and **Western Pacific** (☎ 800/930-3030).

We've always enjoyed Southwest's relaxed attitude and their service leaves few complaints. However, they mostly feature first-come, first-served seating, so if you want to avoid that, you can't go wrong with United.

FINDING THE BEST AIRFARE

Generally, the least expensive fares (except for special packages and special-promotion discount fares you see announced in newspaper travel sections) are **advance-purchase fares** that involve certain restrictions. For example, in addition to paying for your ticket 3 to 21 days in advance, you may have to leave or return on certain days, stay a maximum or minimum number of days, and so on. Also, advance-purchase fares are often nonrefundable. Nonetheless, the restrictions are usually within the framework of one's vacation plans, and savings of $500 and more are not unusual. It's also possible to get a really good airfare combined with your hotel room and perhaps even a car rental by purchasing a **package**.

Another way to find the cheapest fare is by using the Internet to do your searching for you. There are too many companies now to mention, but a few of the better-respected ones are **Travelocity (www.travelocity.com), Microsoft Expedia (www.expedia.com),** and **Yahoo's Flifo Global (travel.yahoo.com/travel).** Each has its own little quirks—Travelocity, for example, requires you to register with them—but they all provide variations of the same service. Just enter the dates you want to fly and the cities you want to visit, and the computer looks for the lowest fares. The Yahoo site has a feature called "Fare Beater," which will check flights on other airlines or at different times or dates in hopes of finding an even cheaper fare. Expedia's site will e-mail you the best airfare deal once a week if you so choose. Travelocity uses the SABRE computer reservations system that most travel agents use, and has a "Last Minute Deals" database that advertises really cheap fares for those who can get away at a moment's notice.

Great last-minute deals are also available directly from the airlines themselves through a free e-mail service called **E-savers.** Each week, the airline sends you a list of discounted flights, usually leaving the upcoming Friday or Saturday, and returning the following Monday or Tuesday. You can sign up for all the major airlines at once by logging on to **Epicurious Travel (travel.epicurious.com/travel/c_planning/02_airfares/email/signup.html),** or go to each individual airline's Web site. See our appendix of useful toll-free numbers and Web sites for specific site addresses.

THE LAS VEGAS AIRPORT

Las Vegas is served by **McCarran International Airport,** 5757 Wayne Newton Blvd. (☎ **702/261-5743;** TDD 702/261-3111; www.mccarren.com). It's just a few minutes' drive from the southern end of the Strip. This big, modern airport—with a brand-new, $500 million dollar expansion—is rather unique in that it includes a casino area with more than 1,000 slot machines. Although these are reputed to offer lower paybacks than hotel casinos (the airport has a captive audience and doesn't need to lure repeat customers), it's hard to resist throwing in a few quarters while waiting for luggage to arrive. We actually know someone who hit a $250 jackpot there on his way out of town, thereby recouping most of his gambling losses at the last possible moment. He was surprised, too.

AIRPORT TRANSPORTATION   Getting to your hotel from the airport is a cinch. **Bell Trans** (☎ **702/739-7990** or fax 702/384-2283) runs 20-passenger minibuses daily between the airport and all major Las Vegas hotels and motels almost around the clock (4:30am to 2am). There are several other companies that run similar ventures—just stand outside on the curb and one will be flagged down for you. Buses from the airport leave about every 10 minutes. For departure from your hotel, call at least 2 hours in advance (though often you can just flag one down outside any major hotel). The cost is $3.50 per person each way to Strip and Convention Center area hotels, $4.75 to Downtown properties (any place north of the Sahara Hotel and west of I-15).

Even less expensive are **Citizen's Area Transit (CAT)** buses (☎ **702/ CAT-RIDE**). The no. 108 bus departs from the airport and will take you to the Stratosphere, where you can transfer to the 301, which stops close to most Strip and Convention Center area hotels. The no. 109 bus goes from the airport to the Downtown Transportation Center at Casino Center Boulevard and Stewart Avenue. The fare is $1.50, 50¢ for seniors and children. *Note:* If you have heavy luggage, you should know that you might have a long walk from the bus stop to your door (even if it's right in front of your hotel).

RENTING A CAR   All of the major car-rental companies are represented in Las Vegas. We like **Allstate** (☎ **800/634-6186** or 702/736-6148), the least expensive of the airport-based car-rental agencies. Besides the usual mix, their fleet of more than 1,500 vehicles includes an inventory of 15 passenger vans, four-wheel drives, Jeeps, minivans, sports cars, and convertibles. We've found this local, family-owned company (the largest independent operator in Las Vegas) friendly and competent, with an invariably charming staff at the airport. They're open 24 hours. And they've agreed to offer our readers a **20% discount off regular rental rates** at any Allstate location (just show the agent your copy of this book). In addition to McCarran Airport, there are Allstate car desks at the Aladdin, Riviera, Stardust, and Jackie Gaughan's Plaza hotels, and the company offers free pickup anywhere in Las Vegas.

National companies with outlets in Las Vegas include **Alamo** (☎ 800/ 327-9633), **Avis** (☎ 800/367-2847), **Budget** (☎ 800/922-2899), **Dollar** (☎ 800/842-2054), **Enterprise** (☎ 800/325/8007), **Hertz** (☎ 800/654-3131), **National** (☎ 800/227-7368), and **Thrifty** (☎ 800/367-2277).

BY CAR

The main highway connecting Las Vegas with the rest of the country is I-15; it links Montana, Idaho, and Utah with southern California. The drive from Los Angeles is quite popular, and thanks to the narrow two-lane highway, can get very crowded on Friday and Sunday afternoons with hopeful weekend gamblers making their way to and from Vegas. (By the way, as soon as you cross the state line, there are three casinos ready to handle your immediate gambling needs, with two more about 20 minutes up the road, 30 miles before you get to Las Vegas.)

From the East Coast, take I-70 or I-80 west to Kingman, Arizona, and then U.S. 93 north to Downtown Las Vegas (Fremont Street). From the south, take I-10

Driving Distances to Las Vegas (in Miles)			
Chicago	1,766	New York City	2,564
Dallas	1,230	Phoenix	286
Denver	759	Salt Lake City	421
Los Angeles	269	San Francisco	586

west to Phoenix and then U.S. 93 north to Las Vegas. From San Francisco, take I-80 east to Reno and then U.S. 95 south to Las Vegas. If you're driving to Las Vegas, be sure to read the driving precautions under "By Car" in the "Getting Around" section in chapter 4.

PACKAGE DEALS

When you make reservations on any airline, also inquire about money-saving packages with your airfare that include hotel accommodations, car rentals, tours, and so forth.

For instance, at press time, a **Delta Dream Vacation** package leaving from New York could cost as little as $350 per person based on double occupancy, including round-trip coach air transportation, 2 nights at your choice of several major casino hotels, a rental car for 24 hours, airport transfers, and bonus discounts and admissions. At press time Southwest Airlines was offering round-trip airfare from Los Angeles with 2 nights at several different hotels complete with ground transportation; per person based on double occupancy, for the Mirage it was $174, and for the Golden Nugget $119. (Of course, this was midweek.) Similar packages are available from such companies as **American Airlines Fly Away Vacations, America West Vacations,** and **US Airways Vacations.**

Prices vary according to the season, seat availability, hotel choice, whether you travel midweek or on the weekend, and other factors. Since even an advance-purchase round-trip fare between New York and Las Vegas can easily be $100 or $200 more than the above-quoted figure, it seems almost insane not to book a less expensive package that includes so many extras.

CHARTER FLIGHTS

Similar to airline packages, charter flights are booked by tour operators who buy up all (or most of) the seats on an airplane and put together packages that include airfare and other features—perhaps accommodations, shows, meals, car rentals, airport transfers, and/or attractions tickets. The operators then sell these charters through travel agents. It can be worth your while to compare charter offerings to major airline packages. Most travel agents know which tour operators specialize in Las Vegas charters. If yours does not, ask them to investigate packages offered by **Funjet Vacations** (☎ 800/558-3050), **Hamilton, Miller, Hudson and Fang** (☎ 800/669-4466), **MLT Vacations** (☎ 800/328-0025), and **Adventure Tours** (☎ 800/638-9040).

For Foreign Visitors 3

This chapter will provide some specifics about getting to the United States as economically and effortlessly as possible, plus some helpful information about how things are done in Las Vegas, from receiving mail to making a local or long-distance telephone call.

1 Preparing for Your Trip

ENTRY REQUIREMENTS

DOCUMENT REGULATIONS Citizens of **Canada** and **Bermuda** may enter the United States without visas, but they will need to show proof of nationality, the most common and hassle-free form of which is a passport.

The U.S. State Department has a Visa Waiver Pilot Program under which citizens of some countries may enter the country without a visa for stays of fewer than 90 days of holiday travel. At press time they included **Andorra, Argentina, Australia, Austria, Belgium, Brunei, Denmark, Finland, France, Germany, Iceland, Ireland, Italy, Japan, Liechtenstein, Luxembourg, Monaco, the Netherlands, New Zealand, Norway, San Marino, Slovenia, Spain, Sweden, Switzerland,** and the **United Kingdom.** (The program as applied to the U.K. refers to British citizens who have the "unrestricted right of permanent abode in the United Kingdom"— citizens from **England, Scotland, Wales, Northern Ireland,** the **Channel islands,** and the **Isle of Man;** and not, for example, citizens of the British Commonwealth of Pakistan.)

Citizens from these countries need only a valid passport and a round-trip air or cruise ticket in their possession upon arrival. If they first enter the United States, they may then visit Mexico, Canada, Bermuda, and the Caribbean islands and return to the United States without needing a visa. Further information is available from any U.S. embassy or consulate.

Citizens of countries other than those specified above, those traveling to the U.S. for reasons or length of time outside the restrictions of the visa waiver program, or those who require waivers of inadmissibility must have two documents:

- a **valid passport,** with an expiration date at least 6 months later than the scheduled end of the visit to the United States. (Some countries are exceptions to the 6-month validity rule. Contact any U.S. embassy or consulate for complete information.)

- a **tourist visa,** available from the nearest U.S. consulate. To obtain a visa, the traveler must submit (in person or by mail) a completed application form with a 1½-inch-square photo and the required application fee. There may also be an issuance fee, depending on the type of visa and other factors.

Usually you can obtain a visa right away or within 24 hours, but it may take longer during the summer rush period (June to August). If you cannot go in person, contact the nearest U.S. embassy or consulate for directions on applying by mail. Your travel agent or airline office may also be able to provide you with visa applications and instructions. The U.S. consulate or embassy that issues your visa will determine whether you will be issued a multiple- or single-entry visa. The Immigration and Naturalization Service officers at your U.S. port of entry will make an admission decision and determine your length of stay.

MEDICAL REQUIREMENTS　No inoculations are needed to enter the United States unless you are coming from, or have stopped over in, areas known to be suffering from epidemics, particularly cholera or yellow fever.

If you have a disease requiring treatment with medications containing narcotics or drugs requiring a syringe, carry a valid, signed generic prescription from your physician to allay any suspicions that you are smuggling drugs. The prescription brands you are accustomed to buying in your country may not be available in the United States.

CUSTOMS REQUIREMENTS　Every adult visitor may bring in, free of duty: 1 liter of wine or hard liquor; 200 cigarettes or 100 cigars (but no cigars from Cuba) or 3 pounds of smoking tobacco; and $100 worth of gifts. These exemptions are offered to travelers who spend at least 72 hours in the United States and who have not claimed them within the preceding 6 months. It is altogether forbidden to bring foodstuff (particularly cheese, fruit, cooked meats, and canned goods) and plants (vegetables, seeds, tropical plants, and so on) into the country. Foreign tourists may bring in or take out up to $10,000 in U.S. or foreign currency with no formalities; larger sums must be declared to Customs upon entering or leaving.

INSURANCE

Unlike most other countries, the United States does not have a national health system. Because the cost of medical care is extremely high, we strongly advise all travelers to secure health coverage before setting out on their trip. You may want to take out a comprehensive travel policy that covers (for a relatively low premium) sickness or injury costs (medical, surgical, and hospital); loss or theft of your baggage; trip-cancellation costs; guarantee of bail in case you are arrested; and costs of accident, repatriation, or death. Such packages (for example, "Europe Assistance" in Europe) are sold by automobile clubs at attractive rates, as well as by insurance companies and travel agencies.

MONEY

The U.S. monetary system has a decimal base: One American dollar ($1) = 100 cents (100¢). Dollar bills commonly come in $1 (a "buck"), $5, $10, $20, $50, and

$100 denominations (the last two are not welcome when paying for small purchases and are usually not accepted in taxis or at subway ticket booths). There are six coin denominations: 1¢ (one cent or "penny"); 5¢ (five cents or "nickel"); 10¢ (ten cents or "dime"); 25¢ (twenty-five cents or "quarter"); 50¢ (fifty cents or "half dollar"); and the rare $1 piece.

Traveler's checks in U.S. dollars are accepted at most hotels, motels, restaurants, and large stores. Sometimes picture identification is required. American Express, Thomas Cook, and Barclay's Bank traveler's checks are readily accepted in the United States. Do not bring traveler's checks denominated in other currencies.

Credit cards are the method of payment most widely used: Visa (BarclayCard in Britain), MasterCard (EuroCard in Europe, Access in Britain, Chargex in Canada), American Express, Discover, Diners Club, JCB (Japan Credit Bank), and Carte Blanche, in descending order of acceptance. You can save yourself trouble by using "plastic" rather than cash or traveler's checks in almost all hotels, motels, restaurants, and retail stores. You must have a credit or charge card to rent a car. It can also be used as proof of identity or as a "cash card," enabling you to draw money from automated-teller machines (ATMs).

If you plan to travel for several weeks or more in the United States, you may want to deposit enough money into your credit-card account to cover anticipated expenses and avoid finance charges in your absence. This also reduces the likelihood of your receiving an unwelcome big bill on your return.

You can telegraph money, or have it telegraphed to you very quickly, using the **Western Union** system (☎ **800/325-6000**).

SAFETY

While tourist areas are generally safe, crime is on the increase everywhere, and U.S. urban areas tend to be less safe than those in Europe or Japan. Visitors should always stay alert. This is particularly true of large U.S. cities, including Las Vegas.

Remember also that hotels are open to the public, and in a large hotel, security may not be able to screen everyone entering. Always lock your room door—don't assume that once inside your hotel you are automatically safe and no longer need to be aware of your surroundings. In Las Vegas, many hotels check room keys at the elevators at night, providing some extra security. Many Las Vegas hotels also have in-room safes; if yours doesn't and you're traveling with valuables, put them in a safety-deposit box at the front desk.

DRIVING SAFETY   Safety while driving is particularly important. Question your rental agency about personal safety, or ask for a brochure of traveler safety tips when you pick up your car. Obtain written directions, or a map with the route marked in red, from the agency showing how to get to your destination. And, if possible, arrive and depart during daylight hours.

Recently more and more crime has involved cars and drivers. If you drive off a highway into a doubtful neighborhood, leave the area as quickly as possible. If you have an accident, even on the highway, stay in your car with the doors locked until you assess the situation or until the police arrive. If you are bumped from behind on the street or are involved in a minor accident with no injuries and the situation appears to be suspicious, motion to the other driver to follow you to either a police station, gas station, or some other well-populated area. Never get out of your car in such situations.

If you see someone on the road who indicates a need for help, do not stop. Take note of the location, drive to a well-lighted area, and telephone the police by dialing ☎ **911.** Park in well-lighted, well-traveled areas if possible.

Always keep your car doors locked, whether attended or unattended. Never leave any packages or valuables in sight. If someone attempts to rob you or steal your car, do not try to resist the thief/carjacker—report the incident to the police department immediately.

2 Getting to the United States

For an extensive listing of airlines that fly into Las Vegas, see "Getting There" in chapter 2. Travelers from overseas can take advantage of the advance-purchase fares offered by all the major U.S. and European carriers.

A number of U.S. airlines offer service from Europe to the United States. If they do not have direct flights from Europe to Las Vegas, they can book you straight through on a connecting flight. You can make reservations by calling the following numbers in London: **American** (☎ 0181/572-5555), **Continental** (☎ 4412/9377-6464), **Delta** (☎ 0800/414-767), and **United** (☎ 0181/990-9900).

And of course many international carriers serve LAX and/or San Francisco International Airport. Helpful numbers to know include **Virgin Atlantic** (☎ 0293/747-747 in London), **British Airways** (☎ 0345/222-111 in London), and **Aer Lingus** (☎ 01/844-4747 in Dublin, or 061/415-556 in Shannon). **Qantas** (☎ 008/177-767 in Australia) has flights from Sydney to Los Angeles and San Francisco; you can also take United from Australia to the West Coast. **Air New Zealand** (☎ 0800/737-000 in Auckland, or 643/379-5200 in Christchurch) also offers service to LAX. Canadian readers might book flights on **Air Canada** (☎ 800/268-7240 in Canada or 800/361-8620), which offers direct service from Toronto, Montreal, Calgary, and Vancouver to San Francisco and Los Angeles.

The visitor arriving by air, no matter what the port of entry, should cultivate patience and resignation before setting foot on U.S. soil. Getting through immigration control may take as long as 2 hours on some days, especially summer weekends, so have your guidebook or something else handy to read. Add the time it takes to clear Customs and you will see you should make a very generous allowance for delay in planning connections between international and domestic flights—figure on 2 to 3 hours at least.

In contrast, for the traveler arriving by car or by rail from Canada, the border-crossing formalities have been streamlined to the vanishing point. And for the traveler by air from Canada, Bermuda, and some places in the Caribbean, you can sometimes go through Customs and Immigration at the point of departure, which is much quicker.

3 Getting Around the United States

On their transatlantic or transpacific flights, some large U.S. airlines (for example, TWA, American, Northwest, United, and Delta) offer travelers special discount tickets under the name **Visit USA,** allowing travel between U.S. destinations at minimum rates. They are not on sale in the United States and must be purchased before you leave your point of departure. This system is the best, easiest, and fastest way to see the United States at low cost. You should obtain information well in advance from your travel agent or the office of the airline concerned, since the conditions attached to these discount tickets can be changed without advance notice.

Bus travel in the United States can be both slow and uncomfortable; however, it can also be quite inexpensive. **Greyhound** (☎ **800/231-2222**), the sole nationwide bus line, offers an **Ameripass** for unlimited travel throughout the United

States. At press time, prices were $179 for 7 days, $289 for 15 days, $399 for 30 days, and $559 for 60 days. Though bus stations are often located in undesirable neighborhoods, the one in Las Vegas is conveniently located in a safe part of Downtown.

There is currently no **rail** service to Las Vegas.

FAST FACTS: For the Foreign Traveler

Automobile Organizations   Auto clubs will supply maps, suggested routes, guidebooks, accident and bail-bond insurance, and emergency road service. The major auto club in the United States, with hundreds of offices nationwide, is the **American Automobile Association (AAA).** Members of some foreign auto clubs have reciprocal arrangements with AAA and enjoy its services at no charge. If you belong to an auto club, inquire about AAA reciprocity before you leave. AAA can provide you with an **International Driving Permit** validating your foreign license, although drivers with valid licenses from most home countries don't really need this permit. You may be able to join AAA even if you are not a member of a reciprocal club. To inquire, call the nearest office in Carson City (☎ **702/883-2470**). In addition, some car-rental agencies now provide these services, so you should inquire about their availability when you rent your car.

Automobile Rentals   To rent a car you need a major credit or charge card. A valid driver's license is required, and you usually need to be at least 25 years old. Some companies do rent to younger people but add a daily surcharge. Be sure to return your car with the same amount of gas you started out with; rental companies charge excessive prices for gasoline. For car-rental companies in Las Vegas, see "Renting a Car" in chapter 2.

Business Hours   Offices are usually open weekdays from 9am to 5pm. Banks are open weekdays from 9am to 3pm or later, although there's 24-hour access to the automated-teller machines (ATMs) at most banks and other outlets. In Las Vegas, money is also available around the clock at casino cages—and every casino has at least one ATM machine. Shops, especially those in shopping complexes, tend to stay open late: until about 9pm weekdays and until 6pm weekends.

Climate   See "When to Go" in chapter 2.

Currency   See "Preparing for Your Trip" earlier in this chapter.

Currency Exchange   The "foreign-exchange bureaus" so common in Europe are rare in the United States. They're at major international airports, and there are a few in most major cities, but they're nonexistent in medium-size cities and small towns. Try to avoid having to change foreign money, or traveler's checks denominated other than in U.S. dollars, at small-town banks, or even at branches in a big city; in fact, leave any currency other than U.S. dollars at home (except the cash you need for the taxi or bus ride home when you return to your own country); otherwise, your own currency may prove more nuisance to you than it's worth.

Las Vegas casinos can exchange foreign currency, usually at a good rate.

Drinking Laws   The legal age to drink alcohol is 21.

Electric Current   The United States uses 110–120 volts AC (60 cycles), compared to 220–240 volts AC (50 cycles), as in most of Europe. Besides a 100-volt converter, small appliances of non-American manufacture, such as hair dryers or shavers, will require a plug adapter with two flat, parallel pins. The easiest solution to the power struggle is to purchase dual-voltage appliances that operate on both 110 and 220 volts and then all that is required is a U.S. adapter plug.

Embassies & Consulates   All embassies are located in the nation's capital, Washington, D.C. In addition, several of the major English-speaking countries also have consulates in San Francisco or in Los Angeles.

The embassy of **Australia** is at 1601 Massachusetts Ave. NW, Washington, DC 20036 (☎ **202/797-3000**); a consulate-general is at 1 Bush St., Suite 700, San Francisco, CA 94104 (☎ **415/362-6160**). The embassy of **Canada** is at 501 Pennsylvania Ave. NW, Washington, DC 20001 (☎ **202/682-1740**); the nearest consulate is at 300 South Grand Ave., 10th Floor, California Plaza, Los Angeles, CA 90071 (☎ **213/346-2700**). The embassy of the **Republic of Ireland** is at 2234 Massachusetts Ave. NW, Washington, DC 20008 (☎ **202/462-3939**); a consulate is at 44 Montgomery St., Suite 3830, San Francisco, CA 94104 (☎ **415/392-4214**). The embassy of **New Zealand** is at 37 Observatory Circle NW, Washington, DC 20008 (☎ **202/328-4848**); the nearest consulate is at 12400 Wilshire Blvd., Suite 1150, Los Angeles, CA 90025 (☎ **310/207-1605**). The embassy of the **United Kingdom** is at 3100 Massachusetts Ave. NW, Washington, DC 20008 (☎ **202/462-1340**); the nearest consulate is at 1 Sansome St., Suite 850, San Francisco, CA 94104 (☎ **415/981-3030**).

If you are from another country, you can get the telephone number of your embassy by calling "Information" (directory assistance) in Washington, D.C. (☎ **202/555-1212**).

Emergencies   Call ☎ **911** for fire, police, and ambulance. If you encounter such travelers' problems as sickness, accident, or lost or stolen baggage, call **Traveler's Aid,** an organization that specializes in helping distressed travelers. In Las Vegas, there is an office in **McCarran International Airport** (☎ **702/798-1742**), which is open daily from 8am to 5pm. Similar services are provided by **Help of Southern Nevada,** 953-35B E. Sahara Ave., Suite 208, at Maryland Parkway in the Commercial Center on the northeast corner (☎ **702/369-4357**). Hours are Monday to Friday 8am to 4pm.

Holidays   On the following national legal holidays, banks, government offices, post offices, and many stores, restaurants, and museums are closed: January 1 (New Year's Day), third Monday in January (Martin Luther King Jr. Day), third Monday in February (Presidents' Day), last Monday in May (Memorial Day), July 4 (Independence Day), first Monday in September (Labor Day), second Monday in October (Columbus Day), November 11 (Veterans Day/Armistice Day), fourth Thursday in November (Thanksgiving Day), and December 25 (Christmas Day). The Tuesday following the first Monday in November is Election Day and is a legal holiday in presidential election years (the next one is 2000).

Legal Aid   If you are stopped for a minor infraction (for example, of the highway code, such as speeding), never attempt to pay the fine directly to a police officer; you may be arrested on the much more serious charge of attempted bribery. Pay fines by mail, or directly into the hands of the clerk of the court. If accused of a more serious offense, it is best to say and do nothing before consulting a lawyer. Under U.S. law, an arrested person is allowed one telephone call to a party of his or her choice. Call your embassy or consulate.

Mail   You may receive mail c/o General Delivery at the main post office of the city or region where you expect to be. The addressee must pick it up in person, and must produce proof of identity (driver's license, credit card, passport).

Mailboxes are blue with a red-and-white logo, and carry the inscription U.S. MAIL. Within the United States, it costs 21¢ to mail a standard-size postcard. Letters that weigh up to 1 ounce cost 32¢ (33¢ beginning January 10, 1999), plus 24¢ for each additional ounce. A postcard to Mexico costs 35¢, a half-ounce letter 46¢; a postcard to Canada costs 40¢, a 1-ounce letter 52¢. A postcard to Europe, Australia, New Zealand, the Far East, South America, and elsewhere costs 50¢, while a 1-ounce letter is $1. In Las Vegas, the closest post office to the Strip is behind the Stardust Hotel at 3100 S. Industrial Rd., between Sahara Avenue and Spring Mountain Road (☎ **800/297-5543**). The **main post office** is at 1001 E. Sunset Rd., same phone number. It's open Monday to Friday 8:30am to 5pm. You can also mail letters and packages at your hotel, and there's a full-service U.S. Post Office in the Forum Shops in Caesars Palace.

Medical Emergencies   See "Emergencies" above.

Taxes   In the United States there is no VAT (value-added tax) or other indirect tax at a national level. There is a $10 Customs tax, payable upon entry to the United States, and a $6 departure tax. Sales tax of 7% is levied on goods and services by state and local governments, however, and is not included in the price tags you'll see on merchandise. There is also a hotel tax of 8%. These taxes are not refundable.

Telephone & Fax   Pay phones can be found on street corners, as well as in bars, restaurants, public buildings, stores, and at service stations. Some accept 20¢, but most are 25¢, for a local call. If the telephone accepts 20¢, you may also use a quarter (25¢), but you will not receive change.

In the past few years, many American companies have installed "voice-mail" systems, so be prepared to deal with a machine instead of a receptionist if calling a business number. Listen carefully to the instructions (you'll probably be asked to dial 1, 2, or 3 or wait for an operator to pick up); if you can't understand, sometimes dialing 0 will put you in touch with an operator within the company. It's frustrating even for locals!

For long-distance or international calls, it's most economical to charge the call to a telephone charge card or a credit card, or you can use a lot of change. The pay phone will instruct you how much to deposit and when to deposit it into the slot on the top of the telephone box.

For **long-distance calls in the United States,** dial 1 followed by the area code and the number you want. For **direct overseas calls,** first dial 011, followed by the country code (Australia, 61; Republic of Ireland, 353; New Zealand, 64; South Africa, 27; United Kingdom, 44; and so on), and then by the city code (for example, 71 or 81 for London, 21 for Birmingham, 1 for Dublin) and the number of the person you wish to call.

Before calling from a hotel room, always ask the hotel phone operator if there are any telephone surcharges. There almost always are, and they often are as much as 75¢ or $1, even for a local call. These charges are best avoided by using a public phone, calling collect, or using a telephone charge card.

For **reversed-charge or collect calls** and for **person-to-person calls,** dial 0 (zero, not the letter "O") followed by the area code and number you want; an operator will then come on the line, and you should specify that you are calling collect, or person-to-person, or both. If your operator-assisted call is international, immediately ask to speak with an overseas operator.

Telephone Directory   The local phone company provides two kinds of telephone directories. The general directory, called the **white pages,** lists businesses and personal residences separately, in alphabetical order. The first few pages are devoted to community-service numbers, including a guide to long-distance and international calling, complete with country codes and area codes.

The second directory, the **yellow pages,** lists all local services, businesses, and industries by type, with an index at the back. The listings cover not only such obvious items as automobile repairs by make of car, or drugstores (pharmacies), often by geographical location, but also restaurants by type of cuisine and geographical location, bookstores by special subject and/or language, places of worship by religious denomination, and other information that a visitor might otherwise not readily find. The yellow pages also include city plans or detailed area maps, often showing postal ZIP codes and public transportation.

For local directory assistance ("Information"), dial ☎ **411;** for long-distance information dial 1, then the appropriate area code and **555-1212.**

Most hotels have fax machines available for their customers, and there is usually a charge to send or receive a facsimile. You will also see signs for public faxes in the windows of small shops.

Time   Nevada is on Pacific time, which is 3 hours earlier than on the U.S. East Coast. For instance, when it is noon in Las Vegas, it is 3pm in New York and Miami; 2pm in Chicago, in the central part of the country; and 1pm in Denver, Colorado, in the midwestern part of the country. Nevada, like most of the rest of the United States, observes daylight saving time during the summer; in late spring, clocks are moved ahead 1 hour and then are turned back again in the fall. This results in lovely long summer evenings, when the sun sets as late as 8:30 or 9pm.

Tipping   Some rules of thumb: bartenders, 10% to 15%; bellhops, at least 50¢ per bag, or $2 to $3 for a lot of luggage; cab drivers, 10% of the fare; chambermaids, $1 per day; checkroom attendants, $1 per garment; hairdressers and barbers, 15% to 20%; waiters and waitresses, 15% to 20% of the check; valet parking attendants, $1; showroom maître d's, see chapter 10 for details; casino dealers, a few dollars if you've had a big win.

Getting to Know Las Vegas 4

Located in the southernmost precincts of a wide, pancake-flat valley, Las Vegas is the biggest city in the state of Nevada. Treeless mountains form a scenic backdrop to hotels awash in neon glitter. For tourism purposes, the city is quite compact.

1 Orientation

VISITOR INFORMATION

All major Las Vegas hotels provide comprehensive tourist information at their reception and/or sightseeing and show desks. Other good information sources are: the **Las Vegas Convention and Visitors Authority,** 3150 Paradise Rd., Las Vegas, NV 89109 (☎ **800/332-5333** or 702/892-0711; www.lasvegas24hours.com), open Monday to Friday 8am to 6pm, Saturday and Sunday 8am to 5pm; the **Las Vegas Chamber of Commerce,** 711 E. Desert Inn Rd., Las Vegas, NV 89109 (☎ **702/735-1616**), open Monday to Friday 8am to 5pm; and, for information on all of Nevada, including Las Vegas, the **Nevada Commission on Tourism** (☎ **800/638-2328**), open 24 hours.

FOR TROUBLED TRAVELERS

The **Traveler's Aid Society** is a social-service organization geared to helping travelers in difficult straits. Their services might include reuniting families separated while traveling, feeding people stranded without cash, or even emotional counseling. If you're in trouble, seek them out. In Las Vegas there is a Traveler's Aid office at McCarran International Airport (☎ **702/798-1742**). It's open daily from 8am to 5pm. Similar services are provided by **Help of Southern Nevada,** 953-35B E. Sahara Ave. (Suite 208), at Maryland Parkway in the Commercial Center (☎ **702/369-4357**). Hours are Monday to Friday 8am to 4pm.

CITY LAYOUT

There are two main areas of Las Vegas: the **Strip** and **Downtown.** For many people, that's all there is to Las Vegas. But there is actually more to the town than that; maybe not as glitzy and glamorous—okay, definitely not—but you will find still more casino action on Paradise Road and in east Las Vegas, mainstream and alternative culture shopping on Maryland Parkway, and different restaurant choices all over the city. Confining yourself to the Strip and Downtown is fine for the first-time visitor, but repeat customers (and you will be) should get out there and explore. Las Vegas Boulevard South (the Strip) is Ground Zero for addresses; anything crossing it will start with 1 East and 1 West (and go up from there) at that point.

THE STRIP

The Strip is probably the most famous 3½-mile stretch of highway in the nation. Officially Las Vegas Boulevard South, it contains most of the top hotels in town and offers almost all of the major showroom entertainment. We divide the Strip into three sections: **South Strip** can be roughly defined as the portion of the Strip south of Harmon Avenue, including the MGM Grand, the Monte Carlo, New York New York, and the Luxor hotels. **Mid-Strip** is a long stretch of the street between Harmon Avenue and Spring Mountain Road, including Caesars, the Mirage and Treasure Island, Bally's, the Flamingo Hilton, and Harrah's. **North Strip** stretches north from Stardust Road all the way to the Stratosphere Tower and includes the Stardust, Sahara, Riviera, Desert Inn, and Circus Circus. It's on the Strip where first-time visitors will, and probably should, spend the bulk of their time. If mobility is a problem, then it's probably the South and Mid-Strip locations that are the best bets.

EAST OF THE STRIP/CONVENTION CENTER

This area has grown up around the Las Vegas Convention Center. Las Vegas is one of the nation's top convention cities, attracting more than 2.9 million convention-eers each year. The major hotel in this section is the Las Vegas Hilton, but in recent years Marriott has built Residence Inn and Courtyard properties here, and the Hard Rock Hotel has opened. You'll find many excellent smaller hotels and motels south-ward along Paradise Road. All of these offer close proximity to the Strip.

DOWNTOWN

Also known as **"Glitter Gulch"** (narrower streets make the neon seem brighter), downtown Las Vegas, which is centered on Fremont Street between Main and 9th streets, was the first section of the city to develop hotels and casinos. With the exception of the Golden Nugget, which looks like it belongs in Monte Carlo, this area has traditionally been more casual than the Strip. But with the advent of the **Fremont Street Experience** (see chapter 7 for details), Downtown is experiencing a revitalization. The area is clean, the crowds low-key and friendly, and the light show overhead as silly as anything on the Strip. Don't overlook it. Las Vegas Boulevard runs all the way into Fremont Street downtown (about a 5-minute drive from the Stratosphere if traffic is good).

BETWEEN THE STRIP & DOWNTOWN

The area between the Strip and Downtown is a seedy stretch dotted with tacky wedding chapels, bail-bond operations, pawnshops, and cheap motels.

However, the area known as the **Gateway District** (roughly north and south of Charleston Boulevard to the west of Las Vegas Boulevard South) is slowly but surely gaining a name for itself as an actual artists' colony. Studios, small cafes, and other signs of life are springing up, and it is hoped this movement will last.

2 Getting Around

It shouldn't be too hard to navigate your way around. For the most part, you won't have to.

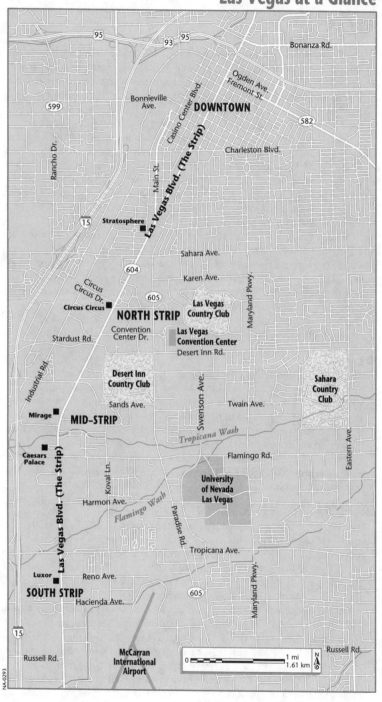

95
93 95
Bonanza Rd.

599

Rancho Dr.

Bonnieville Ave.

Ogden Ave.
Fremont St.

DOWNTOWN

582

Casino Center Blvd.

Charleston Blvd.

Main St.

15 Stratosphere

Las Vegas Blvd. (The Strip)

Sahara Ave.

604

Karen Ave.

Maryland Pkwy.

Circus
Circus Dr.

605

Las Vegas
Country Club

Circus Circus

NORTH STRIP

Stardust Rd.

Convention
Center Dr.

Las Vegas
Convention Center

Desert Inn Rd.

Industrial Rd.

Desert Inn
Country Club

Sands Ave.

Swenson Ave.

Twain Ave.

Sahara
Country Club

Mirage

MID-STRIP

Tropicana Wash

Eastern Ave.

Caesars
Palace

Koval Ln.

Flamingo Rd.

Las Vegas Blvd. (The Strip)

Flamingo Wash

Harmon Ave.

**University
of Nevada
Las Vegas**

Paradise Rd.

Tropicana Ave.

Luxor

Reno Ave.

605

Maryland Pkwy.

SOUTH STRIP

Hacienda Ave.

15

Russell Rd.

**McCarran
International
Airport**

0   1 mi
1.61 km

N

Russell Rd.

NA-0293

BY CAR

We highly recommend a rental car for Vegas tourists. The Strip is too spread out for walking, Downtown is too far away for a cheap cab ride, and public transportation is ineffective at best. Plus, further visits call for exploration in still more parts of the city, and a car brings freedom. You should note that places with addresses some 60 blocks east or west from the Strip are actually less than a 10-minute drive—provided there is no traffic. However, if you plan to confine yourself to one part of the Strip (or one cruise down to it) or to Downtown, your feet will suffice.

Note: If you can, avoid driving during peak rush hours, especially if you have to make a show curtain. Parking is usually a pleasure, since all casino hotels offer valet service. That means that for a mere $1 tip you can park right at the door (though the valet usually fills up on busy nights). Furthermore, though bus tours are available to nearby attractions, a car lets you explore at your own pace rather than according to a tour schedule. See "Renting a Car" in chapter 2 for information and toll-free numbers of companies with offices in Las Vegas.

Since driving on the outskirts of Las Vegas—for example, coming from California—involves desert driving, you must take certain precautions. It's a good idea to check your tires, water, and oil before leaving. Take at least 5 gallons of water in a clean container that can be used for either drinking or the radiator. Pay attention to road signs that suggest when to turn off your car's air conditioner. And don't push your luck with gas—it may be 35 miles, or more, between stations. If your car overheats, do not remove the radiator cap until the engine has cooled, and then remove it only very slowly. Add water to within an inch of the top of the radiator.

BY TAXI

Since cabs line up in front of all major hotels, an easy way to get around town is by taxi. Cabs charge $2.20 at the meter drop and 30¢ for each additional one-fifth of a mile. A taxi from the airport to the Strip will run you $8 to $12, from the airport to Downtown $15 to $18, and between the Strip and Downtown about $7 to $10. You can often save money by sharing a cab with someone going to the same destination (up to five people can ride for the same fare).

If you want to call a taxi, any of the following companies can provide one: **Desert Cab Company** (☎ 702/376-2688), **Whittlesea Blue Cab** (☎ 702/384-6111), and **Yellow/Checker Cab/Star Company** (☎ 702/873-2000).

BY PUBLIC TRANSPORTATION

The no. 301 bus operated by **Citizens Area Transit** (☎ 702/CAT-RIDE) plies a route between the Downtown Transportation Center (at Casino Center Boulevard and Stewart Avenue) and a few miles beyond the southern end of the Strip. The fare is $1.50 for adults, 50¢ for seniors (62 and older) and children 5 to 17, and free for those under 5. CAT buses run 24 hours a day and are wheelchair accessible. Exact change is required, but dollar bills are accepted.

Or you can hop aboard a classic streetcar replica run by **Las Vegas Strip Trolley** (☎ 702/382-1404). These old-fashioned dark green vehicles have interior oak paneling and are comfortably air-conditioned. Like the buses, they run northward from Hacienda Avenue, stopping at all major hotels en route to the Sahara, and then looping back via the Las Vegas Hilton. They do not, however, go to the Stratosphere Tower or Downtown. Trolleys run about every 15 minutes daily between 9:30am and 2am. The fare is $1.30 (free for under age 5), and exact change is required.

Chopper Tom's Traffic Hot Spots

"Chopper" Tom Hawley has watched Las Vegas grow since he was a little kid catching lizards in the desert back in the '60s. A self-described "traffic geek," Tom's traffic reports can be seen mornings and afternoons in Las Vegas on Channel 3. He also co-anchors "The Morning Report" from 7 to 9am on radio station KVBC (105.1 FM).

- **Spring Mountain/I-15 Interchange:** This interchange will be undergoing reconstruction through early 1999. Your best bet is the Desert Inn Superarterial to get over I-15. Use Tropicana or Sahara to get onto the Interstate.

- **Flamingo and the Strip:** Pedestrian underpasses here should have been built by August 1998, but the project fell apart in a squabble between Mirage Resorts and Caesars Palace. Now overhead walkways are being built and probably won't be done until sometime in 1999.

- **U.S. 95 on the West Side of Town:** A huge freeway expansion is planned, but it won't be done until well after the year 2000. During rush hour, try surface streets like Charleston Boulevard or Lake Mead Boulevard.

- **The Strip:** If you want to get a good look at the spectacular hotels, this is the only way to go, and you'll probably even enjoy taking plenty of time waiting at the lights. But if you just want to get to your destination fast, use Okavol Lane or Paradise Road.

- **I-215/Lake Mead Dr./Green Valley Pkwy.:** This three-way interchange is under construction to give motorists a quick new route for driving between Henderson and South Las Vegas. But until the work wraps up around the beginning of 1999, it will be a mess.

- **The Spaghetti Bowl:** If you want pasta, try **Battista's Hole in the Wall,** 4041 Audrie St. (☎ **702/733-3950**). The Spaghetti Bowl is what locals call the mess where I-95 intersects U.S. 95. The whole thing is being completely redesigned right now, but most of the detours are in the overnight hours.

- **Ride the Rails:** At this writing, battles are being fought over which rails will go where. Right now, monorails already exist between MGM and Bally's and between Treasure Island and the Mirage. A system between Bellagio and Monte Carlo should open in fall 1998, and another one is being planned between Bally's and the Las Vegas Hilton.

- **Stay Above It All:** Overhead pedestrian walkways at Tropicana and the Strip were completed a couple of years ago, dramatically improving vehicle traffic and pedestrian safety. Other walkways are under construction on the Strip at both Flamingo and Spring Mountain.

- **The Age of Industrial:** An upgrade of Industrial Road was completed last year, with extra lanes and smooth travel all the way from Russell Road to Oakey. It's a great alternative when I-15 and the Strip are backed up.

- **Do D.I. Direct:** The Desert Inn Superarterial was finished in March 1995, with 2 miles of nonstop travel between Paradise and Valley View. It goes up over I-15 and down under the Strip. The biggest thrill ride this side of the New York New York roller coaster!

> ### ❷ Did You Know?
>
> - Las Vegas (Sin City) has more churches per capita than any other city in America.
> - Illusionists Siegfried and Roy have sawed a woman in half more times than anyone else.
> - Visitors on a trail ride once brought a horse into the crowded casino of the Thunderbird Hotel. They put a pair of dice between his lips at the craps table, and he threw a natural 7.
> - In January, a Las Vegas visitor can ski the snowy slopes of Mount Charleston and water-ski on Lake Mead in the same day.
> - Former President Ronald Reagan performed at the Last Frontier in 1954. Those who saw him said he was a pretty good song-and-dance man.
> - Bandleader Xavier Cugat and Spanish bombshell singer Charo were the first couple to exchange vows at Caesars Palace, 2 days after its 1966 opening.

FAST FACTS: Las Vegas

Ambulances   See "Emergencies," below.

Area Code   702.

Baby-sitters   Contact **Around the Clock Child Care** (☎ **800/798-6768** or 702/365-1040). In business since 1985, this reputable company clears its sitters with the health department, the sheriff, and the FBI, and carefully screens references. Charges are $38 for 4 hours for one or two children, $7.50 for each additional hour, with surcharges for additional children and on holidays. Sitters are on call 7 days a week, 24 hours a day, and they will come to your hotel. Call at least 2 hours in advance.

Banks   Banks are generally open 9 or 10am to 3pm, and most have Saturday hours. See also "Cash & Credit," below.

Car Rentals   See "Getting Around," above.

Cash & Credit   It's extremely easy, too easy, to obtain cash in Las Vegas. Most casino cashiers will cash personal checks and can exchange foreign currency, and just about every casino has a machine that will provide cash on a wide variety of credit cards.

Climate   See "When to Go" in chapter 2.

Convention   Las Vegas is one of America's top convention destinations. Much of the action takes place at the **Las Vegas Convention Center,** 3150 Paradise Rd., Las Vegas, NV 89109 (☎ **702/892-0711**). The largest single-level convention center in the world, its 1.3 million square feet includes 89 meeting rooms. And this immense facility is augmented by the **Cashman Field Center,** 850 Las Vegas Blvd. N., Las Vegas, NV 89101 (☎ **702/386-7100**). Under the same auspices, Cashman provides another 98,100 square feet of convention space.

Dentists & Doctors   Hotels usually have lists of dentists and doctors should you need one. In addition, they are listed in the Centel Yellow Pages.

For dentist referrals you can also call the **Clark County Dental Society** (☎ **702/255-7873**), weekdays 9am to noon and 1 to 5pm; when the office is closed, a recording will tell you who to call for emergency service.

Alert

The area northeast of Harmon and Koval has had increased gang activity of late and should be avoided or at least approached with caution.

For physician referrals, call **Desert Springs Hospital** (☎ **800/842-5439** or 702/733-6875). Hours are Monday to Friday 8am to 5pm.

Drugstores   **Sav-on** is a large 24-hour drugstore and pharmacy close to the Strip at 1360 E. Flamingo Rd., at Maryland Parkway (☎ **702/731-5373** for the pharmacy, 702/737-0595 for general merchandise). **White Cross Drugs,** 1700 Las Vegas Blvd. S. (☎ **702/382-1733**), open daily 7am to 1am, will make pharmacy deliveries to your hotel during the day.

Dry Cleaners   Things spill, and silk stains. When in need, come to **Steiner Cleaners,** 1131 E. Tropicana, corner of Maryland Parkway, in the Vons Shopping Center (☎ **702/736-7474**), open Monday to Friday 7am to 6:30pm, Saturday 8am to 6pm; closed Sunday. Not only did they clean all the costumes for the movie *Casino* but they were Liberace's personal dry cleaner for years.

Emergencies   Dial ☎ **911** to contact the police or fire departments or to call an ambulance.

Emergency services are available 24 hours a day at **University Medical Center,** 1800 W. Charleston Blvd., at Shadow Lane (☎ **702/383-2661**); the emergency room entrance is on the corner of Hastings and Rose streets. **Sunrise Hospital and Medical Center,** 3186 Maryland Pkwy., between Desert Inn Road and Sahara Avenue (☎ **702/731-8080**), also has a 24-hour emergency room. For more minor problems, if you are on the Strip, the Imperial Palace has a 24-hour urgent care facility, the **Resorts Medical Center,** an independently run facility on the 8th floor, with doctors and X-ray machines; it's located at 3535 Las Vegas Blvd. S., between the Sands and Flamingo (☎ **702/731-3311**).

Highway Conditions   For recorded information, call ☎ **702/486-3116.**

Hot Lines   The Rape Crisis Center (☎ **702/366-1640**), Suicide Prevention (☎ **702/731-2990**), and Poison Emergencies (☎ **800/446-6179**).

Libraries   The largest in town is the **Clark County Library branch** at 1401 Flamingo Rd., at Escondido Street, on the southeast corner (☎ **702/733-7810**). Hours are Monday to Thursday 9am to 9pm, Friday and Saturday 9am to 5pm, Sunday 1 to 5pm.

Liquor & Gambling Laws   You must be 21 to drink or gamble. There are no closing hours in Las Vegas for the sale or consumption of alcohol, even on Sunday.

Newspapers & Periodicals   There are two Las Vegas dailies: the *Las Vegas Review Journal* and the *Las Vegas Sun.* The *Review Journal*'s Friday edition has a helpful "Weekend" section with a comprehensive guide to shows and buffets. There are two free alternative papers, with club listings and many unbiased restaurant and bar reviews. *City Life* is weekly and *Scope* is biweekly. And at every hotel desk, you'll find dozens of free local magazines, such as *Vegas Visitor, What's On in Las Vegas, Showbiz Weekly,* and *Where to Go in Las Vegas,* that are chock-full of helpful information—although probably of the sort that comes from paid advertising. The International Newsstand carries a vast selection of virtually ever major U.S. city newspaper and many international ones; they probably don't have everything, but we tried and couldn't find one they had missed. They're in Citibank Plaza at 3900 Maryland Pkwy. (☎ **702/796-9901**), open Monday to Sunday from 8:30am to 9pm.

Parking   Valet parking is one of the great pleasures of Las Vegas and well worth the dollar tip (given when the car is returned) to save walking a city block from the far reaches of a hotel parking lot, particularly when the temperature is over 100°. Another summer plus: The valet will turn on your air-conditioning, so you don't have to get in an "oven on wheels."

Police   For nonemergencies call ☎ **702/795-3111.** For emergencies call ☎ **911.**

Post Office   The most convenient post office is immediately behind the Stardust Hotel at 3100 Industrial Rd., between Sahara Avenue and Spring Mountain Road (☎ **800/297-5543**). It's open Monday to Friday 8:30am to 5pm. You can also mail letters and packages at your hotel, and there's a full-service U.S. Post Office in the Forum Shops in Caesars Palace.

Safety   In Las Vegas, vast amounts of money are always on display, and criminals find many easy marks. Don't be one of them. At gaming tables and slot machines, men should keep wallets well concealed and out of the reach of pickpockets, and women should keep handbags in plain sight (on laps). Outside casinos, popular spots for pickpockets and thieves are restaurants and outdoor shows, such as the volcano at the Mirage or at the Treasure Island pirate battle. Stay alert. Unless your hotel room has an in-room safe, check your valuables in a safety-deposit box at the front desk.

Show Tickets   See chapter 10 for details on obtaining show tickets.

Taxes   Clark County hotel room tax is 8%; the sales tax is 7%.

Time Zone   Las Vegas is in the Pacific time zone, 3 hours earlier than the East Coast, 2 hours earlier than the Midwest.

Veterinarian   If Fido or Fluffy gets sick while traveling, go to the **West Flamingo Animal Hospital.** It's open 24 hours and they take Discover, MasterCard, Visa, and have an ATM machine; 5445 Flamingo near Decatur (☎ **702/876-2111**).

Weather & Time   Call ☎ **702/248-4800.**

Weddings   Las Vegas is one of the easiest places in the world to tie the knot. There's no blood test or waiting period, the ceremony and license are inexpensive, chapels are open around the clock, and your honeymoon destination is right at hand. More than 101,000 marriages are performed here each year. Get a license Downtown at the Clark County Marriage License Bureau, 200 S. 3rd St., at Bridger Avenue (☎ **702/455-3156**). Open 8am to midnight Monday to Thursday and from 8am Friday through midnight Sunday. On legal holidays they're open 24 hours. The cost of a marriage license is $35; the cost of the ceremony, another $35.

Accommodations 5

If there's one thing Vegas has, it's hotels. Big hotels. Here you'll find 19 of the 20 largest hotels in the world. And rooms: 110,000 rooms, to be exact—or at least exact at this writing. Every 5 minutes, or so it seems, someone is putting up a new giant hotel, or adding another 1,000 rooms to an already existing one. So finding a place to stay in Vegas should be the least of your worries.

Or is it?

When a convention, a fight, or some other big event is happening—and these things are always happening—darn near all of those 110,000 rooms are going to be sold out. (Over the course of last year, the occupancy rate for hotel rooms in Las Vegas ran at about 90%.) A last-minute Vegas vacation can turn into a housing nightmare. If possible, plan in advance so that you can have your choice: Ancient Egypt or Ancient Rome? New York or New Orleans? Strip or Downtown? Luxury or economy? Vegas has all that and way too much more.

The bottom line is that with a few sometimes subtle differences, a hotel room is a hotel room is a hotel room. After you factor in location, price, and whether you have a pirate-loving kid, there isn't that much difference between rooms, except for perhaps size and the quality of their surprisingly similar furnishings. Price isn't even always a guideline; prices in Vegas are anything but fixed, so you will notice wild ranges (the same room can routinely go for anywhere from $60 to $250, depending on demand), and even that range is negotiable if it's a slow time (though such times are less and less common thanks to the influx of conventions).

Yes, if you pay more you will probably (but not certainly) get a "nicer" establishment and clientele to match (perhaps not so many loud drunks in the elevators). On the other hand, if a convention is in town the drunks will be there; they will just be wearing business suits and/or funny hats. And frankly, the big hotels, no matter how fine, are mass-producing rooms; at 3,000 or more a pop, they are the equivalent of '60s tract housing. Consequently, even in the nicest hotels you can (and probably will) encounter plumbing noises, overhear conversations from other rooms, or get woken by the maids as they knock on the doors next to yours that don't have the DO NOT DISTURB sign up.

Shifting Sands—Tribute to a Las Vegas Legend

The Sands Hotel, closed in 1996, had been a Las Vegas landmark since 1952. It was the seventh resort to open on the Strip. New York show producer and Copacabana nightclub owner Jack Entratter was one of its original backers, and he used his showbiz contacts to bring superstar entertainment and gorgeous showgirls to the Copa Room stage. Danny Thomas was the room's opening headliner; Jimmy Durante, Red Skelton, Debbie Reynolds, and Jerry Lewis were among those who made regular appearances; and Louis Armstrong and Metropolitan Opera star Robert Merrill performed together for a memorable 2 weeks in 1954. Entrater's efforts not only put the Sands on the map but helped establish Las Vegas as America's entertainment capital.

However, the Sands was probably most famous as the home of the notorious Rat Pack (Frank Sinatra, Sammy Davis Jr., Dean Martin, Peter Lawford, and Joey Bishop) and the site of their 3-week "Summit Meeting" in January 1960. No other Las Vegas show tickets have ever been more coveted or difficult to obtain. One night Sinatra picked up Sammy Davis Jr. bodily and said, "Ladies and gentlemen, I want to thank you for giving me this valuable NAACP trophy." He then dropped Davis into the lap of a man in a ringside seat who happened to be Sen. John F. Kennedy. Davis looked up and quipped, "It's perfectly all right with me, Senator, as long as I'm not being donated to George Wallace or James Eastland." The Rat Pack returned to the Copa stage in 1961 for an onstage birthday party for Dean Martin with a 5-foot-high cake in the shape of a whisky bottle. Martin threw the first slice, and a food fight ensued. The riotous clan kept Las Vegas amused during most of the decade. By the way, Frank Sinatra and Mia Farrow were married at the Sands several eons ago.

Fittingly, perhaps, on the site of the Sands will be the new Venetian Resort. Planned as the largest hotel in the world, it should make Vegas history again. But will it do it with as much style?

1 Best Bets

- **Best for Conventioneers/Business Travelers:** The **Las Vegas Hilton,** 3000 Paradise Rd. (☎ **800/732-7117**), adjacent to the Las Vegas Convention Center and the setting for many on-premises conventions, offers extensive facilities along with helpful services such as a full business center.
- **Best Elegant Hotel:** Country club elegance is the keynote of the **Desert Inn Country Club Resort and Casino,** 3145 Las Vegas Blvd. S. (☎ **800/634-9606**). In its European-style casino, gaming tables are comfortably spaced; the glitzy glow of neon is replaced by the glitter of crystal chandeliers; and the scarcity of slot and video poker machines eliminates the usual noisy jangle of coins. Extensive facilities are complemented by attentive personal service. This is the most prestigious hotel address in town.
- **Best Archetypically Las Vegas Hotel:** By the end of 1998, there aren't going to be any. Las Vegas hotels are one and all doing such massive face-lifts that the archetype is going to be but a memory. Still, despite some major changes, **Caesars Palace,** 3570 Las Vegas Blvd. S. (☎ **800/634-6661**), will probably continue to embody the excess and, well, downright silliness that used to characterize Vegas—and to a certain extent still does.

- **Best Swimming Pool:** The **Mirage,** 3400 Las Vegas Blvd. S. (☎ **800/ 627-6667**), and the **Flamingo Hilton,** 3555 Las Vegas Blvd. S. (☎ **800/ 732-2111**), probably tie for most stunning; both feature lushly landscaped areas, with trees galore, amorphously shaped pools with water slides and waterfalls, plus kiddie pools, Jacuzzis, and, in the case of the Flamingo, swan- and duck-filled ponds and islands of flamingos and African penguins. Far more Vegas, however, is the **Tropicana Resort & Casino,** 3801 Las Vegas Blvd. S. (☎ **800/ 634-4000**), where you'll also find a swim-up bar/blackjack table.

- **Best Health Club:** Like sumptuous swimming pools, deluxe state-of-the-art health clubs are the rule in Las Vegas hotels. Most exclusive (the fee is $20 per visit) and extensively equipped is the club at the **Mirage** (see above), offering a full complement of machines—some with individual TVs (headphones are supplied), free weights, private whirlpool rooms as well as a large whirlpool and saunas, a thoroughly equipped locker room, and comfortable lounges in which to rest up after your workout. An adjoining salon offers every imaginable spa service. Steve Wynn works out here almost daily, as do many celebrity guests.

- **Best Hotel Dining/Entertainment:** Food aficionados will be thrilled with the nationally renowned celebrity chefs at the **MGM Grand Hotel/Casino,** 3799 Las Vegas Blvd. S (☎ **800/929-1111**). You'll find restaurants by Mark Miller, Emeril Lagasse, and Wolfgang Puck, as well as one of the best restaurants in Vegas: the Grand's gourmet room Gatsby's. There's also a re-creation of Hollywood's famed Brown Derby here.

- **Best for Twentysomethings to Baby Boomers:** The **Hard Rock Hotel & Casino,** 4455 Paradise Rd. (☎ **800/437-ROCK**), which bills itself as the world's "first rock 'n' roll hotel and casino" and "Vegas for a new generation." Aficionados of Hard Rock clubs won't mind the noise level, but we aren't sure about everyone else.

- **Best Interior:** For totally different reasons, it's a tie between **New York New York Hotel & Casino,** 3790 Las Vegas Blvd. S. (☎ **800/693-6763**), and the **Mirage** (see above). The latter's tropical rain forest and massive coral-reef aquarium behind the registration desk may not provide as much relaxation as a Club Med vacation, but they're a welcome change from the general hubbub that is usual for Vegas. Speaking of hubbub, New York New York has cornered the market on it, but its jaw-dropping interior, with its extraordinary attention to detail (virtually every significant characteristic of New York City is re-created somewhere here), makes this a tough act to beat. Ever.

- **Best for Families:** It's a classic: **Circus Circus Hotel/Casino,** 2880 Las Vegas Blvd. S. (☎ **800/444-CIRC**), has almost unlimited activities for kids—ongoing circus acts, a vast video-game arcade, a carnival midway, and a full amusement park.

- **Best Rooms:** On the strip, they're at the **Mirage** (see above); Downtown, they're at the **Golden Nugget,** 129 E. Fremont St. (☎ **800/634-3454**). The rooms actually look almost identical, though the former are done in more earth tones, while golds are the hallmark of the latter. In both hotels, each room has a marble entryway, a half-canopy bed, a dressing table with lighted lamp, comfortable overstuffed chairs in the single-bed rooms, and a lush (if average-sized) marble bathroom. You feel special in them.

- **Best Noncasino Hotel:** The very upscale **Alexis Park Resort,** 375 E. Harmon Ave. (☎ **800/582-2228**), is the choice of many visiting celebrities and headliners. Many of its rooms have working fireplaces and/or Jacuzzis, and guests are cosseted with can-do concierge service.

- **Best Casinos:** Our favorite places to gamble are anywhere we might win. But we also like the **Mirage** (lively, beautiful, and not overwhelming), **Caesars Palace** (because the cocktail waitresses are dressed in togas), **New York New York** (because of the aforementioned attention to detail; it almost makes losing fun!), and **Main Street Station,** 200 N. Main St. (☎ **800/465-0711**) (because it's about the most smoke-free casino in town, and because it's pretty).
- **Best Downtown Hotel:** It's a tie. The upscale **Golden Nugget** (see above) is exceptionally appealing in every aspect. The **Main Street Station** (see above), which has done a terrific job of renovating an older space, now evokes turn-of-the century San Francisco, with great Victorian details everywhere, solidly good restaurants, and surprisingly nice rooms for an inexpensive price.
- **Best Views:** From high-floor rooms at the **Stratosphere Las Vegas,** 2000 Las Vegas Blvd. S. (☎ **800/99-TOWER**), you can see the entire city.

2 Coming Attractions

The recent hotel building boom has meant that several legendary old-timers—the Dunes, Sands, and Hacienda hotels, all Strip residents of 4 decades or more—have bit the dust recently. Locals vainly decry the loss of historic properties in this current climate (even Bugsy Siegel's vast suite at the Flamingo, complete with trap-door escape routes and tunnels, has been demolished), but the process is unstoppable. Actually, by the end of 1998, nothing on the Strip will be original, since the Aladdin has been demolished for a from-the-ground-up renovation, and Caesars and the Sahara will have changed their facades, as the Flamingo and others did long ago, and the last of the old hotels will be but memories. In August 1998, due to bankruptcy proceedings, the Debbie Reynolds Hotel was sold at auction to the World Wrestling Federation, which intends to completely redo it in their own inimitable vision. (One can only imagine what that will entail, but then again, one doesn't really want to.)

The new era of hotels was ushered in by the Mirage, and everyone since then has been trying to up the ante. The year 1997 saw the opening of the Orleans just before the New Year (contributing over 800 new rooms with plans already afoot to double that) along with New York New York, which set yet another level of stupendous excess, which will surely remain unmatched. At least until the Venetian, complete with canals and gondolas, makes the scene in 1999. And then something else will come along and top that. It's one of the things you can count on in Vegas. By the year 2001, you can expect another 20,000 hotel rooms to be added.

Here's what's on tap for the next couple of years:

- You may have seen some pictures on the news in '98 of **The Aladdin,** the famous hotel where Elvis and Priscilla were married, being imploded. It is scheduled to return by the year 2000 as part of a billion-dollar rebuilding project. Included in the plans are an adjacent **Planet Hollywood Hotel & Casino,** complete with a music venue and over 1,000 rooms.
- In late 1999 you'll be able to go from New York to France in just a few minutes as Bally's opens its 3,000-room **Paris Casino Hotel** next door to its existing property. It plans on being a faithful re-creation of "The City of Lights" at the turn of the century, complete with a 540-foot replica of the Eiffel Tower.
- The mother of all new projects is **The Venetian** and will be the largest hotel in the world with over 6,000 rooms. It may also be the most expensive to build,

as its canals-and-gondolier theme is supposed to rack up a price tag near $2 billion. It is under construction on the former site of the Sands directly across the street from the Mirage and phase one is supposed to be complete sometime in 1999.

3 Three Questions to Ask Before You Book a Room

WHERE SHOULD I STAY?

Your two main choices for location are the Strip and Downtown. The Strip is undeniably the winner, especially for the first-timers, if only by sheer overwhelming force. On the other hand, it is also crowded, overly confining, and strangely claustrophobic. The hotels only look close together; in reality, those are mostly large properties, and it's a long (and often very hot or very cold) walk from one place to the next.

Contrast that with Downtown, which is nowhere near as striking, but 5 minutes can put you in about 17 different casinos. The Fremont Street upgrade has turned a rapidly declining area into a very pleasant place to be, and the crowds reflect that: They just seem nicer and more relaxed, with the result that a better time can be had there. Since it's only a 5-minute ride by car between Downtown and Strip hotels (the Convention Center is more or less in between), there's no such thing as a bad location if you have access to a car. If money is no object, a $10 cab ride separates the Strip from Downtown.

For those of you depending on public transportation: While the bus ride between Downtown and the Strip is short in distance, it can be long in time if stuck in traffic. You should also be aware that the buses become quite crowded once they reach the Strip and may pass by a bus stop if no one signals to get out and the driver does not wish to take on more passengers. Without a car, your ease of movement between areas of town is, therefore, limited.

But for first timers, frankly, there probably isn't any point to staying anywhere but the Strip; you are going to spend most (if not all) of your time there anyway. For future visits, however, strongly consider Downtown.

But even the Strip location isn't the end of the debate. Staying on the **South Strip** end means an easy walk (sometimes in air-conditioned comfort) to the MGM Grand, New York New York, Tropicana, Luxor, and Excalibur—all virtually on one corner. **Mid-Strip** has Caesars, the Mirage, Treasure Island, Bally's, the Flamingo Hilton, Harrah's, and so forth. The **North Strip** gets you the Riviera, Desert Inn, Sahara, Stardust, and Circus Circus, though with a bit more of a walk between them. For this reason, if mobility is a problem and you want to see more than just your own hotel casino, probably the South and Mid-Strip locations are the best bets.

WHAT AM I LOOKING FOR IN A HOTEL?

Consider also what you want from a hotel. If gambling is not your priority, what are you doing in Vegas? Just kidding. But if you want something quieter, consider a hotel without a casino. Make certain it has a pool, however, especially if you need some recreation; there is nothing so boring as a noncasino, nonpool Vegas hotel. Particularly if you have kids.

Casino hotels, by the way, are not always a nice place for children. It used to be that the casino was a separate section in the hotel and children were not allowed inside (we have fond memories of standing just outside the casino line, watching our dads put quarters in a slot machine "for us"). But in almost all the new hotels,

Reservations Services

If you get harried when you have to haggle, use a free service offered by **Reservations Plus,** 2275 A Renaissance Dr., Las Vegas, NV 89119 (☎ **800/805-9528;** fax 702/795-8767). They'll find you a hotel room in your price range that meets your specific requirements. Because they book rooms in volume, they are able to get discounted rates. Not only can they book rooms but they can arrange packages (including meals, transportation, tours, show tickets, car rentals, and other features) and group rates.

The **Las Vegas Convention and Visitors Authority** also runs a room reservations hotline (☎ **800/332-5334**), which can be helpful. They can apprise you of room availability, quote rates, contact a hotel for you, and tell you when major conventions will be in town.

For those of you hooked up to the Internet, there are a variety of online reservations systems that can help you get a room and make all the appropriate travel arrangements for you.

- www.180096hotel.com
- www.lasvegashotel.com
- www.lasvegasreservations.com
- www.lasvegasrooms.com
- www.lvholidays.com

A couple of words of warning: Make sure they don't try to book you into a hotel you've never heard of. Try to stick with the big names or ones listed in this book. Always get your information in writing and then make some phone calls just to confirm that you really have the reservations that they say they've made for you.

you have to walk through the casino to get anywhere—the lobby, the restaurants, the outside world. This makes sense from the hotel's point of view; it gives you many opportunities to stop and drop a quarter or $10 in a slot.

But this often major, crowded trek gets wearying for adults; it's far worse for kids. The rule is that kids can walk through the casinos, but they can't stop, even to gawk for a second at someone hitting a jackpot nearby. The casino officials who will immediately hustle said child away are just doing their job, but, boy, it's annoying.

So take this (and what a hotel offers that kids might like) into consideration when booking a room. Note also that those gorgeous hotel pools are often cold and not very deep; they look like places you would want to linger, but often (from a kid's point of view) they are not. Plus, the pools close early. (Hotels want you inside gambling, not outside swimming.)

Ultimately, though, if the town is busy, nab any room you can, especially if you get a price you like. How much time are you going to spend in the room anyway?

WHAT WILL I HAVE TO PAY?

As far as prices go, keep in mind that our price categories are rough guidelines at best. If you see a hotel that appeals to you, even if it seems out of your price range, give them a call anyway. They might be having a special, a slow week, some kind of promotion, or they may just like the sound of your voice (we have no other explanation for it). You could end up with a hotel in the "expensive" category offering you a room for $35 a night. Since it's a toll-free call, it's a worth a try.

The Laughlin Alternative

Okay, worst-case scenario: There is not a hotel room to be had for love or money in all of Las Vegas. Well, maybe for money, but you just can't count that high. Consider this seemingly radical alternative: the little town of Laughlin. Less than an hour away by car, Laughlin is also a gambling town. What it offers you are name-brand hotels like the Flamingo Hilton, Harrah's, and Golden Nugget, among many others. On a recent Super Bowl weekend, when most rooms in Vegas were sold out, outrageously priced, or both, Laughlin had plenty of rooms available in the $25 to $45 range. Even taking in account the cost of rental car and gas, this still allows you to have full day's and evening's worth of gambling in Vegas and a budget-conscious place to stay. The only thing you miss out on is being able to walk outside and immediately be on the Strip, but there's enough neon here that you can pretend. One caveat is the narrow two-lane road that you have to take to get there can be intimidating if you aren't used to such roads, but plans are in the works to upgrade it to a four-lane divided highway.

For more information call **Reservations Plus** (☎ **800/805-9528**).

You can also call the **Las Vegas Convention and Visitors Authority** (☎ **800/332-5333**) to find out if an important convention is scheduled at the time of your planned visit; if so, you might want to change your date. Some of the most popular conventions are listed under "When to Go" in chapter 2. Remember also that the best deals are offered midweek by the hotels, when prices can drop dramatically. If possible, go then.

We've classified all our hotel recommendations based on the average rack rate you can expect to be quoted for a double room on an average night (*not* when the Consumer Electronics Show is in town, *not* on New Year's Eve). Expect to pay a little less than this if you stay only Sunday to Thursday and a little more than this if you stay Friday and Saturday.

Of course, you can expect significant savings if you book a money-saving package deal, like those described in chapter 2. And on any given night when business is slow, you might be able to stay at a "very expensive" hotel for a "moderate" price.

4 South Strip

VERY EXPENSIVE

Carriage House. 105 E. Harmon Ave., between Las Vegas Blvd. S. and Koval Lane, Las Vegas, NV 89109. ☎ **800/221-2301** or 702/798-1020. Fax 702/798-1020, ext. 112. 154 units. A/C TV TEL. $135 studio for 1 or 2; $165 one-bedroom condo for up to 4; $275 two-bedroom condo for up to 6. Inquire about lower-priced packages. AE, DISC, MC, V. Free self-parking.

Housed in a 9-story stucco building fronted by palm trees, this friendly, low-key resort hotel has a loyal repeat clientele. It's entered via a large, comfortably furnished lobby where guests enjoy a complimentary Monday afternoon manager's reception with hors d'oeuvres and wine. And the hotel caters to kids with welcome bags of cookies at check-in and gratis VCRs and movies upon request; the front desk maintains a nice-size movie library.

Attractive suites, with brass-trimmed lacquer or bleached-oak furnishings, have small sitting areas and fully equipped kitchenettes (most with dishwashers). One-bedroom units have full living rooms and dining areas, with phones, radios, and

TVs in both rooms. Two-bedroom/two-bath condominiums have a king-size bed in each bedroom and a queen sleeper sofa in the living room. Both the rooms and the public areas are immaculate. Free local phone calls are a plus.

Dining/Diversions: Kiefers, perched on the ninth floor, offers a romantic, candlelit setting and superb skyline views via a wall of windows. Tuesday to Saturday a pianist entertains in an adjoining lounge with a small dance floor. The menu highlights steak, seafood, and pasta dishes. Breakfast and dinner only.

Amenities: Complimentary transportation 7am to 10:30pm to/from airport, pay-per-view movies, tour and show desks, coin-op washers/dryers, Har-Tru tennis court lit for night play (no charge for play, balls, or racquets), swimming pool/ sundeck, whirlpool.

EXPENSIVE

Mandalay Bay. Las Vegas Blvd. S., at Hacienda.

Due to open in early 1999 on the site of the old Hacienda, Mandalay Bay, named for the Rudyard Kipling poem, promises to be "1890s Burma"–themed. Plans include for the top few floors to be a Four Seasons, complete with its own separate entrance (and, presumably, rates), and for a branch of the House of Blues nightclub. No more details were available at press time—though the building does look quite spiffy on the outside—but the phrase makes us think of Southwest Asia in the days of the Raj, tigers, jungle, British colonial tea plantations, and political unrest. It does not, however, make us think of casinos, but time will tell.

✪ **MGM Grand Hotel/Casino.** 3799 Las Vegas Blvd. S., at Tropicana Ave., Las Vegas, NV 89109. ☎ **800/929-1111** or 702/891-7777. Fax 702/891-1112. www.mgmgrand.com. 5,005 units. A/C TV TEL. $69–$119 standard double; $79–$129 concierge-floor double with breakfast; $99–$2,500 suite. Extra person $10. Children under 12 stay free in parents' room. AE, DC, DISC, MC, V. Free self- and valet parking.

The MGM Grand has recently completed one of the most amusing renovations in Vegas. When it first opened, the billion-dollar property, spread over 112 acres, had a *Wizard of Oz* theme. The outside was a shocking shade of emerald green, some door handles had "Oz" on them, rainbows were everywhere, and right in the center was a giant Animatronic reenactment of MGM's most famous movie. Outside was a theme park, which initially charged an exorbitant entry fee.

That has changed. The outside is still green, but now the MGM Grand is The City of Entertainment, which means the theme is *all* MGM movies, not just one specific film beloved by children. Gone is the Oz attraction (though it may reappear at a later date in a different, less prominent part of the hotel), replaced by a Rain Forest Cafe and Studio 54, both of which are accessed through an ornate circular domed room, full of replicated '30s glamour, glitz, and gilded statues. Obviously, this is all more appealing to adults. Relegated to a basement location is the large arcade. Gone is the cartoonish lion at the entrance, replaced by a 9-story-tall, more classy, bronze Leo, part of a new facade that while certainly more glamorous, also looks tacked on (which it is) to the rest of the hotel. Leo is overlooked by 80-foot video screens so that as your plane comes in for a landing you can watch Tom Jones performing. Really. Gone, too, is much of the theme park, replaced by a convention center. Why? Well, probably because the great "Vegas Is for Families" experiment failed. But if you ask anyone in town on the record, they will deny ever catering to families. Given the original look of the MGM and what is coming in its place, that seems especially disingenuous.

But practical. The MGM did seem a bit cheesy (particularly if you contrast it to the even older, original MGM Grand, the elegant place that was destroyed in one

South Strip Accommodations

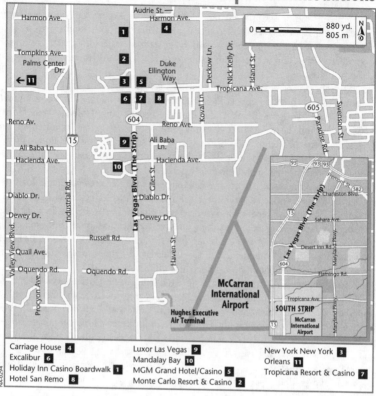

Carriage House **4**
Excalibur **6**
Holiday Inn Casino Boardwalk **1**
Hotel San Remo **8**

Luxor Las Vegas **9**
Mandalay Bay **10**
MGM Grand Hotel/Casino **5**
Monte Carlo Resort & Casino **2**

New York New York **3**
Orleans **11**
Tropicana Resort & Casino **7**

NA-0294

of the worst hotel fires in history). As one of the world's largest hotels, it was also overwhelming and hard to navigate. The eighty 42-inch TV monitors (apprising registering guests of hotel happenings) in the otherwise lovely and vast white marble lobby only added to the chaotic confusion a guest might feel.

But the renovations sought to fix all that. The TV monitors remain, but the lobby is now immediately accessible from outside. The redesign will attempt to create some more intimate corners, and has already made navigating the still immense place somewhat easier. (It's actually kind of amusing how they are now backing away from bragging about their size and moving more toward trying to hide that fact.) And the staff, confirms a recent guest, couldn't be more helpful and friendly. Throughout, the theme of The City of Entertainment is repeated, as old movies are evoked in the decor (though considerable green and the odd rainbow still remain). In certain areas (like the restaurant row), the look is meant to suggest a behind-the-scenes view of a film studio back lot.

The rooms will give no cause for complaint. They are decorated in four distinct motifs. Most glamorous are the Hollywood rooms furnished in two-tone wood pieces (bird's-eye maple on cherry), with gold-flecked walls (hung with prints of Humphrey Bogart, Marilyn Monroe, and Vivien Leigh as Scarlett), gilded moldings, and beds backed by mirrors. Oz-themed rooms still have emerald-green rugs and upholstery, silver-and-gold star-motif wallpaper, bright poppy-print bedspreads, and tasseled green drapes; walls are hung with paintings of Dorothy and friends. In the Casablanca rooms—decorated in earth tones with shimmery fabrics and pecan/walnut furnishings and moldings—artworks depict Moroccan scenes such as an Arab marketplace. And the cheerful Old South rooms feature 18th-century–style furnishings and faux-silk beige damask walls hung with paintings of southern belles and scenes from *Gone With the Wind*. All rooms offer gorgeous marble baths.

Dining/Diversions: MGM houses the most prestigious assemblage of dining rooms of any hotel in town. Four cutting-edge stars in the Las Vegas culinary galaxy—the **Wolfgang Puck Café,** Emeril Lagasse's **New Orleans Fish House, Gatsby's,** and Mark Miller's **Coyote Café**—along with buffet offerings, are described in chapter 6. Indeed, Emeril's and Gatsby's vie for the honor of best restaurant in Vegas. In addition, the following dining facilities comprise a restaurant row between the casino and the theme park.

Heralding the restaurant area's new Hollywood theme is the plush and luxurious **Brown Derby,** modeled after the legendary Los Angeles celebrity haunt where Louella Parsons and Hedda Hopper held court in the 1940s. It's not in a giant hat, though. Like the original, its walls are lined with caricatures of celebrities (a caricaturist on the premises draws customers for a fee), and signature dishes on its largely steak/chops/seafood menu include Cobb salad and grapefruit cake. A handsome mahogany-paneled bar adjoins. Lunch and dinner are served.

Another new facility here consists of two distinct dining areas: **La Scala** and **Tre Visi.** Both serve regional Italian fare. The very elegant La Scala (named for the Milan opera house) has walls hung with opera posters and antique musical instruments. It's open for dinner only. Fronted by an imposing Doric colonnade suggestive of a Roman ruin, with columned archways inside framing scenes of ancient Rome, the more casual Tre Visi serves lunch and dinner.

Dragon Court is an elegant restaurant with textured gold wall coverings and purple-and-gold fleur-de-lis pattern carpeting. Eclectic Chinese fare is featured. Only dinner is served.

A food court, done in a Farmer's Market outdoor theme, features **McDonald's, Hamada's Orient Express, Mamma Ilardo's Pizzeria, Nathan's** (hot dogs and fries), and a **Häagen-Dazs** ice-cream outlet that also features espresso and cappuccino. The **Stage Deli Express,** a cafeteria-style offshoot of the New York original, serves up traditional deli sandwiches; seating overlooks race and sports book action.

Benninger's, off the casino, provides gourmet coffees and scrumptious fresh-baked pastries (great bear claws here). In addition, there are many restaurants and fast-food places in the theme park.

The **Center Stage** and **Betty Boop** lounges offer entertainment nightly. The circular **Flying Monkey Bar** and the **Santa Fe Lounge** offer live music. A talking robotic horse and jockey spout sports data at the **Turf Club Lounge** in the race and sports book area.

Amenities: 24-hour room service, foreign currency exchange, guest relations desk, shoe shine (in men's rooms), casino; MGM Grand Adventures Theme Park; full-service health spa and health club; full-service unisex hair/beauty salon; four night-lit tennis courts with pro shop (lessons available); huge beach-entry swimming pool with waterfall; a vast sundeck area with a Jacuzzi, pool bar, and cabanas equipped with cushioned chairs and towels that rent for $20 per day; a 30,000-square-foot video arcade (including virtual-reality games); carnival midway with 33 games of skill; business center; florist; shopping arcade; two wedding chapels (in the theme park); show/sports event ticket desks; car-rental desk; sightseeing/tour desks; America West airline desk.

Impressions

For the grand debut of Monte Carlo as a resort in 1879 the architect Charles Garnier designed an opera house for the Place du Casino and Sarah Bernhardt read a symbolic poem. For the debut of Las Vegas as a resort in 1946 Bugsy Siegel hired Abbott and Costello, and there, in a way, you have it all.
—Tom Wolfe, *Las Vegas (What?) . . . (Can't hear you! Too noisy) Las Vegas!!!!*

The **MGM Grand Youth Center,** a first-rate facility for children ages 3 to 16, has separate areas for different age groups. The center has a playhouse and tumbling mats for toddlers, a game room, extensive arts-and-crafts equipment, video games, a dining area, and a large-screen TV/VCR for children's movies. Accompanied by professional counselors, youngsters can visit the theme park or the swimming pool, take excursions to nearby attractions, have meals, and participate in all sorts of entertainment and activities (☎ **702/891-3200** for details and prices).

Monte Carlo Resort & Casino. 3770 Las Vegas Blvd. S., between Flamingo Rd. and Tropicana Ave., Las Vegas, NV 89109. ☎ **800/311-8999** or 702/730-7777. Fax 702/730-7250. www.monte-carlo.com. 3,014 units. A/C TV TEL. Sun–Thurs $69–$199 double, Fri–Sat $99–$269 double; $139–$339 suite. Extra person $15. Children under 12 stay free in parents' room. AE, CB, DC, DISC, MC, V. Free self- and valet parking.

The newest resort on the Strip, the massive Monte Carlo is the world's seventh largest hotel. It's fronted by Corinthian colonnades, triumphal arches, splashing fountains, and allegorical (and slightly naughty) statuary, with an entranceway opening on a bustling casino. A separate entrance in the rear of the hotel leads to a splendid marble-floored, crystal-chandeliered lobby evocative of a European grand hotel. Palladian windows behind the registration desk overlook a salient feature: the hotel's 20,000-acre pool area, a lushly landscaped miniature water park with a 4,800-foot wave pool, a surf pond, waterfalls, and a "river" for tubing. Also notable is the Monte Carlo's spa, offering extensive workout facilities, hot and cool whirlpools, steam and sauna, and numerous services (massage, facials, sea-salt scrubs, seaweed wraps, and more). Workout clothing and toiletries are provided.

Spacious rooms with big marble baths exude a warmly traditional European feel. Striped tan wallpapers with fleur-de-lis friezes create a neutral backdrop for rich cherrywood furnishings and vivid floral-print fabrics and carpeting. Cable TVs are equipped with hotel information channels, keno, and pay-movie options. A concierge level for VIPs is on the 32nd floor.

Dining/Diversions: The Monte Carlo's **Pub and Brewery and Dragon Noodle Company** are described in chapter 6. In addition, there is now a branch of the classic Downtown French restaurant **Andre's,** reviewed in chapter 6, in the hotel.

A wall of stained-glass windows, beveled mirrors, rich mahogany paneling, plush leather booths, and elegantly appointed tables lit by shaded candle lamps set an opulent tone at **Blackstone's Steak House.** Dinner only; entrees include mesquite-grilled steaks, seafood, prime rib, and roast duck Grand Marnier.

At the **Market City Caffe,** a tempting antipasto bar (with dozens of items ranging from roasted potato salad to mussels marinara), a display kitchen housing an oak-burning pizza oven, and wooden bins overflowing with fruits and vegetables create a warmly colorful interior. Lunch and dinner daily.

The plant-filled, sky-ceilinged 24-hour **Cafe** has a whimsical magic/fantasy theme; delightful murals depict clowns, court jesters, and harlequins. Additional venues include a food court (with branches of **Nathan's, McDonald's, Sbarro,**

Häagen-Dazs, and a first-rate bagel bakery), a pool-area snack bar, and several lounges, most notably the plush **Houdini's,** its magic theme honoring illusionist Lance Burton, who headlines at the hotel's showroom.

Amenities: 24-hour room service, foreign currency exchange, shoe shine, limo rental, casino, car-rental desk, four tennis courts, sightseeing/tour/show desk, barber/beauty salon, vast swimming pool, kiddie pool, whirlpool, water attractions (see above), wedding chapel, full business center, large video-game arcade, large shopping arcade.

✪ **New York New York Hotel & Casino.** 3790 Las Vegas Blvd. S., at Tropicana Ave., Las Vegas, NV 89109. ☎ **800/693-6763** or 702/740-6969. Fax 702/740-6920. www. nynyhotelcasino.com. 2,034 units. A/C TV TEL. Sun–Thurs from $89 double, Fri–Sat from $129 double. Extra person $20. AE, CB, DC, DISC, MC, V. Free self- and valet parking.

Just when you think Las Vegas has it all and has done it all, they go and do something like this. New York New York is just plain spectacular. Even the jaded and horrified have to admit it. You can't miss the hotel; it's that little (Hah!) building on the corner of the Strip and Tropicana that looks like the New York City skyline: the Empire State Building, the Chrysler Building, the Public Library, down to the 150-foot Statue of Liberty and Ellis Island, all built to approximately one-third scale. And as if that isn't enough, they threw in a roller coaster running around the outside and into the hotel and casino itself.

And inside, it all gets better. There are details everywhere—so many, in fact, that the typical expression on the face of casino-goers is slack-jawed wonder. If you enter the casino via the Brooklyn Bridge (the walkway from the Strip), you find yourself in a replica of Greenwich Village, down to the cobblestones, the manhole covers, the tenement buildings, and the graffiti. (Yes, they even re-created that. You should see the subway station.) The main casino area is done as Central Park, complete with trees, babbling brooks, streetlamps, and footbridges. The change carts are little Yellow Cabs. The reception area and lobby are done in belle epoque, art deco, golden age of Manhattan style; you feel like breaking out into a 1930s musical number while standing there. It really is impossible to adequately describe the sheer mind-blowing enormity of the thing. So we are just going to leave it at: *Wow.* The word *subtle* was obviously not in the lexicon of the designers. It's hard to see how Vegas can ever top this, but then again that's been said before.

Upstairs—oh, yes, there's much more—is the arcade, which is Coney Island–themed (naturally), and just as crowded as the real thing, as kids play boardwalk games in the hopes of winning tickets redeemable for cheap prizes. (This helps them learn about gambling at an early age.) The line for the roller coaster (lengthy at this writing) is here. There are many restaurants, all housed in buildings that fit the theme of whatever New York neighborhood is represented in that particular part of the hotel.

Rooms are housed in different towers, each with a New York–inspired name. (Disappointingly, they are not inside the buildings of the skyline—it would have been quite fun to stay in the Empire State Building.) Truthfully, the place is so massive that finding your way to your room can take a while. There are 64 different styles of rooms, and they are all smashing. Each essentially is done up in a hard-core art deco style: various shades of inlaid wood, rounded tops to the armoires and headboards, usually shades of brown and wood colors. However, some of the rooms are downright tiny (just like New York again!), and in those all this massively detailed decoration could be overwhelming, if not suffocating. The bathrooms are also small, but with black marble–topped sinks, which again lend a glamorous '20s image. The amenities come in bottles shaped like the NYC skyline—these are the sort you want to stash in your suitcase to take home!

The march to the pool will in some cases trot you right down that Central Park bridge—wave to all the restaurant patrons as you parade in your swimsuit. The pool is the only disappointment; though fairly large with a waterfall, it's shallow and ringed on one side by the parking garage. The roller coaster regularly screams by overhead.

Cranks would have us note that coming here is not like going to the real New York. On the other hand, given how crowded it is (everyone wants to come check it out, and stays to play) and how noisy, it kind of is just like being in New York. Especially with the all-too-realistic traffic and parking nightmares. In short, New York New York is not only overcrowded but perhaps not as efficient as it should be. Though staying here seems irresistible, it may be worth waiting until some of the newness has worn off (although that should have happened by now and hasn't) or certainly until another new, fabulous place opens up. But this hasn't stopped many from staying here; a mere 6 months after opening, hotel representatives announced they were doing so well they were planning to add another 1,000 rooms.

Dining/Diversions: As mentioned above, even though New York New York has been around for over a year, everyone is going there, which means the restaurants and snack bars are almost always crowded, particularly within 2 hours (in either direction) of mealtimes. This translates to long lines and waits, and occasionally less-than-terrific service. Too bad; the food looks tasty, and they have several brand-name restaurants here that provide a welcome relief from some of the dreck found in Vegas hotels. Plan to either bring a book, eat at really off hours, or skip it altogether until (again) the newness has worn off.

The **Motown Cafe** is described in chapter 6.

Il Fornaio is a reliable chain, featuring nouvelle Italian cuisine (meaning lighter sauces based on olive oil rather than tomatoes). They also make their own delicious bread and some terrific pastries.

Chin-Chin is another chain, somewhat less reliable (it gets mixed reviews from diners), featuring Szechuan and Cantonese, with some Polynesian and Pacific Rim tossed in.

Gallagher's Steak House is an upscale steak house, most notable for the huge cuts of raw meat that are in the windows, attracting many bemused looks.

America is the 24-hour coffee shop. Scattered throughout the property are also a pizza place (featuring slices and long lines), a deli, barbecue, Mexican, and **Nathan's** hot dogs, which no New York–themed hotel should be without (though the dogs cost quite a bit more than the buck they will set you back in NYC). **Schraft's Ice Cream** has also been resurrected here; at $2.50 for a scoop, it's pricey, but so good it's worth it.

There are several festive and beautifully decorated bars throughout the property. At the **Bar at Times Square,** a lighted ball drops every night at midnight, to re-create the famous New Year's Eve event in the real location. New Year's Eve every night: A terrific promotion, or hell on earth?

A production show entitled **MADhattan** is reviewed in chapter 10.

Amenities: Concierge, courtesy limo, currency exchange, dry cleaning, express checkout, laundry, newspaper delivery, room service, safety-deposit boxes, video rentals, valet and self-parking, beauty salon, car rental, casino, arcade, pool, tour desk. The spa is smaller than average and merely adequate, but at $15 a day it is slightly cheaper than other major hotels.

🎡 Family-Friendly Hotels

As repeatedly mentioned in their individual listings, most of the hotels are backing away from being perceived as a place for families. Still, anything with a serious theme and/or outlets for kids, as the following all have, is probably better than a regular hotel.

Circus Circus Hotel/Casino *(see p. 85)* Centrally located on the Strip, this is our first choice if you're traveling with the kids. The hotel's mezzanine level offers ongoing circus acts daily from 11am to midnight, dozens of carnival games, and an arcade with more than 300 video and pinball games. And behind the hotel is a full amusement park.

Excalibur *(see p. 55)* Also owned by Circus Circus, Excalibur features a whole floor of midway games, a large video-game arcade, crafts demonstrations, free shows for kids (puppets, jugglers, magicians), and thrill cinemas. It has child-oriented eateries and shows (details in chapter 10).

Luxor Las Vegas *(see p. 58)* Another Circus Circus property. Kids will enjoy VirtuaLand, an 18,000-square-foot video-game arcade that showcases Sega's latest game technologies. Another big attraction here is the "Secrets of the Luxor Pyramid," a high-tech adventure/thrill ride using motion simulators and IMAX film.

MGM Grand Hotel, Casino, & Theme Park *(see p. 48)* This resort is backed by a 33-acre theme park and houses a state-of-the-art video-game arcade and carnival midway. A unique offering here is a youth center for hotel guests ages 3 to 16, with separate sections for different age groups. Its facilities range from a playhouse and tumbling mats for toddlers to extensive arts-and-crafts equipment for the older kids.

Tropicana Resort & Casino. 3801 Las Vegas Blvd. S., at Tropicana Ave., Las Vegas, NV 89109. ☎ **800/634-4000** or 702/739-2222. Fax 702/739-2469. www.tropicana.lv.com. 1,874 units. A/C TV TEL. $79–$229 double. Extra person $15. Children under 18 stay free in parents' room. AE, CB, DC, DISC, MC, V. Free self- and valet parking.

This longtime denizen of the Strip is looking great since a major renovation in 1995. The entranceway is now a colorful Caribbean village facade; there are nightly laser light shows on the Outer Island corner facing the Strip; pedestrian skywalks across the Strip link the Trop with the MGM Grand, the Excalibur, and the Luxor; and the resort's resident bird and wildlife population has dramatically increased. The Trop today comprises a lush landscape of manicured lawns, towering palms, oleanders, weeping willows, and crepe myrtles. There are dozens of waterfalls, thousands of exotic flowers, lagoons, and koi ponds. And flamingos, finches, black swans, mandarin ducks, African crown cranes, cockatoos, macaws, toucans, and Brazilian parrots live on the grounds. There's even a wildlife walk (home to pygmy marmosets, boa constrictors, and others) inside the resort itself.

Rooms in the Paradise Tower are traditional, with French provincial furnishings and turn-of-the-century wallpapers. Island Tower rooms, more befitting a tropical resort, are decorated in pastel colors like pale pink and sea-foam green, with splashy print bedspreads and bamboo furnishings; some have beds with mirrored walls and ceilings. Motel rooms out back can be tiny and oddly shaped. All Trop rooms have sofas and safes; TVs offer Spectravision movies, account review, video checkout, and channels for in-house information.

Dining/Diversions: Mizuno's, a beautiful teppanyaki dining room, is detailed in chapter 6, as are the Trop's buffet offerings.

El Gaucho is an elegantly rustic Argentine steak house, with rough-hewn log beams overhead and pecky-pine walls hung with cowhides, antlers, serapes, branding irons, and gaucho gear. Steaks, chops, prime rib, and seafood come with traditional accompaniments. Dinner only.

Papagayo's is a colorful Mexican eatery behind a wrought-iron gate, where cream stucco walls are adorned with Mexican rugs and Diego Rivera prints. Lunch and dinner.

Peitro's is the hotel's new gourmet room.

Calypso's, the Trop's 24-hour coffee shop, is the most cheerful in town. Decorated in bright island colors, it has a wall of windows overlooking waterfalls, weeping willows, and palm-fringed ponds filled with ducks and flamingos. Traditional (and very tasty) coffee-shop fare is augmented by interesting items ranging from Caribbean shrimp sate to bacon-stuffed cheese quesadillas. An extensive Chinese menu is available nightly from 6pm to midnight.

The **Players Deli,** sandwiched between the casino and the pool, is a unique cafeteria-cum-gaming room where slot and video poker machines are equipped with handy pullout dining ledges. Gamblers can also snack here at poker tables or in a small keno lounge or sports book. Hot and cold sandwiches, salads, and snack fare (nachos, chicken wings) are featured. Open daily from 10am to 10pm.

Down a level from the casino, in the Atrium Shopping area, is a **Baskin-Robbins** ice-cream parlor. The **Atrium Lounge** in the casino offers a variety of live music nightly after 5pm. The **Coconut Grove Bar** serves the pool area, and the **Tropics Bar** is between the two towers on the wildlife walk.

Amenities: 24-hour room service, shoe shine, casino, health club (a range of machines, treadmills, exercise bikes, steam, sauna, Jacuzzi, massage, and tanning room), video-game arcade, tour and show desks, wedding chapel, car-rental desk, beauty salon and barbershop, business center, travel agent, shops (jewelry, chocolates, women's footwear, logo items, women's fashions, sports clothing, gifts, newsstand).

Three swimming pools (one Olympic size) and three whirlpool spas are located in a 5-acre garden with 30 splashing waterfalls, lagoons, and lush tropical plantings. One pool has a swim-up bar/blackjack table.

MODERATE

Excalibur. 3850 Las Vegas Blvd. S., at Tropicana Ave., Las Vegas, NV 89109. ☎ **800/937-7777** or 702/597-7777. Fax 702/597-7040. www.excalibur-casino.com. 4,032 units. A/C TV TEL. $49–$119 for up to 4 people. Children under 17 stay free in parents' room; children over 17 pay $12. Rates are higher during holidays and convention periods. AE, CB, DC, DISC, MC, V. Free self- and valet parking.

Now this is kitsch. One of the largest resort hotels in the world, Excalibur (aka "the Realm") is a gleaming white, turreted castle complete with moat, drawbridge, battlements, and lofty towers. And it's huger than huge. Apparently, the creators thought there were a lot of Arthur and Guinevere wannabes out there. And probably they are right; but do we really need a medieval, forest-themed, knights-running-amok hotel in which to act out our fantasies?

Needless to say, this is not historically accurate. But it is hilarious. What it is not, is comfortable, which is actually historically accurate, since big castles were not traditionally warm, cozy, inviting places. Excalibur is just too darn big, a chaotic frenzy at all times. Even the must-see factor fades quickly.

But do check it out. And while you are at it, have fun by having the hotel page you and your friends: "Lady Doe to the white courtesy phone" or "Sir Jones to the house phone." Really, they do this. The second floor holds the recently refurbished

---

Our Top Five Ideas for New Hotels

Perhaps one of the most fascinating things about this city is the fact that its identity is stolen from other locations. Within city limits you have (or will have) New York, Paris, Venice, New Orleans (many times over), Rio de Janeiro, ancient Rome, Algiers, medieval Europe, Egypt, Monte Carlo, the French Riviera, and the old West. Note, please, that you will not see a Las Vegas–themed anything in any of these places. Or anywhere else for that matter. No, Vegas seems determined to re-create skylines as opposed to building one of its own. With that in mind, we offer a few suggestions for the latest and greatest amusement park, er, hotel/casino. (And lest you think we went overboard, remember, there is an Ellis Island Casino already.)

- **Butte, Montana, Hotel and Casino** Imagine the wonder of Montana's Big Sky country with a whole lot of neon added. An Animatronic buffalo stampede happens out front every hour for free, and the explosive roller coaster, the Unabombadier, offers unparalleled thrills. Just be careful crossing the driveways and in the parking garages—there are no speed limits.
- **Hotel Seattle** Bill Gates's first foray into the casino and hotel business.
- **Dakota** The centerpiece here is the life-size re-creation of Mount Rushmore that comes to Animatronic life every 15 minutes to pass out 2-for-1 coupons at the Dakota Buffet.
- **St. Louis Theme Park** Located behind the St. Louis Hotel and Casino, don't miss the Arch Coaster (which only makes one loop, but it's a doozie), the Arch Sling-Shot, the Arch Water Ride, and Pirates of the Arch.
- **Hoover Dam Hotel & Casino** Why drive 30 miles? See a quarter-scale replica right here on the Las Vegas Strip!

Medieval Village site of Excalibur's restaurants and quaint shops along winding streets and alleyways, a sort of permanent Renaissance Faire. Which could be reason enough to stay away. On the Village's Jester's Stage, jugglers, puppeteers, and magicians amuse guests with free 20-minute performances throughout the day. Up here you can access the newly enclosed, air-conditioned, moving sidewalk that connects with the Luxor.

Below the casino level is the Fantasy Faire, housing a very dark and large video-game arcade, dozens of medieval-themed carnival games, and two "magic motion machine" theaters featuring high-tech visual thrills; the thrills include simulated roller-coaster and runaway train adventures and an outer-space demolition derby directed by George Lucas, enhanced by hydraulically activated seats that synchronize with the on-screen action.

The rooms maintain the Arthurian motif with walls papered to look like stone castle interiors. Oak furnishings are heraldically embellished; mirrors are flanked by torchier sconces; bedspreads have a fleur-de-lis theme; and prints of jousting knights adorn the walls. Guests who have stayed in Tower 2 have complained about the noise from the roller coaster across the street at New York New York. It shuts down at 11pm, so early birds should probably stay in a different part of the hotel.

Note: If you should accidentally drop your wallet exiting a cab outside the Excalibur, don't expect to ever see it again. But that is probably true for any Vegas hotel.

Dining/Diversions: Camelot, Excalibur's fine dining room, offers continental fare in a rustic castle setting, with murals of Camelot's pristine lakes and verdant forests forming an idyllic backdrop. Dinner only.

Sir Galahad's, a prime rib restaurant, occupies a candlelit "castle" chamber with massive oak beams and wrought-iron candelabra chandeliers overhead. The specialty is prime rib, carved tableside and served with soup or salad, mashed potatoes, creamed spinach, and Yorkshire pudding. Dinner only.

Wild Bill's, a Western-themed restaurant and dance hall, has beveled-glass doors punctured by "bullet holes," walls adorned with rodeo murals, and booths separated by large wagon wheels. A rustic bar nestles in one corner. Country music is played during the day; at night there's live music for dancing. No, we don't know what it has to do with King Arthur either. Entrees include steak, ribs, catfish, and burgers. Dinner only.

Lance-a-Lotta Pasta replicates a flamboyant Italian village, complete with strolling guitarists. The menu lists pizzas and pastas, subs and hero sandwiches. They serve huge portions, and many locals say this is their favorite place in town for pasta. Dinner only.

Café Expresso, a window operation off Lance-a-Lotta Pasta, serves espresso, cappuccino, and pastries. It has several tables in the Medieval Village.

The **Sherwood Forest Cafe,** its entrance guarded by a sentry of lavender dragons (kids love to climb on them), is Excalibur's 24-hour facility. A low-priced children's menu is a plus.

Another heraldic dining room is **Excalibur's Round Table Buffet.** Other facilities include three snack bars. The **Village Pub** is an Alpine-themed bar in the Medieval Village; the **Minstrel's Theatre Lounge** offers live entertainment nightly (during the day, movies and sporting events are shown on a large-screen TV); there are several bars in the casino (most interesting of these is **King George's,** featuring international beers and microbrews); and a snack and cocktail bar serves the North pool.

Amenities: 24-hour room service, free gaming lessons, shoe shine, foreign currency exchange, casino, tour and show desks, state-of-the-art video-game arcade, wedding chapel (you can marry in medieval attire), unisex hairdresser, car-rental desk, a parking lot that can accommodate RVs, shops (see chapter 9). There are two large, beautifully landscaped swimming pools complete with waterfalls and water slides and an adjoining 16-seat whirlpool spa.

Holiday Inn Casino Boardwalk. 3750 Las Vegas Blvd. S., between Harmon and Tropicana aves., Las Vegas, NV 89109. ☎ **800/HOLIDAY,** 800/635-4581, or 702/735-2400. Fax 702/730-3166. www.hiboardwalk.com. 655 units. A/C TV TEL. $39–$109 double; $250–$495 one-bedroom suite, $495–$895 two-bedroom suite. Extra person $15. Rates may be higher during special events. Children 19 and under stay free in parents' room. AE, DC, DISC, JCB, MC, V. Free self- and valet parking.

This is just like a Holiday Inn, only in Vegas you *gotta* have a theme, and the hotel underwent an extensive renovation to give it a more attractive Coney Island and Boardwalk flavor, inside and especially out. The facade is kind of fun, with clowns and games and mannequins dressed in turn-of-the-century clothes. Of course, this is completely eclipsed by New York New York just a few doors (in Strip terms) down. After all, the roller coaster on the outside of this hotel is just a facade. Meanwhile, at press time, Steve Wynn's Mirage Corp. had just purchased the property, with assurances that nothing will change for the time being (with the possible exception that the aforementioned mannequins may be coming down). Given Wynn's dominance of the Strip, it seems likely the future of this hotel is somewhat in doubt.

Still, for the time being, it's a Holiday Inn, which means you know what you are getting in terms of quality, and the Strip location is a good one. Also, you don't have to walk through the casino to get to the lobby, which is a plus. On the other hand, it's a bit pricey, at the high end for what are standard Holiday Inn hotel rooms. The ones in the new 16-story tower, decorated in vibrant colors with cherrywood furnishings and prints of Coney Island adorning the walls, are perhaps a bit nicer than the older units, which are pleasantly done up in soft pastels with blond wood furnishings. All offer cable TVs with pay-movie options. Irons and ironing boards are in the rooms.

Dining/Diversions: A big draw is the **Cyclone Coffee Shop,** a 24-hour facility decorated with murals of the Coney Island boardwalk and adorable roller-coaster-motif lighting fixtures. Well worth a visit even if you're staying elsewhere, it has some of the best bargain meals in town (see chapter 6 for details).

Coney's, totally replicating the feel of a beach restaurant, serves boardwalk fare: fresh roasted corn on the cob, fresh-cut fries, pizza, and cheesesteak sandwiches. Other facilities include a 24-hour deli in the casino, an ice-cream/yogurt parlor, and two casino bars; a buffet room is under construction.

Amenities: 24-hour room service, shoe shine, casino, two small swimming pools, shops, coin-op washers/dryers, video-game arcade and shooting gallery, sight-seeing/show/tour desk, car-rental desk. Guests can use health club facilities nearby.

✪ **Luxor Las Vegas.** 3900 Las Vegas Blvd. S., between Reno and Hacienda aves., Las Vegas, NV 81119. ☎ **800/288-1000** or 702/262-4000. Fax 702/262-4452. www.luxor.com. 4,988 units. A/C TV TEL. Sun–Thurs $49–$259 double, Fri–Sat $99–$299 double; $179–$279 concierge level; $99–$329 Jacuzzi suite, $500–$800 for other suites. Extra person $10. Children under 12 stay free in parents' room. AE, CB, DC, DISC, MC, V. Free self- and valet parking.

The Luxor has just completed a $300 million renovation and expansion. Cheese fans will be disappointed to learn that the Egyptian fantasma that set the pace for all others isn't all that tacky anymore. Oh sure, the main hotel is still a 30-story bronze pyramid, complete with a really tall, 315,000-watt light beam at the top. (The Luxor says that's because the Egyptians believed their souls would travel up from heaven in a beam of light; we think it's really because it gives them something to brag about: "The most powerful beam on earth!") Sure, replicas of Cleopatra's Needle and the Sphinx still grace the outside, but the interior redesign has been made much more inviting, classier, and functional.

Guests now enter on the casino level (as opposed to one level up in the past) and are adjunct to the lobby, which used to be a hike away. The lobby has been redone in marble and cherrywood—vaguely art deco, which was influenced by Egyptian Revival anyway. It's one of the nicest lobbies in town. There is also a separate lobby in the two new towers, which is exclusively for tour groups. Even the Egyptian touches that remain have taken on a grand air rather than that of a theme park. (The tacky and overpriced Cleopatra's Barge ride down the "Nile" is gone for good.) It's kind of impressive, unless of course you've actually been to Egypt and seen the real statues of Ramses. Don't fear: The talking Animatronic camels are back.

The rooms have had a freshening up in the pyramid. High-speed "inclinator" elevators run on a 39° angle, making the ride up to your room a bit of a thrill. Sloped window walls remind you that you're in a pyramid. *Note:* In the pyramid, most baths have showers only, no tubs. The rooms are probably better in the new tower. Featuring fine art deco and Egyptian furnishings, they were full of nice touches. Huge armoires house not only the TV but closet space. The marble bathrooms have phones, vanity mirrors, and hair dryers. Even the floor lamps are interesting. This is one of the few rooms in Las Vegas that stands out. You know you are in the Luxor when you are in these rooms, as opposed to the cookie-cutter decor usually found in town. Especially desirable are a group of suites with glamorous art deco elements, private sitting rooms, refrigerators, and, notably, Jacuzzis by the window (enabling you to soak under the stars at night). And we would love to meet whomever is going to rent the new 4,000-square-foot luxury suite at the top of the tower.

Alternative culture denizens might be made aware that at least one multiply tattooed and pierced soul was asked to leave the Luxor gift shop, despite an armload of packages, because they "don't allow gang activity in the casino." This may be what happens when you upgrade your image.

Dining/Diversions: The Luxor's **Pharaoh's Pheast** buffet is discussed in chapter 6.

To enter **Isis**, a gourmet room, you'll pass through a colonnade of caryatid statues. Within, replicas of artifacts from King Tutankhamen's tomb are on display in glass cases, and a golden statue of Osiris forms a visual centerpiece. A harpist plays during dinner. The classic continental menu features items such as braised breast of pheasant filled with foie gras and pistachio. Dinner only.

The **Sacred Sea Room** has gold walls adorned with murals and hieroglyphics depicting fishing on the Nile. Turquoise mosaic tiles on the ceiling suggest ocean waves, and the dining-at-sea ambience is further enhanced by a central ship's hull and mast. Fresh- and saltwater seafood arrives daily from both coasts. Dinner only.

The **Luxor Steakhouse** breaks the Egyptian theme with a club-room style dining area and features adequate but ultimately overpriced steak-house fare.

The 24-hour **Pyramid Café**—its booths flanked by palm trees and foliage—replicates the interior of a pyramid. Like the decor, the menu has an Egyptian theme with a small nod to Middle Eastern cuisine. Most menu items, however, are of the predictable Las Vegas hotel coffee-shop genre. A $3 late-night breakfast of sirloin steak, eggs, hash browns, and toast is served daily except Wednesday from 11pm to 6am.

Other venues are a deli off the casino and a food court on the attraction level that includes Swenson's ice-cream shop, McDonald's, Little Caesar's pizza, and Nathan's hot dogs.

The hotel's new high-tech nightclub **Ra** is reviewed in chapter 10. The plush Nefertiti's Lounge features live bands for dancing nightly; off-hours sporting events are aired on a large-screen TV. The Obelisk Bar and Anteroom Lounge serve the casino. Tut's Hut specializes in Polynesian drinks and Otemanu Hot Rock samplers (seafood, tenderloin, chicken, pork, or vegetables grilled at your table and served with plum, peanut, mustard, and teriyaki dipping sauces). The Sportsbook Lounge, adjoining the race and sports book, airs sports action on TV monitors overhead. And the Oasis Terrace and Bar provides poolside food and drinks.

Amenities: 24-hour room service, foreign currency exchange, shoe shine, casino; full-service unisex hair salon; complete spa and health club (with a full range of machines, free weights, steam, sauna, and Jacuzzi; massage, facials, herbal wraps, and other beauty treatments available); VirtuaLand, an 18,000-square-foot video arcade that showcases Sega's latest game technologies; car-rental desk; tour/show/sightseeing desks.

The hotel has five pools, with the main one an immense palm-fringed swimming pool (palms even grow right in the pool) with outdoor whirlpool, kiddie pool, pool-accessories shop, and luxurious cabanas (cooled by misting systems and equipped with rafts, cable TVs, phones, ceiling fans, tables and chairs, chaise longues, and refrigerators stocked with juices and bottled water) that rent for $75 a day.

San Remo. 115 E. Tropicana Ave., just east of the Strip, Las Vegas, NV. ☎ **800/522-7366** or 702/736-1120. $69–$299 double. A/C TV TEL. AE, CB, DC, DISC, JCB, MC, V. Free self- and valet parking.

Located right behind the Tropicana, this is a good Strip alternative, since it puts you right at one of the most active corners, for a much better rate than usually found on the Strip. Plus, they always seem to have a $4 prime rib deal going on, which is very Vegas indeed. The rooms are quite nice, done in a French Provincial style, and are larger than normal. Some come with convertible sofas and dressing areas, and 40% of tower rooms even have balconies. The "minisuites" are larger than the standard rooms by half, adding a sitting area and desks.

Dining/Diversions: Luigi's Deli serves Italian sandwiches. **Paparazzi's Grille** is an upscale steak and seafood house. **Ristorante DeiFiori** is a 24-hour coffee shop. The sushi bar is called, wait for it, **Sushi Bar.** Casual Italian can be found at **Pasta Remo.** There are two bars in the casino, a bar/lounge with live entertainment afternoons and evenings, a very small showroom, and a small video arcade.

Amenities: 24-hour room service, laundry service, bell desk, show desk, gift shop, casino, pool with poolside service.

INEXPENSIVE

✪ **Orleans.** 4500 W. Tropicana Ave., west of Strip and I-15, Las Vegas, NV 89103. ☎ **800/ORLEANS** or 702/365-7111. Fax 702/365-7505. www.orleanscasino.com. 870 units. A/C TV TEL. $39–$89 standard double; $175–$225 one-bedroom suite. AE, DC, DISC, MC, V. Free self- and valet parking.

Just opened in December 1997, the Orleans is owned by the same company that owns the Barbary and Gold Coast casinos. It's a little out of the way, but with a 12-screen movie complex, complete with food court and day care center, this becomes an increasingly attractive option to staying on the hectic Strip. Its facade is aggressively fake New Orleans, more reminiscent of Disneyland than the Big Easy. Inside it's much the same. But a bright casino (complete with Cajun and zydeco music over the loud speakers) and a policy of handing out Mardi Gras beads at all the restaurants and bars (ask if you haven't gotten yours) make for a pleasantly festive atmosphere. However, we could do without those scary mannequins simulating Mardi Gras fun leaning over French Quarter–style railings above the casino.

If the prices hold true (as always, quotes vary), this hotel is one of the best bargains in town, despite the location. The rooms are particularly nice—the largest in town, so the hotel claims, next to Rio's. They all have a definite New Orleans French feel. They are L-shaped with a seating alcove by the windows, and come complete with slightly turn-of-the-century–style overstuffed chair and sofa. The beds have brass headboards, the lamps (including some funky iron floor lamps) look antique, and lace curtains flutter at the windows. The one drawback is that all these furnishings, and the busy floral decorating theme, make the room, particularly down by the seating area in front of the bathrooms, seem crowded. Still, it's meant to evoke a cozy, warm Victorian parlor, which traditionally is very overcrowded, so maybe it's successful after all. The medium-size bathrooms are also nice, but there is no closet, only a rod for hanging clothes. Suites are, depending on your taste, even more grand and spectacular, but they have a different look, so they could also be disappointing. They have a grand-looking wood bar and richly upholstered chairs; the bathrooms are very fancy with dark wood and marble and a big oval tub. They also have four TVs!

Dining/Diversions: You would think something called Orleans would open up their Louisiana restaurants first, but that is not the case. First came **Vito's** Italian, a fancy Italian place complete with piano bar from 1pm to 3am.

Canal St. Grill is a modern steak-and-seafood place.

Don Miguel's, a basic but satisfying Mexican restaurant, makes its own tortillas, and you can watch.

Courtyard Cafe is the 24-hour coffee shop. **Terrible Mike's** offers fast food. **Kate's Korner** has ice cream. Five bars are throughout the property, plus the **Bourbon St. Lounge,** which features live bands at night.

The **Branson Theater** is their 827-seat theater featuring live entertainment.

Amenities: Room service, safety-deposit boxes, courtesy bus to/from airport and the Strip, casino, beauty salon, business center, game room/arcade, 70-lane bowling alley, wedding chapel, 40,000 square feet of meeting space (with more on the way), two medium-size pools with grass and cabanas.

5 Mid-Strip

VERY EXPENSIVE

Bally's Las Vegas. 3645 Las Vegas Blvd. S., at Flamingo Rd., Las Vegas, NV 89109. ☎ **800/634-3434** or 702/739-4111. Fax 702/794-2413. www.ballyslv.com. 2,804 units. A/C TV TEL. $95–$135 double; $35 more for concierge floor (including breakfast); $300–$2,500 suite. Extra person $15. Children 18 and under stay free in parents' room. AE, CB, DC, JCB, MC, V. Free self- and valet parking.

Bally's recently completed a $72 million renovation, which included the construction of a monorail that whisks passengers from its downstairs shopping level (a bit of a hike from the casino) to the MGM Grand. More noticeable is its elaborate new facade, a plaza containing four 200-foot people movers that transport visitors to and from the Strip via a neon-lit arch surrounded by cascading waters and lush landscaping. Light, sound, and water shows take place here every 20 minutes after dark.

The minute you step from its glittering entranceway into its light and airy casino, you'll notice that Bally's is one of the most cheerful hotels on the Strip. A whimsical mural of Las Vegas scenes backs the registration desk. A virtual "city within a city," Bally's offers a vast array of casino games, superb restaurants, entertainment options, shops, and services. During your Las Vegas stay, you need never step outside.

Large rooms are decorated in teal, mauve, and earth tones. All have sofas. TVs offer video checkout, not to mention cash-advance capability for your credit card. The 22nd floor is a concierge level.

Dining/Diversions: Seasons, its interior modeled after a grand salon at Versailles, is an ornate setting of crystal chandeliers, gilded plasterwork and trellises, and elegantly draped private alcoves backed by gilt-framed mirrors. Cuisine is continental. Dinner only.

Bally's Steakhouse exudes an aura of substantial comfort. Gleaming brass chandeliers are suspended from a gorgeous oak-and-mahogany ceiling, and diners are ensconced in leopard-skin booths and black leather armchairs. A traditional steak-and-seafood menu is complemented by an extensive wine list. Dinner only.

Al Dente has an expanse of marble flooring and art-deco maple and black lacquer columns where planters of greenery create intimate dining areas. Its menu offers delicious pastas, thin-crust pizzas with California-style toppings, and other Italian entrees. Dinner only.

Las Olas is a charming candlelit Mexican eatery fronted by a lounge with a tiered fountain. The dining area, its walls hung with rugs and embroideries, displays Mexican statuary and pottery in wall niches. Breakfast, lunch, and dinner are served.

There's also a bright and cheerful 24-hour coffee shop, a newly opened Chinese resaurant (Chang's) and food outlets in the shopping mall include a branch of New York's **Stage Deli.**

The mermaid-themed Bubbles Bar serves the casino. In addition, On the Rocks, a poolside bar with a lovely terrace cooled by ceiling fans, specializes in tropical drinks and wines by the glass. And the Terrace Café, a seasonal poolside eatery, offers light fare during the day. See also "Buffets & Sunday Brunches" in chapter 6.

Amenities: 24-hour room service, guest services desk, shoe shine, foreign currency exchange, casino, tour and show desks, car-rental desk, small video-game arcade, shopping arcade (see chapter 9), wedding chapel, men's and women's hair salons, state-of-the-art health spa and fitness center, eight night-lit tennis courts and pro shop (lessons available), two basketball courts.

A gorgeous palm-fringed sundeck surrounds an Olympic-size swimming pool, one of the most beautiful in Las Vegas. There's a whirlpool, and guests can rent private cabanas with stocked refrigerators, TVs, ceiling fans, rafts, and private phones for $60 to $85 a day.

Bellagio. 3600 Las Vegas Blvd. S., at the corner of Flamingo Rd., Las Vegas, NV 89109. ☎ **888/987-6667.** www.bellagiolasvegas.com. 3,270 units. A/C TV TEL. $129–$499 double. Extra person $30. AE, CB, DC, DISC, MC, V. Free self- and valet parking.

Steve Wynn's latest amazing upscale resort is due to open in late 1998, on the site of the legendary Dunes Hotel. The $1.6 billion resort is inspired by the eponymous Italian village that overlooks Lake Como. For the price, it better be good. Knowing Wynn, it will be.

The front of the property, in keeping with Wynn hotels, is spectacular. It features an 8-acre lake, the setting for a choreographed water-ballet extravaganza (more free shows!), and a replica of an Italian village. The grounds will be some of the most lushly landscaped, with classical gardens, fountains, and pools. Rooms are to be appointed with "custom European-style furnishings, art, and antiques" plus heavily marbled bathrooms. There will be a shopping gallery featuring such high-class names as Chanel, Hermès, Tiffany & Co., Giorgio Armani, Gucci, and Prada. Plans are also for a Gallery of Fine Art that will exhibit paintings and sculptures from the 1870s Impressionist movement and ending with the 1970s and abstract expressionism. Apparantly, there is a hefty entrance fee planned. Cirque de Soleil will mount an entirely new $70 million extravaganza—if it's anywhere near the level of *Mystère* (and there is no reason to think it won't be), this will rival that sister production as the best show in town. There will be a monorail to carry guests between Bellagio and Monte Carlo. *Note:* This is meant to be an expensive playground for adults only, and at this time, they are not permitting children as guests.

Dining/Diversions: Plans are for a variety of dining options, from casual cafes and bistros, to branches of the legendary Le Cirque, and the famed Boston restaurant, Olives.

✪ **Caesars Palace.** 3570 Las Vegas Blvd. S., just north of Flamingo Rd., Las Vegas, NV 89109. ☎ **800/634-6661** or 702/731-7110. Fax 702/731-6636. www.caesars.com. 2,471 units. A/C TV TEL. From $99 standard double, $109–$500 "run of house deluxe" double; $549–$1,000 suite. Extra person $20. Children under 12 stay free in parents' room. AE, CB, DC, DISC, MC, V. Free self- and valet parking.

Since 1966, Caesars has stood as simultaneously the ultimate in Vegas luxury and the nadir (or pinnacle, depending on your values) of Las Vegas cheese. It's the most Vegas-style hotel you'll find. Or at least it was. Caesars has completed a massive $300 million renovation, inside and out. Don't worry, the Roman theme remains. But as with everything else in Vegas, it has been upgraded to, let's say, a nicer neighborhood in Rome.

When Caesars was originally built to reflect Roman decadence, its designers probably had no idea how guffaw-inducing this would be some years later. It's the

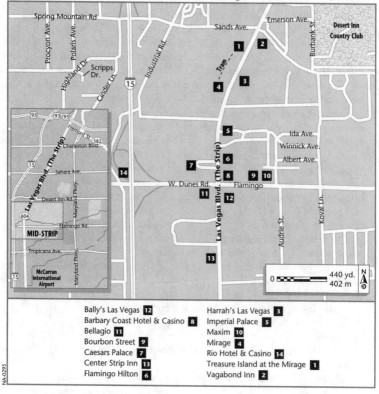

Bally's Las Vegas **12**
Barbary Coast Hotel & Casino **8**
Bellagio **11**
Bourbon Street **9**
Caesars Palace **7**
Center Strip Inn **13**
Flamingo Hilton **6**

Harrah's Las Vegas **3**
Imperial Palace **5**
Maxim **10**
Mirage **4**
Rio Hotel & Casino **14**
Treasure Island at the Mirage **1**
Vagabond Inn **2**

level of kitsch all should aspire to: Roman colonnades, Roman pillars, gigantic faux marble Roman statues, staff attired in gladiator outfits—it's splendidly ridiculous. It's what Vegas ought to be.

But all things change, and Caesars has been outshined over the years by more modern glamour. And frankly, that facade was looking dated 2 decades ago. So, like all of Vegas, they upgrade. The dark and smoky Romanesque design is being replaced by a brighter, more upscale theme; tacky '70s neon and mirrors have been replaced by beiges, earth tones, and hand-painted murals (specially commissioned). It's all generally lighter, brighter, and perhaps closer to the elegance Caesars originally sought to evoke. But never fear, the Roman statues still remain, as do the toga'd cocktail waitresses, and so does Caesar's giggle factor. Unfortunately, the fate of the entrance fountains (which landed permanently in Vegas legend when Evel Knievel attempted to jump over them) remains in question.

Past or future, Caesars remains spectacular. From the Roman temples, heroic arches, golden charioteers, and 50-foot Italian cypresses of its entrance, to the overwhelming interiors, it's the spectacle a good Vegas hotel should be. A moving sidewalk carries you into the Forum Shops and the casino. (*Note:* Plans are to turn that area into yet another shop addition, so by sometime in 1999 that moving sidewalk will be gone.) The shops are in the grandest mall you can imagine (think of the *La Dolce Vita* walk on the Via Veneto), covered by a sky that is supposed to change during the day to reflect the passing of time. (How Vegas is that, by the way, that you can't see the real sky, but we will simulate it for you?) These high-rent boutiques (Armani, Versace) lead to a group of Animatronic Roman statues that come to life every hour to mumble something about bacchanals and the good life. That is probably supposed to subliminally make you want to gamble more and otherwise live it up, provided of course Caesars benefits. It's somewhat creepy, but the crowd eats it up. Another hall leads to more expensive shops, and a fountain that performs another show with somewhat better production values, during which Atlantis literally rises from the deep and the room is transformed into a sound, light, and fire extravaganza. It runs every 1½ hours.

Caesars is also known for its luxurious rooms and service. (Long lines at the reservations desk are sometimes relieved by gratis champagne.) The lobbies that lead to the rooms are stunning, all marble, dark greens and mahogany trim. Accommodations occupy (ultimately) four towers, and there are too many decorator schemes to describe here. You'll likely enjoy a lavish bath with marble floor, European fixtures, and oversized marble tubs (about half are Jacuzzis). (*Note:* Some of the rooms have lavish tubs in the middle of the room, which can be uncomfortable if you want to shower and don't want this to turn into a spectator sport.) Art in the rooms keeps to the Greco-Roman theme (some have classical sculptures in niches); furnishings tend to neoclassic styles; Roman columns, pilasters, and pediments are common. Many rooms have four-poster beds with mirrored ceilings, and all are equipped with three phones (bedside, bath, and desk), cable TVs with HBO, a gaming instruction channel (with cameo appearances by hotel headliners like Natalie Cole and Johnny Mathis), and in-house information stations. All rooms have private safes, hair dryers, irons and ironing boards, and lighted closets.

Then there is the brand-new 32-story Tower. The rooms there lack the cutesy Roman touches, but make up for them with additional luxury. Expect all the above touches, plus more, including his-and-her baths and an eco-friendly, computer-programmed climate-control system monitored at the front desk.

Still more things to take advantage of, in addition to the fine restaurants and the aforementioned Forum Shops (which are quite pleasant to stroll through), are the OMNIMAX Theatre (described in chapter 7), the Atlantis Ride (described in chapter 7), and Caesars Magical Empire (described in chapter 7).

Dining/Diversions: Caesars has a well-deserved reputation for superior in-house restaurants. There are nine in the hotel, plus dining facilities in the Forum shopping area. All are highly recommended.

The hotel's premier restaurant, the exquisite **Palace Court,** and **Bacchanal,** which re-creates a multicourse Roman feast, and the sushi restaurant, **Hyakumi,** are described in chapter 6 along with the hotel's food court and buffets.

Neros, specializing in prime-aged steaks and fresh seafood at dinner, has an extensive wine list. Its lunch menu features international contemporary fare. The restaurant's newly refurbished octagonal design is a contemporary interpretation of the Spanish Madejar style, with an eight-pointed star radiating from the ceiling. Padded, sound-absorbing walls make for a more intimate dining experience.

Terraza specializes in rustic Italian cuisine. A shady and cool garden spot with doors that open to the pool, it's perfect for brunch.

Cafe Roma, Caesars' comfortable, 24-hour casual dining venue, offers international buffets and a menu that runs the gamut from filet mignon to chicken quesadillas, as well as burgers, salads, and sandwiches. A Chinese menu is available from 5pm to 1:15am.

Restaurants in the Forum Shops arcade include **Spago, Chinois** (both Wolfgang Puck's famed establishments), **The Palm, Planet Hollywood,** and the **Stage Deli**—all discussed in chapter 6. In the new Atlantis section, there is a

Caviartorium—a place to sample high-priced fish eggs, and a **Cheesecake Factory.** Some new additions will arrive by late 1998.

There are several casino lounges, among them the **Olympic Lounge** and **La Piazza Lounge** offering nightly live entertainment in the Olympic Casino. The **Palace Court Terrace** (an ultraelegant, romantic piano bar) is one of our favorite Las Vegas nightspots. See also **Cleopatra's Barge Nightclub** in chapter 10.

Amenities: 24-hour room service, shoe shine, complimentary gaming lessons, valet and dry cleaning services, three casinos, two extensive shopping arcades (see chapter 9), state-of-the-art video arcade, American Express office, show desks, car-rental desk.

Having spent over $100 million renovating their **"Garden of the Gods,"** Caesars has created a tasteful, although undeniably Caesars, masterpiece. With three pools measuring a total of 22,000 square feet, there is plenty of space for frolicking in the hot sun. Inspired by the healing Baths of Caracalla in Rome, each of the pools is adorned with griffins or sea horses and inlaid with classic granite and marble mosaics. To feel even more regal, there are also 16 shaded cabanas that offer phones, TV, and air-conditioning for $150 a day. (Reserve them early.) Several amenities are also available by the pool area including Caribbean massage, two Jacuzzis, three tennis courts, the Neptune Bar, and of course a Snackus Maximus.

The **Caesars Spa** is another gorgeous facility, offering full salon services (a large range of facials, massages, wraps, and other beauty treatments), saunas, steam rooms and whirlpool tubs, plus an incredibly well-supplied health club with state-of-the-art machinery. Go work off some of that Caesars indulgence and then get a little pampered.

Also under construction are 113,000 square feet of meeting space and 250,000 square feet of additional retail space for the Forum Shops. These should be finished by the time you read this.

EXPENSIVE

✪ **Flamingo Hilton.** 3555 Las Vegas Blvd. S., between Sands Ave. and Flamingo Rd., Las Vegas, NV 89109. ☎ **800/732-2111** or 702/733-3111. Fax 702/733-3353. www.hilton. com. 3,999 units. A/C TV TEL. $69–$205 double; $250–$580 suite. Extra person $16. Children 18 and under stay free in parents' room. Inquire about packages and time-share suites. AE, CB, DC, DISC, JCB, MC, V. Free self- and valet parking.

The Flamingo has changed a great deal since Bugsy Siegel opened his 105-room oasis "in the middle of nowhere" in 1946. It was so luxurious for its time that even the janitors wore tuxedos. Jimmy Durante was the opening headliner, and the wealthy and famous flocked to the tropical paradise of swaying palms, lagoons, and waterfalls. While the Flamingo is a senior citizen on the Strip with a colorful history, a fresh, new look, enhanced by a recent $130 million renovation and expansion, has made Siegel's "real class joint" better than ever. Still, reaching the outside world (the Strip and Flamingo competitors) can be difficult; there is a lot of casino between you and the lobby, and then again between you and the street.

For those planning some leisure time outside the casino, the Flamingo's exceptional pool area, spa, and tennis courts are a big draw. One of the two best in Vegas, the pool is smashing, with countless trees and foliage, live birds, two water slides, waterfalls, and so on. Although the water can be a little chilly, kids should be able to spend hours in there.

Rooms occupy six towers and are variously decorated. Some are done up in soft blues and peach for a resort look enhanced by pretty fabrics, light painted-wood furnishings, and lovely watercolors of tropical scenes. Others use soft earth tones, forest green, or coral. All accommodations offer in-room safes; TVs have in-house information and gaming instruction stations, a keno channel, video checkout, message retrieval, and account review.

Dining/Diversions: The Old West **Beef Baron,** heralded by golden steer heads and a mural of a cattle roundup, bills itself as "a steak house forged in the spirit of our first great cattle ranchers." They usually offer steak and seafood specials for a decent price. Dinner only.

Fronted by a tiered terra-cotta fountain, **Alta Villa** is designed to suggest an Italian village, with a vaulted ceiling, a trellised grape arbor under a painted sky, and grapevine-motif carpeting. A pretty ceramic-tiled exhibition kitchen is a focal point. A traditional Italian menu is featured. Dinner only.

Peking Market's interior simulates an open marketplace in a bustling Chinese city. A central wood-burning brick oven casts a warm glow. Dinner only.

The candlelit **Flamingo Room** is adorned with murals of flamingos, flamingo sculptures, and glass etched with flamingos; it offers piano-bar music at dinner. One of the draws here is an extensive salad bar supplemented by smoked whitefish and salmon, and crab and shrimp salads. The menu highlights steak and seafood dishes. Dinner only.

Hamada of Japan is a softly lit, teak-beamed restaurant centered by a small rock garden. Some of the seating is at teppanyaki grill tables, and there's also a sushi bar. Come by for a Japanese breakfast of fish, raw egg, sticky beans, rice, soup, pickles, vegetables, and seaweed. It's open for all meals.

Lindy's Deli, a pleasant and spacious 24-hour coffee shop, offers appetizing smoked fish platters (salmon, whitefish, sturgeon) with bagels and cream cheese, corned beef and pastrami sandwiches, matzo ball soup, and other traditional Jewish deli items in addition to typical Las Vegas coffee-shop fare.

Bugsy's Deli, offering sandwiches on fresh-baked breads, is a casual self-service eatery just off the casino. The **Pool Grille** serves up light fare, and a snack bar serves the race and sports book area. **Bugsy's Bar,** festooned with orange and pink neon flamingo feathers, occupies a central position in the casino. And the **Rainbow Bar,** off the casino, has a wall of windows overlooking palm trees and waterfalls.

The **Flamingo's Paradise Garden Buffet** is described in chapter 6.

Amenities: 24-hour room service, guest services desk, translation services (interpreters are available for more than 35 languages; gaming guides are available in six languages), casino, car-rental desk, tour and show desks, full-service beauty salon/barber shop, wedding chapel, four night-lit championship tennis courts with pro shop and practice alley (tennis clinics and lessons are available), shopping arcade (see chapter 9 for details).

Five gorgeous swimming pools, two Jacuzzis, water slides, and a kiddie pool are located in a 15-acre Caribbean landscape amid lagoons, meandering streams, fountains, waterfalls, a rose garden, and islands of live flamingos and African penguins. Ponds are filled with ducks, swans, and koi, and a grove of 2,000 palms graces an expanse of lawn.

A health club offers a variety of Universal weight machines, treadmills, stair machines, free weights, sauna, steam, a TV lounge, and hot and cold whirlpools. Exercise tapes are available, and spa services include massage, soap rub, salt glow, tanning beds, and oxygen pep-up.

✪ **Harrah's Las Vegas.** 3475 Las Vegas Blvd. S., between Flamingo and Spring Mountain rds., Las Vegas, NV 89109. ☎ **800/HARRAHS** or 702/369-5000. Fax 702/369-5008. www.harrahs.lv.com. 2,700 units. A/C TV TEL. $75–$289 standard double, $99–$329 deluxe double; $195–$1,000 suite. Extra person $15. Children 12 and under stay free in parents' room. AE, CB, DC, DISC, MC, V. Free self- and valet parking.

A recent radical face-lift has completely transformed Harrah's. It used to look like a Mississippi River showboat, but now it looks nothing like that. It's more elegant, with a European carnival theme. Everywhere there are large murals celebrating different international festivals accented by lots of marble, bright colors, mirrors, and gold trim. A neat trick involving the confetti-strewn pattern carpeting and the fiber-optic fireworks on the ceiling combine to make a festive effect. They have removed Jackson Square, an outdoor shopping area, and replaced it with Carnaval Court, which is a festive, palm-fringed shopping/entertainment plaza where strolling entertainers perform.

Overall, Harrah's has done a terrific job with its remodeling, creating a comfortable and fun environment while somehow eschewing both kitsch and the haughtiness that follows in the wake of other hotel conversions' more upscale images.

The rooms are also light and festive, with marble fixtures and light wood accents. All the rooms are larger than average; the points that emerge from both the old and the new tower wings translate inside into an extra triangle of space for a couch and table. Spacious minisuites in this section, offering large sofas and comfortable armchairs, are especially desirable. In all rooms, TVs offer hotel information and keno channels, pay movies, Nintendo, and video account review and checkout.

Dining/Diversions: The plush **Claudine's** is a romantic turn-of-the-century setting for steak and seafood meals. After you dine, relax over drinks in the adjoining piano bar lounge. Dinner only.

The Range steak house is one of the few hotel restaurants that overlooks the Strip and is reviewed in chapter 6. **Asia** features a mixture of Chinese and other Asian cuisines. The **Garden Cafe** is a 24-hour coffee shop. **Club Cappocino** serves specialty coffees and home-baked pastries. **Andreotti's** serves Italian foods in an outdoor Tuscan-inspired atmosphere. **Winning Streaks,** the sports book restaurant and pub, features solid hamburgers.

Several new bars have also opened. Of special mention, **La Playa** is an open-air lounge with a beach-gone-crazy theme. It is the only bar on the Strip with outdoor seating, right on the Strip, and features live Caribbean reggae bands.

In the lobby are a **TCBY** and an espresso/pastry cart for quick breakfasts.

See also the buffet listings in chapter 6.

Amenities: 24-hour room service (including a special pizza and pasta menu), complimentary gaming lessons, casino, car-rental desk, tour and show desks, nice-size video-game arcade, coin-op laundry, shops (see chapter 9 for details), unisex hair salon.

Harrah's has a beautiful, Olympic-size swimming pool and sundeck area with waterfall and trellised garden areas, a whirlpool, kids' wading pool, cocktail and snack bar, and poolside shop selling T-shirts and sundries.

The hotel's health club has doubled in size. One of the better facilities on the Strip, it has a spa offering a full range of services and a health club with Lifecycles, treadmills, stair machines, rowing machines, lots of Universal equipment, free weights, plus there are two TVs and a VCR for which aerobic exercise tapes are available.

✪ **Mirage.** 3400 Las Vegas Blvd. S., between Flamingo Rd. and Sands Ave., Las Vegas, NV 89109. ☎ **800/627-6667** or 702/791-7111. Fax 702/791-7446. www.themirage.com. 3,323 units. A/C TV TEL. Sun–Thurs $79–$399 double, Fri–Sat and holidays $159–$399 double; $250–$3,000 suite. Extra person $30. AE, CB, DC, DISC, MC, V. Free self- and valet parking.

Supercalafragilisticexpialadocious!
                    —Governor Bob Miller's reaction upon first visiting the Mirage

We really like this place. Actually, ask around; most visitors and locals agree. Even if they haven't stayed here, the majority consider it the most beautiful hotel in Vegas. From the moment you walk in and breathe the faintly tropically perfumed air (we think it's vanilla) and enter the lush rain forest, you just know that you are on vacation. It's a totally different experience from most Vegas hotels, where you step inside the door and are immediately the victim of a sensory assault.

The Mirage was Steve Wynn's first from-the-ground-up project; it seems funny now, but back in 1989 this was considered a complete gamble that was sure to be a failure. That was before the hotel opened, mind you. On opening day the crowds nearly tore the place down getting inside, and the Mirage soon made its money back. Now it is the model all recent hotels follow.

Occupying 102 acres, the Mirage is fronted by more than a city block of cascading waterfalls and tropical foliage centering on a very active "volcano," which, after dark, erupts every 15 minutes, spewing fire 100 feet above the lagoons below. To be honest, it's not very volcanolike; if you've seen the movie, you are going to be disappointed. Instead of lava flow, expect a really neat light show, and you won't mind a bit. (In passing, that volcano cost $30 million, which is equal to the entire original construction cost for Caesars next door.) The lobby is dominated by a 53-foot, 20,000-gallon simulated coral reef aquarium stocked with more than 1,000 colorful tropical fish, including six sharks. This gives you something to look at while waiting (never for long) for check-in. We miss Sidney, the increasingly large grouper who was the star of the tank since its opening, and whose leisurely progress through the coral was very Zen-like. Alas, Sidney finally outgrew his home and retired with honors to the larger, public Long Beach Aquarium.

Next it's through the rain forest, which occupies a 90-foot domed atrium—a path meanders through palms, banana trees, waterfalls, and serene pools. If we must find a complaint with the Mirage, it's with the next bit, as you have to negotiate 8 miles (or so it seems) of casino mayhem to get to your room, the pool, food, or the outside world. (On the other hand, the sundries shop is located right next to the guest room elevators, so if you forgot toothpaste you don't have to travel miles to get more.) The formerly tropical-themed rooms have been redone in varying neutrals, with liberal use of muted gold. A marble entryway, mirrors, vanity table, and canopy over the bed's headboard give even the standards a luxurious appearance. The bathrooms are marble and slightly on the small size, depending on the room. Oak armoires house 25-inch TVs, and phones are equipped with fax and computer jacks. Further up the price scale are superdeluxe rooms with whirlpool tubs. By the way, when you ring anywhere in the hotel (front desk, restaurant reservations, the spa) whomever answers the phone greets you by name ("How can I help you, Ms. Jones?"), thanks, apparently, to a sophisticated caller-ID system. It takes you aback at first, but one has to admit it is a nice personal touch in a large facility. The staff continues the helpful touches; any problems that may arise are quickly smoothed out.

Off the casino is a habitat for Siegfried and Roy's white tigers, a plaster enclosure that allows for photo taking and "aaaahhhs." Out back is the pool, one of the nicest in Vegas; it has a quarter-mile shoreline, a tropical paradise of waterfalls, trees, water slides, and so forth. It looks inviting, but truth be told it is sometimes on the chilly side and isn't very deep. But it's so pretty you hardly care. Behind the pool is the dolphin habitat and the new Siegfried and Roy's Secret Garden, which has a separate admission.

Dining/Diversions: The **Noodle Kitchen,** a very authentic Asian restaurant, and the **Mirage Buffet** are detailed in chapter 6.

Kokomo's, situated in the tropical rain forest atrium, offers seating under bamboo-thatched roofing and trellised bougainvillea vines. Some tables overlook lagoons and waterfalls. The menu highlights steaks, chops, prime rib, and seafood. This is a beautiful place to eat, certainly, but somewhat pricey for the privilege. All meals are served.

Mikado, under a starlit sky, offers diners a candlelit setting with a sunken tropical rock garden, lotus pond, and sheltering pines. Teppanyaki cooking is featured along with à la carte Japanese specialties and a sushi bar. Dinner only.

At **Moongate,** also under the stars, seating is in an open courtyard defined by classical Chinese architectural facades and tiled rooflines. White doves perch on cherry tree branches, and intricately hand-carved walls frame a moongate tableau. The menu offers Cantonese and Szechuan specialties. Dinner only.

A cobblestone passage evoking a European village street leads to **Restaurant Riva,** a very pretty dining room. Candlelit at night, its walls are hung with gilt-framed still-life paintings and its windows with swagged draperies. Sophisticated northern Italian fare is served. Dinner only.

Off the same quaint street is the new **Melange,** a fine French eatery in a courtyard setting enhanced by original works by Picasso.

A branch of **California Pizza Kitchen,** under a thatch-roofed dome, is in the center of the casino overlooking the race and sports book. A bank of video monitors lets you follow the action while dining on oak-fired pizzas with toppings ranging from duck sausage to goat cheese. Calzones, salads, and pasta dishes are here, too. All entrees are under $11.

The **Caribe Café,** a festive 24-hour coffee shop, adheres to the tropical theme. It's designed to suggest an open-air Caribbean village. Additional food and beverage facilities include an ice-cream parlor; the **Paradise Café,** an alfresco terrace with umbrella tables overlooking the pool (drinks and light fare are served); the **Lagoon Saloon** in the rain forest, specializing in tropical drinks and offering live music for dancing until 1am Sunday to Wednesday; the **Baccarat Bar,** where a pianist entertains nightly (jackets required for men); the poolside **Dolphin Bar;** and the **Sports Bar** in the casino.

Amenities: 24-hour room service, overnight shoe shine upon request, morning newspaper delivery, casino, car-rental desk, shops (Siegfried and Roy and Cirque du Soleil merchandise and others), unisex hairdresser and salon offering all beauty services, video arcade, business services center. A free tram travels between the Mirage and Treasure Island almost around the clock.

The **Mirage Day Spa** teems with friendly staff anxious to pamper the customers, bringing you iced towels to cool you during your workout and refreshing juices afterward. After a workout in the gym, soak in the soothingly darkened Jacuzzi, take a steam, a sauna, a shower, and you'll be prepared for an evening of wild abandon. All the regular spa services are available, but a flat $20 charge for use of the above facilities is sufficient to make you relaxed and happy. Aveda and other fancy, name-brand products in the dressing room, along with hair dryers, an endless supply of towels, cold drinks, and encouragement, make this a blessed retreat in a wild town.

Free swimming lessons and water aerobics classes take place daily at the pool. Private poolside cabanas (equipped with phones, TVs, free snacks and soft drinks, refrigerators, misting systems, rafts, and radios) can be rented for $85 a day.

Rio Suites. 3700 W. Flamingo Rd., at I-15, Las Vegas, NV 89103. ☎ **800/752-9746** or 702/252-7777. Fax 702/252-0080. www.playrio.com. 2,582 units. A/C TV TEL. $95 Sun–Thurs, $149 Fri–Sat. Extra person $15. Inquire about golf packages. AE, CB, DC, MC, V. Free self- and valet parking.

The Rio Hotel confounded expectations by not only succeeding in an area somewhat removed from the Strip but by also thriving there. It recently completed an immediately popular $200 million addition: a 41-story tower and the Masquerade Village. Diverging from the rest of the tropically themed hotel, this latter simulates a European village, complete with shops, restaurants, and a bizarre live-action show in the sky. The addition is actually quite nice—not only is the architecture, in its faux way, aesthetically pleasing, but this part of the casino is much more airy, thanks to the very tall ceilings.

Rio pushes itself as a "carnival" atmosphere hotel, which in this case means the same hectic, crowded, noisy conditions you can expect to find in Brazil during carnival time. The older section's low ceilings only seem to accentuate how crowded the area is in both the number of people and the amount of stuff (slot machines, gaming tables). Out back is a pool with a sandy beach, and two new pools in imaginative fish and shell shapes that seem inviting until you get up close and see how small they are. It could be especially disappointing after you have braved the long, cluttered walk (particularly from the new tower rooms) to get there.

The rooms are touted because of their size; every one is a "suite," which does not mean two separate rooms but rather one large one with a sectional, corner sofa, and coffee table at one end. The dressing areas are certainly larger than average and feature a number of extra amenities, such as refrigerators (unusual for a Vegas hotel room), coffeemakers, and small snacks. Windows, running the whole length of the room, are floor to ceiling, with a pretty impressive view. The furniture does not feel like hotel room standard, but otherwise the decor (shades of green) is fairly bland and nothing to get excited about. Expect, by the way, a long wait on the phone for reservations, and a not very helpful staff.

Attempting to compete with Treasure Island's free pirate show, and to keep shoving that party, carnival theme down your throat, there is a new, live-action show called *The Masquerade Show in the Sky*. Three differently themed shows alternate, from noon to 10pm Sunday to Tuesday, from 1 to 11pm Thursday to Saturday (it's dark Wednesday). Sets modeled after Mardi Gras floats (sort of) move on grids set in the ceiling, filled with costumed performers who lip sync to songs designed to rev up the crowd but not continue the theme (Motown hits, for example). These floats are best viewed from the second floor of the Village. Down below, dancers do their thing on a stage, while even stranger costumes (ostriches, dragons) prance next to them. Guests can also don costumes and ride a float, but you have to pay for the privilege. All this party atmosphere, by the way, is strictly for adults; they actively discourage guests from bringing children.

Dining/Diversions: Fiore (the Rio's premier restaurant), the **All American Bar and Grille,** and the hotel's first-rate buffet are all described in chapter 6.

In the elegant **Antonio's,** an Italian restaurant, the centerpiece of the room is a marble-columned rotunda in which a crystal chandelier is suspended from a recessed Mediterranean-sky ceiling. Other focal points are an exhibition kitchen and a magnificent marble display table brimming with tempting antipasto selections. Dinner only.

Napa is a new addition, featuring country French gourmet cuisine. They have more than 600 selections of wine, and you can watch food preparation in the kitchen. Dinner only is served, Wednesday to Sunday.

Mask is an Asian restaurant set in a simulated rain forest. Dinner only.

Mama Marie's Cuccini is a moderately priced Italian restaurant catering to "family-style dining." It features extremely ordinary Italian food. Lunch and dinner are served.

Bamboleo is a combination Brazilian/Argentinean/Mexican place, open for lunch and dinner.

The **Voodoo Cafe,** set atop the 41st floor of the new Tower, promises to offer New Orleans–style food, live jazz and dancing, along with a view.

Buzio's Seafood Restaurant overlooks a palm-fringed pool. Massive alabaster chandeliers and flowering plants are suspended from a lofty canvas-tent ceiling, and a marble counter faces an exhibition kitchen. Lunch and dinner are available daily.

The **Beach Cafe,** also overlooking the pool and sandy beach, is the Rio's tropically festive 24-hour facility. Besides regular coffee-shop fare, it features Mexican, Italian, and Polynesian/Chinese specialties. Delicious fresh-baked desserts are a plus.

Toscano's Deli, off the casino, not only looks like a New York delicatessen but serves up a creditable pastrami or corned beef on rye. It also features pizza, pastas, and a wide array of first-rate fresh-baked breads, cakes, and pastries.

Stroll through the **Nawlins** store, which features beignets (French donuts liberally covered in powdered sugar; make sure they give you lots and eat all of them) made from genuine Café Du Monde mix. They cost a bit more than at the real McCoy, but you aren't at the real McCoy, anyway.

You might consider checking out the **Wine Cellar Tasting Room,** which bills itself as "the world's largest and most extensive collection of fine wines." Maybe, maybe not. Tasting here costs about $15 for three wines; open daily.

The **Voodoo Lounge** and **Club Rio** are discussed in chapter 10. The **Ipanema Piano Bar** features live music Sunday through Friday. **Mambo's Entertainment Lounge** in the casino has dancing from 9pm to 3am (except Sunday). Another casino bar is under a fantasy coral reef with fish swimming overhead. Drinks, tropical and otherwise, are available poolside from the open-air **Coco-Bana** or a service window off Buzio's.

Amenities: 24-hour room service, guest services desk, foreign currency exchange, shoe shine, complimentary shuttle bus to/from the MGM and the Forum Mall, casino, tour and show desks, unisex hair salon (all beauty services, including massage and facials), small video-game arcade, fitness room (stair machine, rowing machine, Lifecycle, four-station exercise machine), shops (gifts, clothing for the entire family, logo merchandise). Three whirlpool spas nestle amid rocks and foliage, there are two sand volleyball courts, and blue-and-white-striped cabanas (equipped with rafts and misting coolers) can be rented for $8 per hour or $25 per day.

✪ Treasure Island at the Mirage. 3300 Las Vegas Blvd. S., at Spring Mountain Rd., Las Vegas, NV 89177-0711. ☎ **800/944-7444** or 702/894-7111. Fax 702/894-7446. www. treasureislandlasvegas.com. 2,891 units. A/C TV TEL. From $69 double; from $109 suite. Extra person $30. Inquire about packages. AE, DC, DISC, JCB, MC, V. Free self- and valet parking.

They will deny it now if you ask them, but Treasure Island was originally conceived (more or less) as the family alternative to the more grown-up Mirage. Why else would you build a hotel that is essentially a blown-up version of Disneyland's Pirates of the Caribbean? But that's all behind them. Sure, the pirate theme remains

Treasures of the Romanovs

The Rio will be offering an unusual diversion in the form of a collection of Russian art objects. A display of Romanov Dynasty–era treasures never before seen outside of Russia, this exhibition, featuring everything from paintings to Faberge eggs exhibited in 13 galleries, looks fairly legitimate, with genuine historical and artistic significance. It will be up from November 7, 1998, to April 15, 1999.

with a vengeance, complete with plenty of skulls, crossbones, treasure chests, pirate ships' figureheads, Animatronic skeletons, and pirate nautical paraphernalia. But a $25 million face-lift has added more marble and gilded the bones, so to speak (actually, literally in some cases). It's still Pirates of the Caribbean, but with lots and lots of money thrown at it. Despite this, it still remains a top family choice and many kids are often running about, which some vacationers may not find desirable.

This is modern Vegas kitsch; not nearly as out there as, say, Excalibur, but loads of fun to gawk at anyway. The outside is an entire 18th-century pirate village, with the front consisting of a wooden dock from which spectators can view the free live-action pirate stunt show that plays every 90 minutes. The rooms continue the Caribbean theme; in other words, expect a lot of sand. And parchment. It's not quite as opulent as the Mirage, but comfortable. They do have a modern phone system with icons on the buttons so that you can easily get connected to the spa or make dinner reservations without fumbling for the right extension. Turndown service is available if you request it. For those of us who get disoriented in these giant hotels, the hallways have different wallpaper patterns, so you know instantly which of the several choices is yours. Best of all, Strip-side rooms have a view of the pirate battle—views are best from the sixth floor on up. The pool is nothing special—medium to large but with none of the massive foliage and other details that makes the one at the Mirage stand out.

Dining/Diversions: The hotel's premier restaurant, the **Buccaneer Bay Club,** is described in chapter 6, as are its buffet offerings.

Madame Ching's, luxurious, romantically lit (red silk globe lights are suspended from lotus medallions), and adorned with Chinese paintings, ceramics, sculpture, and lacquer screens, is a good choice for intimate dining. The regional Chinese fare is excellent, and Western pastries are a dessert option. Madame Ching, by the way, was a notorious 19th-century female pirate. Dinner only.

The Plank, designed on the unlikely theme of a pirate's library, comprises a warren of cozy rooms where books and curios are displayed in leaded-glass cases. Its ambience is a mix of gleaming brass, polished burl, and musty leather-bound volumes. The menu features seafood and mesquite-grilled steaks and prime rib. Dinner only; no children allowed.

The **Black Spot Grille,** its name notwithstanding, is an Italian "sidewalk cafe" set off from the shopping arcade by lacy iron grillwork. Its Italian village ambience is reflected in a Venetian *putti* (cherub) fountain, festival lanterns strung overhead, and faux bougainvillea draped from terra-cotta eaves. It's a good place for a tasty, late-night snack. Lunch and dinner; almost all menu items are under $10.

The very comfortable **Lookout Café,** Treasure Island's 24-hour coffee shop, has an arched beamed ceiling suggestive of a ship's underdeck. Walls are hung with muskets, daggers, and pirate booty from the seven seas, and amber broken-bottle sconces provide soft lighting. From 4pm to midnight, a full prime rib dinner is $10.

Just across from Mutiny Bay (the video-game arcade) is **Sweet Revenge,** an ice-cream/frozen yogurt parlor. The **Quarterdeck Deli,** a cafeteria off the casino, serves items ranging from pastrami to potato pancakes. And the **Island Snack Bar** offers light fare and nonalcoholic specialty drinks by the pool.

Captain Morgan's Lounge is a piano bar that overlooks the casino. The **Battle Bar,** in the casino near the race and sports book, airs athletic events on TV monitors overhead and offers live music nightly except Monday. More importantly, it provides patio seating overlooking Buccaneer Bay; for the best possible view of the ship battle, arrive at least 45 minutes before the show and snag a table by the railing. The ornate, crystal-chandeliered **Swashbuckler's** specializes in ice-cream drinks and a 24-ounce rum concoction served in a skull mug; you can play progressive video poker while imbibing. And in the pool area is the simpatico **Island Bar** offering frozen specialty drinks; it's cooled by a misting system in summer.

Amenities: 24-hour room service, limo rental, foreign currency exchange, shoe shine (in men's room in the lobby and casino), casino, tour and sightseeing desks, car-rental desk, travel agency, Mutiny Bay (an 18,000-square-foot, state-of-the-art video-game arcade and carnival midway; one highlight is a full-size Mazda Miata motion-simulator ride), two wedding chapels, full-service unisex salon (days of beauty are an option), and a shopping arcade (for details, see chapter 9). A full-service spa and health club with a complement of machines, sauna, steam, whirlpool and massage, on-site trainers, TVs and stereos with headsets, and anything else you might need (including a full line of Sebastian grooming products in the women's locker rooms). A free tram travels between Treasure Island and the Mirage almost around the clock. For a good photo op, sit in the front of the first car; as you leave the loading dock, note how the Mirage, palm trees, and a bit of the New York New York skyline are framed in an attractive, and nearly surreal, manner.

A large free-form swimming pool with a 230-foot loop slide has a beautifully landscaped sundeck area amid palms and flower beds. There's a kiddie pool and whirlpool, and cabanas (equipped with overhead fans, small refrigerators, phones, cable TVs, rafts, tables, and chairs) can be rented for $75 a day.

MODERATE

Barbary Coast Hotel & Casino. 3595 Las Vegas Blvd. S., at Flamingo Rd., Las Vegas, NV 89109. ☎ **800/634-6755** or 702/737-7111. Fax 702/737-6304. 200 units. A/C TV TEL. Sun–Thurs $39–$75 double, Fri–Sat and holidays $100 double. Extra person $10. Children under 12 stay free in parents' room. AE, CB, DC, DISC, JCB, MC, V. Free self- and valet parking.

Evoking the romantic image of turn-of-the-century San Francisco but not quite as nicely as Main Street Station Downtown, the Barbary Coast enjoys a terrific Strip location. The casino is adorned with $2 million worth of magnificent stained-glass skylights, and the extremely charming, Victorian-style rooms make for an opulent setting. The latter, decorated in shades of rose and gray, have half-canopied brass beds, gaslight-style lamps, lace-curtained windows, and pretty floral carpets. All accommodations include little sitting parlors with entrances framed by floral chintz curtains.

Dining/Diversions: Drai's, a new upscale restaurant, is covered in detail in chapter 6.

Michael's, the Barbary Coast's premier restaurant, is flamboyantly Victorian—an intimate dining room with white marble floors, red satin damask wall coverings, plush red velvet booths, and a gorgeous stained-glass dome overhead. The menu highlights steaks and seafood. Dinner only.

The **Victorian Room,** open 24 hours, is another attractive, turn-of-the-century venue. Its extensive menu runs the gamut from burgers to broiled Alaskan crab legs; in addition, Chinese entrees are offered at lunch and dinner.

Two bars serve the casino.

Amenities: 24-hour room service, shoe shine, casino, Western Union office, tour and show desks, gift shop.

Bourbon Street. 120 E. Flamingo, between the Strip and Koval Lane, Las Vegas, NV 89109. ☎ **800/634-6956** or 702/737-7200. Fax 702/794-3490. 167 units. A/C TV TEL. $39–$99 standard double; $59–$109 minisuite; $69–$209 executive suite. AE, CB, DC, DISC, MC, V. Free self- and valet parking.

Note: At press time, this hotel was without a casino. Plans are afoot to restore the gaming license, so it should be back in operation by 1999.

A small hotel located just steps from one of the busiest corners of the Strip (Caesars, Bally's, Flamingo Hilton), Bourbon Street is a cheap alternative to its fancier neighbors. It has a common New Orleans theme (don't you wonder how many hotels in New Orleans have a Vegas theme?) that is a bit worn in places but not shabby. Presently the empty casino area is disconcerting and is probably what is giving the hotel a ghost-town air. That's nothing that a few dozen slot machines and a couple of loud craps tables won't cure.

The rooms are basic, functional, and not particularly memorable. However, they are clean, well decorated, and the windows open (which is always nice); there are coffeemakers, modem hookups, in-room movies, and, perhaps most importantly, they can be really cheap. What more do you want?

Dining/Diversions: A very inexpensive 24-hour restaurant that specializes in Italian fare and one bar.

Amenities: Baby-sitting, laundry/dry cleaning, and room service, tour desk, meeting space, nonsmoking floors.

Imperial Palace. 3535 Las Vegas Blvd. S., between Sands Ave. and Flamingo Rd., Las Vegas, NV 89109. ☎ **800/634-6441** or 702/731-3311. Fax 702/735-8328. www.imperialpalace. com. 2,700 units. A/C TV TEL. $49–$99 double; $79–$149 "luv tub" suite, $159–$299 other suites. Extra person $15. Inquire about packages. AE, CB, DC, DISC, MC, V. Free self- and valet parking.

Though appearing even older than its 17 years, the Imperial Palace has much more going for it than the first impression might give. The Strip location, right in the middle of the action, can't be beat. The standard rooms are just that, but they all have balconies, which is exceedingly rare in Vegas. The "luv tub" rooms are a great deal; for the price, you get a larger bedroom (with a mirror over the bed!) while the larger-than-usual bathroom features a 300-gallon sunken "luv tub" (with still more mirrors). A perfect Vegas hoot. Given the slightly larger size of the "luv tub" rooms, that $59 low-end fee plus the location make them one of the best bargains on the Strip. The room amenities are all environmentally aware; biodegradable paper containers featuring cruelty-free products. They are in an "ongoing" process of upgrading the furniture. TVs offer in-house information channels, video message review and checkout, and pay-per-view movies. The hotel spa, while perhaps nothing hugely special, is more than adequate for exercise needs and is relatively inexpensive—$10 for all day. And the hotel also has a well-appointed 24-hour urgent care clinic, open to the public, which given the location—in the middle of the aforementioned action—is well worth knowing about. The pool is fairly large, with a waterfall and a Jacuzzi. From April to October, they hold "luaus" at night out here, a Polynesian revue and buffet. Expect tiki torches.

A unique feature is the Imperial Palace Auto Collection of more than 800 antique, classic, and special-interest vehicles spanning a century of automotive history (details in chapter 7). Don't forget the Breathalyzers on the way to the parking garage.

Dining/Diversions: Embers, the Imperial Palace's plush gourmet room, has burgundy silk-covered walls, spacious candlelit booths, and a smoked-mirror ceiling with recessed pink neon. The menu features steak and seafood entrees, along with pasta dishes; flambé desserts are a specialty. Dinner only.

The **Ming Terrace,** fronted by a bamboo ricksha, achieves additional Eastern ambience from Chinese screens and painted fans. The menu features Mandarin, Cantonese, and Szechuan specialties. Dinner only.

The **Rib House** is a rustic setting with exposed-brick walls and heavy oak dividers defining seating areas. A warm, cozy glow emanates from frosted-glass sconces, candlelit tables, and a working fireplace. Barbecued ribs and chicken are specialties. Dinner only.

The **Seahouse,** a casual nautically themed restaurant softly lit by ship's lanterns, features fresh seafood; if you're not a fish fancier, you might order filet mignon béarnaise or charbroiled chicken breast with sautéed mushrooms. Dinner only.

The 24-hour pagoda-like **Teahouse** offers (in addition to the usual burgers, salads, sandwiches, and full entrees) buffet brunches weekdays ($6) and champagne Sunday brunches ($6.50) from 8am to 3pm. A prime rib and champagne dinner is featured nightly from 5 to 10pm for $8.

Pizza Palace is an ordinary Italian eatery with checkered tablecloths and big tufted-leather booths. It serves regular and deep-dish pizzas, Italian sandwiches, and pasta dishes. An antipasto salad bar is a plus. Lunch and dinner are offered.

The **Emperor's Buffet,** on the third floor, has a South Seas decor composed of thatched roofing, bamboo and rattan paneling, and Polynesian carvings. All meals are served.

Betty's Diner, in the shopping arcade, serves sandwiches, pizza, nachos, hot dogs, malts, and ice-cream sundaes. **Burger Palace** is attractively decorated with sports-themed murals. Adjoining it is the **Sports Bar,** where you can follow the races over cocktails. There are a total of 10 cocktail bars/lounges in the hotel, including the **Mai Tai Lounge** on the main floor and the **Poolside Bar** (both specializing in exotic Polynesian drinks), and the **Ginza, Geisha, Sake, and Kanpai bars** serving the casino.

Amenities: 24-hour room service, free gaming lessons, shoe shine in casino, casino, health club (machines, free weights, sauna, steam, massage, tanning, TV lounge), show and tour desks, car-rental desk, travel agency, unisex hairdresser, wedding chapel, shopping arcade. An Olympic-size swimming pool is backed by a rock garden and waterfalls, and its palm-fringed sundeck area also has a Jacuzzi.

Maxim. 160 E. Flamingo Rd., between the Strip and Koval Lane, Las Vegas, NV 89109. ☎ **800/634-6987** or 702/731-4300. Fax 702/735-3252. 795 units. A/C TV TEL. $25–$209 double. Extra person $10. Children under 4 stay free in parents' room. AE, DC, DISC, MC, V. Free self- and valet parking.

Note: At press time, the Maxim had filed for bankruptcy. Attempts to deal with this situation are in play, but the future of the hotel must remain in some doubt.

Another older hotel, the Maxim has a dark interior and seems stuck in the '70s (check out the glitzy lights in the casino). Most of Maxim's business is senior citizens, but pop culture buffs and the ghoulish will note it was just outside on the street where rapper Tupac Shakur was fatally shot. The recently redone rooms are small and standard hotel, though the colors are more modern. All offer TVs with pay-movie options and in-house information channels. If you prefer, you can rent a "players suite" with a whirlpool tub in the bedroom and a separate living room with wet bar.

The pool is very small, and the deck area often looks shabby (the sun's reflection off the hotel ages the surfacing fast). Still, Maxim's is only a block off the Strip, so the location is a definite advantage. And as far as ambience, consider Maxim's the neighborhood bar of casinos. Frankly, sometimes a smaller hotel is also a boon; after all, when you tell your friends, "Meet me by the elevator," they don't ask which one.

Dining/Diversions: The Treehouse is the Maxim's 24-hour coffee shop, a dimly lit facility (it's a bit claustrophobic actually) with many tables overlooking the casino. The portions are large, and the waitresses tell you to finish all your food and bring you chicken soup if you have a cold. In addition to the requisite coffee-shop fare, it features daily specials such as a New York steak or prime rib dinner for $5.

More cheerful is **Jack's Colossal Deli,** a plant-filled self-service "sidewalk cafe" with a window wall and red-and-green-striped booths under an awning. There's also an interior room. Light fare (fresh-baked breakfast pastries, tacos, chili, salads, sandwiches, homemade soups) is served daily. All meals are served.

The **Grand Buffet,** served on the mezzanine level, is rather elegant, especially at dinner when tables are candlelit and a pianist entertains on a baby grand. Dinner ($7) is served nightly, plus a weekday brunch buffet and Saturday and Sunday champagne brunch ($8).

There are two casino cocktail lounges: the **Waterfall** and **Cloud Nine.**

Amenities: Room service, shoe shine, casino, car-rental desk, tour and show desks, small video-game arcade, gift shop (it also carries resort wear, liquor, luggage, jewelry, and logo items), beauty salon/barbershop, pool and sundeck with seasonal poolside bar.

INEXPENSIVE

Center Strip Inn. 3688 Las Vegas Blvd. S., at Harmon Ave., Las Vegas, NV 89109. ☎ **800/777-7737** or 702/739-6066. Fax 702/736-2521. 156 units. A/C TV TEL. Sun–Thurs $40–$50 double, Fri–Sat and holidays from $80 double; Sun–Thurs $80 suite (for up to 4), higher Fri–Sat and special events. Rates include continental breakfast. Mention you read about the Center Strip in Frommer's for a $5 discount Sun–Thurs. AE, DC, DISC, MC, V. Free parking at your room door.

This centrally located little motel is owned and operated by Robert Cohen, who is usually on the premises making sure guests are happy. He's a bit of an eccentric, and his hotel doesn't fit into any expected budget-property pattern. For example, the rooms have video-cassette players, and a selection of about 1,000 movies can be rented for just $2 each. Local calls and use of a fax machine are free. Breakfast consists of bagels, Danish, juice, and coffee, and free coffee is available in the lobby all day. A free pasta dinner is offered daily (subject to availability). Also available at the front desk: irons, hair dryers, and gratis bath amenities.

The rooms, situated in 2-story white stucco buildings, are standard motel units equipped with small refrigerators and safes. Suites offer kitchenettes, tubs with whirlpool jets, and steam rooms.

There's no on-premises restaurant, but numerous hotel restaurants (including ultimately Bellagio) are within easy walking distance, and you can have pizza delivered to your room. You'll also get a coupon for an all-you-can-eat $6 buffet for two at the Aladdin across the street. Facilities include a swimming pool and sundeck and a car-rental desk; the front desk can arrange tours.

Cohen also operates two Downtown properties: **Crest Budget Inn,** 207 N. 6th St., Las Vegas, NV 89101 (☎ **800/777-1817** or 702/382-5642); and **The Downtowner,** 129 N. 8th St., Las Vegas, NV 89101 (☎ **800/777-2566** or 702/384-1441). If you mention this book, you'll pay just $25 a night Sunday to Friday, $40 Saturday. However, you get what you pay for.

Vagabond Inn. 3265 Las Vegas Blvd. S., just south of Sands Ave., Las Vegas, NV 89109. ☎ **800/828-8032**, 800/522-1555, or 702/735-5102. Fax 702/735-0168. 126 units. A/C TV TEL. Sun–Thurs $42–$95 standard double, $65–$125 king room; Fri–Sat $52–$110 standard double, $72–$150 king room. Rates include continental breakfast. AE, CB, DC, DISC, MC, V. Free self-parking.

A central location just across the street from Treasure Island (a cool place from which to watch the pirate battle—drag out a lawn chair), plus clean, nicely decorated, basic motel rooms, make this a viable choice. One-third of the rooms have patios or balconies, and all offer cable TVs with pay-movie options. King rooms have wet bars and refrigerators. A wide selection of complimentary bath amenities is available at the front desk, and free coffee is served in the lobby around the clock, as is a daily continental breakfast of juice, fruit, and pastries. Facilities include coin-op washers and dryers. There's a swimming pool but no restaurant. A gratis airport shuttle and free local calls are pluses.

6 North Strip

VERY EXPENSIVE

✪ **Desert Inn Country Club Resort & Casino.** 3145 Las Vegas Blvd. S., between Spring Mountain Rd. and Convention Center Dr., Las Vegas, NV 89109. ☎ **800/634-6906** or 702/733-4444. Fax 702/733-4744. 702 units. A/C TV TEL. $175–$185 double; $215–$225 minisuite; $350–$555 suite. Extra person $35. Children under 12 stay free in parents' room. AE, CB, DC, DISC, JCB, MC, V. Free self- and valet parking.

The Desert Inn has long been the most glamorous and gracious of Vegas hotels; coming here means leaving the hectic Strip action behind. The Desert Inn considers itself more a resort than a hotel, and the property and prices reflect this. The property has just undergone a serious renovation. The look now reflects a turn-of-the-century Palm Beach resort, with elegant, clean, and spare lines. (Frankly, the time period of the decor is not turn-of-the-century in many parts, but let's not be picky.) As with most Vegas renovations, the look of everything is lighter, brighter, and cleaner—apparently, in the '90s, sand tone, rather than dark, means glamour. The clientele this attracts is middle to upper class, with a large convention crowd, thanks to their close proximity to the Sands Convention Center.

The Desert Inn's history dates from its opening in 1950, with Edgar and Charlie McCarthy premiering in the showroom. Howard Hughes (and later his estate) owned the hotel from 1967 to 1988, and he lived here in the late 1960s. (Actually, legend has it that from the day he checked in to the day he left, via a back door, he was never seen by a single hotel employee. It was during this time that he may or may not have been picked up on the highway outside of town by Melvin Drummar and may or may not have rewarded Melvin by making him his heir.) Since this is more resort than hotel, expect first-rate service all the way (indeed, when a mix-up happened with a spa reservation, the matter was dealt with much more efficiently and sweetly than at other hotels in Vegas). Travelers, too, like the on-site golf course, which is quite a good one. And there are five tournament-class tennis courts, all lit for night play; expert instruction and practice ball machines are available.

The newly redone rooms (in light golds and greens) feel spacious, with comfortable armchairs and matching hassocks. The fluffy bed coverings appear lusher than usual, and the mattresses are very firm. Rooms have views of either the Strip or the golf course (the latter really helps give the feel of a getaway), and some even have small balconies, though they are more for air currents than actual standing. Each room has a very big closet with an iron and ironing board. Business travelers will be pleased that the phone lines have modem connections. Cable TVs feature

Fun Facts

In Martin Scorsese's movie *Casino,* starring Robert De Niro, Joe Pesci, and Sharon Stone, the Riviera stood in for the fictional Tangiers.

pay-movie options as well as gaming instruction and hotel information channels. The bathrooms are perhaps the best in Vegas: beautiful and large, done in black and gray granite with double sinks, a separate enclosure for the toilet, and a glass shower separate from the tub. Amenities include a big basket of Neutrogena products, a phone, and a hair dryer.

Dining/Diversions: See chapter 6 for details on the opulent **Monte Carlo Room.**

Portofino, previously a northern Italian restaurant, is now upscale Mediterranean cuisine. It overlooks the casino (which isn't very noisy).

At **Ho Wan,** an upscale Cantonese/Szechuan restaurant, a traditional Chinese interior is currently undergoing total renovation to a more contemporary Asian decor, and a new menu is also in the works.

Terrace Pointe, a delightful plant-filled 24-hour coffee shop with a windowed wall overlooking the pool, offers an American/continental à la carte menu along with Asian specialties and buffet breakfasts and lunches. An omelet station is featured every morning, and, at lunch, there's a carving station.

A posh new steak house is also in the works. The newly remodeled **Starlight Theatre,** a plush casino lounge, features name entertainment at night; it's a romantic setting for cocktails and dancing, one of two casino bars. And even the furthest booth has a fine view of the stage.

Amenities: 24-hour room service, concierge, shoe shine, golf course, five tennis courts, swimming pool (some suites have private swimming pools).

The Desert Inn Spa is very beige, large, and pristine. The well-equipped gym has the benefit of actual windows and natural light—something you rarely see in Las Vegas unless you're outside. The placement of the soaking pools in another area with bright, natural light makes the sauna experience feel a little less private than at other spas, but since the other naked women don't resemble showgirls, it's not in the least uncomfortable. If a staff person offers to blend you a complimentary smoothie, don't turn her down. As you sit wrapped in a thick robe, waiting to be called for your massage, that smoothie will taste especially delicious.

Other facilities include a casino, tour and show desks, car-rental desk, beauty salon/barbershop, business center, shops, including golf and tennis pro shops.

EXPENSIVE

Riviera Hotel & Casino. 2901 Las Vegas Blvd. S., at Riviera Blvd., Las Vegas, NV 89109. ☎ **800/634-6753** or 702/734-5110. Fax 702/794-9451. 2,136 units. A/C TV TEL. $59–$95 double; $125–$500 suite. Extra person $20. Inquire about "Gambler's Spree" packages. AE, CB, DC, MC, V. Free self- and valet parking.

As a reaction to the ultimately futile attempt to restyle Vegas as a "family resort," the Riviera began to promote itself as an "alternative for grown-ups" and an "adult-oriented hotel." In addition to absolutely no attractions for kids, what this means is that they aren't shy about plastering posters of their flesh-intensive, naughty show *Crazy Girls* over most surfaces. Parents should probably take the hint and take their tykes elsewhere.

Opened in 1955 (Liberace cut the ribbon and Joan Crawford was the official hostess of opening ceremonies), at 9 stories the Riviera was the first "high-rise" on

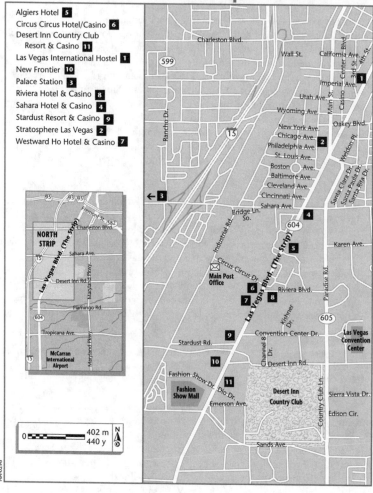

Algiers Hotel 5
Circus Circus Hotel/Casino 6
Desert Inn Country Club
  Resort & Casino 11
Las Vegas International Hostel 1
New Frontier 10
Palace Station 3
Riviera Hotel & Casino 8
Sahara Hotel & Casino 4
Stardust Resort & Casino 9
Stratosphere Las Vegas 2
Westward Ho Hotel & Casino 7

the Strip. Today, it tries to evoke the Vegas of the good old days—"come drink, gamble, and see a show"—and while it is appropriately dark and glitzy, it's also very crowded and has a confusing layout. Don't miss your chance to take your photo with the bronze memorial to the Crazy Girls, and their butts, outside on the Strip.

Rooms have recently been redone; gone are the dark tones and heavy appointments, in favor of muted florals, sandstone, and foam. It's less old-fashioned, but also has less character. Half the rooms offer pool views. Amenities include in-room safes and cable TVs with pay-movie options and in-house information stations.

Dining/Diversions: Kristofer's, an elegant, tropically themed steak-and-seafood restaurant, overlooks the pool. The adjoining lounge serves poolside fare. Dinner only.

Ristorante Italiano, a romantic setting under a simulated starlit sky, has a window wall backed by murals of Venice. Classic Italian specialties are featured. Dinner only.

Kady's is the Riviera's very cheerful 24-hour restaurant, with a wall of windows overlooking the pool as well as outdoor patio seating. Along with the usual coffee-shop fare, Kady's menu offers Jewish deli specialties.

Rik' Shaw (don't ask me what the punctuation means) features Chinese fare in an elegant candlelit room with crystal chandeliers and mirrored columns. The fan-shaped menu lists traditional Cantonese specialties. Dinner only.

An excellent choice for families is the **Mardi Gras Food Court,** which, unlike most of its genre, is extremely attractive. White canvas umbrella tables and Toulouse-Lautrec–style murals create a comfortable French cafe ambience. Food choices are wide-ranging, including burgers, pizza, gyros, falafel, and Chinese fare.

There are two casino bars: the **Splash Bar** and **Le Bistro Lounge;** the latter offers nightly live entertainment.

Amenities: 24-hour room service, shoe shine, casino (one of the world's largest), large arcade with carnival and video games, well-equipped health club (full complement of cardio and weight machines, free weights, steam, sauna, tanning, facials, salt/soap rubs, massage), Olympic-size swimming pool and sundeck, wedding chapel, beauty salon/barbershop, comprehensive business services center, America West airlines desk, tour and show desks, car-rental desk, shops (see chapter 9 for details), two Har-Tru tennis courts lit for night play. A unique feature here: a wine-tasting booth operated by Nevada's only winery. Be careful with the booth by the Strip entrance to the casino that offers free or discounted tickets to many shows; it's a time-share deal and you must go look at property to get your reward.

MODERATE

New Frontier. 3120 Las Vegas Blvd. S., at Fashion Show Dr. ☎ **800/634-6966** or 702/ 794-8200. Fax 702/794-8401. 986 units. A/C TV TEL. Sun–Thurs $49 double, Fri–Sat $75 double; Sun–Thurs $85 atrium minisuite, Fri–Sat $115 atrium minisuite. AE, MC, V. Free outdoor parking.

For a long time, conscientious travelers avoided the Frontier, which was afflicted with a 6½-year-long labor strike. But it finally ended (and over 50% of the work force came back, which tells you something), and between that and new owners (the old ones fired Siegfried and Roy!), the venerable hotel is back. Staying here is fun simply because it is the oldest extant hotel on the Strip, dating back to 1942. (In Vegas terms, that's practically the Acropolis.) But that doesn't mean sacrificing all the fabulous comforts of new Las Vegas: In the works is one of those much vaunted total renovations that should take better advantage of the 41 acres of property (one of the largest sites in Vegas). As this is a process that will be going on throughout 1998 and 1999, expect the place to look very different, though retaining the country-western theme. Further, by 1999, the New Frontier will be a Radisson flagship property.

Currently, it's still in great shape for an older hotel, but expect the old-fashioned dark reds to turn into "upscale western," which will be in keeping with other Vegas trends, brighter and lighter. It seems they won't change the setup, which, thanks to that older hotel layout, means you don't have to walk through the casino in order to get to your room or the lobby. The atrium wing is built around a lush garden oasis, with waterfalls and palm trees. The entire wing has natural, fresh air circulating through it—quite a treat. Rooms and suites are large, comfortable, and done in tasteful colors, with coffeemakers and irons in every unit and windows that open. The atrium rooms, all minisuites, are some of the best-kept secrets in town thanks to that fresh air and the view of the atrium. The pool is more like Palm Springs than Vegas—it's not showy, but simply a nice, relaxed pool.

Dining/Diversions: Phil's Angus Steakhouse is covered in chapter 6. **Margerita's Mexican Cantina** serves Mexican food. **Cattleman's Buffet** is a buffet and coffee shop, the latter open 24 hours.

Among the planned upgrades is to install a **Gilly's,** the club from *Urban Cowboy,* which will be a dance hall complete with mechanical bull and a barbecue and regular performances by country-western stars.

Amenities: Room service 6am to 11pm, casino, outdoor pool, dry cleaning, beauty shop, arcade, cable TV.

Palace Station. 2411 W. Ave, Las Vegas, NV 89102. ☎ **800/634-3101** or 702/367-2411. Fax 702/221-6510. 1,029 units. A/C TV TEL. $59–$169 double; $95–$1,000 suite. AE, CB, DC, DISC, MC, V. Free self- and valet parking.

Another in the series of early California, vaguely Victorian-influenced hotels, the Palace Station is situated by itself, which makes it ideal for those looking to keep away from the bustle of the Strip and Downtown. A train theme runs through, complete with old train artifacts. In the lobby are several antique slot machines, which are always fun to look at (nope, you can't play them, but the odds probably stink anyway). The Palace Station comes off as slightly more stylish than some Downtown hotels. The larger-than-it-appears casino (it's actually quite big) attracts many locals, which makes for a more relaxed atmosphere.

The hotel is split into two parts, consisting of the original buildings plus the newer (1991) tower. The older section is out back, a motel-style building by the pool. The rooms in this section have a mix of newer and slightly chipped dark-wood furniture. With views only of the parking lot, they are small, dark, and only have showers. For the price, they aren't worth it. Better are the Tower rooms, which are larger, brighter, and newer in feel (possibly thanks to the lighter color schemes—the decor is along the same lines). Floors 6 and above have mountain and Strip views. The corner rooms have extra-large bathrooms (though all are spacious enough and have bathtubs), with a separate changing room that has two sinks. The suites, mostly along the Victorian line, are quite nice indeed, prettily decorated, spacious, and quite luxurious. This is a place best to stay in if you can get the low-end price or you want to stay away from the crush of the Strip or Downtown.

Dining/Diversions: Guadalajara Bay is their Mexican restaurant, featuring 15 different kinds of salsas.

Pasta Palace features Italian food. Dinner only.

The **Iron Cafe** is their 24-hour coffee shop that also serves Chinese food until 11pm. Scattered throughout the property is a Burger King, Pizza Place, and TCBY. There are two bars that make large margaritas for 99¢.

Amenities: Room service, laundry and dry cleaning, express checkout, casino, pool, beauty salon, car rental, game room/arcade, tour desk.

Sahara Hotel & Casino. 2535 Las Vegas Blvd. S., at E. Sahara Ave., Las Vegas, NV 89109. ☎ **800/634-6666** or 702/737-2111. Fax 702/737-2027. 2,035 units. A/C TV TEL. $35–$55 standard double, $55–$85 deluxe double; $200–$600 suite. Extra person $10. Children under 14 stay free in parents' room. AE, CB, DC, DISC, MC, V. Free self- and valet parking.

One of the few venerable hotel casinos remaining in Vegas (it's come a long way since it opened in 1952 on the site of the old Club Bingo), the Sahara has just finished a major face-lift. Unfortunately, this includes the loss of the landmark sign, once the tallest in Vegas. (The new one, featuring a camel, is frankly going to look just as dated even more quickly.) The point is not only to keep up with the Joneses—as the newer, glitzy hotels make the old ones seem not just quaint but shabby—but also to attempt to unify the theme. This means trying to make things more like Morocco, though the reality seems to include all of North Africa (hence towers called Tangiers, Egyptian artwork, and so on). A new entrance features an arched neon dome with Moroccan detail, with plenty of marble and chandeliers, plus little tiles and other Arabian Nights details. This entrance is quite a hike from the actual registration area—be sure to bring your camel.

The room decor suffers from overkill, with stars and stripes assaulting the eyes and not looking terribly Moroccan (but then again, neither does Morocco). The boldly striped bedspreads on the otherwise comfortable beds are a particular mistake. The windows open, which is unusual for Vegas.

There is a handsome Olympic-size pool, done in Moroccan mosaic tiles, and misters on the palm trees. Unfortunately, it is also right by the parking garage, which means you might be giving some casino-bound tourist an eyeful. It should be noted that the Sahara feels they are not as well equipped as other hotels for children and discourage you from bringing yours.

Dining/Diversions: Sahara Steakhouse is just what the name implies, serving steaks and seafood in an upscale surrounding. The **Sahara Oasis Buffet** is detailed in chapter 6.

Paco's Hideaway serves Mexican food. Dinner only. The adjoining cantina, backed by a tropical aquarium, serves margaritas, Mexican beers, and light fare.

The **Caravan Coffee Shop,** a 24-hour facility off the casino with windows overlooking the pool, serves all the requisite coffee-shop fare. A steak-and-lobster dinner with salad, potato, and vegetable is just $7.77. A steak-and-eggs breakfast served from 11pm to 6am is $3.

Bar/lounges include a 24-hour casino bar (the **Safari Bar**), plus the **Casbah Lounge,** offering top-notch live entertainment daily from 2 to 6pm and 7pm to 4am.

Amenities: 24-hour room service, casino, beauty salon/barbershop, car-rental desk, tour and show desks, shops, video-game arcade. The Sahara has a large swimming pool and sundeck with a pool shop and poolside bar in nearby thatched-roof structures. A smaller pool shares the same courtyard setting.

Stardust Resort & Casino. 3000 Las Vegas Blvd. S., at Convention Center Dr., Las Vegas, NV 89109. ☎ **800/634-6757** or 702/732-6111. Fax 702/732-6257. www.stardustlv.com. 2,495 units. A/C TV TEL. $60–$1,000 Tower rooms and suites; $36–$200 Motor Inn rooms (2-person max). Extra person $10. Children 12 and under stay free in parents' room. AE, CB, DC, DISC, JCB, MC, V. Free self- and valet parking.

Opened in 1958, the Stardust is a longtime resident of the Strip, its 188-foot starry sign one of America's most recognized landmarks. Today, fronted by a fountain-splashed exterior plaza, the Stardust has kept pace with a growing city. In 1991, it added a 1,500-room tower and a 35,000-square-foot state-of-the-art meeting and conference center, part of a comprehensive $300 million expansion and renovation project. It's a likable hotel, but has no personality, despite being the only star of *Showgirls.* (It was probably chosen for its oh-so-Vegas lightbulb-intensive facade, which turns up in just about every Vegas establishing shot called for by commercials, TV, or movies. The movie *Swingers* also had a number of scenes here.)

Rooms in the Towers are perfectly adequate, nice even, but frankly, completely forgettable. If you must know more, the 32-story West Tower rooms are decorated in rich, earth tones with black accents and bedspreads and drapes in bold abstract prints. East Tower rooms are light, airy, and spacious, with peach carpeting and attractive green floral-print bedspreads, upholstered headboards, and draperies. You can rent an adjoining parlor room with a sofa bed, Jacuzzi tub, refrigerator, and wet bar—a good choice for families. Also quite nice are Villa rooms in 2-story buildings surrounding a large swimming pool. Decorated in soft Southwestern pastels, they have private shaded patios overlooking the pool. The least expensive rooms are in the Stardust's Motor Inn—four 2-story white buildings with shuttered windows set far back on the property. In the past, they were rundown motel rooms but have been redecorated in more cheerful colors. A suite can be better, but it is a long walk to your hotel. Motor Inn guests can park at their doors. All Stardust accommodations offer in-room safes, and TVs have Spectravision movie options and in-house information channels.

Dining/Diversions: William B's is an elegant steak-and-seafood restaurant fronted by a handsome bar/lounge. Flambé desserts are a house specialty. Dinner only.

Tres Lobos is an attractive restaurant designed to resemble the open courtyard of a hacienda. A plush adjoining lounge specializes in many-flavored margaritas.

Toucan Harry's Coffee Shop, the Stardust's 24-hour facility, is a lushly tropical setting under a tented fabric ceiling. In addition to a vast array of sandwiches, salads, and full entrees (including many low-fat, low-cholesterol items), Harry's features a full Chinese menu with more than 50 dishes.

Ralph's Diner reflects America's current nostalgia craze. Fifties rock 'n' roll tunes emanate from an old-fashioned jukebox, and waitresses garbed in classic white diner uniforms sometimes dance to the music. It's not a quiet place. All-American fare is served, an old-fashioned soda fountain turns out desserts, and low-priced blue-plate specials are offered daily. All meals served; everything is under $10 (most dishes are under $7).

Tony Roma's, which you may know from other locations, has a home at the Stardust; more about it, and the Stardust's **Warehouse Buffet,** in chapter 6.

The **Short Stop** is a snack bar in the race and sports book area of the casino. There are eight bars and cocktail lounges in the hotel, including the **Terrace Bar** in the casino with an alfresco seating area overlooking the pool, and the **Starlight Lounge,** featuring live music nightly.

Amenities: 24-hour room service, shoe shine, free ice on every floor, casino, beauty salon/barbershop, video-game arcade, car-rental desk, show desk, shops (gifts, candy, clothing, jewelry, logo items, liquor). There are two large swimming pools: one in the Villa section, the other between the East and West Towers. Both have attractively landscaped sundecks and poolside bars; the Towers pool area has three whirlpool spas. Guests can use the Las Vegas Sporting House directly behind the hotel, a state-of-the-art, 24-hour health club; its extensive facilities are detailed in chapter 7.

✪ **Stratosphere Las Vegas.** 2000 Las Vegas Blvd. S., between St. Louis St. and Baltimore Ave., Las Vegas, NV 89104. ☎ **800/99-TOWER** or 702/380-7777. Fax 702/383-5334. www.grandcasinos.com. 1,500 units. A/C TV TEL. Sun–Thurs $39–$93 double, Fri–Sat $59–$129 double; $69–$400 suite. Extra person $15. Children 18 and under stay free in parents' room. Rates may be higher during special events. AE, CB, DC, DISC, JCB, MC, V. Free self- and valet parking.

A really neat idea, in that Vegas way, in a really bad location. At 1,149 feet, it's the tallest building west of the Mississippi. In theory, this should have provided yet another attraction for visitors; climb (okay, elevator) to the top and gaze at the stunning view. But despite being on the Strip, it's a healthy walk from anywhere—the nearest casino is the Sahara, which is 5 very long blocks away. This and possibly the hefty price charged for the privilege of going up in said Tower may have conspired to keep the crowds away. Stay away they did; the hotel is in severe financial trouble, and construction on additions and upgrades has halted.

But in an effort to lure crowds back, prices have dropped, and some changes have been made. The casino has been toned down (previously it was a World's Fair theme; now it's more temperate and adult-looking). The shopping arcade, again with a "major cities" theme, has been expanded slightly. You can still ride the incredible thrill rides (provided the wind isn't blowing too hard that day) on top of the tower: the world's highest roller coaster (it careens around the outer rim of the tower 909 feet, 108 stories, above ground) and the Big Shot, a fabulous free-fall ride that thrusts passengers up and down the tower at speeds of up to 45 miles per hour. (One thrill-ride aficionado called the Big Shot the scariest thing he had ever ridden.) Indoor and outdoor observation decks offer the most stunning city views you will ever see, especially at night.

The rooms are furnished in handsome, Biedermeier-style cherrywood pieces with black lacquer accents. Enhanced by bright abstract paintings, they offer TVs with in-house information channels and pay-movie options, safes, phones with modem ports, and hair dryers and cosmetic mirrors in the bath. Ask for a high floor when you reserve to optimize your view.

Dining/Diversions: Two notable restaurants here are the revolving **Top of the World,** featuring panoramic vistas of Las Vegas from 800 feet, and **Big Sky Steak House,** offering all-you-can-eat barbecue dinners. They're described in chapter 6, where you'll also find details about the hotel's buffet room.

At the delightful **Ferraro's,** sky-painted ceilings, trompe l'oeil effects, and stunning murals create the illusion that you're dining in an Italian courtyard.

The 24-hour **Sister's Cafe and Grille,** its corrugated tin roofing and bayou murals designed to suggest a rustic Louisiana fishing camp, adds Cajun/Creole specialties to the more traditional Las Vegas coffee-shop fare.

A **Nathan's, McDonald's,** and **Rainforest Cafe** are in the Tower Shops area, along with a pizzeria, **Jitters** (a gourmet coffee shop), and a **Häagen-Dazs** outlet. **Roxy's Diner** is a '50s-themed eatery.

Bars and lounges include the **Images Cabaret;** the **L'Isles Bar** featuring live Caribbean/reggae music and tropical drinks; a cocktail lounge on the 107th floor; and the **Big Sky Lounge** adjacent to the restaurant, which features country music nightly after 8pm.

Amenities: 24-hour room service, foreign currency exchange, casino, guest services desk, tour and show desk, video-game arcade, shopping arcade, three wedding chapels (offering incredible views from the 103rd floor), car-rental desk. An exercise facility, child care center, and vast resort-style pool and sundeck are in the works.

INEXPENSIVE

Algiers Hotel. 2845 Las Vegas Blvd. S., between Riviera Blvd. and Sahara Ave., Las Vegas, NV 89109. ☎ **800/732-3361** or 702/735-3311. Fax 702/792-2112. 106 units. A/C TV TEL. Sun–Thurs from $40 double, Fri–Sat and holidays from $55 double. Extra person $10. Children under 12 stay free in parents' room. AE, CB, DC, DISC, MC, V. Free self-parking at your room door.

A venerable denizen of the Strip, the Algiers opened in 1953. However, a recent multimillion-dollar renovation—including landscaping (note the lovely flower beds out back) and a new facade with a 60-foot sign—brought rooms and public areas up to date. There's no casino here, though you can play video poker in the bar. Neat 2-story, aqua-trimmed peach stucco buildings house nice-size rooms (with dressing areas) that are clean and spiffy looking. Free local calls are a plus. Facilities include a medium-size pool and palm-fringed sundeck.

Impressions

The Circus Circus is what the whole hep world would be doing on Saturday night if the Nazis had won the war.

—Hunter S. Thompson, *Fear and Loathing in Las Vegas*

The cozy Algiers Restaurant and Lounge is a local hangout frequented by state and city politicians and journalists. It has a copper-hooded fireplace and walls hung with historic Las Vegas photographs of pretower Strip hotels (Dunes, Sands, Flamingo), Liberace cutting the ribbon at the opening of the Riviera, Clara Bow and Joey Adams with the owner of the now-defunct Thunderbird, and many more. A glassed-in cafe overlooks the pool. The restaurant serves all meals, including many steak and seafood specialties, barbecued baby-back ribs, and low-calorie dishes. There are souvenir shops, a jeweler, and a car-rental office out front. Also on the premises is the famed Candlelight Chapel, where many celebrities have tied the knot over the last 3 decades.

The Algiers is a good choice for families, right across the street from Circus Circus with its many child-oriented facilities and a half block from Wet 'n' Wild. It's also within walking distance of the Las Vegas Convention Center and the Stratosphere Tower.

✪ **Circus Circus Hotel/Casino.** 2880 Las Vegas Blvd. S., between Circus Circus Dr. and Convention Center Dr., Las Vegas, NV 89109. ☎ **800/444-CIRC**, 800/634-3450, or 702/734-0410. Fax 702/734-2268. www.circuscircus.com. 3,744 units. A/C TV TEL. Sun–Thurs $39–$79 double, Fri–Sat $59–$99 double. AE, CB, DC, DISC, MC, V. Free self- and valet parking.

Perhaps the strongest evidence that things are changing in Las Vegas is the massive remodeling and renovation of this classic hotel and casino. The circus theme remains, but Jumbo the Clown has been replaced by commedia dell'arte harlequins. In other words, like everyone else, even the venerable Circus Circus, once the epitome of kitsch, is trying to be taken more seriously. Gone are the bright primary colors and garish trims (murals, carpeting) and instead are subtle, muted tones and more high-rent touches that appeal less to big-top buffs and more to the Cirque de Soleil crowd.

Don't come expecting an adult atmosphere; the circus theme remains and the kid appeal along with it. The midway level features dozens of carnival games, a large arcade (more than 300 video and pinball games), trick mirrors, and ongoing circus acts under the big top from 11am to midnight daily. The world's largest permanent circus according to the *Guinness Book of World Records,* it features renowned trapeze artists, stunt cyclists, jugglers, magicians, acrobats, and high-wire daredevils. Spectators can view the action from much of the midway or get up close and comfy on benches in the performance arena. There's a "be-a-clown" booth where kids can be made up with washable clown makeup and red foam rubber noses. They can grab a bite to eat in **McDonald's** (also on this level), and since the mezzanine overlooks the casino action, they can also look down and wave to Mom and Dad—or more to the point, Mom and Dad can look up and wave to the kids without having to stray too far away from the blackjack table. Circus clowns wander the midway creating balloon animals and cutting up in various ways.

There is also the upgraded Grand Slam Canyon indoor theme park out back and an all-new shopping arcade decorated with replicas of turn-of-the-century circus posters.

The thousands of rooms here occupy sufficient acreage to warrant a free Disney World–style aerial shuttle (another kid pleaser) and minibuses connecting its many components. Tower rooms have brand-new, just slightly better than average furnishings, and offer safes and TVs with in-house information and gaming instruction stations. The Manor section comprises five white 3-story buildings out back, fronted by rows of cypresses. Manor guests can park at their doors, and a gate to the complex that can be opened only with a room key assures security. These rooms are usually among the least expensive in town, but we've said it before and we'll say it again: You get what you pay for.

All sections of this vast property have their own swimming pools; additional casinos serve the main tower and Skyrise buildings; and both towers provide covered parking garages.

Dining/Diversions: Highly esteemed by locals, the **Steak House** is elegant and candlelit, its cherry-paneled walls hung with gilt-framed oil landscapes. Shelves of books and green glass chandeliers create a clubby look. A plush lounge adjoins. Open for dinner and Sunday brunch.

The very reasonably priced **Pink Pony** is Circus Circus's cheerful bubble-gum pink and bright red 24-hour eatery, with big paintings of clowns on the walls and pink pony carpeting. It offers a wide array of coffee-shop fare, including a number of specially marked "heart-smart" (low-fat, low-cholesterol) items.

Stivali Italian Restaurant is its new fancy Italian dining room, located in the new shopping arcade. Lunch and dinner are served.

The brass-railed **Pizzeria** is in the main casino. **Latte Express,** featuring gourmet coffees, adjoins. Two 24-hour eateries, the **Westside Deli** (in the Main Tower's casino) and the **Skyrise Snack Bar** (near the race and sports book), round out food options here. The **Promenade Cafe** is the new coffee shop in the shopping arcade.

In addition, there are seven casino bars throughout the Circus Circus complex, notably the carousel-themed **Horse-A-Round Bar** on the midway level.

Circus Circus Buffet is discussed in chapter 6.

Amenities: 24-hour room service (continental breakfast and drinks only), shoe shine, three casinos, wedding chapel, tour and show desks, car-rental desk, unisex hairdresser, two swimming pools, two video-game arcades, shops (see chapter 9), Grand Slam Canyon Theme Park (see chapter 7).

Adjacent to the hotel is **Circusland RV Park,** with 384 full-utility spaces and up to 50-amp hookups. It has its own 24-hour convenience store, swimming pools, saunas, Jacuzzis, kiddie playground, fenced pet runs, video-game arcade, and community room. The rate is $12 Sunday to Thursday, $16 Friday and Saturday, $18 holidays.

Westward Ho Hotel & Casino. 2900 Las Vegas Blvd. S., between Circus Circus Dr. and Convention Center Dr., Las Vegas, NV 89109. ☎ **800/634-6803** or 702/731-2900. 777 units. A/C TV TEL. $37–$56 double; $76 suite. Extra person $10. MC, V. Free parking at your room door.

Located next door to Circus Circus, the Westward Ho is fronted by a vast casino, with rooms in 2-story buildings that extend out back for several city blocks. In fact, the property is so large that a free bus shuttles regularly between the rooms and the casino 24 hours a day. There are three swimming pools and three whirlpool spas to serve all areas.

The rooms are clean and adequately furnished motel units. A good buy here: two-bedroom suites with 1½ baths, living rooms with sofa beds, and refrigerators; they sleep up to six people.

There's a 24-hour restaurant in the casino under a stained-glass skylight dome. It serves a buffet breakfast, brunch and dinner, as well as an à la carte menu featuring traditional coffee-shop fare. Other facilities include a tour desk, free airport shuttle, a gift shop, a casino lounge where a three-piece country band entertains Monday to Saturday from 7pm to 1am, and a deli in the casino serving sandwiches, ribs, and half-pound extra-long hot dogs.

7 East of the Strip

In this section we've covered hotels close by the Convention Center, along with those farther south on Paradise Road, Flamingo Road, and Tropicana Avenue.

VERY EXPENSIVE

✪ **Alexis Park Resort.** 375 E. Harmon Ave., between Koval Lane and Paradise Rd., Las Vegas, NV 89109. ☎ **800/582-2228** or 702/796-3300. Fax 702/796-4334. 500 units. A/C MINIBAR TV TEL. $99–$139 one-bedroom suite, $175–$250 one-bedroom loft suite, $350–$1,500 larger suite. Extra person $15. Children 18 and under stay free in parents' room. AE, CB, DC, DISC, JCB, MC, V. Free self- and valet parking.

A low-key atmosphere, luxurious digs, and superb service combine to make Alexis Park the hotel choice of many showroom headliners and visiting celebrities. Alan Alda, Alec Baldwin, Whitney Houston, Robert de Niro, Dolly Parton, and Garth Brooks are just a few of the superstars who've chosen this resort's discreet elegance over the glitzier Strip hotels. It's the kind of place where you can get a phone at your restaurant table or your suit pressed at 3am.

You'll sense the difference the moment you approach the palm-fringed entranceway, fronted by lovingly tended flower beds and a rock waterfall. The elegant lobby has comfortable sofas amid immense terra-cotta pots of ferns, cacti, and calla lilies, and there's notably fine artwork throughout the public areas.

Spacious suites are decorated in light resort colors with taupe lacquer furnishings. Loft suites have cathedral ceilings. All are equipped with refrigerators, wet bars, two-line phones (one in each room of your suite) with computer jacks, and TVs (also one in each room) with HBO and pay-movie options. More than a third of the suites have working fireplaces and/or Jacuzzi tubs.

Dining/Diversions: Pegasus, an exquisite award-winning gourmet dining room, is described in chapter 6.

The **Pisces Bistro,** under a 30-foot domed ceiling with planters of greenery cascading from tiers overhead, provides live entertainment Tuesday to Saturday nights (see chapter 10) and serves drinks, pizzas, salads, sandwiches, a few full entrees (steak, seafood, pasta), and desserts, both inside and on a patio overlooking the pool.

Amenities: 24-hour room service, concierge, gift shop, unisex hair salon, health club (including a good complement of workout equipment, whirlpool, massage, steam, and sauna).

Behind the hotel are beautifully landscaped grounds with palm trees and pines, streams and ponds spanned by quaint bridges, gazebos, rock gardens, flower beds, and oleanders. Here you'll find a large fountain-centered swimming pool, two smaller pools, cabana bars, three whirlpool spas, umbrella tables, table tennis, and a nine-hole putting green.

Courtyard Marriott. 3275 Paradise Rd., between Convention Center Dr. and Desert Inn Rd., Las Vegas, NV 89109. ☎ **800/321-2211** or 702/791-3600. Fax 702/796-7981. www.marriott.com. 159 units. A/C TV TEL. Sun–Thurs $109 double, Fri–Sat $119 double;

$119–$129 suite. Convention rates can be higher. AE, CB, DC, DISC, MC, V. Free parking at your room door.

Housed in 3-story terra-cotta–roofed stucco buildings, in an attractively landscaped setting of trees, shrubbery, and flower beds, the Courtyard is a welcome link in the Marriott chain. The concept for these limited-service, lower-priced lodgings (though not especially low-priced for Las Vegas) was developed in the 1980s, and this particular property opened in 1989. Although the services are limited, don't picture a no-frills establishment. This is a beautiful hotel, with a pleasant, plant-filled lobby and very nice rooms indeed.

Like its public areas, the rooms, most with king-size beds, still look spanking new. Decorated in shades of gray-blue, mauve, and burgundy, with sofas and handsome mahogany furnishings (including large desks), they offer TVs with multiple On-Command movie options. All rooms have balconies or patios.

Dining/Diversions: Off the lobby is a light and airy plant-filled restaurant with glossy oak paneling and tables. It serves buffet breakfasts, as well as à la carte lunches (mostly salads and sandwiches); light fare is available from 5 to 10pm. Adjoining is a comfortable lobby lounge with plush furnishings, a large-screen TV, and a working fireplace. Drinks are served here from 4 to 10pm. You can also enjoy breakfast in this lounge and catch a morning TV news show.

Amenities: Room service 4 to 10pm, complimentary airport shuttle, small exercise room, medium-size swimming pool with adjoining whirlpool, picnic tables and barbecue grills, coin-op washers/dryers.

Crowne Plaza Holiday Inn. 4255 Paradise Rd., just north of Harmon Ave., Las Vegas, NV. ☎ **800/2-CROWNE** or 702/369-4400. Fax 702/369-3770. A/C TV TEL. $149–$189 double. AE, CB, DC, DISC, MC, V. Free self-parking. No valet parking.

The upscale link in the Holiday Inn chain, this business-oriented hotel is right next to the Hard Rock, and so it might provide a more sober place to stay rather than that Gen-X destination. Each room is technically a suite, but apparently after building their 5-story atrium they didn't have a lot of space left for the rooms, and so each is on the small side, made more so by the sheer amount of stuff crammed into them. Expect a wet bar, a sitting area complete with convertible sofa bed, a fridge, and a desk. Nice touches include robes and full-size ironing board and iron. Summertime can find calypso bands playing by the pool, making it a party spot for the many flight crews who regularly stay here.

Dining/Diversions: The **Atrium Bar and Grille** is a "European Coffeeshop," but despite the name is fairly standard. There is a pool bar during the summer.

Amenities: Room service 6am to 10pm, laundry, dry cleaning, concierge, tour desk, 24-hour airport shuttle, transportation to and from the Strip, sundry/gift shop, baby-sitting services, pool, hot tub, wet and dry sauna, small workout facility with Nautilus machines, weights, and treadmills.

✪ **Hard Rock Hotel & Casino.** 4455 Paradise Rd., at Harmon Ave., Las Vegas, NV 89109. ☎ **800/473-ROCK** or 702/693-5000. Fax 702/693-5010. www.hardrock.com. 340 units. A/C TV TEL. Sun–Thurs $75–$250 double, Fri–Sat $145–$300 double; from $250 suite. Extra person $25. Children 12 and under stay free in parents' room. AE, DC, MC, V. Free self- and valet parking.

Owner Peter Morton, who bills his Hard Rock Hotel and Casino as "Vegas for a New Generation," sent out invitations to the property's March 1995 opening inscribed on casino chips bearing the image of Jimi Hendrix. Dozens of celebrities flew in for the festivities, which included concerts by the Eagles and Sheryl Crow. Everything here is rock-themed, from the Stevie Ray Vaughan quote over the entrance ("When this house is a rocking, don't bother knocking, come on in") to

Alexis Park Resort **12**

Best Western Mardi Gras Inn **5**

Courtyard Marriott **4**

Crowne Plaza Holiday Inn **10**

Emerald Springs Holiday Inn **8**

Fairfield Inn by Marriott **6**

The Hard Rock Hotel & Casino **11**

La Quinta Inn **7**

Las Vegas Hilton **1**

Marriott Suites **3**

Motel 6 **13**

Residence Inn by Marriott **2**

Sam's Town **14**

Super 8 Motel **9**

the vast collection of music memorabilia displayed in public areas. The house is always "a rocking" (the pulsating beat emanates from hundreds of speakers throughout the property), and the cheerful casino features piano-shaped roulette tables and guitar-neck-handle slot machines. Even the walls of the bell desk are lined with gold records.

Large, attractive rooms, decorated in earth tones with photographs of rock stars adorning the walls, have beds with leather headboards and French windows that actually open to fresh air (a rarity in Las Vegas). Uncharacteristically large 27-inch TVs (most hotel sets are smaller since they want you in the casino, not staring at the tube) offer pay-movie options and special music channels.

A new expansion is underway, due to be finished in 1999, that should double the size of the hotel.

Dining/Diversions: The Hard Rock's premier restaurant, **Mortoni's,** is a beauty. Parchment-yellow walls are hung with vintage photographs such as a tuxedoed James Dean at a Hollywood party; Humphrey Bogart, Frank Sinatra, and Grace Kelly at Chasen's in the 1940s; and stills from Las Vegas movies. Furnishings are butter-soft plush red leather. Large windows overlook the pool area, where, weather permitting, you can dine outdoors at umbrella tables. The fare is Italian, and portions are vast. Dinner only.

Mr. Lucky's 24/7 is the hotel's round-the-clock coffee shop, displaying rock memorabilia and old Las Vegas hotel signs. California-style entrees and pizzas are offered in addition to the usual Las Vegas menu.

The **Hard Rock Cafe** (details in chapter 6) is adjacent to the hotel.

Orbit, the hotel's late-night weekend dance club, is discussed in chapter 10. The Center Bar in the casino is under a glowing purple dome, from which a globe inscribed with the words "One Love, One World" is suspended. The **Beach Club Bar** serves light fare and frozen drinks poolside. And the **Viva Las Vegas Lounge,** off the casino, has a video wall where four monitors display rapid-paced rock footage.

Amenities: 24-hour room service, concierge, casino, small video-game arcade, gift/sundry shop and immense Hard Rock retail store, show desk (for **The Joint** only; tickets to other shows can be arranged by the concierge), health club (offering a full complement of Cybex equipment, stair machines, treadmills, massage, and steam rooms).

The Hard Rock has one of the most gorgeous pool areas in Las Vegas, complete with a palm-fringed sandy beach, grassy expanses of lawn, a vast, free-form sand-bottomed pool with a water slide and 150 speakers providing underwater music, several whirlpools, and raft rentals. Luxurious poolside cabanas (equipped with TVs, phones, misters, and refrigerators) can be rented for $55 to $85 a day.

⭐ **Las Vegas Hilton.** 3000 Paradise Rd., at Riviera Blvd., Las Vegas, NV 89109. ☎ **800/ 732-7117** or 702/732-7111. Fax 702/732-5790. www.lvhilton.com. 3,479 units, A/C TV TEL. $95–$279 double. Extra person $25. Children of any age stay free in parents' room. Inquire about attractively priced golf and other packages. CB, DC, DISC, ER, MC, V. Free self- and valet parking.

This is really quite a classy hotel, which is probably why so many business travelers prefer it. (That, and the location next to the convention center.) The lobby, glittering with massive chandeliers and gleaming marble, is lovely, and the casino is actually separate from it. There are quite a few terrific restaurants, plus the largest hotel convention and meeting facilities in the world. Their nightclub (called The Nightclub) is a great place to hang in the evening and features regular sets by dance music star Kristine W. Col. Tom Parker's memorial service was held here in the hotel. And one of Elvis's sequined jumpsuits is enshrined in a glass case in the front (he played here).

A serious renovation has added a number of new shops, plus **Star Trek: The Experience,** a themed attraction and accompanying space-themed casino. They want to start attracting more of a leisure crowd, but you do have to wonder how all these additions might change the otherwise high-rent atmosphere.

The newly remodeled rooms have partly marble floors and slightly larger marble bathtubs. Each has a small dressing area outside the bathroom. The rooms are nothing particularly special in terms of decor, but they are very comfortable. Some have views of the adjacent 18-hole golf course. They feature automatic checkout on the TV and a hotline number on the phone that sends you directly to housekeeping. All offer TVs (cached in handsome armoires) with HBO, On-Command pay-movie options, an in-house information channel, and video checkout capability.

Dining/Diversions: Bistro Le Montrachet is reviewed in chapter 6.

Most dramatic of the Hilton's restaurants is **Benihana Village,** a pagoda-roofed Oriental fantasyland with cascading waterfalls and meandering streams, spanned by quaint wooden bridges. You'll enjoy dancing water displays and fiber-optic fireworks while you dine. The Village houses three restaurants and a lounge. On one side of the central waterway is the **Garden of the Dragon,** its entrance presided over by a fiery-eyed dragon atop a pagoda. The menu offers regional Chinese specialties. Dinner only.

Across the stream is the **Seafood Grille,** fronted by a colorful Asian marketplace aclutter with barrels of eggs (above which are animated hens in wooden cages) and displays of fish, fruits, and vegetables. Seating is under a pagoda eave, walls are hung with fishing nets, and wooden columns are embellished with Chinese kites. Dinner only.

At the far end, occupying two dining levels, is a branch of **Benihana,** with a restrained Japanese shoji-screen decor and teppanyaki-grill tables. It's solid Japanese food, but that show, with the chef slicing, dicing, and whirling away at your table, is still a kitsch thrill. Dinner only.

Near the entrance to this exotic restaurant complex is the **Kabuki Lounge,** an inviting setting for cocktails.

The **Hilton Steakhouse,** which also serves seafood and chops, offers a warmly intimate wood-paneled interior with candlelit tables. Dinner only.

Another beef eatery is the **Barronshire Room,** where an English club ambience is created by high-backed burgundy leather booths and armchairs, crystal chandeliers and sconces, and walls hung with gilt-framed oil paintings. The restaurant is patterned after the renowned Barronshire Inn in southern England. Dinner only.

At the simpatico **MargaritaGrille,** Mexican music, pots of cacti, and displays of papier-mâché birds and pottery combine to create a south-of-the-border ambience. The **Grille's** bar is quite popular for cocktails and Mexican appetizers. Dinner only.

Andiamo, a charming Italian *ristorante,* seats diners amid planters of ficus trees and terra-cotta columns. Above the brass- and copper-accented exhibition kitchen is a colorful display of Italian food products. All pasta and bread served here is made fresh on the premises. Dinner only.

Finally there's the **Coffee Shop,** a Southwestern 24-hour facility where lush faux foliage, including hibiscus draped from driftwood beams overhead, gives the room a cheerful ambience. Traditional Las Vegas coffee-shop fare is supplemented by Mexican specialties.

Additional facilities include a branch of **TCBY** and a cappuccino and pastry cart in the lobby. There are seven bar/lounges at the Hilton. In addition, the **Garden**

Snack Bar serves the pool deck; the **Paddock Snack Bar** in the race and sports book features pizza, sandwiches, and other light fare items (not oats); and the **Nightclub,** a first-rate casino lounge, has live entertainment nightly. See also the buffet listings in chapter 6. *Note:* Children 12 and under dine in any Hilton restaurant for half the listed menu prices.

Amenities: 24-hour room service, foreign currency exchange, two casinos, car-rental desk, tour desk, travel agency, shops, small video-game arcade, business service center (faxing and express mail), multiservice beauty salon/barbershop, jogging trail, 18-hole golf course.

The third-floor roof comprises a beautifully landscaped 8-acre recreation deck with a large swimming pool, a 24-seat whirlpool spa, six Har-Tru tennis courts lit for night play, Ping-Pong, and a putting green. Also on this level is a luxurious, 17,000-square-foot, state-of-the-art health club offering Nautilus equipment, Life-cycles, treadmills, rowing machines, three whirlpool spas, steam, sauna, massage, and tanning beds. Guests are totally pampered: All toiletries are provided; there are comfortable TV lounges; complimentary bottled waters and juices are served in the canteen; and beauty services include facials, oxygen pep-up, and spa body treatments.

Marriott Suites. 325 Convention Center Dr., Las Vegas, NV 89109. ☎ **702/650-2000.** Fax 702/650-9466. www.marriot.com. 278 units. A/C TV TEL. $159 suite. AE, CB, DC, DISC, MC, V. Free outdoor parking.

Oh, sure, you don't lack for Marriotts in Las Vegas, but it is a reliable chain, and you can't fault the location of this one—just 3 blocks off the Strip (a 10-minute walk at most, though in 100°F heat, that may be too far) and not much more than that from the Convention Center. Obviously, this is a solid choice for business travelers, but families might like the lack of casino and accompanying mayhem, not to mention the extra-large, quite comfortable rooms. Each suite has a sitting area separated from the bedroom (with a king-size bed) by French doors, a minifridge, and phones with data port. In passing, it's worth coming by here simply for the gorgeous prints on the walls; far, far better than you would expect in a hotel, much less in a chain.

Dining: Allie's American Grille is reviewed in chapter 6. **Windows Lobby Bar** serves light fare and beverages.

Amenities: All rooms have minirefrigerators, coffeemakers, data-port phones, and in-room movies. Free newspaper, complimentary airport shuttle, outdoor pool with Jacuzzi, health club, 24-hour room service, business center, valet laundry service, sundry shop, guest laundry, ballroom and banquet hall.

EXPENSIVE

La Quinta Inn. 3970 Paradise Rd., between Twain Ave. and Flamingo Rd., Las Vegas, NV 89109. ☎ **800/531-5900** or 702/796-9000. Fax 702/796-3537. www.laquinta.com. 181 units. A/C TV TEL. $85–$95 standard double, $89–$99 executive double; $115–$125 suite. Rates include continental breakfast; inquire about seasonal discounts. AE, CB, DC, DISC, MC, V. Free self-parking.

A remodeling process to be completed in 1999 may remove some of the pleasant grounds of this mission-style hotel. Nonetheless, it's still a tranquil alternative to Strip hubbub, featuring a courtyard, a charming stone fountain, rustic benches, lawn games (croquet, badminton, volleyball), barbecue grills, and picnic tables. The staff is terrific—friendly and incredibly helpful. The rooms are immaculate and attractive. Executive rooms feature one queen-size bed, a small refrigerator, a wet bar, and a microwave oven. Double queens are larger but have no kitchen facilities.

And two-bedroom suites are not just spacious—they are really full apartments. They contain large living rooms (some with sofa beds), dining areas, and full kitchens. Ground-floor accommodations have patios, and all accommodations feature baths with oversized whirlpool tubs. TVs offer satellite channels and HBO.

Dining/Diversions: Complimentary continental breakfast (juice, bagels, cereal, muffins, fresh fruit, beverages) is served daily in the Patio Café.

Amenities: Car rentals/tours arranged at the front desk, coin-op washers/dryers, medium-size swimming pool and adjoining whirlpool. A free 24-hour shuttle offers pickup and return to and from the airport and several Strip casino hotels.

✪ **Residence Inn by Marriott.** 3225 Paradise Rd., between Desert Inn Rd. and Convention Center Dr., Las Vegas, NV 89109. ☎ **800/331-3131** or 702/796-9300. www.marriott.com. 192 units. A/C TV TEL. $89–$169 studio; $109–$219 penthouse. Rates include continental breakfast. AE, CB, DC, DISC, MC, V. Free self-parking.

Staying here is like having your own apartment in Las Vegas. The property occupies 7 acres of perfectly manicured lawns, tropical foliage, and neat flower beds. It's a great choice for families and business travelers. Monday to Friday, they offer a free light dinner with beer, wine, and soda.

Accommodations, most with working fireplaces, are housed in condolike, 2-story wood-and-stucco buildings, fronted by little gardens. Studios have adjoining sitting rooms with sofas and armchairs, dressing areas, and fully equipped eat-in kitchens complete with dishwashers. Every guest receives a welcome basket of microwave popcorn and coffee. TVs offer visitor information channels and VCRs (you can rent movies nearby), and all rooms have balconies or patios. Duplex penthouses, some with cathedral ceilings, add an upstairs bedroom (with its own bath, phone, TV, and radio) and a full dining room.

Dining/Diversions: A big continental buffet breakfast (fresh fruit, yogurt, cereals, muffins, bagels, pastries) is served each morning in the gatehouse, a delightful cathedral-ceilinged lobby lounge with a working fireplace. There's comfortable seating amid planters of greenery. Daily papers are set out here each morning; there's a large-screen TV and a stereo for guest use; and a selection of toys, games, and books is available for children. Weekday evenings from 5:30 to 7pm, complimentary buffets with beverages (beer, wine, coffee, soda), fresh popcorn, and daily varying fare (soup/salad/sandwiches, tacos, Chinese, barbecue, spaghetti, and so on) are served in the gatehouse. This cocktail-hour spread affords an opportunity to socialize with other guests, a nice feature if you're traveling alone.

Amenities: Local restaurants deliver food, and there's also a complimentary food-shopping service. Maids wash your dishes; car-rental desk, barbecue grills, coin-op washers/dryers, sports court (paddle tennis, volleyball, basketball). There's a good-size swimming pool and whirlpool with a sundeck. Guests can use the health club next door at Courtyard Marriott (details above).

MODERATE

Best Western Mardi Gras Inn. 3500 Paradise Rd., between Sands Ave. and Desert Inn Rd., Las Vegas, NV 89109. ☎ **800/634-6501** or 702/731-2020. Fax 702/733-6994. 315 units. A/C TV TEL. $40–$125 double. Extra person $8. Children 18 and under stay free in parents' room. AE, CB, DC, DISC, JCB, MC, V. Free parking at your room door.

Opened in 1980, this well-run little casino hotel has a lot to offer. A block from the convention center and close to major properties, its 3-story building sits on nicely landscaped grounds with manicured lawns, trees, and shrubbery. There's a gazebo out back where guests can enjoy a picnic lunch.

Accommodations are all spacious, queen-bedded minisuites with sofa-bedded living room areas and eat-in kitchens, the latter equipped with wet bars, refrigerators, and coffeemakers. All are attractively decorated and offer TVs with HBO and pay-movie options. Staying here is like having your own little Las Vegas apartment.

Dining/Diversions: A pleasant restaurant/bar off the lobby, open from 6:30am to 11pm daily, serves typical coffee-shop fare; a 12-ounce prime rib dinner here is just $9.

Amenities: Free transportation to/from airport and major Strip hotels, small casino (64 slots/video poker machines), small video-game arcade, car-rental desk, tour and show desks, coin-op washers/dryers, unisex hairdresser, gift shop, RV parking. The inn has a large swimming pool with a duplex sundeck and whirlpool.

Emerald Springs Holiday Inn. 325 E. Flamingo Rd., between Koval Lane and Paradise Rd., Las Vegas, NV 89109. ☎ **800/732-7889** or 702/732-9100. Fax 702/731-9784. 150 units. A/C TV TEL. $69–$99 studio; $99–$129 Jacuzzi suite, $129–$175 hospitality suite. Extra person $15. Children 18 and under stay free in parents' room. AE, CB, DC, DISC, MC, V. Free self-parking.

Housed in three mauve-trimmed peach stucco buildings, Emerald Springs offers a friendly, low-key alternative to the usual glitz and glitter. It's entered via a charming, marble-floored lobby with a waterfall fountain and lush, faux tropical plantings under a domed skylight. Off the lobby is a comfortably furnished lounge with a large-screen TV and working fireplace. Typical of the inn's hospitality is a bowl of apples for the taking at the front desk. And weeknights from 10:30pm to midnight you can "raid the icebox" at the **Veranda Café,** which offers complimentary cookies, peanut butter and jelly sandwiches, and coffee, tea, or milk. Although your surroundings here are serene, you're only 3 blocks from the heart of the Strip.

Public areas and rooms here are notably clean and spiffy. Pristine hallways are hung with nice abstract paintings and have small seating areas on every level, and rooms are beautifully decorated in teal and mauve with bleached-oak furnishings. Even the smallest accommodations (studios) offer small sofas, desks, and armchairs with hassocks. You also get two phones (desk and bedside), an in-room coffeemaker (with gratis coffee), and a wet bar with refrigerator. TVs (concealed in an armoire) have HBO and pay-movie options; VCRs are available upon request. There's a separate dressing room and a hair dryer in the bath. Suites add a living-room area with a large-screen TV to the above, an eat-in kitchenette with a microwave oven, a larger dressing room, and a Jacuzzi tub. Hospitality suites feature sitting room areas and dining tables.

Dining/Diversions: Just off the lobby (you can hear the splashing of the fountain and waterfall), the **Veranda Café** offers both indoor and alfresco dining, the latter on a covered patio overlooking the pool. It serves buffet breakfasts and à la carte lunches (burgers, salads, deli sandwiches) and dinners (light fare plus entrees). A comfortable bar/lounge with video poker games adjoins.

Amenities: Concierge, complimentary limousine transportation to and from the airport and nearby casinos between 6:30am and 11pm (van service available 11pm to 6:30am), room service, business services, gratis newspapers available at the front desk, fitness room, nice-size pool/sundeck and whirlpool in an attractively landscaped setting.

Fairfield Inn by Marriott. 3850 Paradise Rd., between Twain Ave. and Flamingo Rd., Las Vegas, NV 89109. ☎ **800/228-2800** or 702/791-0899. Fax 702/791-2705. www.marriot. com. 129 units. A/C TV TEL. $62–$150 for up to 5 people. Rates include continental breakfast. AE, CB, DC, DISC, MC, V. Free self-parking.

East of the Strip 95

This pristine property, opened in 1990, is a pleasant place to stay. It has a comfortable lobby with sofas and armchairs, a simpatico setting in which to plan your day's activities over a cup of coffee, tea, or hot chocolate (provided gratis all day).

Rooms are cheerful. Units with king-size beds have convertible sofas, and all accommodations offer well-lit work areas with desks; TVs have free movie channels as well as pay-movie options. Local calls are free.

Breakfast pastries, fresh fruit, juice, and yogurt are served in the lobby each morning, and many restaurants are within easy walking distance. Facilities include a pool/whirlpool and sundeck with umbrella tables. A free shuttle goes to and from the airport every 30 minutes between 6am and midnight. Car rentals and tours can be arranged. The front desk offers warm hospitality.

✪ **Sam's Town Hotel & Gambling Hall.** 5111 Boulder Hwy., at Flamingo Rd., Las Vegas, NV 89122. ☎ **800/634-6371** or 702/456-7777. Fax 702/454-8014. 648 units. A/C TV TEL. $50–$100 double; $140–$240 suite. Extra person $5. AE, CB, DC, DISC, MC, V. Free self- and valet parking.

Just 5 miles from the Strip (which means it's not precisely near anything, but if you have a car, it's also not far) and western-themed, Sam's Town is immensely popular with locals and tourists alike. Its friendly atmosphere and nightly laser shows make it a good choice for families. The property occupies 58 acres, with accommodations surrounding one of its biggest selling points: Mystic Falls, a lush 25,000-square-foot indoor park under a 9-story skylight. Here, amid leafy trees, fern gullies, fountains, and flower beds, are meandering streams, rock waterfalls, and wildlife, both real (including a dam-building beaver) and Animatronic (chirping birds). Lovely year-round, the park is an especially welcome setting in summer when 100°F-plus temperatures make it impossible to spend any time outdoors; in this controlled setting, it's always a comfortable 70°F. There is a coffeehouse (**Java in the Park**), and a bar overlooking the waterfall, plus chairs and benches, as well as a log pagoda where you can sit in tranquil comfort and read a book, a novelty in this town.

Large, high-ceilinged accommodations overlooking the park or mountains are also notably appealing, with rustic light-wood furnishings, Native American–motif carpeting, cowhide-shaded lighting fixtures, and western art on the walls. Each room has a large desk and a cable TV offering pay-movie options, keno, and a hotel information channel. At night the park is lit by lanterns, and trees are strung with thousands of tiny lights.

Dining/Diversions: Papamios Italian Kitchen and Sam's Town, **The Great Buffet** are described in chapter 6.

Diamond Lil's, an opulent Old West/Victorian crystal-chandeliered gourmet room, seats diners in plush booths lit by fringe-shaded oil lamps. Dinner only. A bar/lounge adjoins.

At **Billy Bob's Steak House and Saloon,** also highlighting steak, prime rib, and seafood, log and stone walls are hung with rusty farm implements and paintings of the Old West. A waterwheel in one room creates a pleasant splashy backdrop. Dinner only. The **Silver Dollar Bar,** embellished by a display of animal horns, adjoins.

Willy and Jose's is a "Mexican cantina" with fading wallpapers and neon beer signs over the bar serving traditional Mexican (not Tex-Mex) fare. Twelve-ounce margaritas are 95¢. Dinner only.

Mary's Diner, open for all meals, conforms to the traditions of its genre, complete with counter seating and small jukeboxes adjoining its comfortable red leatherette booths. The menu includes Yankee pot roast, meat loaf with real mashed potatoes, homemade chili, and the like.

Cheap Hotel Alternatives

If you are determined to come to Vegas during a particularly busy season and you are finding yourself shut out of the prominent hotels, here is a list of moderate to very inexpensive alternatives. We haven't inspected all the rooms or evaluated the service at these places, but most of these are major hotel chains, which encourages a certain amount of quality control. All are located in decent neighborhoods, and a drive-by indicates that they seem to be well cared for.

On or Near the Strip
Budget Suites of America, 1500 Stardust; ☎ **702/732-1500**
Budget Suites of America, 4205 W. Tropicana; ☎ **702/889-1700**
Comfort Inn, 211 E. Flamingo; ☎ **800/634-6774**
Howard Johnson Hotel, 3111 W. Tropicana; ☎ **800/654-2000**
Quality Inn, 377 E. Flamingo; ☎ **800/221-2222**
Rodeway Inn, 167 E. Tropicana; ☎ **702/795-3311**
Travelodge, 3735 S. Las Vegas Blvd.; ☎ **800/225-3050**

Paradise Road & Vicinity
Budget Suites of America, 3684 Paradise Rd.; ☎ **702/699-7000**

Downtown & Vicinity
Best Western Main Street, 100 N. Main St.; ☎ **800/528-1234**
Best Western Mariana, 1322 E. Fremont; ☎ **800/528-1234**
Budget Inn, 301 S. Main St.; ☎ **702/385-5560**
Econo Lodge, 520 S. Casino Center; ☎ **800/233-7706**
Econo Lodge, 1150 S. Las Vegas Blvd.; ☎ **800/424-4777**

East Las Vegas & Vicinity
Budget Suites of America, 4625 Boulder Hwy.; ☎ **702/454-4625**
Budget Suites of America, 4855 Boulder Hwy.; ☎ **702/433-3644**
Motel 6 Boulder Highway, 4125 Boulder Hwy.; ☎ **800/466-8356**
Super 8 Motel, 5288 Boulder Hwy.; ☎ **800/825-0880**

West Las Vegas & Vicinity
Motel 6, 5085 Industrial Rd. (South Las Vegas); ☎ **800/466-8356**
EZ-8 Motel, 5201 S. Industrial Rd. (South Las Vegas); ☎ **800/32-MOTEL**

Smokey Joe's Cafe and Market is the hotel's 24-hour facility, another western setting with knotty-pine booths, faux windows overlooking a cowboy town mural, and walls hung with washboards and antique farm implements. Coffee-shop fare is supplemented by a full Chinese menu. Great deals here include inexpensive buffets at breakfast and terrific all-you-can-eat salad bars at lunch and dinner, not to mention graveyard specials such as three eggs, a three-quarter-pound ham steak, hash browns, and toast served from 11pm to 11am for $3.

Another 24-hour facility is the **Final Score Sports Bar,** where you'll find pool tables, darts, pinball, air hockey, and a basketball cage; sporting events are aired on more than 30 TV monitors, and there's occasionally live music for dancing. Light fare (burgers, wings, nachos) is available, and there's patio seating overlooking the pool.

Roxy's Saloon, one of 13 bars on the premises, offers live entertainment (C&W) for dancing daily from noon to the wee hours. Rounding out facilities here are a deli

Motel 6

At press time there were plans to turn a portion or all of this property into a new 1940s gangster-themed hotel called Bugsy's. A portion of Motel 6 may still be operating or may be entirely closed by the end of 1999.

---

in the race and sports book area, a bowling alley snack bar, a food court, an ice-cream parlor, and a rotating bar in the park.

The **Sunset Stampede** is a laser and water show that takes place four times daily (2, 6, 8, and 10pm) in the Mystic Falls Park. It begins with a howl from an Animatronic wolf atop the waterfall, and then water spurts in sync with orchestral themes, as lasers fire random pretty colors around the room. As a 10-minute show, it's not long enough or special enough to be worth the drive from the Strip (though there are free buses to transport you—call for details). If you are already out there, grab a seat at the bar early. This is particularly important for kids, as it gets pretty crowded and it is tough to see the show unless you are close up.

Amenities: Room service, foreign currency exchange, shoe shine; free shuttle bus to/from the Stardust, MGM, Bally's, Fremont, and California hotels; casino, two RV parks ($14 a night with complete hookup), 56-lane bowling alley open 24 hours, 25,000-square-foot western shop, dance hall, gift/logo shop, sand volleyball court, country dance hall.

INEXPENSIVE

Motel 6. 195 E. Tropicana Ave., at Koval Lane, Las Vegas, NV 89109. ☎ **800/4-MOTEL-6** or 702/798-0728. Fax 702/798-5657. 602 units. A/C TV TEL. Sun–Thurs $34 single, Fri–Sat $52 single. Extra person $6. Children under 17 stay free in parents' room. AE, CB, DC, DISC, MC, V. Free parking at your room door.

Fronted by a big neon sign, Las Vegas's Motel 6 is the largest in the country, and it happens to be a great budget choice. Most Motel 6 properties are a little out of the way, but this one is quite close to major Strip casino hotels (the MGM is nearby). It has a big, pleasant lobby, and the rooms, in 2-story cream stucco buildings, are clean and attractively decorated. Some rooms have showers only; others, tub/shower baths. Local calls are free and your TV offers HBO.

Dining: Three restaurants (including a pleasant 24-hour family restaurant called **Carrows**) adjoin.

Amenities: A large, well-stocked gift shop, vending machines, a tour desk, two nice-size swimming pools in enclosed courtyards, a whirlpool, and coin-op washers/dryers.

Super 8 Motel. 4250 Koval Lane, just south of Flamingo Rd., Las Vegas, NV 89109. ☎ **800/800-8000** or 702/794-0888. 290 units. A/C TV TEL. Sun–Thurs $41–$43 double, Fri–Sat $56–$58 double. Extra person $8. Children 12 and under stay free in parents' room. Pets $8 per night (1 pet only). AE, CB, DC, DISC, MC, V. Free self-parking.

Billing itself as "the world's largest Super 8 Motel," this friendly property occupies a vaguely Tudor-style stone-and-stucco building. Coffee is served gratis in a pleasant little lobby furnished with comfortable sofas and wing chairs. Rooms are clean and well maintained. Some have safes, and TVs offer free movie channels.

Dining/Diversions: The nautically themed **Ellis Island Restaurant,** open 24 hours, offers typical coffee-shop fare at reasonable prices. In the adjoining bar—a library-like setting with shelves of books and green marble tables—sporting events are aired on TV monitors. There's also a bar in the casino with a karaoke machine.

Amenities: Limited room service via Ellis Island, free airport transfer, casino (actually located next door at Ellis Island; race book and 50 slot/poker/21 machines), small kidney-shaped pool/sundeck and adjoining whirlpool, car-rental desk, coin-op washers/dryers.

8 Downtown

EXPENSIVE

✪ **Golden Nugget.** 129 E. Fremont St., at Casino Center Blvd., Las Vegas, NV 89101. ☎ **800/634-3454** or 702/385-7111. Fax 702/386-8362. www.mirageresorts.com. 1,907 units. A/C TV TEL. $49–$299 double; $275–$500 suite. Extra person $20. AE, CB, DC, DISC, MC, V. Free self- and valet parking.

The Golden Nugget opened in 1946, the first building in Las Vegas constructed specifically for casino gambling. Steve Wynn took it over as his first major project in Vegas, in 1973. He gradually transformed the Old West/Victorian interiors (typical for Downtown) into something more high rent; marble and brass gleam, and the whole package seems considerably more resortlike and genuinely luxurious, especially for Downtown Vegas. The sunny interior spaces are a welcome change from the Las Vegas tradition of dim lighting. Don't forget their mascot (well, it ought to be): the world's largest gold nugget. The Hand of Faith nugget weighs in at 61 pounds, 11 ounces.

If the decor of the Mirage sounded appealing to you and you want to stay Downtown, come here, since the same people own them and the rooms look almost identical. In keeping with the name, the color scheme in the newly refurbished rooms is gold (rather than the beiges of the Mirage), but features they do share include the marble entryways, half-canopy beds, vanity tables with magnifying make-up mirrors, armoires, and marble bathrooms complete with hair dryers. Cable TVs feature pay-movie options. In the North Tower, the rooms are slightly larger than in the South (and also slightly larger than at the Mirage). Suites are done in darker colors and include a good-size parlor with a wet bar. Each has two different bathrooms, one for men and one for women (the latter has Jacuzzi jet tubs and potpourri!), each with its own TV. You don't have to walk through the casino to get to your room, but you do have to walk a distance to get to the pool. During the winter, they put up a pavilion over part of the pool deck space to allow for more interior space.

Dining/Diversions: The **Carson Street Cafe,** the Nugget's 24-hour restaurant, and its superb buffets and 24-hour Sunday brunch are described in chapter 6.

Stefano's, off a gorgeous marble-floored courtyard, offers a festive setting for northern Italian cuisine, complete with singing waiters. Murals of Venice behind trellised "windows" are designed to look like scenery, and baroque elaboration includes cupids, ornate columns, and gilt-framed mirrors. The wait staff sings Italian opera. Dinner only.

The opulent **Lillie Langtry's** is adorned with beveled and gilt-framed mirrors, gilded wood flowers, Chinese art, and a lovely painting of swans. It's a lovely setting, softly lit and enhanced by a backdrop of piano and harp music. The menu is Chinese and mesquite-grilled steaks. Dinner only.

This branch of the **California Pizza Kitchen** is a plush precinct with an exhibition kitchen housing an oak-burning pizza oven. In addition to pizzas with trendy toppings, the menu offers calzones, salads, pasta, and other entrees. Open for lunch and dinner daily.

In addition, a 24-hour snack bar in the casino offers deli sandwiches, pizza, and light fare, and there are four casino bars including the elegant **Claude's** and the **38 Different Kinds of Beer Bar.**

Accommodations Downtown

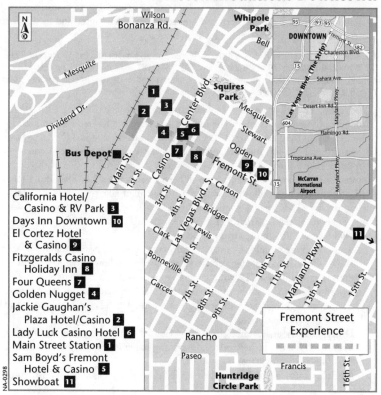

California Hotel/ Casino & RV Park **3**
Days Inn Downtown **10**
El Cortez Hotel & Casino **9**
Fitzgeralds Casino Holiday Inn **8**
Four Queens **7**
Golden Nugget **4**
Jackie Gaughan's Plaza Hotel/Casino **2**
Lady Luck Casino Hotel **6**
Main Street Station **1**
Sam Boyd's Fremont Hotel & Casino **5**
Showboat **11**

NA-0298

Amenities: 24-hour room service, shoe shine, concierge, casino, car-rental desk, full-service unisex hair salon, shops (gifts, jewelry, designer fashions, sportswear, logo items), video-game arcade.

The Nugget's top-rated health club offers a full line of Universal equipment, Lifecycles, StairMasters, treadmills, rowing machines, Gravitron, free weights, steam sauna, tanning beds, and massage. Salon treatments include everything from leg waxing to seaweed-mask facials. Free Sebastian products are available for sprucing up afterward. The spa's opulent Palladian-mirrored foyer is modeled after a salon in New York's Frick Museum.

The entrance to the hotel's immense swimming pool and outdoor whirlpool spa is graced by elegant marble swans and bronze fish sculptures. Fountains, palm trees, and verdant landscaping create a tropical setting, and a poolside bar serves the sundeck.

MODERATE

Days Inn Downtown. 707 E. Fremont St., at 7th St., Las Vegas, NV 89101. ☎ **800/ 325-2344,** 800/325-2525, or 702/388-1400. Fax 702/388-9622. www.daysinn.com. 147 units. A/C TV TEL. $40–$65 one bedroom; $45–$80 two bedrooms (rates are for up to 4 people; may be higher during special events). "Super Saver" rate (Sun–Thurs $39, Fri–Sat $50) if you reserve 30 days in advance via ☎ 800/325-2525 (subject to availability). AE, CB, DC, DISC, MC, V. Free self-parking.

Opened in 1988, this Days Inn still looks quite new. Rooms, in a U-shaped 3-story building, are cheerfully decorated and have TVs offering pay movies. On-premises facilities comprise a rooftop pool and sundeck, a few video games, and the Culinary Restaurant, serving coffee-shop fare at all meals.

✪ **Fitzgeralds Casino Holiday Inn.** 301 Fremont St., at 3rd St., Las Vegas, NV 89101. ☎ **800/274-LUCK** or 702/388-2400. Fax 702/388-2181. 652 units. A/C TV TEL. $40–$85 double; $60–$105 suite. Extra person $10. Children under 19 stay free in parents' room. AE, CB, DC, DISC, MC, V. Free self- and valet parking.

Fitzgeralds recently became a Holiday Inn franchise and has upgraded all their rooms to fit said chain's code. The result is attractive and has received an award for Best Redesign from the Governor's Conference. Outside, a model of Mr. O'Lucky, their very tall (45-foot) leprechaun mascot, oversees a new sign; neon coins pour from a rainbow into a pot of gold. (Elsewhere, you can rub a piece of the Blarney stone for luck.) The restaurants have all been given serious face-lifts, and a sort of Irish country village walkway, complete with big giant fake tree, leads to the room elevators. Fitzgerald's has the only balcony in Downtown from which you can watch the Fremont Street Experience. You can also sit in their McDonald's and gawk at the light show through the atrium windows.

The look in the rooms is clean and comfortable, standard hotel room decor, done in shades of green (no, the leprechaun theme does not follow in here). Because this is the tallest building in Downtown (34 stories), you get excellent views: either snow-capped mountains, Downtown lights, or the Strip. Jacuzzi tub rooms are $20 more and are slightly larger with wrap-around windows. All offer safes and 25-inch TVs with pay-movie options.

Dining/Diversions: Limericks, an upscale Irish pub, is described in chapter 6.

Vincenzo's is a moderately priced, unexciting Italian/seafood restaurant designed to look like a Tuscan village.

Molly's Country Kitchen is their coffee shop and looks like an Irish cottage (sort of).

The balcony of the second-floor **Lookout Lounge** (featuring Irish drinks) is a good vantage point for viewing the Fremont Street Experience. A **McDonald's** and three bars are on the casino floor.

Amenities: 24-hour room service, complimentary gaming lessons, casino, tour and show desks, car-rental desk, gift shop, jewelry shop.

✪ **Four Queens.** 202 Fremont St., at Casino Center Blvd., Las Vegas, NV 89101. ☎ **800/634-6045** or 702/385-4011. Fax 702/387-5122. www.savenet.com/702/4queen.htm. 700 units. A/C TV TEL. $29–$179 double; $119–$350 suite. Extra person $15. AE, CB, DC, DISC, MC, V. Free self- and valet parking.

Opened in 1966 with a mere 120 rooms, the Four Queens (named for the owner's four daughters) has evolved over the decades into a major Downtown property occupying an entire city block. You walk past their glittering lights facade and into their small but elegant—in a slightly faded, slightly dated way (with mirrors and huge chandeliers)—lobby and you just know you are in old Las Vegas. And are glad. As the staff says, this is the place to stay if you just want to gamble. Their clientele is on the older side (50-plus), who are not coming to Las Vegas for the first time.

Notably nice rooms, decorated in basic hotel-room style, are located in 19-story twin towers. Especially lovely are the North Tower rooms, decorated in a Southwestern motif and, in most cases, offering views of the Fremont Street Experience. South Tower rooms are done up in earth tones with dark-wood furnishings and wallpaper in small floral prints. Minisuites, decorated in traditional styles, have living rooms (separated from the bedrooms by a trellised wall) and dining areas, double-sink baths, and dressing areas. All accommodations offer TVs with in-house

---

Impressions
_____

There was a magic in this place. It was like stepping back into the frontier. Casino owners were king. They owned the town. They were glamorous. They had beautiful women and lots of money.

—Steve Wynn, on Las Vegas when he visited as a boy

---

information and pay-movie channels. Some rooms are equipped with small refrigerators and coffeemakers.

Dining/Diversions: Hugo's Cellar is described in chapter 6.

At **Lailani's Island Café,** a whimsical Hawaiian cafeteria with colorful tropical murals on its walls, diners are entertained by island music, a 3-foot talking macaw, dancing flowers in dugout canoes, a five-headed totem pole with eyes that light up, and a fiber-optic light show overhead. Lunch and dinner are served.

Pastina's Italian Bistro is somewhat more traditional, though it, too, has a vaulted fiber-optic ceiling with shooting stars and swirling galaxies. The menu features a choice of pastas and traditional Italian entrees. Dinner only.

Magnolia's Veranda, a 24-hour dining facility overlooking the casino, has three sections: a casual plant-filled cafe, an adjoining "courtyard," and a rather elegant crystal-chandeliered dining area adorned with murals of New Orleans. The same menu is offered throughout. Besides the requisite coffee-shop fare, Magnolia's offers Hawaiian specialties. A great deal here is the $5 prime rib dinner served from 6pm to 2am.

Hugo's has a cozy lounge with a working fireplace, and two bars serve the casino.

Amenities: 24-hour room service, gift shop, car-rental desk, tour and show desks, small video-game arcade, plus a basic workout room that is free.

INEXPENSIVE

California Hotel/Casino & RV Park. 12 Ogden Ave., at 1st St., Las Vegas, NV 89101. ☎ **800/634-6255** or 702/385-1222. Fax 702/388-2660. 855 units. A/C TV TEL. Sun–Thurs $50 double, Fri–Sat $60 double; holidays $70 double. Extra person $5. Children 12 and under stay free in parents' room. AE, CB, DC, DISC, MC, V. Free self- and valet parking.

This is a hotel with a unique personality. California-themed, it markets mostly in Hawaii, and since 85% of the guests are from the "Aloha State," it offers Hawaiian entrees in several of its restaurants and even has an on-premises store specializing in Hawaiian foodstuff. You'll also notice that dealers are wearing colorful Hawaiian shirts. Of course, everyone is welcome to enjoy the aloha spirit here.

The rooms, however, reflect neither California nor Hawaii. Decorated in contemporary-look burgundy/mauve or apricot/teal color schemes, they have mahogany furnishings and attractive marble baths. In-room safes are a plus, and TVs offer pay-per-view movies and keno channels.

Dining/Diversions: With its redwood paneling and massive stone fireplace, the **Redwood Bar and Grill,** featuring steak and seafood, looks like an elegant ski lodge. There's piano bar entertainment in the adjoining lounge. Dinner only.

The **Pasta Pirate,** themed to suggest a coastal cannery warehouse, has a corrugated-tin ceiling and exposed overhead pipes. Walls are hung with neon signs and historic pages from the *San Francisco Chronicle.* Italian, steak, and seafood entrees are featured. Dinner only.

Also evoking San Francisco is the rather charming **Market Street Café,** a 24-hour facility. The menu lists all the expected coffee-shop fare, as well as Hawaiian items and specially marked "heart-smart" choices.

The **Cal Club Snack Bar,** a casual cafeteria/ice-cream parlor, serves sundaes, along with Hawaiian soft drinks (flavors like guava and island punch) and Chinese/Japanese snack fare.

There are two 24-hour casino bars: the **Main Street Bar** and the **San Francisco Pub. Dave's Aloha Bar** on the mezzanine level is a tropical setting for exotic cocktails, liqueur-spiked coffees and ice-cream drinks, and international beers.

Amenities: Room service (breakfast only), casino, car-rental desk, car wash, small rooftop pool, small video-game arcade, shops (gift shop, chocolates). A food store carries items popular with Hawaiians and there are several umbrella tables outside where these snacks can be eaten.

El Cortez Hotel & Casino. 600 Fremont St., between 6th and 7th sts., Las Vegas, NV 89101. ☎ **800/634-6703** or 702/385-5200. 428 units. A/C TV TEL. $32 double; $40 minisuite. Extra person $3. AE, CB, DC, DISC, JCB, MC, V. Free self- and valet parking.

This small hotel is popular with locals for its casual, "just-folks" Downtown atmosphere and its frequent big-prize lotteries (up to $50,000) based on Social Security numbers. The nicest accommodations are the enormous minisuites in the newer 14-story tower. Some are exceptionally large king-bedded rooms with sofas; others have separate sitting areas with sofas, armchairs, and tables, plus small dressing areas. The rooms in the original building are furnished more traditionally and with less flair, and they cost less. Local calls are just 25¢.

Dining/Diversions: Roberta's Café is an elegant candlelit restaurant featuring charbroiled steaks and seafood. Dinner only.

There's also a large 24-hour coffee shop called the **Emerald Room,** where you can enjoy a bacon-and-eggs breakfast with hash browns, toast, and coffee for $1. A "soup-to-nuts" 18-ounce porterhouse steak dinner is $6.45 here. Four bars serve the casino.

Amenities: Small video-game arcade, beauty salon, gift shop, and barbershop.

Under the same ownership is **Ogden House,** just across the street, with rooms that go for just $18 a night.

Jackie Gaughan's Plaza Hotel/Casino. 1 Main St., at Fremont St., Las Vegas, NV 89101. ☎ **800/634-6575** or 702/386-2110. Fax 702/386-2378. 1,037 units. A/C TV TEL. $40–$120 double; $80–$150 suite. Extra person $8. Children under 12 stay free in parents' room. AE, DC, DISC, MC, V. Free self- and valet parking.

Built in 1971 on the site of the old Union Pacific Railroad Depot, the Plaza, a double-towered, 3-block-long property, permanently altered the Downtown skyline. Las Vegas's Amtrak station (currently unused) is right in the hotel, and the main Greyhound terminal adjoins it. Fremont Street literally ends right at the Plaza's front door, so you can't fault the location.

Accommodations are spacious and attractively decorated, with king rooms offering plush sofas. The suites in particular are huge, and the two-bedroom suite would be a terrific option for a large party of friends to share. Rooms in the North Tower look down on the Fremont Street Experience.

Dining/Diversions: The **Center Stage** restaurant, offering fabulous views of Glitter Gulch and the Fremont Street Experience, is described in chapter 6.

The '50s-motif **Plaza Diner,** open 24 hours a day and agleam with chrome, features red leatherette booths and a Wurlitzer-style jukebox stocked with oldies. Typical diner fare is featured, everything from a BLT to a stack of hotcakes. A noteworthy special is the full-roast prime rib dinner for $6, available from 10am to midnight (midnight to 10am it's just $5).

At the **Back Stage,** comfortable leather booths, walls hung with still-life oil paintings, stained-glass windows, and brass candelabra chandeliers combine to create a warmly inviting ambience. Open for breakfast and lunch, the latter featuring sandwiches, salads, and Cajun specialties.

Other food and beverage facilities include an ice-cream parlor, **Coffee and Cravings,** for gourmet coffees and fresh-baked goods; a 24-hour casino snack bar; several casino cocktail bars; and the **Omaha Lounge,** offering live entertainment in the casino almost around the clock.

Amenities: Guest services desk (also handles in-house shows), tour desk, casino, car-rental desk, shops, a wedding chapel, beauty salon/barbershop. There's a sports deck with a nice-size swimming pool, a quarter-mile outdoor jogging track, and four Har-Tru tennis courts.

Lady Luck Casino Hotel. 206 N. 3rd St., at Ogden Ave., Las Vegas, NV 89101. ☎ **800/523-9582** or 702/477-3000. Fax 702/382-2346. www.lady-luck.com. 792 units. A/C TV TEL. $40–$155 double; Sun–Thurs $55–$75 junior suite, Fri–Sat $70–$105 junior suite. Extra person $8. AE, CB, DC, DISC, JCB, MC, V. Free self- and valet parking.

What is today Lady Luck opened in 1964 as Honest John's, a 2,000-square-foot casino with five employees, five pinball machines, and 17 slots. Today that casino occupies 30,000 square feet, and the hotel, including sleek 17- and 25-story towers, is a major Downtown player taking up an entire city block. What it retains from earlier times is a friendly atmosphere, one that has kept customers coming back for decades. Eighty percent of Lady Luck's clientele is repeat business.

Neon tubing overhead around the casino and hotel is color coded to your room key, so you know which way to the particular tower where you are staying. This is good as one of those towers is actually across the street (an over-the-street enclosed walkway takes you there). Tower rooms are decorated in a variety of attractive color schemes, mostly using muted Southwestern hues and handsome oak furnishings. It's all larger, brighter, and lighter than you might expect (though again, a variation on familiar hotel-room decor). Rooms also have full-length mirrors. The bathroom amenities come in a red plastic, heart-shaped container. All rooms are equipped with small refrigerators and TVs with pay-per-view movie options. Junior suites in the West Tower have parlor areas with sofas and armchairs, separate dressing areas, and baths with whirlpool tubs. The original Garden Rooms are a little smaller and less spiffy-looking in terms of decor; on the plus side, they're right by the pool, which is not heated, by the way (but there aren't a lot of pools in Downtown).

Dining/Diversions: The **Burgundy Room** evokes Paris in the 1930s, with plush velvet-upholstered booths and a display of period art including lithographs and original prints by Erté, Poucette, and Salvador Dalí. Elegantly appointed tables are lit by Venetian hurricane lamps. The menu highlights steak, pasta, and fresh seafood. Dinner only.

Marco Polo is a fine Italian restaurant that serves dinner only, Thursday to Monday 4 to 10pm.

At the Southwestern-themed, 24-hour **Winners' Café,** a basic coffee-shop menu is augmented by Mexican and Polynesian specialties.

In addition, there is a daily buffet (details in chapter 6), and ESPN is aired on three TV monitors in the **Casino Bar.**

Amenities: 24-hour room service, multilingual front desk, and complimentary airport shuttle, casino, tour and show desks, car-rental desk, gift shop, unheated swimming pool and sundeck.

✪ **Main Street Station.** 200 N. Main St., between Fremont and I-95, Las Vegas, NV 89101. ☎ **800/465-0711** or 702/387-1896. Fax 702/386-4466. 406 units. A/C TV TEL. Sun–Thurs $45 double; Fri–Sat $55 double; holidays and conventions $65 double. AE, CB, DC, DISC, MC, V. Free self- and valet parking.

Though not actually on Fremont Street, the Main Street Station is just 2 short blocks away, barely a 3-minute walk. Considering how terrific it is, this is hardly an inconvenience. Having taken over an abandoned hotel space, the Main Street Station reopened in November 1996 to become, in our opinion, one of the nicest hotels in Downtown and one of the best bargains in the city. The overall look is, admittedly as usual for Downtown, turn-of-the-century San Francisco. However, unlike everywhere else, the details here are outstanding, producing a beautiful hotel by any measure. Outside, gas lamps flicker on wrought-iron railings and stained-glass windows. Inside are hammered tin ceilings, ornate antique-style chandeliers, and lazy ceiling fans. The small lobby is filled with wood panels, long wooden benches, and a front desk straight out of the Old West with an old-timey key cabinet with beveled-glass windows. (Check out the painting of a Victorian gambling scene to the left of the front desk.) Even the cashier cages look like antique brass bank tellers' cages. Over the casino bar, rattan blade fans rotate horizontally rather than vertically. It's all very Victorian, and even though faux, it feels authentic. It's also incredibly appealing and just plain pretty.

Though a small-size hotel, they pack a lot in. The stylish microbrew pub is described in detail in chapter 10. The setting for both the buffet and the Pullman Grille restaurant are uncommonly pretty, especially for Downtown. And the casino, thanks to some high ceilings, is one of the most smoke-free around. An enclosed bridge connects the hotel with the California across the street, where you will find shopping and a kids' arcade.

The long and narrow rooms are possibly the largest in Downtown. The ornate decorating downstairs does not extend up here. White-painted, wooded plantation shutters replace the usual curtains; each room has a very large gilt-framed mirror; the simple but not unattractive furniture is vaguely French provincial, done in medium-tone neutrals. It's all clean and in good taste. The bathrooms are small but well appointed. It should be noted that rooms on the north side overlook the freeway, and the railroad track is nearby. The soundproofing seems quite strong—we couldn't hear anything when inside, but then again, we are from Los Angeles. A few guests have complained about noise in these rooms, but the majority have had no problems. If you are concerned, request a room on the south side. Each room has Nintendo for a charge and movies for free.

Dining/Diversions: Triple 7 Brew Pub is described in detail in chapter 10. The excellent buffet is described in chapter 6.

The **Pullman Grille** is the steak-and-seafood place, and is much more reasonably priced than similar (and considerably less pretty) places in town. The doors leading to the mahogany dining room are made of massive wood with copper relief figures on them, recycled from a turn-of-the-century mansion, as was the ornate bar and large stone fireplace. Part of the restaurant is a real Pullman train car. It has been turned into the cigar car, where a choice of smokes will be offered to guests who are ensconced in cushy Victorian furniture. All the old details are here, including some lovely velvet drapes. Strangely, when empty, the car does not smell like smoke, and it certainly does not trickle into the restaurant proper. (That was the whole idea of having a separate smoking car.)

The **Cascade Cafe** is a 24-hour coffee shop. You order a variety of cheap meals (including some Asian cuisine) at a window.

Amenities: Dry cleaning and laundry service, in-room massage, safety-deposit boxes, casino, gift shop, show desk, shopping and game-room arcade at California Hotel accessible via connecting walkway.

Sam Boyd's Fremont Hotel & Casino. 200 E. Fremont St., between Casino Center Blvd. and 3rd St., Las Vegas, NV 89101. ☎ **800/634-6182** or 702/385-3232. Fax 702/385-6229. 452 units. A/C TV TEL. $35–$80 double. Extra person $8. Children under 12 stay free in parents' room. AE, CB, DC, DISC, JCB, MC, V. Free valet parking.

When it opened in 1956, the Fremont was the first high-rise in Downtown Las Vegas. Wayne Newton got his start here, singing in the now-defunct Carousel Showroom. Of course, one merely steps out the front door to be on the Fremont Street Experience. There is also a free shuttle to Sam's Town, if you want to check out Mystic Falls. Large, comfortable, and more peaceful rooms than you might expect offer safes and TVs with in-house information channels and pay-movie options. They encourage environmental awareness by only changing linens every other day; upon request, it can be more often, but why not help out the earth a bit?

Dining/Diversions: The Fremont boasts a gorgeous oak-paneled art deco restaurant called the **Second Street Grill,** which is reviewed in chapter 6.

A branch of **Tony Roma's** offers scrumptious barbecued chicken and smoky, fork-tender baby-back ribs, juicy charbroiled steaks, and fresh seafood. A children's menu is a plus. The walls of this handsome plant-filled restaurant are hung with historic photographs of Las Vegas. Dinner only.

The **Lanai Cafe** is a comfortable 24-hour coffee shop, with a wide-ranging American and Chinese menu. Specials here include a full prime-rib dinner ($6) or a steak-and-lobster-tail dinner ($10). The **Lanai Express,** a tiny cafeteria also featuring American and Chinese fare, adjoins.

The Fremont also has a great buffet (see chapter 6 for details). There are bars in the casino, race and sports book, and keno lounge.

Amenities: Room service at breakfast only, casino, 24-hour gift shop. Guests can use the swimming pool and RV park at the nearby California Hotel, another Sam Boyd enterprise.

Showboat. 2800 Fremont St., between Charleston Blvd. and Mojave Rd., Las Vegas, NV 89104. ☎ **800/826-2800** or 702/385-9123. Fax 702/383-9238. 456 units. A/C TV TEL. $29–$139 double; $149–$189 one-bedroom suite, $195–$215 two-bedroom suite. Extra person $10. Children under 12 stay free in parents' room. AE, CB, DC, DISC, MC, V. Free self- and valet parking.

Near to neither the Strip nor Downtown, the 40-year-old Showboat is easy to miss, but a recent renovation makes it worth a look, if location isn't an issue. Instead of the "showboat" look of old, it has gone more in a Mardi Gras/old-time Louisiana direction, with Victorian interiors (moldings, distressed paint, and other touches) plus murals of Mississippi plantations and riverboats, and stunning Venetian-glass chandeliers in the lobby. The result is very clean, bright, and pretty. It's a good-looking hotel, with a casino popular with locals. Opened in 1954, it was the first hotel to offer buffet meals and bingo, not to mention a bowling alley. And the bowling alley, North America's largest, hosts major PBA tournaments.

The rooms are small but follow the same New Orleans theme with appropriate wall finish and wallpaper borders. They have dressing areas equipped with cosmetic mirrors. You'll find a hair dryer and extra phone in the bath, and TVs offer pay-movie and hotel information stations. The medium-size pool is nothing special.

Dining/Diversions: The **Plantation** keeps to the garden theme. One room evokes a veranda with white porch railings backed by exquisite botanical murals; the other is more elegant, with Palladian windows and ornate Victorian chandeliers. Together they comprise a lovely setting in which to enjoy mesquite-grilled steaks and seafood specialties. Dinner only.

DiNapoli diverges from the New Orleans theme with Roman frescoes, columns, and classical statuary. The menu features California-inspired southern Italian cuisine as well as seafood specialties. Dinner only.

And the delightful 24-hour Mardi Gras–themed **Showboat Coffee Shop** extends into the casino with cafe seating.

There's also an adequate buffet here (details in chapter 6), and a snack bar and a bar/lounge are located in the Bowling Center. Several bars serve the casino, including the **Mardi Gras Room,** which features quality lounge acts and occasional bigger names such as Juice Newton, Sha Na Na, Chubby Checker, and Lacy J. Dalton. When headliners appear, there's a two-drink minimum.

Amenities: 24-hour room service, shoe shine, casino, gift shop, beauty salon/barbershop, 24-hour Bowling Center with 106 lanes, bowling pro shop, video-game arcade, Olympic-size swimming pool in a courtyard setting.

9 Henderson

About 6 miles from the Strip (though it can be up to a half-hour drive) is the town of Henderson. Formally most noted (and we use that term loosely) for its factory tours, two large resorts have recently opened up there, offering still more alternatives to Strip hustle and bustle.

Reserve Hotel and Casino. 777 W. Lake Mead Dr., Henderson, NV 89015 (from the Strip take I-95 S and exit at Lake Mead Dr.). ☎ **888/899-7770** or 702/558-7000. Fax 702/567-7373. 224 units. A/C TV TEL. Sun–Thurs $49–$79 double, Fri–Sat $69–$99 double. AE, DC, DISC, MC, V.

This new resort has taken advantage of the space to be found in the community of Henderson, about a 20-minute drive from Las Vegas proper. It's perfect if you want to avoid the mayhem of central Vegas. However, with no transportation either to the airport or the Strip and with a minimum amount of facilities, the Reserve is probably more a choice for business travelers (provided they don't mind a lack of room service) or the socially shy.

The theme is the African Serengeti plains, which translates to the exterior of the building covered in murals of giraffes, elephants, and lions roaming sawgrass-covered grounds. The casino ceiling is painted and lit to reflect the ever-changing African sky, and animal sounds surround you as you walk across the paw-printed carpet. Hutlike structures hang over the gaming tables adorned with cobras fanning their hoods. In the corner is the crashed six-seater plane of Congo Jack, the hotel's own mythological hero.

The standard rooms are just that, standard. The small rooms continue the jungle theme with tacky leopard-printed curtains and bedspreads. There is an option for two queens or a king-size bed. If you want a view of the Strip, you need to reserve a room above the sixth floor on the west side—otherwise your view is of the hotel roof and piping. All rooms include a coffeemaker, movies, and a game player. A small pool overlooks the freeway.

Dining/Diversions: Pasta Mombasa is an Italian restaurant open only for dinner, as is the **Wildfire Steakhouse. Congo Jack's Cafe** serves American food 24 hours a day. All meals can be had at the **Grand Safari Buffet.** Local bands play in the lounge every night.

Amenities: Pool, 24-hour dry cleaning and laundry.

Sunset Station. 1301 W. Sunset Rd., at U.S. 93/95, Henderson, NV 89104. ☎ **888/ 786-7389.** Fax 702/221-6510. 450 units. A/C TV TEL. $49–$119 standard double; $69–$159 petite suite, $109–$219 king suite. AE, DC, MC, V. Free self- and valet parking.

With a 97,000-square-foot casino, 13 movie theaters, a roller hockey rink, 13 restaurants, an outdoor amphitheater—with top-name acts—a large pool, and a state-of-the-art arcade, Sunset Station is more like an entertainment complex than a casino. There is even "Kids Quest," where you can drop your kids off to make their own music videos, watch movies, or climb on an extensive gym while you gamble. And if all of this isn't enough for you, there is a mall across the street. Because of the range of activities, this is a favorite gathering spot of the local yuppie crowd. Certainly, it's a better choice for travelers than the Reserve, since both are located in beautiful downtown. There are shuttles going to and from the south end of the Strip hourly, should you not find enough to do here.

The theme is a little scattered, not quite pulling off the desired Mediterranean and Spanish complex. Actually, from the '40s art deco Gaudi bar to the coat-of-arms banners hanging in the Sports and Racing Bar to the old train replica in the lobby, there are so many different design elements in this enormous complex that it is hard to even find that Mediterranean theme.

Despite its size, though, this is an incredibly easy hotel to navigate. The hotel has a separate entrance from the casino, which makes it easy to maneuver in. Thankfully, the theme muddle does not extend to the rooms, with the result that they are basic with no particular personality. If you want a view, go above the 17th floor. The king suites include a Jacuzzi tub, large bar, safe, two bathrooms, and a large living area. They are perfect for families or business meetings. All rooms include a coffeemaker and movies.

Dining/Diversions: Previously Gordon Biersch, the **Sunset Brewing Company** serves up chicken wings, burgers, pizza, and pasta. And, of course, beer. There is also a large selection of cigars in the cigar lounge out front.

Costa Del Sol Seafood Restaurant and Oyster Bar serves up fresh lobster and crab at reasonable prices. On weekend nights the Oyster Bar is packed, so be prepared to wait.

Capri, a cozy Italian restaurant, is one of the few places that actually does have a Mediterranean feel. There is a nice "open-air" patio, complete with a painted sky and umbrellas overlooking the casino. A perfect spot for people-watching.

Rosalita's Mexican Cantina is a family-style Mexican restaurant and the **Sunset Cafe** is a 24-hour coffee shop. Since the **Feast Around the World Buffet** caters to locals as well as tourists, the food here is a cut above the average. The buffet offers plenty of low-fat alternatives along with a large fruit and salad bar as well as your standard pile-your-plate fare.

There are also six fast-food restaurants: **Viva Salsa, Capri Pizza Kitchen, Fatburger, Manhattan Bagel, Kenya's "Cakes of the Stars,"** and **Ben and Jerry's.**

Amenities: Airport shuttle, 24-hour room service, tour and show desk, Sega video arcade, Kids Quest, casino, pool.

Sunset Station's **Outdoor Amphitheater** is basically a large poolside lawn that holds up to 2,000 chairs, attracting big names such as Pauli Shore, Glen Frey, and the queen of party tears herself, Leslie Gore. Call for an upcoming schedule. There is also a roller hockey rink and 13 movie theaters.

10 Airport Vicinity

In most cities, the airport is somewhat away from the regular action. In Vegas, however, it is less than a mile from the Strip. Consequently, staying at an airport hotel makes little sense, unless you are truly flying in and flying out, or really, really want to avoid casinos. It just seems silly to stay at the basic chain offerings when you can simply drive an extra 6 blocks and hit some fabulous resort hotel. But if you are determined, here is a list of reliable chains down airport way.

- **Best Western McCarren,** 4970 Paradise Rd.; ☎ **800/528-1234**
- **Comfort Inn South,** 5075 Koval Lane; ☎ **800/221-2222**
- **Days Inn Airport,** 5100 Paradise Rd.; ☎ **800/634-6439**
- **Howard Johnson Airport,** 5100 Paradise Rd.; ☎ **800/446-4656**

11 A Hostel

Las Vegas International Hostel. 1208 Las Vegas Blvd. S., 1 block south of Charleston Blvd., Las Vegas, NV 89104. ☎ **702/385-9955.** 60 beds. A/C. $14 bed in a dorm room with shared bath accommodating 4 people; $28 private room with shared bath. There's a $2 surcharge for 1-night stays on weekends. AYH and AAIH members and guests with student ID receive discounted rates. No credit cards. Free self-parking.

This American Association of International Hostels (AAIH) facility, the only legitimate hostel in town, houses clean but spartan rooms in a 2-story building. It's a dive, but a clean and friendly dive. However, it is on a bad part of the Strip, a 20-minute walk from the closest Strip property, the Stratosphere, so don't walk; use the Strip bus to get around. Guests don't hang out as much as in regular hostels; they are off playing elsewhere, so it tends to be quiet at night.

Although rooms are sparse (four iron beds and nothing else), upstairs rooms are a tad nicer, with balconies and polished pine floors (ceramic tile downstairs). You get a free sheet and pillowcase and pay $1 for a top sheet, blanket, and towels. The beds themselves are basically a board with a thin mattress—but what do you expect from a youth hostel? Gratis coffee, tea, and lemonade are available in the lounge throughout the day. There is one lounge offering TV, VCR (and tapes), books, and games. Other facilities include coin-op washers/dryers and a fully equipped kitchen with a fridge you can store food in (but don't totally expect it to be there when you return). The host arranges excursions to Hoover Dam; Red Rock Canyon; Mount Charleston; Valley of Fire; and Bryce, Zion, and Grand canyons; and the friendly staff is knowledgeable about local sights and restaurants.

July and August are the busiest months for the hostel, though these are the slowest months elsewhere in town. Hence, if you want to stay here because you like hosteling as a way of life, reserve several weeks in advance. On the other hand, if you're considering a hostel only to save money, try bargaining with Strip hotels in their off-season; you might be able to obtain very low rates.

Dining 6

Among the many images that people have of Las Vegas is cheap food deals, bargains so good the food is practically free. They think of the buffets—all a small country can eat—for only $3.99!

All that is true, but frankly, eating in Las Vegas is no longer something you don't have to worry about budgeting for. The buffets are certainly there—no good hotel would be without one—as are the cheap meal deals, but you get what you pay for. Some of the cheaper buffets, and even the more moderately priced ones, are mediocre at best, ghastly and inedible at worst. And we don't even want to think about those 69¢ beef stew specials.

Also, in terms of fine dining, for the most part, Vegas is stuck in an unimaginative time warp. A hotel's star restaurant will more than likely be yet another overpriced steak-and-seafood joint. *Gourmet* here means anything à la orange or flambéed. On top of all this, anything cheap (a buffet, a special meal deal) or any place located in a popular hotel-casino will certainly attract a long line. Sometimes you can wait more than an hour for the privilege of paying too much for a disappointing meal.

Which is not to say there isn't hope. Little by little, quality restaurants have been sneaking into Las Vegas. Wolfgang Puck's **Spago** and **Chinois,** Emeril Lagasse's **Emeril's New Orleans Fish House** (serving stunning Creole seafood), **Gatsby's** (the MGM Grand's gourmet restaurant, which even hard-core foodie snobs say serves some of the best food they've ever eaten), and Mark Miller's **Coyote Cafe** all would be standouts in any other major city. Reliable small chains such as **Lawry's** and **Il Fornaio** have crept in during the last year. The **Enigma Cafe,** located in the slowly burgeoning Gateway artists' district (right between the Strip and Downtown, so it's accessible to both), offers up healthful, interesting food at prices comparable to some of the best hotel meal deals in town. Best of all, if you look, there are small ethnic joints popping up all over the place. (Though many close nearly as abruptly. Call in advance, just to make sure.) Get off the Strip and go looking for them.

Which is actually part of the problem. Staying on the Strip, if you don't have the mobility of a car, severely limits your food options. Getting outside of those enormous hotel resorts is a major proposition (and don't think that's not done on purpose), which is why so often visitors settle for what the hotel has to offer—long lines and diminished quality. Walking to another hotel—on the Strip, yet another major investment of time—means probably encountering much the same thing. But not always. Once, faced with dismal breakfast choices, we went from the Mirage over to Caesars, landing in their Forum Shops where the Stage Deli stood, largely empty and with considerably better munchie options.

OUR BEST LAS VEGAS RESTAURANT ADVICE

GETTING IN   There are tricks to surviving dining in Vegas. If you can, make reservations in advance, particularly for the better restaurants (you might well get to town, planning to check out some of the better eateries, only to find they are totally booked throughout your stay). Eat as much as you can during off hours, which admittedly are hard to find. But you know that noon to, say, 1:30 or 2pm is going to be prime for lunch, and 5:30 to 8:30pm (and just after the early shows get out) for dinner. Speaking of time, give yourself plenty of it, particularly if you have to catch a show. We once tried to grab a quick bite in the Riviera, before running up to *La Cage*. The only choice was the food court, where long lines in front of all the (fast-food chains only) stands left us with about 5 minutes to gobble something decidedly unhealthy.

STAYING HEALTHY   *Unhealthy* is the watchword here; if you don't care about your heart or your waistline, you will do just fine in Vegas. (And really, what says "vacation" more than a cream sauce?) But slowly, salads are making their way silently on to the menus, and some more health-conscious restaurants are opening. You just have to look for them. (The reviews below may give you some hints.) You can always stick to brand names; every fast-food restaurant is here, usually in several places, and a number of reliable coffee-shop chains are also around. And we certainly don't mean to take away any enjoyment of those extravagant buffets; heck, that's a major part of the fun of Vegas! We insist on indulging at least once during every visit we make. Excess is the watchword here, and what better symbol is there than mounds of shrimp and unlimited prime rib?

SAVING MONEY   The late-night specials—a complete steak meal for just a couple dollars—are also an important part of a good, decadent Vegas experience (and a huge boon for insomniacs). And having complained about how prices are going up, you still can eat cheaply and decently (particularly if you are only looking upon food as fuel) all over town. The locals repeatedly say that they almost never cook, because in Vegas it is always cheaper to eat out. To locate budget fare, see "Great Meal Deal" (page 129) and check local newspapers (especially Friday editions) and free magazines (such as *Vegas Visitor* and *What's On in Las Vegas*), which are given away at hotel reception desks (sometimes these sources also yield money-saving coupons).

You should also look at our coffeehouse listings in chapter 10, because a number of them serve light and inexpensive food, such as the **Jazzed Cafe,** which serves authentic Italian food until 3am.

ABOUT THEME RESTAURANTS   It shouldn't be too surprising to learn that a town devoted to themes (what hotel worth its salt doesn't have one, at this point?) is full of virtually every theme restaurant there is (Hard Rock Cafe, All Star Cafe, Planet Hollywood). For the most part, these establishments glorify some aspect of pop culture: movies, sports, rock music, and so forth. Almost all have prominent celebrity co-owners and tons of "memorabilia" on the walls, which in virtually every case means throwaway items from blockbuster movies, or some article of clothing a celeb wore once (if that) on stage or on the playing field. Almost all have virtually identical menus and have gift shops full of logo items.

This sounds cynical, and it is—but not without reason. Theme restaurants are for the most part noisy, cluttered, overpriced places that are strictly tourist traps. Their celebrity owners pretend they eat there regularly. But given, say, the hectic film production schedules of Bruce Willis and Arnold Schwarzenegger—and the nearly dozen branches of Planet Hollywood worldwide—that seems highly unlikely. (Of course, should said celebs find themselves in Vegas, it is quite likely they would pop into their joint at least once.) But if you eat at one of these places, you've eaten at them all. We don't want to be total killjoys. Fans should have a good time checking out the stuff on the walls of the appropriate restaurant. And while the food won't be the most memorable ever, it probably won't be bad. But that's not really what you go for.

ABOUT PRICE CATEGORIES   The restaurants in this chapter are arranged first by location, then by the following price categories (based on the average cost of a dinner entree): **Very Expensive,** more than $20; **Expensive,** $15 to $20; **Moderate,** $10 to $15; **Inexpensive,** under $10 (sometimes well under). In expensive and very expensive restaurants, expect to spend no less than twice the price of the average entree for your entire meal with a tip; you can usually get by on a bit less in moderate and inexpensive restaurants. Buffets and Sunday brunches are gathered in a separate section at the end of this chapter.

A FINAL WORD   If you can, get in your car and check out some of the options listed below that are a bit off the beaten track. And be sure to patronize small ethnic places as much as you can. Show Vegas you demand flavor *now!*

1 Best Bets

- **Best All-Around:** It's a toss-up between **Gatsby's** (☎ 702/891-7337) and **Emeril's New Orleans Fish House** (☎ 702/891-7374), both located on the South Strip in the MGM Grand, and both of which vie for the unofficial "Best Restaurant in Vegas" title. Emeril's features Creole seafood, while Gatsby's is nouvelle and slightly Asian influenced. Both are superb dining experiences. Both offer tasting menus for about $75, not counting a tasting menu of terrific wine. It adds up. Always feeling free to spend your money for you, we can say they are worth it.

- **Best Buffet:** For the Strip, it's the **Mirage Buffet** (☎ 702/791-7111). Not at all the cheapest in town, but the quality goes up accordingly. The salad bar comes loaded with countless possibilities, including a variety of cold salads (when was the last time you saw gefilte fish on a buffet?). And the gigantic mound of shrimp is the right sort of decadent touch you want in a Vegas buffet. Downtown, the new **Main Street Station Garden Court,** 200 N. Main St. (☎ 702/387-1896), has an incredible buffet; all live-action stations, wood-fired brick-oven pizzas, fresh lovely salsas and guacamole in the Mexican section, and better-than-average desserts. Nowhere else in Downtown comes even close (though they are outstripped on Sunday by the Golden Nugget's Sunday brunch).

- **Best Sunday Champagne Brunch:** It's Midstrip's **Bally's** lavish **Sterling Sunday Brunch** (☎ 702/739-4111), where display tables embellished with floral arrangements and ice sculptures are laden with everything from mounds of fresh shrimp to sushi and sashimi, and fancy entrees include the likes of roast duckling with black-currant and blueberry sauce.

- **Best Graveyard Dinner Deal:** Downtown, **Binion's Horseshoe Coffee Shop,** 128 E. Fremont St., at Casino Center Blvd. (☎ 702/382-1600), offers a complete New York steak dinner served with potato, roll, and salad for just $3 from 10pm to 5:45am.

- **Best Cheap Breakfast:** Make your first stop of the day at the South Strip's **Cyclone Coffee Shop,** 3750 Las Vegas Blvd. S., at the Holiday Inn Casino Boardwalk, where a $1.29 breakfast includes two eggs, bacon or sausage, hash browns, and toast. It's served around the clock.
- **Best Spot for a Romantic Dinner:** In Mid-Strip, the Rio's warmly elegant **Fiore** (☎ 702/252-7702), with its gorgeous interior and arched windows overlooking the palm-fringed pool, is the most simpatico setting for a leisurely romantic dinner. Brilliant cuisine, a great wine cellar, and superb service combine to create a memorable evening.
- **Best Spot for a Celebration:** On the South Strip at the Tropicana, **Mizuno's** (☎ 702/739-2713) teppanyaki grills are ideal for small parties, with the chef's theatrics comprising a tableside show. Additionally, MGM Grand's elegant **Gatsby's** (see above) with its superlative food would make a fine spot for a wedding supper.
- **Best Free Show at Dinner:** At Treasure Island's **Buccaneer Bay Club** (☎ 702/894-7350) everyone rushes to the window when the ship battle begins.
- **Best Wine List:** The distinguished cellar at **Gatsby's** (see above) houses 600 wines in all price ranges and has a friendly master sommelier on hand to guide you in your selections. Trust him; he knows his stuff.
- **Best View:** See all of Las Vegas from the revolving **Top of the World** (☎ 702/380-7711), at the Stratosphere, North Strip, 106 stories up.
- **Best California Cuisine:** Wolfgang Puck's **Spago** (☎ 702/369-6300) didn't invent California cuisine (or did it?), but it might as well have. Find it Mid-Strip at Caesars.
- **Best Chinese Cuisine: Chin's,** 3200 Las Vegas Blvd. S. (☎ 702/733-8899), where piano bar music enhances an ambience of low-key elegance, offers scrumptious and authentic Cantonese fare, including some original creations such as deep-fried battered chicken served with strawberry sauce and fresh strawberries.
- **Best Deli:** The **Stage Deli** (☎ 702/893-4045) in Caesars will give no cause for complaints. You might also try the new deli in **New York New York,** which has been winning raves.
- **Best Healthy/Veggie Conscious:** The **Enigma Cafe,** 918½ S. Fourth St. (☎ 702/386-0999), in the Gateway District, which makes it convenient for both the Strip and Downtown, offers a large selection of really cheap sandwiches, salads, and smoothies, all fresh and interesting. (They have hummus!) That, plus their enormous menu of coffees and other specialty drinks, and their pretty, relaxing setting, make this a great Vegas find.
- **Best Italian Cuisine:** The chain **Il Fornaio** (☎ 702/650-6500) in New York New York is the best for a moderately priced meal, and **Fiore** (see above) in the Rio for something quite a bit more dear.
- **Best New Orleans Cuisine:** One of Las Vegas's newest celebrity chef venues, **Emeril's New Orleans Fish House** (see above) at the MGM Grand, offers total authenticity combined with culinary brilliance.
- **Best Southwestern Cuisine:** The fact that it's the only notable Southwestern restaurant in town doesn't make the MGM Grand's **Coyote Cafe** (☎ 702/891-7349) any less impressive. Superstar Santa Fe chef Mark Miller brings contemporary culinary panache to traditional Southwestern cookery, and the results are spicy and spectacular.

- **Best Steak and Seafood: Lawry's The Prime Rib,** 4043 Howard Hughes Pkwy. (☎ **702/893-2223**), has such good prime rib, it's hard to ever imagine having any better. And you'll enjoy nothing but the best cuts of beef and the freshest seafood at East Las Vegas's **The Tillerman,** 2245 E. Flamingo Rd. (☎ **702/731-4036**), a gorgeous restaurant with candlelit tables amid an indoor grove of ficus trees and tree-trunk pillars.

2 Restaurants by Cuisine

AMERICAN
All-American Bar & Grille (Mid-Strip, Rio, M)
All Star Cafe (South Strip, Showcase Mall, M)
Binion's Horseshoe (Downtown, Binion's Horseshoe, I)
Buccaneer Bay Club (Mid-Strip, Treasure Island, VE)
Carson Street Café (Downtown, Golden Nugget, I)
Dive! (North Strip, Fashion Show Mall, M)
Hard Rock Cafe (East of the Strip, M)
Harley Davidson Cafe (South Strip, M)
Spago (Mid-Strip, Caesars Palace, VE)
Top of the World (North Strip, Stratosphere, VE)

ASIAN
Dragon Noodle Co. (South Strip, Monte Carlo, M)
Spago (Mid-Strip, Caesars Palace, VE)

BAGELS
Einstein Bros. Bagels (East of the Strip, I)

BARBECUE
Big Sky Steak House (North Strip, Stratosphere, I)
Country Star (South Strip, M)
Tony Roma's—A Place for Ribs (Downtown, Sam Boyd's Fremont, M)
Tony Roma's—A Place for Ribs (North Strip, Stardust, M)

BUFFETS/BRUNCHES
Bally's Big Kitchen Buffet (Mid-Strip, M)
Bally's Sterling Sunday Brunch (Mid-Strip, VE)
Caesars Palace Palatium Buffet (Mid-Strip, M)
Circus Circus Buffet (North Strip, I)
Excalibur's Round Table Buffet (South Strip, I)
Flamingo Hilton Paradise Garden Buffet (Mid-Strip, I)
Golden Nugget Buffet (Downtown, M)
Harrah's Fresh Market Buffet (Mid-Strip, M)
Lady Luck Banquet Buffet (Downtown, I)
Las Vegas Hilton Buffet of Champions (East of the Strip, M)
Luxor's Pharoah's Pheast Buffet (South Strip, I)
Main Street Station Garden Court (Downtown, I)
MGM Grand Buffet (South Strip, I)
Mirage Buffet (Mid-Strip, M)
Monte Carlo Buffet (South Strip, I)
Rio's Carnival World Buffet (Mid-Strip, I)
Sahara Oasis Buffet (North Strip, I)
Sam Boyd's Fremont Paradise Buffet (Downtown, I)
Sam's Town, The Great Buffet (East of the Strip, I)
Showboat Captain's Buffet (Downtown, I)

Key to abbreviations: VE = Very Expensive; E = Expensive; M = Moderate; I = Inexpensive

Stardust Warehouse Buffet (North Strip, I)

Stratosphere Buffet (North Strip, I)

Treasure Island Buffet (Mid-Strip, I)

Tropicana Island Buffet (South Strip, M)

CALIFORNIA

Enigma Cafe (West Las Vegas, I)

Gordon-Biersch Brewing Company (East of the Strip, M)

Planet Hollywood (Mid-Strip, Caesars Palace, M)

Rain Forest Cafe (South Strip, MGM Grand, M)

Wolfgang Puck Café (South Strip, MGM Grand, M)

CHINESE

Cathay House (West Las Vegas, M)

Chin's (North Strip, Fashion Show Mall, E)

Noodle Kitchen (Mid-Strip, Mirage, M)

CONTEMPORARY CREOLE

Emeril's New Orleans Fish House (South Strip, MGM Grand, VE)

CONTINENTAL

Bacchanal (Mid-Strip, Caesars Palace, VE)

Buccaneer Bay Club (Mid-Strip, Treasure Island, VE)

Cafe Nicolle (West Las Vegas, E)

Top of the World (North Strip, Stratosphere, VE)

CUBAN

Rincon Criollo (North Strip, I)

DELI

Celebrity Deli (East of the Strip, I)

Stage Deli (Mid-Strip, Caesars Palace, M)

DESSERTS

Freed's Bakery (East of the Strip, I)

Luv-It Frozen Custard (North Strip, I)

DINER

Green Shack (East of the Strip, I)

Liberty Cafe at the Blue Castle Pharmacy (North Strip, I)

Poppa Gar's (West Las Vegas, I)

DONUTS

Krispy Kreme Donuts (West Las Vegas, I)

Ronald's Donuts (West Las Vegas, I)

EURASIAN

Chinois (Mid-Strip, Caesars Palace, VE)

Gatsby's (South Strip, MGM Grand, VE)

FOOD COURT

Food Court (South Strip, Monte Carlo, I)

La Piazza Food Court (Mid-Strip, Caesars Palace, I)

FRENCH

Andre's (Downtown, VE)

Bistro Le Montrachet (East of the Strip, Las Vegas Hilton, VE)

Monte Carlo Room (North Strip, Desert Inn, VE)

Palace Court (Mid-Strip, Caesars Palace, VE)

Pamplemousse (East of the Strip, E)

INDIAN

Shalimar (East of the Strip, Citibank Plaza, M)

INTERNATIONAL

Garlic Cafe (West Las Vegas, E)

Hugo's Cellar (Downtown, Four Queens, VE)

Second Street Grill (Downtown, Fremont Hotel, E)

ITALIAN

Fiore (Mid-Strip, Rio, VE)

Papamios Italian Kitchen (East of the Strip, Sam's Town, M)

Pegasus (East of the Strip, Alexis Park Resort, VE)

JAPANESE
Ginza (East of the Strip, M)
Kabuki (East of the Strip, M)
Mizuno's (South Strip, Tropicana, E)

MEDITERRANEAN
Enigma Cafe (West Las Vegas, I)
Mediterranean Cafe and Market (East of the Strip, I)
Pegasus (East of the Strip, Alexis Park Resort, VE)

MEXICAN
Dona Maria Tamales (North Strip, I)
Ricardo's (East of the Strip, M)
Toto's (East of the Strip, I)
Viva Mercados (West Las Vegas, M)

MOROCCAN
Mamounia (East of the Strip, M)
Marrakech (East of the Strip, M)

PROVENÇALE
Fiore (Mid-Strip, Rio, VE)

PUB FARE
Monte Carlo Pub & Brewery (South Strip, Monte Carlo, I)

SOUL FOOD
Sadie's Soul Kitchen (East of the Strip, I)

SOUTHWESTERN
Allie's American Grille (East of the Strip, Marriott Suites, M)

Country Star (South Strip, M)
Coyote Cafe (South Strip, MGM Grand, VE)
Motown Cafe (South Strip, New York New York, M)

STEAK/SEAFOOD
Center Stage (Downtown, Jackie Gaughan's, I)
Drai's (Mid-Strip, Barbary Coast, VE)
Lawry's The Prime Rib (East of the Strip, E)
Limerick's (Downtown, Fitzgeralds, E)
Morton's of Chicago (North Strip, Fashion Show Mall, VE)
The Palm (Mid-Strip, Caesars Palace, VE)
Phil's Angus Steakhouse (North Strip, New Frontier, VE)
The Range (Mid-Strip, Harrah's, VE)
The Tillerman (East of the Strip, VE)

SUSHI
Dragon Sushi (West Las Vegas, I)
Hyakumi (Mid-Strip, Caesars Palace, E)

TEX-MEX
Z Tejas Grill (East of the Strip, M)

THAI
Komol (East of the Strip, M)
Thai Spice (West Las Vegas, M)

3 South Strip

VERY EXPENSIVE

✪ **Coyote Cafe.** MGM Grand, 3799 Las Vegas Blvd. S. ☎ **702/891-7349.** Reservations suggested for the Grill Room, not accepted for the Cafe. Grill Room main courses $15–$32. Cafe main courses $7.50–$17.50 (many are under $10). AE, CB, DC, DISC, JCB, MC, V. Grill Room daily 5:30–10pm. Cafe daily 7:30am–11pm. SOUTHWESTERN.

In a town where restaurant cuisine often seems stuck in a 1950s time warp, Mark Miller's Coyote Cafe evokes howls of delight. His robust regional cuisine combines elements of traditional Mexican, Native American, Creole, and Cajun cookery with cutting-edge culinary trends. The main dining room is fronted by a lively cafe/bar, in which an exhibition cooking area houses a *cazuela* (casserole) oven and *comal* grill under a gleaming ceramic tile hood. The adobe-walled Grill Room offers a more tranquil setting. Tables are candlelit; etched-glass partitions by Santa Fe artist Kit Carson depict whimsical scenes (such as a coyote and a horse dining in a restaurant). A warm glow emanates from innovative sconces that filter light through multicolored Japanese rice paper.

The Grill Room menu changes monthly. If you're lucky, you might find the heavenly "painted soup"—half garlicky black bean, half beer-infused smoked Cheddar—"painted" with chipotle cream and garnished with salsa fresca and de árbol chili powder. A reliable main course is the salmon fillet crusted with ground pumpkin seeds and corn tortillas topped with roasted chile/pumpkin-seed sauce and presented on a bed of spinach-wrapped spaghetti squash studded with pine nuts, corn kernels, scallions, and morsels of sun-dried tomato. Desserts include chocolate banana torte served on banana crème anglaise and topped with a scoop of vanilla ice cream. The wine list includes many by-the-glass selections, including champagnes and sparkling wines, which nicely complement spicy Southwestern fare; Brazilian daiquiris are a house specialty.

The Cafe menu offers similar but somewhat lighter fare. Southwestern breakfasts ($6 to $9.50) range from huevos rancheros to blue-corn pancakes with toasted pine nuts, honey butter, and real maple syrup.

✪ **Emeril's New Orleans Fish House.** MGM Grand, 3799 Las Vegas Blvd. S. ☎ **702/ 891-7374.** Reservations suggested. Main courses $12–$18 lunch, $18–$28 dinner (more for lobster). AE, CB, DC, DISC, MC, V. Daily 11am–3pm and 5:30–10:30pm. CONTEMPORARY CREOLE.

Tucked into an almost unseen corner of the MGM Grand is one of the very finest restaurants in the city. Chef Emeril Lagasse of New Orleans's Emeril's and NOLA (and an extremely popular TV chef on cable's Food Network) has brought his cuisine to town. The restaurant's quiet and comforting decor provides the stage for creative, exciting, "BAM!" food.

Although Lagasse caters to the tastes of everyone from poultry lovers to vegetarians, seafood is the specialty here, flown in from Louisiana or from anywhere that he finds the quality of the ingredients to be the very finest. We started off with the most recent edition of Lagasse's legendary savory "cheesecakes," the Lobster Cheesecake with tomato-tarragon coulis, topped with a dollop of succulent Louisiana choupique caviar. It's a heady, rich appetizer that may be completely unlike anything you've ever had. Oysters on the half shell are also a favorite, served with two tangy dipping sauces. And try the barbecued shrimp, which come in a garlic-and-herb butter sauce that will have you mopping your plate with bread.

Our entrees did not fail to elicit a "Wow!" from everyone at the table. A Creole-seasoned seared ahi steak was stuffed with Hudson Valley foie gras and served in a bed of Lagasse's famous "smashed" potatoes, creamy and rich, with roasted shallots and a part-shallot reduction—absolutely luxurious. A medley of seafood, from caviar to shrimp to mussels and clams, came over pasta in a delicious and very spicy broth. And in a dish that bordered on the sinful, there was a marvelously seasoned filet mignon stuffed with a crawfish dressing and topped with Bordelaise sauce with crawfish tails and sliced andouille sausage. Meat eaters will also be very happy with the utterly tender and flavorful filet of beef with tasso Hollandaise sauce and homemade Worcestershire.

It would be difficult to recommend one particular dessert from the vast menu since they're all fabulous, but if it's your first visit, a slice of the banana cream pie with banana crust and caramel drizzle is one of the finest desserts you will ever have. And if your capacity for rich food is depleted by the end of your meal, there's a trio of house-made sorbets (mixed berry, apple, and root beer the night we dined there), which provide a lovely finish to your meal without necessarily pushing you over the

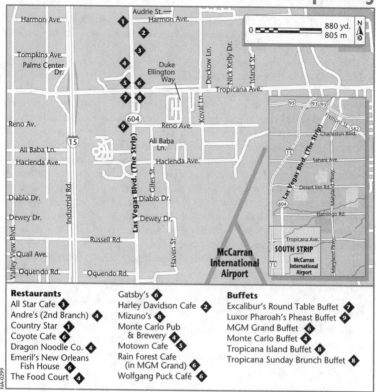

Restaurants

All Star Cafe	**3**
Andre's (2nd Branch)	**4**
Country Star	**1**
Coyote Cafe	**6**
Dragon Noodle Co.	**4**
Emeril's New Orleans Fish House	**6**
The Food Court	**4**

Gatsby's	**6**
Harley Davidson Cafe	**2**
Mizuno's	**8**
Monte Carlo Pub & Brewery	**4/5**
Motown Cafe	**5**
Rain Forest Cafe (in MGM Grand)	**6**
Wolfgang Puck Café	**6**

Buffets

Excalibur's Round Table Buffet	**7**
Luxor Pharoah's Pheast Buffet	**9**
MGM Grand Buffet	**6**
Monte Carlo Buffet	**4**
Tropicana Island Buffet	**8**
Tropicana Sunday Brunch Buffet	**8**

NA-0299

edge of the abyss. If you're feeling adventurous, don't miss the Chef's Degustation, a seven-course tasting menu. It usually features smaller portions (thank heavens) of the most exciting dishes from the regular menu, plus some specials of the evening.

✪ **Gatsby's.** MGM Grand, 3799 Las Vegas Blvd. S. ☎ **702/891-7337.** Reservations suggested. Jackets suggested for men. Main courses $29–$58. Degustation (tasting) menu $75, $95 with selected wines accompanying each course. AE, CB, DC, DISC, MC, V. Wed–Mon 6pm, with last seating at 9:30pm. EURASIAN.

This is a very expensive restaurant but on par with the swankiest establishments in more food-oriented cities. Since you're on vacation anyway, set aside some of those blackjack winnings and prepare to discover exactly how exquisite, interesting, and flavorful a meal can be. Gatsby's Chef de Cuisine, Terence Fong, has quite a conundrum to solve: How do you please the generally food-conservative Las Vegas customer and offer an innovative, exciting dining experience that invigorates everyone involved? Provide the expected but don't let it dictate preparation; combine familiar ingredients with more unusual ones to subtly educate the unadventurous; use only fresh, lovely, seasonal items. This means, for example, that Fong's lobster bisque, a rich soup you'll find on many a local menu, presented here with perhaps two lumps of divinely sweet meat and a few bites of equally sugar-rich roasted corn, awakens one to the difference between the ordinary and the extraordinary. It means starting with aromatic yet familiar jasmine and basmati rice, but adding toasted orzo, wheat berries, and quinoa (a rather trendy but very healthful and tasty grain) to produce a delicious confetti of flavors rather than a safe side dish. It means that the gracious wait staff brings unexpected treats to tease diners into anticipation, such as tiny cilantro crêpe purses of beluga caviar and vodka crème fraîche, or perfectly smoked salmon on half-dollar-size blini.

Anything from this kitchen that includes foie gras is worth ordering. This delicacy might show up on the menu in more than one guise, accompanied with pan-roasted stuffed quail and a lentil-corn salad, or with Perigourd truffles and organic greens dressed in a port wine vinaigrette. Maine lobster might be simply sautéed and served with lobster-ginger butter to gild the already sumptuous meat; ahi tuna gets an Asian preparation with a sesame-seed crust and a spicy wasabi butter. Fans of exotic meats, or anyone curious to try ostrich or buffalo, are in the right place. The grilled domestic ostrich, bathed in a red wine–shallot reduction and served with wild mushroom risotto, is a lovely dish, tender and not the least bit gamey. Duck is well treated here, as well. It's slow roasted, so the slices are as tender and lean as possible, garnished with an Asian-style sauce and pretty little vegetables. Vegetarians will find dinner just as lush. Along with the chef's vegetable plate, replete with couscous or risotto or that wonderful rice confetti and lots of recently plucked delicacies, vegetable broth–based soups, a couple of salads, and appetizers such as the vegetable spring rolls will profoundly satisfy your appetite and expectations.

It's painful to recall the dessert menu, living so far from the source. Melanie Bonnano, the pastry chef, takes great delight in whimsical presentations like a Cup of Java, a treat that fulfills coffee and chocolate lovers on a number of levels. Her coffee-and-cream granita-laden chocolate cup will have you examining your freezer in a new light. Soufflés available in five flavors are a house specialty, but chocolate cake mysteriously filled with fresh raspberries and wrapped in filo pastry is a feast for the eyes and tongue.

Everything, from the lavish crackers and bread to the sorbets presented in the center of ice flowers, is made in-house. If you are curious to see the kitchen, a special chef's table sits in a little room separated from the activity by glass windows—when you make reservations, you can request this spot, although it's hard to concentrate on conversation when you're craning your neck to watch the pastry chef. It's also possible to request a special tasting menu ($75), which will truly give you a sense of the restaurant's possibilities. For an extra $30, the enthusiastic sommelier will pair wines from the luxuriously stocked cellar with each course. While spending a few hundred dollars on dinner for two may seem extravagant, the experience is worth that and more. At Gatsby's, unlike most places in Las Vegas, there's no possible way to lose.

EXPENSIVE

✪ **Mizuno's.** Tropicana Resort and Casino, 3801 Las Vegas Blvd. S. ☎ **702/739-2713.** Reservations suggested. Full Samurai dinners mostly $15–$20, Shogun combination dinners $25–$39. AE, CB, DC, DISC, MC, V. Daily 5–10:30pm. JAPANESE.

This stunning, marble-floored restaurant is filled with authentic Japanese artifacts, among them an ancient temple bell, a 400-year-old vase from Tokyo, and antique scrolls and shoji screens. One of the latter depicts the restaurant's theme, the exchange of cultures between the East and West as exemplified by the silk and tea trade. A meandering glass "stream" is lit by tiny twinkling lights to suggest running water, and cut-glass dividers are etched with graceful cherry blossoms, irises, and plum trees. Food is prepared at marble teppanyaki grill tables where you're seated with other patrons; together you comprise the "audience" for a highly skilled chef, who, wielding cooking knives with the panache of a samurai swordsman, rapidly trims, chops, sautés, and flips the food onto everyone's plates. This being Las Vegas, his dazzling display of dexterity is enhanced by a flashing light show over the grill.

Entrees comprised of tasty morsels of New York strip steak, filet mignon, shrimp, lobster, chicken, or shrimp and vegetable tempura, and various combinations of the above, come with miso soup or consommé (get the tastier miso), salad with ginger dressing, an array of crispy flavorful vegetables stir-fried with sesame seeds and spices, steamed rice, and tea. Though it's a lot of food, an appetizer of shrimp and mushrooms sautéed in garlic butter with lemon soy sauce merits consideration. And a bottle of warm sake is recommended. Ginger or red bean ice cream make for a fittingly light dessert. A great bargain here: a full early-bird dinner served from 5 to 6pm for just $10.

MODERATE

See also the listing for **Coyote Cafe** (p. 115), an expensive restaurant fronted by a more moderately priced cafe.

All Star Cafe. 3785 Las Vegas Blvd. S., at Tropicana Ave., in the Showcase Mall, next to the MGM Grand. ☎ **702/795-8326.** Reservations accepted. Main courses $6–$18. AE, DC, DISC, JCB, MC, V. Sun–Thurs 11am–midnight, Fri–Sat 11am–1am. AMERICAN.

This is the sports-theme restaurant, filled with memorabilia from hundreds of different sports legends, covering just about every sport you can imagine. Buffs should be pleased. The co-owners are Vegas resident Andre Agassi, Monica Seles, Wayne Gretzky, Ken Griffey Jr., Joe Montana, Shaquille O'Neal, and new wunderkind Tiger Woods (who recently joined as an investor). The menu is "All American" and includes pasta specialties, salads, and the usual hamburgers and hot dogs.

Country Star. 3724 Las Vegas Blvd. S., at Harmon Ave. ☎ **702/740-8400.** Reservations for large parties only. Main courses $6–$22 (most under $14). AE, MC, V. Sun–Thurs 11am– 10pm, Fri–Sun 11am–11pm. BARBECUE/SOUTHWESTERN.

This would be the country music entry, attempting to cash in on the success of the Hard Rock. Restaurant principals include Reba McEntire, Vince Gill, Tracy Lawrence, Neal McCoy, Lorianne Crook, and Charlie Chase. Music memorabilia (Merle Haggard's boots, a Minnie Pearl hat with dangling price tag, Dolly Parton's wedding dress, gold records, Grand Ole Opry posters) adds to the atmosphere. It's more low-key and friendly than, say, Hard Rock or Planet Hollywood. Dozens of video monitors, including several embedded in the entranceway floor, play nonstop C&W music videos. The food here is pretty good and the barbecue sauce is terrific (bottles are on the tables).

Dragon Noodle Co. Monte Carlo Resort, 3770 Las Vegas Blvd. S., between Flamingo Rd. and Tropicana Ave. ☎ **702/730-7965.** Reservations not accepted. Main courses $5.50–$17 (many under $10). AE, CB, DC, DISC, MC, V. Sun–Thurs 11am–10pm, Fri–Sat 11am–11pm. ASIAN FUSION.

Dragon Noodle was designed according to the complex principles of *Feng Shui*, the ancient Chinese art of geomancy used in planning building interiors to maximize prosperity and positive energy. The resulting casual, minimalist interior suggests a marketplace, with displays of Asian foodstuffs and sacks of rice on the floor. Along the back wall is a noteworthy exhibit of Asian teapots and other kitchen antiques.

Order up a platter of pan-seared pot stickers and create your own dipping sauce by mixing hoisin sauce, hot sauce, and vinegar. Other notable dishes here are spicy, wok-seared Mongolian beef served over crispy rice-stick noodles with scallion shreds, crisp-skinned roast duck, and Thai-style barbecued chicken scented with lemongrass, ginger, hot chile, and a hint of curry (it's served with spicy peanut and shallot sauces). With any of the above, we like to order steamed buns and make little sandwiches; try it. Dragon Noodle's extensive selection of teas (equivalent to a carefully crafted wine list) are served in exquisite pots. Other beverage options include more than a dozen wines by the glass, Asian beers, specialty iced teas, and fresh-squeezed juices. Among the Asian-nuanced desserts is a rich coconut cake layered with cream-cheese frosting and topped with toasted coconut.

Harley Davidson Cafe. 3725 Las Vegas S., at Harmon. ☎ **702/740-4555.** Reservations not accepted. Main courses $6–$18. AE, DC, DISC, MC, V. Sun–Thurs 11:30am–midnight, Fri–Sat 11:30am–1am. AMERICAN.

You can't miss the Harley Cafe—it's the one with the giant hog jutting from the facade. Inside is an all-American ode to all things motorcyclish (American-made, naturally). The wait staff are rocker/biker types, the music blares, and the food is basic (burgers, dogs, BBQ) but a tad high in price. Do try the warm chocolate-chip Tollhouse cookie pie.

Motown Cafe. New York New York Hotel, 3790 Las Vegas Blvd. S. ☎ **702/740-6440.** Reservations not accepted. Main courses $7–$18. AE, DISC, JCB, MC, V. Sun–Thurs 7:30am–11:30pm, Fri–Sat 7:30am–2am. SOUTHWESTERN.

The menu at this tribute to Motown record label artists features light Southwestern cuisine (jambalaya, shrimp Creole) probably because no one could figure out what the indigenous cuisine of Detroit was. (This is in addition to the basic burgers and so forth). They also offer a breakfast buffet. And as we all know, Motown music is just about the best there is for dancing, and so the Cafe stays open until 3am on weekdays and 4am on weekends for dancing.

Rain Forest Cafe. MGM Grand, 3799 Las Vegas Blvd. S. ☎ **702/891-8580.** Reservations not required. Main courses $9–$13 breakfast, $10–$19 dinner. AE, DC, DISC, JCB, MC, V. Mon–Thurs 7am–midnight, Fri–Sat 7am–1am, Sun 7am–11pm. CALIFORNIA.

If you've always wanted to eat a meal in the Jungle Cruise ride at Disneyland, here's your chance. Decor-wise, this is possibly the best of the many theme restaurants in town. It's full of faux foliage, Animatronic animals (some of which are not indigenous to rain forests, but oh well), flowers, giant butterflies and so forth. Water splashes, animals roar, music plays, thunderstorms hit periodically—it all adds up to one noisy experience, but not, sadly, a particularly educational one. The food is tasty and imaginative, if somewhat busy variations on the usual pastas, sandwiches, and what-not. The veggie burgers did earn serious raves from connoisseurs of same. Consider checking out the smoothies offered at the bar. Kids will love the sights and the children's menu. You won't love trying to steer them through the gift shop entrance.

✪ **Wolfgang Puck Café.** MGM Grand, 3799 Las Vegas Blvd. S. ☎ **702/895-9653.** Reservations not accepted. Main courses $9–$15. AE, DC, MC, V. Sun–Thurs 8am–11pm, Fri–Sat 8am–midnight. CALIFORNIA.

A brightly colored riot of mosaic tiles and other experiments in geometric design, the Wolfgang Puck Café stands out in the MGM Grand. It's more or less Spago Lite: downscaled salads, pizzas, and pastas, all showing the Puck hand, and while perhaps a little more money than your average cafe, the food is comparably better, if sometimes not *that* special. However, it's all very fresh nouvelle cuisine, which makes a nice change of pace. The specialty pizzas are fun; constructed on crusts topped with fontina and mozzarella cheeses, they're brushed with pesto and layered with embellishments such as spicy jalapeño-marinated sautéed chicken, leeks, and cilantro. (And no, it's not just like eating the Puck brand sold in the frozen food section.) It's always a thrill to get a good salad in Vegas, and there are quite a few on this menu. Worth noting is the signature Chinois chicken salad tossed with crispy fried wontons, julienned carrots, cabbage, and green onions in a Chinese honey-mustard sauce. For something cheap, try the surprisingly large baby greens salad with the goat cheese toast—that and the very fine herb bread that comes gratis is $5, which fills you up in a fairly healthy way for not a lot of money. Dessert highlights include a caramel cheesecake, a warm chocolate soufflé, and a hot chocolate truffle cake with chocolate sauce. There does tend to be a line, particularly after *EFX* lets out just across the casino.

INEXPENSIVE

✪ **Food Court.** Monte Carlo Resort and Casino, 3770 Las Vegas Blvd., between Flamingo Rd. and Tropicana Ave. ☎ **702/730-7777.** Main courses $2–$10. No credit cards. Daily 6am–3am. FOOD COURT.

Food courts are a dime a dozen in Vegas, but the one in the Monte Carlo has some surprisingly good options. Sure, there is the always reliable **McDonald's,** and for sweets there is **Häagen-Dazs,** but they also have a branch of **Nathan's Hot Dogs,** New York's finest. **Golden Bagel** offers another New York staple, big and tasty enough to satisfy even picky natives. **Sbarro** offers enticing pizza slices. It's much more attractively decorated than your usual mall food courts, and with those extended hours (each stand has its own, but they all fall within the listed parameters), there remains little time for anyone to go hungry. If you want a good, cheap meal on the Strip and wish to avoid some of those dubious night-owl specials, come here.

Monte Carlo Pub & Brewery. Monte Carlo Resort, 3770 Las Vegas Blvd. S., between Flamingo Rd. and Tropicana Ave. ☎ **702/730-7777.** Reservations not accepted. Main courses $6–$8. AE, CB, DC, DISC, MC, V. Sun–Thurs 11am–1am, Fri–Sat 11am–3am. PUB FARE.

When the Monte Carlo opened in summer 1996, this large and lively pub immediately became a favorite lunch spot and after-work hangout for local business-people. A working microbrewery (you can view the copper holding tanks and vats through large windows), it has a high-ceilinged warehouse/industrial interior, with exposed-brick and rusty corrugated-tin walls, track lighting, and a network of exposed pipes overhead. An ornate mahogany back bar with beveled mirrors adds a note of elegance. The Pub is cigar-friendly (maintaining a humidor), and rock videos blare forth from a large screen and 40 TV monitors around the room. This is no place for a romantic rendezvous.

The menu features somewhat sophisticated versions of pub fare, doled out in enormous portions. We like the pizza topped with lamb, grilled eggplant, and goat cheese. Other choices include penne pasta with wild mushrooms in garlic cream sauce, a sample platter of sausages served with warm potato salad and whole-grain mustard, sandwiches, burgers, and barbecued baby-back ribs. A microbrew with your meal (or a sampler of five) is de rigueur. Desserts include bread pudding with butterscotch rum sauce and creamy peanut butter pie. After 9pm, only pizza is served, and dueling pianos provide dance music and entertainment.

4 Mid-Strip

VERY EXPENSIVE

Bacchanal. Caesars Palace, 3570 Las Vegas Blvd. S., just north of Flamingo Rd. ☎ **702/731-7110.** Reservations required. Fixed-price dinner $69.50, plus tax and gratuity. AE, CB, DC, DISC, MC, V. Tues–Sat 6–11pm with seatings at 6, 6:30, 9, and 9:30pm. CONTINENTAL.

This is the quintessential Vegas restaurant experience, where the food is considerably less important than the spectacle. A bacchanal is a devotee of the Roman god of wine, Bacchus. As a festival participant, a certain level of debauchery is required. You will be expected to accept a massage from a wine goddess (the toga-clad waitresses who dispense alcohol) or Hercules, be enticed by the belly dancers, show respect and honor for Caesar and Cleopatra, and for pity's sake, eat and drink your fair share. Not for the introverted or inhibited. Giggling is allowed. Being aloof and above it all is not.

Along with everything else in Caesars, Bacchanal has had a face-lift, but it's still its decadent, and silly, self. Your experience will take place in a Roman garden, with a large fountain occupying the center of the room (the belly dancers pose on its edges, batting their eyes at the crowd). The walls are painted with frescoes, featuring tranquil scenes of the Italian countryside. The ceiling is decorated with golden vines and enormous rock crystal torches light the room. The six-course meal (entree, soup, salad, pasta, crudités, and dessert) is certainly plentiful and satisfactory—but you really don't come for the food. You come for the show, the royal service, the personalized greeting by Caesar and Cleopatra, the belly dancing, and of course, the wine goddesses, who keep your glass ever full. But be careful; there are stories of people who have slipped out to the bathroom—which requires a pass through the casino—after several glasses of wine and returned down $20,000. That may be more decadence than you can handle.

✪ **Buccaneer Bay Club.** Treasure Island, 3300 Las Vegas Blvd. S. ☎ **702/894-7350.** Reservations required. Main courses $16–$26. AE, CB, DC, DISC, JCB, MC, V. Daily 5–10:30pm. AMERICAN/CONTINENTAL.

This is a little-known gem (at least, outside of Treasure Island guests) that features a laudable menu more innovative than the standard found at other equivalent hotel restaurants. And it's certainly considerably cheaper.

A meandering layout creates a series of intimate dining nooks (perfect for quiet conversations) all done in a posh pirate theme with a low-beamed ceiling and stucco walls adorned with daggers and pistols. Treasure chests are displayed in wall niches along with a veritable museum of artifacts including a Spanish conquistador's helmet. The whole thing overlooks the hotel's "bay" where a pirate battle is waged every 90 minutes. This probably isn't the best place to view it from (the windows are smallish, and you're behind the action), but the wait staff does notify you at show time and will hold your food service until it's through if you have chosen to watch. It's fun to watch everyone rush to the windows when they announce, "Pirates are on!"

Speaking of the service, it is among the best we've experienced, with an efficient team of friendly, knowledgeable, and almost prescient servers at every table (they anticipated a woman's desire for another glass of wine before she even had finished wistfully vocalizing it).

Appetizers come in both hot (shrimp Jamaica, escargot brioche) and cold (shrimp cocktail, Parma prosciutto) varieties with the savory celery-root flan and the quail being the true standouts. Regarding the latter, it was not on the menu, so be sure to ask about specials. Entrees range from poultry (chicken, duck, pheasant) to beef (filet mignon, prime rib, steak) to seafood (sea bass, lobster, salmon). A favorite here is the Pheasant Charles, which comes with pan-seared, thyme-roasted wild mushroom risotto and is served in a Merlot lingonberry sauce. There's also Colorado Buffalo Prime Rib, which is roasted and grilled over mesquite wood and served with creamy horseradish potatoes. It's hard to get over the thought of eating a buffalo at first, but if you can, it'll be one of the best pieces of cow-based meat

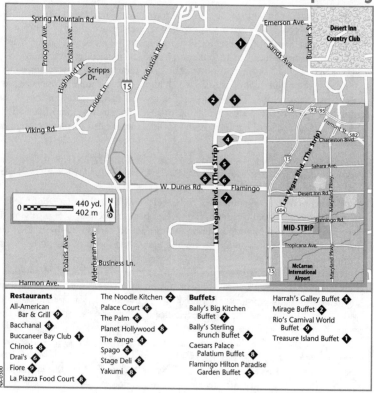

Restaurants

All-American
  Bar & Grill ❾
Bacchanal ❽
Buccaneer Bay Club ❶
Chinois ❽
Drai's ❻
Fiore ❾
La Piazza Food Court ❽

The Noodle Kitchen ❷
Palace Court ❽
The Palm ❽
Planet Hollywood ❽
The Range ❹
Spago ❽
Stage Deli ❽
Yakumi ❽

Buffets

Bally's Big Kitchen
  Buffet ❼
Bally's Sterling
  Brunch Buffet ❼
Caesars Palace
  Palatium Buffet ❽
Flamingo Hilton Paradise
  Garden Buffet ❺

Harrah's Galley Buffet ❸
Mirage Buffet ❷
Rio's Carnival World
  Buffet ❾
Treasure Island Buffet ❶

you'll ever taste. Desserts include apple binets, white chocolate cheesecake with raspberry sauce, and the house specialty apricot or harlequin (Grand Marnier, white and dark chocolate) minisoufflés.

Chinois. 3570 Las Vegas Blvd. S., in the Forum Shops at Caesars Palace. ☎ **702/737-9700.** Reservations suggested. Main courses $11–$16.50 cafe, $19.75–$28 restaurant. AE, JCB, MC, V. Restaurant daily 6–10:30pm; cafe daily 11:30am–midnight. EURASIAN.

From Wolfgang Puck, the man who brought you Spago and gourmet frozen pizzas, comes another entry in the world of fine dining and innovative cuisine. Not the groundbreaker that Spago was, and probably more about presentation than truly remarkable meals, Chinois is still a welcome addition to the Vegas foodie scene.

Demonstrating both modern and Southwestern influences, the food and decor could be called nouvelle Asian. The latter is another phantasm courtesy of Puck's wife's artistically fevered brain. Let's just call it colorful, quirky, and eccentric and be done with it. The downstairs cafe (where sushi and more recognizable, classic Chinese dishes are served) is casual, but even the upstairs dining room, which overlooks the Forum Shops (and is on eyeball level with the giant Trojan horse that forms the entrance to FAO Schwarz—watch him bob his head and blow smoke during your meal) has more of a kicky atmosphere rather than a formal dining one. Food is served family style, which helps spread the rather high prices around some. There are specials every night, but you can count on Chinois "classics" every evening. Appetizers include Szechuan pancakes with stir-fried Peking duck, spring veggies, and wild mushrooms—everything combines into one new savory taste.

Always free to spend your money, we also recommend the lovely sautéed foie gras with rhubarb compote (it has a citrus zing to it) and a sauce made from port wine, figs, and spices. For entrees, keeping in a pricey vein, we are sorry to relate that the Shanghai lobster with a rich coconut curry sauce is marvelous. If you need to get talked out of it, however, the lobster can have some chewy bits. More budget-minded is the whole sizzling catfish, which along with a couple of appetizers will easily feed two people. The Cantonese duck with divine sesame crêpes is also superb, a light, nearly perfect rendering of that difficult fowl. Skip the ordinary Mongolian lamb chops, but save room for the scrumptious chocolate mint gâteau dessert.

Drai's. 3595 Las Vegas Blvd. S., in the Barbary Coast. ☎ **702/737-0555.** Reservations recommended. Main courses $19–$28. AE, MC, V. Sun–Thurs 5:30–9:30pm, Fri–Sat 5:30–10:30pm. STEAK/SEAFOOD.

A famous Los Angeles restaurant has come to L.A. with much fanfare, but one can't help but notice the food is very ordinary. Not bad, just perhaps not justifying the high prices. There are multiple dining rooms done in dark wood—very L.A. fern bar—with leopard prints on the menus and plates, and too loud jazz music blaring throughout.

Peculiarly, the most expensive menu item is Dover sole with mashed potatoes—a cheap fish and a cheap accompaniment. The menu boasts that none of their soups are made with dairy products. They might want to reconsider; the potato leak soup was flat and dull because it really needed cream or butter. Lake Superior whitefish in filo dough with onion marmalade will please those who don't mind their appetizers on the sweet side. On the plus side, duck was crispy and not dry, crab cakes were tasty and with shredded, not puréed crab, and served with a stiff but nice and cheesy risotto. However, the lemon caper sauce had no flavor. Still, it would be worth going to Drai's just for the chocolate mousse dessert—light and delectable, and not overly sweet.

✪ **Fiore.** Rio Suite Hotel, 3700 W. Flamingo Rd., at I-15. ☎ **702/252**-7702. Reservations recommended. Main courses $26–$48. AE, CB, DC, DISC, MC, V. Daily 5–11pm. ITALIAN/PROVENÇALE.

Fiore offers a deliciously simpatico setting for the brilliantly innovative cuisine of chef Kolachai Ngimsangaim. In his spacious, mahogany-ceilinged dining room, with arched windows overlooking a palm-fringed pool, tables are exquisitely appointed with fine silver, flowers, and Villeroy and Boch china in diverse floral patterns. Flower- and fruit-motif carpeting furthers the "fiore" motif, while an exhibition kitchen aglow with wood-burning pizza ovens (nine different hardwoods are used for grilling here) adds warmth and theatricality. We love the interior space, but it's also tempting to dine alfresco on the flower-bordered flagstone terrace (heated in winter, mist-cooled in summer). Light jazz provides a pleasant musical backdrop.

Ngimsangaim's seasonally changing menus complement the culinary elegance of northern Italy with the earthy exuberance of southern France. For an appetizer we had the sautéed herb-crusted prawns in a buttery mustard/anise sauce. This was followed by an entree of barbecued Atlantic salmon in honeyed hickory sauce, served with grilled polenta, portobello mushrooms, roasted Roma tomatoes, and grilled asparagus spears. Fiore's thoughtful list of more than 400 wines in several price ranges is international in scope and includes 45 premium by-the-glass selections. Consult knowledgeable sommelier Barrie Larvin for suggestions. Dine slowly, and consider including a cheese course—excellent cheeses are served with seasonal fruits. But do save room for dessert—perhaps a warm chocolate torte on crème anglaise embellished with raspberry stars and chocolate hearts. In addition to an extensive listing of cognacs, ports, and dessert wines, hand-rolled cigars elegantly presented in a mahogany humidor are a postprandial option on the terrace.

⭐ **Palace Court.** Caesars Palace, 3570 Las Vegas Blvd. S., just north of Flamingo Rd. ☎ **702/734-7110.** Reservations required. Main courses $29–$55. AE, MC, V. Daily sittings at 6, 6:30, 9, and 9:30pm. FRENCH.

The Palace Court has long been considered one of the finest restaurants in town; when it went through a brief slump, foodies were disheartened, particularly since it's not cheap. It's still not cheap, but it is back up to its original standards and is worth the expense again.

It's hard to know where to begin with the lavish menu. The delicious tuna appetizer came with the perfect amount of ginger plus tender, paper-thin radishes—it is, however, not recommended for those on no- or low-salt diets. Sautéed fresh scallops, accompanied by baby asparagus, are perfect scallops, tender and no grit, covered in a light and most mellow tarragon sauce that might have you licking your plate to get the last drop. Salade Riche is an array of leafy colors, some pungent strips of Swiss cheese, chunks of lobster, and a bit of delectable foie gras, all with a light dressing that does not drown out the salad flavors. If red snapper is offered on a special, skip it. Instead, go right to the rack of lamb with fresh goat cheese; "absolutely fabulous" was the comment that followed this amazing combo. Do consider a selection from the vast and beautifully chosen wine list.

Every dessert got a rave, especially the heavy, but not overly so, bittersweet chocolate cake, but the crêpe souffle found even chocolate fans switching allegiances. The meal finishes up with jumbo chocolate-dipped strawberries and a plate of petit fours.

The Palm. Forum Shops at Caesars Palace, 3500 Las Vegas Blvd. S. ☎ **702/732-7256.** Reservations recommended. Main courses $8.50–$14 lunch, $15–$35 dinner. AE, CB, DC, MC, V. Daily 11:30am–11pm. STEAK/SEAFOOD.

A branch of the now wide-reaching venerable New York eatery, which attracts a star-studded clientele fond of the reliable, if not terribly exciting, hearty bill of fare. (The famous may also be hoping to find their faces among the many caricatures that cover the walls.) This is plain, but filling Boy Food, but at Manly prices. Red-meat lovers will be happy with the high quality steaks found here, though those on a budget will shudder in horror. The tendency is to give them a good charring, so if you don't like your meat blackened, you might want to start with it less well done, and send it back for more if necessary. If you hit a jackpot, your money will be well-spent on one of the Palm's Buick-sized lobsters, utterly succulent and outrageously priced, but given their size—they start at 3 pounds—they can easily be shared. If you are worried it won't be enough, add one of the delicious appetizers (plump but high-priced shrimp cocktails, or a perfect prosciutto with melon) or toss in a side of crispy deep-fried onion. Desserts are similarly heavy and unspectacular.

The Range. 3475 Las Vegas Blvd. S., in Harrah's. ☎ **702/369-5000.** Reservations highly recommended. Main courses $19–$27. AE, CB, DC, DISC, MC, V. Daily 5:30–11pm. STEAK.

Part of Harrah's impressive renovation, this is worth eating at if only for the spectacular view of the Strip (few Strip restaurants take advantage of this view, oddly enough) from 40-foot-high wraparound windows. Muted copper and wood tones make for a formal but not intimidating environment and a fine-looking room. The small menu features the usual steak-house offerings—various cuts of beef and some chicken dishes plus a few salads—but at a high medium price. However, the quality is better than the usual Vegas steak house. We particularly liked the filet mignon on a gorgonzola onion croustade. All entrees come with side dishes (changing nightly, but can include such items as marinated mushrooms or horseradish mashed potatoes) served family style. Appetizers are also worth noting. The Five Onion soup is thick, heavy, creamy, and served in a giant, hollowed-out onion. It's delicious, as was a smoked chicken quesadilla. Don't miss the bread, which comes with a sweet and savory apricot-and-basil butter.

✪ **Spago.** Forum Shops at Caesars Palace, 3500 Las Vegas Blvd. S. ☎ **702/369-6300.** Reservations recommended for the dining room; not accepted at the cafe. Dining room main courses $14–$28. Cafe main courses $8.50–$16.50. AE, CB, DC, DISC, JCB, MC, V. Dining room Sun–Thurs 6–10pm, Fri–Sat 5:30–10:30pm. Cafe daily 11am–midnight. AMERICAN/ ASIAN.

Wolfgang Puck's landmark L.A. restaurant provides a rare foodie oasis in Vegas. However, though one of the few truly innovative restaurants in Vegas, Spago has been riding a bit on its reputation. While anything you get here is going to be better and more interesting than what you'd get at the vast majority of Vegas restaurants, you get the feeling they've been far ahead of the pack for just long enough to get comfortable. Which is not to say Spago is not worth the expense—it just means that others have caught up with them (and in some cases, though it may be considered heresy to say it, may have surpassed Puck's baby), and they are no longer the only foodie game in town.

But it's still an experience going there—call it California casual elegance. The postindustrial interior is the very model of a modern major restaurant, while the exterior cafe on the Forum Shops is more relaxed and provides an opportunity for people watching as fine as at any European sidewalk cafe. It's probably not as star-heavy as the celebrated L.A. original, but it's safe to say that any Hollywood muck-a-muck in town would probably be inclined to eat here.

When Nomi Malone, who appeared in the film *Showgirls,* came to eat at the cafe, she peevishly said she didn't "know what any of this stuff is." She must not get out much: The cafe menu features such familiar items as meat loaf and pizza, although glamorized versions—this isn't Country Kitchen, and so this pizza features smoked salmon. Not to mention crème fraîche. It sounds like an unholy hybrid of Italian and deli, but it's sublime. Other cafe specialties include Puck's signature Chinois chicken salad and a superb mesquite-fried salmon served with a tangy toss of soba noodles and cashews in a coconut-sesame-chile paste vinaigrette nuanced with lime juice and Szechuan mustard. The inside menu changes seasonally; examples of potential choices include scallops with a divine basil risotto, an appetizer of tuna sashimi in hot olive oil and sesame, or porcini mushrooms with a truffle sauce. The "signature" dish is a Chinese-style duck, moist but with a perfectly crispy skin. It's about as good as duck gets. It was served with a doughy steamed bun and Chinese vegetables. Desserts range from fresh fruit sorbets in surprising flavors (cantaloupe, honeydew), to a luscious brownie topped with homemade chocolate, whipped cream, and ice cream. The wine list is impressive, but the house wine was a disappointment and possibly not worth the cost.

EXPENSIVE

Hyakumi. Caesars Palace, 3750 Las Vegas Blvd. S. ☎ **702/731-7731.** Reservations recommended. Sushi $6–$7 per order; main courses $25–$60. AE, CB, DC, DISC, MC, V. Restaurant Tues–Sun 6–11pm. Sushi bar Fri–Sat 5pm–midnight, Sun and Tues–Thurs 5–11pm. SUSHI.

Hyakumi (say "Yah-KOO-me") is a quaint little oasis in the midst of a bustling casino. Tastefully decorated with hardwood floors in a tea-garden atmosphere, it is a relaxing respite from the madness of Vegas, as kimono-clad waitresses cater to your every need with a never-ending cup of particularly good green tea plus hot towels to put you in a Zen-like state.

But the setting, as serene and beautiful as it is, is not the reason for a visit to Hyakumi; it's the sushi. Supervised by Executive Chef Hiroji Obayashi, famed for his award-winning Hirozen Gourmet Restaurant in Los Angeles, Hyakumi offers some of the best sushi in town. It's not the cheapest, but it is well worth the extra cost. From the toro tuna to the salmon roll, every bite melts in your mouth. The fish is shipped in daily and is prepared by friendly sushi chefs who obviously love what they do. If sushi isn't your thing, there is also a restaurant serving up tradi-tional (but very expensive) Japanese fare in a lovely garden setting.

MODERATE

See also the listing for **Spago** and **Chinois** (both above), expensive restaurants fronted by more moderately priced cafes.

All-American Bar & Grille. Rio Suite Hotel, 3700 W. Flamingo Rd., at I-15. ☎ **702/ 252-7767.** Reservations recommended. Main courses $6–$13.75 lunch (most under $10), $18–$25 dinner. AE, CB, DC, DISC, MC, V. Daily 11am–11pm. AMERICAN.

This warmly inviting balconied restaurant has two themes: sports and Americana. Mahogany-paneled walls are hung with snowshoes, golf clubs, oars, and croquet mallets; there's a portrait of George Washington and a torch-bearing Statue of Lib-erty; vintage American flags fly from lofty mahogany rafters; and the wait staff is in flag-motif shirts. You can also eat in a lively sunken bar area filled with athletic memorabilia (Roger Staubach's football jersey, and the like), while watching sporting events aired on eight TV monitors.

At lunch, the menu features burgers, salads, and sandwiches. Dinner options include steaks, seafood, and a choice of 27 domestic beers and selected wines by the glass.

A typical meal here might begin with an order of Blue Point oysters, followed by filet mignon and lobster tails (served with soup or salad, warm sourdough bread and butter, grilled vegetables, and a baked potato), with a finale of peach cobbler topped with homemade vanilla ice cream.

Noodle Kitchen. Mirage, 3400 Las Vegas Blvd. S., between Flamingo Rd. and Sands Ave. ☎ **800/456-4564.** Reservations not accepted. Main courses $8–$22.75 (many under $10). AE, CB, DC, DISC, MC, V. Daily 11am–4am. CHINESE.

The Mirage designed the Noodle Kitchen to serve its sizable clientele of Asian high rollers, a clientele desirous of authentic, non-Americanized Chinese fare. Most of the diners here are Asian, but American and European food aficionados will also appreciate the Kitchen's high-quality cuisine. It's really not so much a separate estab-lishment as a section of the hotel's lushly tropical Caribe Café.

Start off with clear soup, flavored with Chinese cilantro and replete with thin egg noodles and dumplings filled with minced shrimp and ear mushrooms. A combi-nation plate of soy chicken slices, roast pork, and tender crisp-skinned roast duck with plum sauce makes a marvelous entree choice, especially when accompanied by delicious al dente steamed vegetables (Chinese broccoli or choy sum) in oyster sauce. If you like to spice things up, you'll find three hot sauces on the table. There are Asian desserts (such as red bean ice delight), but as these are an acquired taste, you might prefer fresh-baked cakes and pies from the Caribe Café menu. Or skip dessert altogether in favor of sweet Vietnamese iced coffee mixed with condensed milk, coconut milk, and shaved ice. All bar drinks, including Chinese and Japanese beers, are available.

Planet Hollywood. Forum Shops at Caesars Palace, 3500 Las Vegas Blvd. S. ☎ **702/ 791-STAR.** Reservations not accepted. Main courses $8–$20 (most under $13). AE, DC, MC, V. Sun–Thurs 11am–midnight, Fri–Sat 11am–1am. CALIFORNIA.

Arnold, Sly, Bruce, and Demi joined forces with some finance buddies to create a movie version of the Hard Rock. It was an instant success and a sure sign of the decline of Western civilization. Some of the objects displayed are worthless; others are sort of amusing—Barbara Eden's genie bottle, chariot wheels from *Ben Hur,* the side of beef Stallone sparred with in *Rocky,* the *Star Trek* control tower. Video monitors are everywhere, showing trailers for soon-to-be-released movies, themed video montages, and footage of Planet Hollywood grand openings around the world (which isn't the least bit self-indulgent and promotional, oh, no). Further reluctant credit is given for the more imaginative than average theme-restaurant menu: blackened shrimp served with Creole mustard sauce; linguine tossed with Thai shrimp, peanuts, and julienned vegetables in spicy sweet chile sauce; white chocolate bread pudding drenched in whisky sauce and topped with white chocolate ice cream.

✪ Stage Deli. Forum Shops at Caesars Palace, 3500 Las Vegas Blvd. S. ☎ **702/893-4045.** Reservations accepted for large parties only. Main courses $10–$14, sandwiches $6–$14. AE, DC, DISC, JCB, MC, V. Sun–Thurs 7:30am–10:30pm, Fri–Sat 7:30am–midnight. DELI.

New York City's Stage Deli—a legendary hangout for comedians, athletes, and politicians—has been slapping pastrami on rye for more than half a century. Its Las Vegas branch retains the Stage's brightly lit, Big Apple essence. Walls are embellished with subway graffiti and hung with Broadway theater posters, bowls of pickles grace the white Formica tables, and, in the New York tradition, comics and celebrities like Buddy Hackett and Arnold Schwarzenegger drop by whenever they're in town.

The deli is often not crowded. In addition to being handy for Caesars guests, if you are staying next door at the Mirage, it's easy to pop over, making it a satisfying breakfast alternative (to often overcrowded, overpriced, and not very good hotel breakfast joints in the area). The huge (we mean it) menu means finding something for even the pickiest of eaters.

Most of the fare—including fresh-baked pumpernickel and rye, meats, chewy bagels, lox, spicy deli mustard, and pickles—comes in daily from New York. The Stage dishes up authentic 5-inch-high sandwiches stuffed with pastrami, corned beef, brisket, or chopped liver. Maybe overstuffed is a better description. Unless you have a hearty appetite, are feeding two, or have a fridge in your room for leftovers, you might want to try the half sandwich and soup or salad combos. Other specialties here include matzo ball soup, knishes, kasha varnishkes, cheese blintzes, kreplach, pirogen, and smoked fish platters accompanied by bagels and cream cheese. Or you might prefer a full meal consisting of pot roast and gravy, salad, homemade dinner rolls, potato pancakes, and fresh vegetables. Desserts run the gamut from rugelach cheesecake to Hungarian-style apple strudel, and available beverages include wine and beer, milk shakes, Dr. Brown's sodas, and chocolate egg creams.

INEXPENSIVE

La Piazza Food Court. Caesars Palace, 3570 Las Vegas Blvd. S., just north of Flamingo Rd. ☎ **702/731-7110.** Complete meals $7–$15. AE, DC, DISC, MC, V. Sun–Thurs 8:30am–11pm, Fri–Sat 9am–midnight. FOOD COURT.

Essentially an upscale cafeteria, this is a great choice for families. Food stations are located along an attractive arched walkway lit by pink neon, and the brass-railed dining area, under massive domes, is rather elegant, with gold-topped columns and

Great Meal Deals

We've already alluded to the rock-bottom budget meals and graveyard specials available at casino hotel restaurants. Quality not assured and Pepto-Bismol not provided. As prices and deals can change with no notice, we are just going to list a few recent examples. Your best bet is to keep your eyes open as you travel through town, as hotels tend to advertise their specials on their marquees. (For example, the **San Remo Hotel** was advertising a $4 prime rib special when we last went by.)

- **Binion's Horseshoe Coffeeshop:** A 16-ounce T-bone steak complete with salad, corn, and a baked potato, $6.75; served 4:45 to 11:45pm.
- **Holiday Inn Casino Boardwalk, Cyclone Coffee Shop:** For $7 your choice of either a 16-ounce porterhouse steak, 1 pound of crab legs, surf and turf combining the two, a full rack of baby-back ribs or prime rib, with baked potato, soup or salad, roll and butter.
- **Imperial Palace, Coffee Shop:** They have a night-owl prime-rib special, quite possibly the cheapest in town, $3; open 11pm to 7am.
- **Jackie Gaughan's Plaza, Plaza Diner:** Between 11pm and 11am, a graveyard special features a 16-ounce ham steak with two eggs, hash browns, toast, and coffee for $4.
- And, of course, all over town are 99¢ shrimp cocktails. Locals favor the one at the **Golden Gate Hotel;** we tried it and can say we safely survived the experience.

comfortable upholstered seating. The food is top quality—terrific deep-dish pizzas, an excellent salad bar, fresh-baked pies and cakes, sushi, smoked fish, immense burritos, Chinese stir-fry, rotisserie chicken, and a New York–style deli, **Häagen-Dazs** bars, and a selection of beverages that includes herbal teas, wine, beer, espresso, and cappuccino. Just about any single beverage you can think of, from virtually all over the world, you can find here. There's something for every dining mood. Waffle cones are baked on the premises, creating a delicious aroma.

5 North Strip

VERY EXPENSIVE

Monte Carlo Room. Desert Inn, 3145 Las Vegas Blvd. S., between Desert Inn Rd. and Sands Ave. ☎ **702/733-4444.** Reservations recommended. Jackets for men required. Main courses $28–$80. AE, CB, DC, DISC, JCB, MC, V. Thurs–Mon 6–11pm. FRENCH.

The delightful Monte Carlo Room is equally renowned for its sublime setting and fine French cuisine. The romantic main dining room has charming murals of Greek youths and nymphs lolling in a classical setting framed by rose bowers and Palladian windows overlooking the palm-fringed pool. The ceiling is painted with cupids frolicking amid fluffy clouds. Diners are comfortably ensconced in tapestried banquettes at tables illumined by white taper candles or pink-shaded crystal lamps.

Excellent appetizer choices include seafood ravioli with champagne-caviar sauce or a terrine of fresh goose liver. We also love the thick, velvety, cognac-laced lobster bisque, full of rich flavor, served in a scooped-out round loaf of bread. For your entree, consider a classic French entrecôte au poivre or duck à l'orange served with apple- and pine-nut–studded wild rice. A mélange of vegetables and a potato dish (perhaps pommes soufflés) accompany entrees. There's an extensive wine list; consult the sommelier for suggestions. Flaming tableside preparations are a specialty, including desserts such as crêpes Suzette and cherries jubilee.

Morton's of Chicago. 3200 Las Vegas Blvd. S., in the Fashion Show Mall (take Spring Mountain Rd. off the Strip, make a right at Fashion Show Dr., and follow the signs). ☎ **702/893-0703.** Reservations recommended. Main courses $18–$30. AE, CB, DC, JCB, MC, V. Mon–Sat 5:30–11pm, Sun 5–10pm. STEAK/SEAFOOD.

This famous gourmet steak chain has a warm, clublike interior. Ecru walls are hung with LeRoy Neiman prints and photographs of celebrity diners, rich mahogany paneling adds a note of substantial elegance, and much of the seating is in roomy, gold leather booths. An exhibition kitchen gleams with copper pots, and wines are stored in a brick-walled rack. Frequent power diners here include most hotel/casino owners as well as Strip entertainers Siegfried and Roy. Robert de Niro and Joe Pesci came in frequently during the filming of *Casino*, and, one night, Tony Curtis joined the wait staff in singing "Happy Birthday" to a guest.

Start off with an appetizer, perhaps a lump crabmeat cocktail with mustard-mayonnaise sauce. Entree choices include succulent prime Midwestern steaks prepared to your exact specifications, plus lemon oregano chicken, lamb chops, Sicilian veal, grilled swordfish, whole baked Maine lobster, and prime rib with creamed horseradish. Side orders such as flavorfully fresh al dente asparagus served with hollandaise or hash browns are highly recommended. Portions are bountiful; plan to share. A loaf of warm onion bread on every table is complimentary. Leave room for dessert, perhaps a Grand Marnier soufflé. There's an extensive wine list, and you may want to retreat to a sofa in the cozy mahogany-paneled bar/lounge for after-dinner drinks.

✪ **Phil's Angus Steakhouse.** 3120 Las Vegas Blvd. S., in the New Frontier Hotel. ☎ **702/794-8233.** Reservations recommended. Main courses $17–$33 (lobster $50). AE, DISC, MC, V. Wed–Sun 5–10pm. STEAK/SEAFOOD.

Every hotel has a steak house, but only a few are worth singling out. This one is so good, we can't wait to eat here again, and even have the menu all planned out. First of all, it's a relief to dine here, thanks to some terrific soundproofing. Though you are right on the edge of the casino, all the noise vanishes when you cross the threshold. The interior is like a library, if it were set in a train car. It's intimate and cozy, and you want to sit back in there and nurse a cognac all night long, particularly as you are pampered by the refined, well-trained staff.

The delicious lump crab cakes were interestingly combined with polenta and a spicy chile crème fraîche. That, and the scotch salmon, make excellent starters, as do the hearty, thick and yet somehow light soups. You can pick your steaks from a platter. The petit filet melts in the mouth, with just the right beef flavor and a béarnaise sauce that was the proper accompaniment. The porterhouse could literally be cut with a fork. Sides are ordered separately; the Yukon mashed potatoes with horseradish were quite tasty, and the sautéed spinach was perfectly done. For dessert, skip the tiramisù in favor of the crème caramel.

✪ **Top of the World.** Stratosphere Las Vegas Hotel, 2000 Las Vegas Blvd. S., between St. Louis St. and Baltimore Ave. ☎ **702/380-7711.** Reservations required. Main courses $13–$21 lunch, $21–$29 dinner. AE, CB, DC, DISC, JCB, MC, V. Daily 11am–3:45pm; Sun–Thurs 4–11pm, Fri–Sat 4pm–midnight. AMERICAN/CONTINENTAL.

Okay, revolving restaurants are the very definition of kitsch. But you know what? We like 'em. And when you've got views like these, well, there is a difference between having good taste and being made of stone.

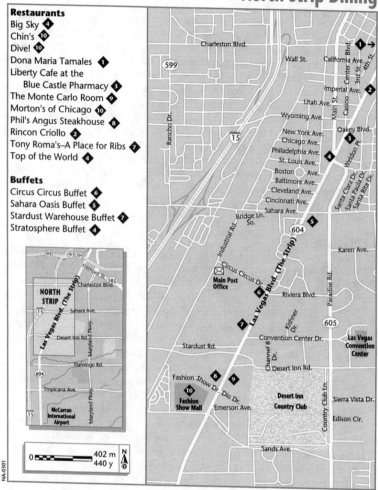

Restaurants
Big Sky ④
Chin's ⑩
Dive! ⑩
Dona Maria Tamales ①
Liberty Cafe at the
   Blue Castle Pharmacy ③
The Monte Carlo Room ⑨
Morton's of Chicago ⑩
Phil's Angus Steakhouse ⑧
Rincon Criollo ②
Tony Roma's–A Place for Ribs ⑦
Top of the World ④

Buffets
Circus Circus Buffet ⑥
Sahara Oasis Buffet ⑤
Stardust Warehouse Buffet ⑦
Stratosphere Buffet ④

Because you are 869 feet in the air, Vegas is stretched out before you in a glittering palette. Who knew this town could be so beautiful? This proves the Stratosphere is good for something. The Top of the World restaurant may not have the best food in Vegas (though some things are actually pretty good), but it has hands down the best view. (It takes about an hour for one revolution.) You will be so busy admiring the Strip, noticing that Vegas goes on much further than you thought, wondering which casino that particular cluster of lights is, and trying to spot your hotel, that you won't even notice what you are eating. It's one of the most romantic spots in town to dine.

But it's expensive, and the entrees, at least, not worth the cost. Having anticipated that customers might want to fill up tables just ordering a small snack, there is a $15 per person minimum. Here's what you do: Order only the generous-size appetizers and desserts. You won't be disappointed, and you can easily make the minimum. The menu changes, but recent appetizers included Southwestern spring rolls (think of a cross between an eggroll and a fajita) filled with chicken and veggies, slightly deep fried to a nice crunch, and served with a fine guacamole. It's tart, crunchy, messy, and fattening, which means it has to be good. There was also an oversized (to the point of silliness) bruschetta (chopped tomato, basil, and garlic covered in olive oil on huge toasted slices of bread) that was tasty if hard to eat. The salads are overpriced and overly fussy, while the entrees are not terribly imaginative. (The filet of almond-crusted salmon did get a thumbs-up on an earlier visit.) The desserts were stellar, with the stand-out being the expensive ($9) but easily shared by two (it's huge and rich) Chocolate Stratosphere Tower. Yep, a chocolate replica of the very building you are sitting in; the top part is filled with a terrific chocolate mousse, and the whole thing gets covered in chocolate sauce, poured by your waiter with great ceremony. It's a gimmick, but chocolate lovers will be thrilled. Additional happiness came with towering *vacherin*, layers of hazelnut meringue filled with Bavarian cream, garnished with fresh berries, and served with crème anglaise and kiwi and raspberry sauces. The service was also impeccable.

EXPENSIVE

✪ **Chin's.** 3200 Las Vegas Blvd. S., in the Fashion Show Mall (turn at the Frontier sign). ☎ **702/733-8899.** Reservations recommended. Main courses $10–$12 lunch, $10–$29.50 dinner. AE, DC, MC, V. Mon–Sat 11:30am–9:30pm, Sun noon–9:30pm. CHINESE.

Chin's has been a Vegas fixture for nearly 20 years and is consistently voted by locals in the *Las Vegas Review* as their favorite Chinese restaurant. It is certainly a surprise for anyone who knows Chinese food solely through take-out or strip malls. The simple, stark decor produces an ambience of low-key elegance. The prices will surprise you, too. This is not $1 Chinese food. But as owner Mr. Chin points out, Chinese food takes so much time to prepare (all that chopping, dicing, splicing, and what not) and to present in the traditionally stylish way (no steam trays here) that it's a wonder anyone would ever charge just a couple dollars for a dish.

Chin is justly proud of his achievements, but he adds as much to his restaurant as the food. You will see him moving from table to table, greeting regulars by name; do try to have him visit with you, if you can. He's full of stories, like how Jerry Lewis and Neil Sedaka are regulars, with a special dish created just for the latter (shrimp with lobster in lobster sauce, no vegetables).

However, anyone with broad experience with Chinese food won't find anything terribly surprising here. Experiments with more radical dishes failed (too-timid tourists?), and so the menu is on the safe side. Which is not to say it isn't good. Stand-outs include strawberry chicken (think lemon chicken but with a different fruit; Chin's created this twist on a familiar dish, and other local restaurants have copied it); an appetizer of sinful deep-fried shrimp puffs (stuffed with minced shrimp and mildly curried cream cheese); splendid spring rolls; and barbecued pork-fried rice that strikes that tricky, careful balance between dry and greasy.

MODERATE

Dive! 3200 Las Vegas Blvd. S., in the Fashion Show Mall. ☎ **702/369-DIVE.** Reservations for large parties only. Main courses $7–$14. AE, CB, DC, DISC, MC. V. Sun–Thurs 11:30am–10pm, Fri–Sat 11:30am–11pm. AMERICAN.

Notable for being one of the few theme restaurants not devoted to memorabilia, Dive! was partly created by Steven Spielberg and movie exec Jeffrey Katzenberg. The outside is admittedly quite fun: yellow submarine crashing through a 30-foot wall of water that cascades into an oversize pool erupting with depth-charge blasts. Its gunmetal-gray interior replicates the hull of a submarine with vaulted cylindrical ceilings, porthole-shaped (albeit neon-accented, since this is Vegas) windows, exposed conduits that burst with steam, sonar screens, and working periscopes. Every hour a high-tech show projected on a 16-cube video wall (and 48 additional monitors throughout the restaurant) simulates a fantasy submarine dive. And overhead, a luxury ocean liner, a manta ray research vessel, exotic fish, a fighting shark, and model subs circumnavigate the room on a computerized track. It's all whimsical and imaginative. Surprise—they serve submarine sandwiches (among other choices). Kids should love it and adults will find it slightly less annoying than, say, Chuck E. Cheese (and with somewhat more sophisticated food).

Tony Roma's—A Place for Ribs. Stardust Resort and Casino, 3000 Las Vegas Blvd. S., at Convention Center Dr. ☎ **702/732-6111.** Reservations not accepted. Main courses $8.25–$13; children's portions $5. AE, CB, DC, DISC, MC, V. Sun–Thurs 5–11pm, Fri–Sat 5pm–midnight. BARBECUE.

Tony Roma's is a popular national chain, and the company has voted this Stardust location the very best of its 140 franchises in terms of service, food quality, and cleanliness—so if you must eat at a chain, this is a satisfactory choice. It's a comfortable place, and a tub with brass faucets sits outside, so you can wash your sticky fingers upon exiting.

This is a great choice for family dining. The house specialty is meaty, fork-tender baby-back ribs barbecued in tangy sauce, but you can also order big, juicy beef ribs, honey- and molasses-basted, Carolina-style pork ribs, or spicy Cajun ribs. A sampler plate is available. There are also hearty platters of barbecued shrimp or chicken, burgers, the catch of the day, steaks, and salads. Consider a side order of onion rings (served in a loaf). Entrees come with coleslaw and a choice of baked potato, french fries, or ranch-style beans. The children's menu lists a choice of four meals in a basket—ribs, burgers, chicken fingers, or chicken drumstick and thighs, all served with fries. For dessert there are fresh-baked chocolate, coconut, and banana cream pies, and all bar drinks are available. There is another Tony Roma's Downtown, at **Sam Boyd's Fremont Hotel and Casino,** 200 E. Fremont St.

INEXPENSIVE

Big Sky Steak House. Stratosphere Las Vegas Hotel, 2000 Las Vegas Blvd. S., between St. Louis St. and Baltimore Ave. ☎ **702/780-7777.** Complete steak dinners from $10, all-you-can-eat barbecue dinner $13, free for children under 6. AE, CB, DC, DISC, JCB, MC, V. Sun–Thurs 5–11pm, Fri–Sat 5pm–midnight. BARBECUE.

Food bargains abound in Las Vegas, and this is one of the best. Big Sky features murals depicting the Old West, oil paintings of cowboys, log handrails, lasso-motif carpeting, and a cashier housed in a chuck wagon. All of this provides a suitably rustic setting for hearty all-you-can-eat family-style feasts. Country music helps set the tone, and service is down-home and friendly.

Entree choices include prime rib with creamed horseradish sauce and a barbecue combination (beef brisket, St. Louis ribs, Carolina-pulled pork, and fried chicken), and steaks. Whatever you select, it will come with a huge salad, scrumptious corn muffins (don't fill up on them; there's lots more food coming), corn on the cob, seasoned steak fries, coleslaw, Texas toast, and baked beans with pork. And when you've eaten your fill, you can waddle over to the dessert table and help yourself to apple cobbler, fresh berries and cream, and bread pudding with rum sauce. There's a full bar.

Dona Maria Tamales. 910 Las Vegas Blvd. S., corner of Charleston Blvd. ☎ **702/382-6538.** Main courses $5.45–$8 breakfast, $6–$13 lunch or dinner. AE, CB, MC, V. Sun–Thurs 8am–10pm, Fri–Sat 8am–11pm. MEXICAN.

Decorated with Tijuana-style Mayan quiltwork and calendars, this is your quintes-sential Mexican diner, convenient to both the north end of the Strip and Down-town. They use lots of lard, lots of cheese, and lots of sauce. As a result, the food is really good—and really fattening. Yep, those health reports showing how bad Mex-ican food can be for your heart probably did some research here. That just makes it all the better, in our opinion. Locals apparently agree; even at lunchtime the place is crowded.

You will start off with homemade chips and a spicy salsa served in a mortar. Meals are so large that it shouldn't be a problem getting full just ordering off the sides, which can make this even more of a budget option. Naturally, the specialty is the fantastic tamales, which come in red, green, cheese, or sweet. They also serve up excellent enchiladas, chile relleños, burritos, and fajitas. All dinners include rice, beans, tortillas, and soup or salad. Sauces are heavy but oh so good. For dessert they have flan, fried ice cream, and Mexican-style pumpkin pie and sweet-potato pie.

✪ **Liberty Cafe at the Blue Castle Pharmacy.** 1700 S. Las Vegas Blvd. ☎ **702/383-0101.** Reservations not accepted. Nothing over $6.50. No credit cards. 24 hours. DINER.

You can go to any number of retro soda fountain replicas (such as Johnny Rockets) and theme restaurants that pretend to be cheap diners, but why bother when the (admittedly, decidedly unflashy) real thing is just past the end of the Strip? The soda fountain/lunch counter at the Blue Castle Pharmacy was Las Vegas's first 24-hour restaurant, and it has been going strong for 60 years. Plunk down at the counter, and watch the cooks go nuts trying to keep up with the orders. The menu is basic comfort food: standard grill items (meat loaf, ground round steak, chops), fluffy cream pies, and classic breakfasts served "anytime"—try the biscuits and cream gravy at 3am. They also serve gyros and the like. But the best bet is a one-third-pound burger and "thick creamy shake," both the way they were meant to be and about as good as they get. At around $5, this is half what you would pay for a com-parable meal at the Hard Rock Cafe. And as waitress Beverly says, "This is really real." Places like this are a vanishing species—it's worth the short walk from the Stratosphere.

Rincon Criollo. 1145 Las Vegas Blvd. S. ☎ **702/388-1906.** Reservations not accepted. Main courses $6.50–$10, paella (for 3) $20. AE, DISC, MC, V. Tues–Sun 11am–10pm. CUBAN.

Located beyond the wedding chapels on Las Vegas Boulevard, Rincon Criollo has all the right details for a good, cheap ethnic joint: full of locals and empty of frills. It's not the best Cuban food ever, but it gets the job done. The main courses (fea-turing Cuban pork and chicken specialties) are hit and miss; try the marinated pork leg or, better still, ask your server for a recommendation. Paella is offered, but only for parties of three or more (and starts at $20). The side-course *chorizo* (a spicy sausage) is excellent, and the Cuban sandwich (roast pork, ham, and cheese on bread, which is then pressed and flattened out) is huge and tasty. For only $3.50, the latter makes a fine change-of-pace meal.

6 East of the Strip

In this section we've covered restaurants close by the Convention Center, along with those farther south on Paradise Road, Flamingo Road, and Tropicana Avenue.

VERY EXPENSIVE

Bistro Le Montrachet. Las Vegas Hilton, 3000 Paradise Rd. ☎ **702/732-5111.** Reserva-tions suggested. Main courses $23–$46. AE, CB, DC, DISC, JCB, MC, V. Wed–Mon 6–10:30pm. FRENCH.

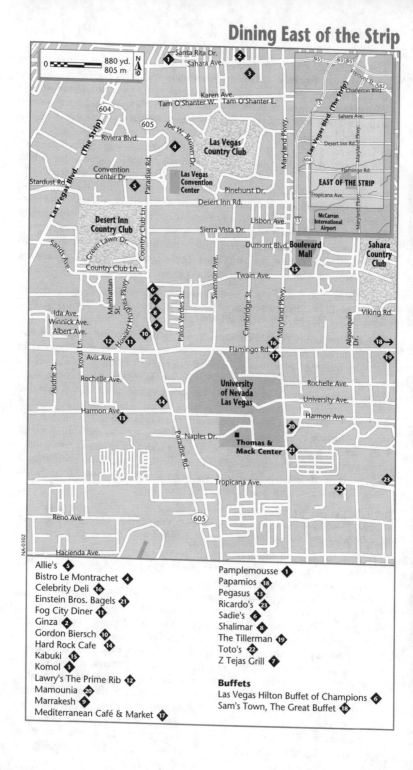

Allie's **5**
Bistro Le Montrachet **4**
Celebrity Deli **16**
Einstein Bros. Bagels **21**
Fog City Diner **11**
Ginza **2**
Gordon Biersch **10**
Hard Rock Cafe **14**
Kabuki **15**
Komol **3**
Lawry's The Prime Rib **12**
Mamounia **20**
Marrakesh **9**
Mediterranean Café & Market **17**

Pamplemousse **1**
Papamios **18**
Pegasus **13**
Ricardo's **23**
Sadie's **6**
Shalimar **8**
The Tillerman **19**
Toto's **22**
Z Tejas Grill **7**

Buffets
Las Vegas Hilton Buffet of Champions **6**
Sam's Town, The Great Buffet **18**

This ultraelegant French restaurant seats diners under a dome bathed in a flattering pink light, an effect enhanced by the discreet glow emanating from shaded Chinese lamps. The room centers on a templelike circle of massive walnut columns wherein a large floral arrangement graces an ornate marble table. Rich, mahogany-paneled walls are hung with landscapes and still-lifes; a crystal chandelier and beveled mirrors add sparkle.

Dishes are exquisitely presented and prepared. You might begin with chilled duck foie gras served on toast points. Also noteworthy are creamy lobster bisque and the salad "Le Montrachet," a refreshing mélange of Belgian endive, watercress, julienned beets, and enoki mushrooms in a Gorgonzola/walnut oil dressing. Entree choices range from roasted breast of Muscovy duck (served with white and black beans and currants in a crème de cassis sauce) to broiled live Maine lobster removed from the shell and served atop herbed Moroccan couscous with crab dressing and drawn butter. Among desserts, we're partial to the rich crème brûlée complemented by seasonal fruits, berries, and petits fours. The restaurant's wine cellar stocks more than 400 wines from vineyards spanning the globe.

Pegasus. Alexis Park Resort, 375 E. Harmon Ave., between Koval Lane and Paradise Rd. ☎ **702/796-3300.** Reservations recommended. Main courses $13–$19. AE, DC, DISC, MC, V. Daily 6–10pm. MEDITERRANEAN/ITALIAN.

This low-key luxury resort attracts many visiting celebrities and Strip headliners, and its premier restaurant is a fitting venue for such an upscale clientele. Its splashing fountains and mist of diffused lighting on etched mirrors make us feel like we're dining in an underwater kingdom. Planters of greenery, pots of ferns, and a large floral centerpiece further beautify this serene setting, as does a wall of arched windows overlooking a fountain-splashed rock garden.

A new menu features Mediterranean and Italian dishes, all with a gourmet flair. Options include Italian pasta and bean soup, lobster wonton and shrimp eggroll (very Italian!), and California-style pizzas (all under $10). Main courses include fresh ahi tuna; fresh salmon fillet grilled or poached and laced with a citrus-and-dill beurre blanc; chicken ravioli; and steak. There's an extensive wine list (including many Italian wines) with choices in varying price ranges.

✪ **The Tillerman.** 2245 E. Flamingo Rd., at Channel 10 Dr., just west of Eastern Ave. ☎ **702/731-4036.** Reservations recommended. Main courses $20–$39. AE, CB, DC, DISC, MC, V. Daily 5–11pm; bar/lounge until midnight. STEAK/SEAFOOD.

The Tillerman is on any number of locals "best of Vegas" lists, and while we agree the food is terrific, the high prices and somewhat snooty attitude make us feel we can spend our money better elsewhere.

Of the four main seating rooms, the center is the best, with a high ceiling and filled with plants, trees, and a huge circular stained-glass window. There's additional seating on the mezzanine level, where diners enjoy treetop views. The meal begins with a relish tray and a basket of delicious oven-fresh breads. Also complimentary is a Lazy Susan salad bar served at your table with a choice of homemade dressings, including a memorable chunky blue cheese. Portions are immense, so appetizers are really not necessary, but then again, they're too good to pass up. Especially notable: crab cake garnished with carrot chips, superb filet medaillons in a spicy red sauce, and yellowfin tuna blackened and served almost rare in a spicy mustard sauce. For entrees, regulars most often order the crab legs, which are excellent, as is the swordfish and halibut. Try also the shrimp in garlic cream sauce. The wine list is huge but expensive; the cheapest glass is $8. After such a large meal, a lighter dessert like the

Have You Heard the One About the Belly Dancer?

If you have never tried Moroccan food, you should. Not only are you in for some new taste treats, but the action-packed presentation and gluttonous portions are very appropriate to Vegas. A full Moroccan feast (which is what most U.S. Moroccan restaurants feature) is an event. Vegas has two notable Moroccan establishments: **Marrakech,** 3900 Paradise Rd., at Howard Hughes Dr. (☎ **702/737-5611**), where a six-course meal will cost you $25 per person (reservations recommended; American Express, Discover, Diners Club, MasterCard, Visa accepted; open Monday to Sunday 5:30 to 11pm); and **Mamounia,** 4632 S. Maryland Pkwy., between Harmon and Tropicana avenues (☎ **702/ 597-0092**), where a Moroccan feast will set you back $23 per person (reservations recommended; American Express, Discover, MasterCard, Visa accepted; open daily 5 to 11pm).

Both rooms are covered, floor to ceiling, with Moroccan (or Moroccan style) rugs, furnished with low tables made of intricately inlaid wood (from the town of Essaouria). There is some simple tilework on the walls at Marrakech. It all adds up to that Arabian nights den of thieves feel. Diners sit on cushions on the floor or on very low cushioned benches.

Oh, and you eat with your fingers. Yep, that's part of the fun. A waiter comes out and pours water into a brass bowl so that you can wash your hands and passes out huge towels for your lap. You then start a multicourse feast, beginning with a trio of cold salads: marinated carrots, eggplant and tomato and cucumber. Use the bread supplied from a big basket to scoop it up. The salads are relatively simple and supremely tasty. This is followed by shrimp in a garlic sauce that seems more Italian than Moroccan (peculiarly, both restaurants feature this out-of-place item). But if you like garlic and shrimp, you won't complain too much. Next is *b'stilla,* a truly amazing dish if done right. Layers of filo are interspersed with chicken, eggs, and nuts; the whole thing is topped by powdered sugar and cinnamon. The uninitiated raise their eyebrows at it, while their more informed companions dig in. After you try it, you will fight for more than your fair share too. The final course is some kind of fowl (chicken or Cornish game hen), usually in a wonderful lemon and olive sauce. You finish up with some sweet mint tea, poured with great ceremony. All of this adds up to way too much food, so those cushions come in handy as you roll on the floor, holding your stomach and moaning. But what's that sound? It's the belly dancer, who has come out to dazzle you with her gravity-defying shimmy skills, to get the crowd going in a conga line (or, unfortunately, the Macarena), and to accept a tip or two.

This experience is roughly the same at the two restaurants (though it's a lot more fun when the establishment is full; when the belly dancer emerges, a party atmosphere follows), but the food at Marrakech is considerably better. However, they found that the b'stilla was too strange for many patrons, so they turned it into a dessert with a fruit filling; they will make it with chicken if you ask when ordering; trust us and do. In its favor, the Mamounia offers à la carte items (Marrakech is considering this), so you can try other Moroccan specialties such as tajines, which are delicious stews cooked in clay pots.

Bavarian creme with strawberries, might be in order. Skip the carrot cake in favor of the divine chocolate eclair.

ⓘ Family-Friendly Restaurants

Buffets   Cheap meals for the whole family. The kids can choose what they like, and there are sometimes make-your-own sundae machines.

Dive! (see p. 132)   Housed in a submarine and featuring a zany high-tech show every hour projected on a video wall, this is the most fun family-oriented spot of all.

Rain Forest Cafe (see p. 120)   This is like eating in the Jungle Book Ride at Disneyland. Animals howl, thunder wails, everywhere there is something to marvel at, there is a decent kids' menu, and they might even learn a little bit about ecology and the environment.

Hard Rock Cafe (see p. 140)   Kids adore this restaurant, which throbs with excitement and is filled with rock memorabilia.

Planet Hollywood (see p. 128)   This popular chain houses a veritable museum of movie memorabilia, and the action on numerous video monitors keeps kids from getting bored.

Pink Pony   This bubble-gum pink circus-motif 24-hour coffee shop at Circus Circus will appeal to kids. And Mom and Dad can linger over coffee while the kids race upstairs to watch circus acts and play carnival games.

Sherwood Forest Cafe   Kids love to climb on the lavender dragons fronting this 24-hour coffee shop at Excalibur, and they also enjoy numerous child-oriented activities while you're on the premises.

EXPENSIVE

✪ **Lawry's The Prime Rib.** 4043 Howard Hughes Pkwy., at Flamingo Rd., between Paradise Rd. and Koval Lane. ☎ **702/893-2223.** Reservations recommended. Main courses $20–$30. AE, DC, DISC, JCB, MC, V. Sun–Thurs 5–10pm, Fri–Sat 5–11pm. STEAK/SEAFOOD.

If you love prime rib, come here. If you could take or leave prime rib, Lawry's will turn you into a believer. Because Lawry's does one thing, and it does it better than anyone else. Lawry's first opened in Los Angeles in 1938 and still remains a popular tradition. Originally, all Lawry's offered was prime rib, which they did perfectly and with tremendous style. Over the years, they have added three branches, the most recent landing in Las Vegas at the beginning of 1997. Yes, you can get prime rib all over town for under $5. But that's a tuna fish sandwich to Lawry's caviar (if one might mix food metaphors).

Eating at Lawry's is a ceremony, with all the parts played the same for the last 60 years. Waitresses in brown-and-white English maid uniforms, complete with starched white cap, take your order—for side dishes, that is. The real decision, what cut of rib you are going to have, comes later. Actually, that's the only part of the tradition that has changed. Lawry's has added fresh fish (halibut, salmon, or swordfish, depending on the evening) to its menu. Anyway, you tell the waitress what side dishes you might want (sublime creamed spinach, baked potato) for an extra price. Later, she returns with a spinning salad bowl (think of salad preparation as a Busby Berkeley musical number). The bowl, resting on crushed ice, spins as she pours Lawry's special dressing in a stream from high over her head. Tomatoes garnish. Applause follows. Eventually, giant metal carving carts (designed after the original ones) come to your table, bearing the meat. You name your cut (the regular Lawry's, the extra-large Diamond Jim Brady, only for serious carnivores, and the wimpy thin English cut), rare, medium, well. It comes with terrific Yorkshire pudding, nicely browned and not soggy, and some creamed horseradish that is combined with fluffy whipped cream, simultaneously sweet and tart.

Flavorful, tender, perfectly cooked, lightly seasoned, this will be the best prime rib you will ever have. Okay, maybe that's going too far, but the rest is accurate, honest. It just has to be tasted to be believed. You can finish off with a rich dessert (English trifle is highly recommended), but it almost seems pointless. Incidentally, the other Lawry's are decorated English-manor style, but the Vegas branch has instead tried to re-create a 1930s restaurant, with art deco touches all around and big-band music on the sound system.

Pamplemousse. 400 E. Sahara Ave., between Santa Paula and Santa Rita drives, just east of Paradise Rd. ☎ **702/733-2066.** Reservations required. Main courses $17.50–$24.50. AE, CB, DC, DISC, MC, V. Seatings daily at 6–6:30pm and 9–9:30pm. FRENCH.

Evoking a cozy French countryside inn, Pamplemousse is a catacomb of low-ceilinged rooms and intimate dining nooks with rough-hewn beams. Copperware and provincial pottery adorn the walls; candlelit tables, beautifully appointed with Villeroy and Boch show plates and fresh flowers, are draped in pale-pink linen; and classical music or light jazz plays softly in the background. It's all very charming and un-Vegasy. There's additional seating in a small garden sheltered by a striped tent. The restaurant's name, which means grapefruit, was suggested by the late singer Bobby Darin, one of the many celebrity pals of owner Georges La Forge. Strip headliners Wayne Newton, Robert Goulet, Siegfried and Roy, and Englebert Humperdinck are regulars.

The menu, which changes nightly, is recited by your waiter. The meal always begins with a large complimentary basket of crudités (about 10 different crisp, fresh vegetables), a big bowl of olives, and, a nice country touch, a basket of hard-boiled eggs. From there, you might proceed to an appetizer of lightly floured bay scallops sautéed in buttery grapefruit sauce, followed by an entree of crispy duck breast and banana in a sauce of orange honey, dark rum, and crème de banane. Filet mignon, New York steak, and rack of lamb are always featured. For dessert, perhaps there'll be homemade dark chocolate ice cream with pralines in a sabayon sauce. An extensive, well-rounded wine list complements the menu.

MODERATE

✪ **Allie's American Grille.** 325 Convention Center Dr., in Marriott Suites. ☎ **702/650-2000.** Main courses $8.25–$15, sandwiches $6–$9.25. AE, CB, DC, DISC, MC, V. Mon–Fri 6:30am–10:30pm, Sat–Sun 7am–10pm. SOUTHWESTERN.

Don't miss this little treasure. Tucked away on the other side of the bar in the Marriott Suites, Allie's is a coffee shop at breakfast time, but for lunch and dinner it turns into a cafe with a delightful menu best described as nouveau Southwestern. Check out the chicken portobello quesadilla appetizer, or the Pacific Rim yellowfin tuna salad—tuna on crispy Asian vegetables. The salmon BLT is a seared salmon steak over an inch thick with delicious maple pepper bacon, Grey Poupon sauce, and lovely leafy lettuce on a toasted brioche. Served with french fries and a cilantro coleslaw, it was a delicious, inventive take on an old favorite. The salmon was fresh and all the flavors combined perfectly. The rigatoni primavera had fresh spinach, asparagus, and tomatoes in a light, creamy sauce. There is a lovely dessert menu featuring a genuine root-beer float.

Ginza. 1000 E. Sahara Ave., between State St. and Maryland Pkwy. ☎ **702/732-3080.** Reservations for large parties only. Main courses $12.55–$17.50. AE, DC, MC, V. Tues–Sun noon–10pm. JAPANESE.

For almost 2 decades, this charming little restaurant has attracted a devoted clientele of local Japanese and Japanese food aficionados. There's a sushi bar in the front room, and the main dining area has shoji screen–covered windows, tables sheltered by shingled eaves, rice paper lighting fixtures, and cream walls adorned with Japanese fans, paintings, and prints. Four spacious, red-leather booths are the sole concession to Las Vegas style.

You might begin with a shared appetizer of tempura shrimp and vegetables. Entrees such as beef, chicken, or salmon sprinkled with sesame seeds in a thick teriyaki sauce come with soup (miso or egg flower), salad, and green tea. Sushi is a highlight, and there are about 30 à la carte selections from which to choose. Be sure to try an appetizer or entree portion of Ginza's unique Vegas rolls: salmon, tuna, yellowtail, and avocado rolled with seaweed in sesame-studded rice and quickly deep-fried so that the sesame seeds form a crunchy crust. It's served with lemon soy sauce. Also delicious are seaweed-wrapped California rolls. The fish is extremely fresh, and everything here is made from scratch. A bottle of sake is recommended. For dessert there's lemon sherbet or ginger and green tea ice creams.

Gordon-Biersch Brewing Company. 3987 Paradise Rd., just north of Flamingo. ☎ **702/ 312-5247.** Main courses $11–$16. AE, DISC, MC, V. Sun–Thurs 11:30am–10pm, Fri–Sat 11:30am–11pm; bar open until 2am. CALIFORNIA.

This is a traditional brew pub (exposed piping and ducts, but the place is still comfortable and casual), but it's worth going to for a nosh as well. The menu is pub fare meets California cuisine (kids will probably find the food too complicated), and naturally, there are a lot of beers (German-styled lagers) to choose from. Appetizers include satays, pot stickers, calamari, baby-back ribs, delicious beer-battered onion rings, and amazing garlic-encrusted fries. A wood-burning pizza oven turns out California-type toppings—eggplant, shrimp, and so forth. For lunch, there are various pastas, stir-fries, sandwiches, and salads. The dinner menu eliminates the sandwiches and adds rosemary chicken, steaks, fish items, and, just in case you forgot it was a brew pub type joint, beer everything: beer-glazed ham, beer meat loaf, beer BBQ glazed ribs. Doesn't that make you want to order a glass of milk?

Hard Rock Cafe. 4475 Paradise Rd., at Harmon Ave. ☎ **702/733-8400.** Reservations not accepted. Main courses $9–$17; burgers and sandwiches $7.60–8.75. AE, DC, MC, V. Sun–Thurs 11am–11:30pm, Fri–Sat 11am–midnight. AMERICAN.

The original Hard Rock Cafe opened in London as a meeting place for American expatriates and homesick exchange students dying for a good burger. T-shirts then simply said "Hard Rock Cafe," with no identifying city. No need for one. Now that Hard Rocks are everywhere (can it be long before there is one in Tibet?), the cachet is gone.

But this is the only Hard Rock (so far) attached to a hotel and a truly extraordinary casino, so let's cut this branch some slack. Allegedly, some stars do eat here; it's not out of the question because if a big rock act is playing in town, they will be playing at the Hard Rock. And staying there. So it is not at all uncommon to see them wandering the lobby or getting dealt a hand at the blackjack tables. Eating there? Well, sure, maybe. Sheryl Crow, Michael Keaton, The Ramones, Pat Benatar, and Eddie Van Halen have been spotted there over time.

The menu offers some good salads in addition to the burgers. An inexpensive children's menu is a plus for families. Don't be frightened by the line outside—it's usually not for the restaurant but the on-premises Hard Rock merchandise store. The Hard Rock Hotel and Casino is next door (see chapter 5).

Kabuki. 1150 E. Twain at Maryland Pkwy. ☎ **702/733-0066.** Reservations required on weekend nights. Main courses $7–$17. AE, CB, DC, DISC, MC, V. Mon–Sat 11:30am–2pm and 5–10pm. JAPANESE.

Primarily catering to a Japanese clientele, walking into the Kabuki is like getting a taste of Japan. Rice paper covers the windows of this tastefully converted diner while various paintings of Japanese Kabuki actors cover the walls. The service is excellent, starting your meal off with a warm towel and green tea. Yes, they do have a small sushi bar, but what the locals (who voted this their favorite Japanese restaurant in a recent *Review Journal* poll) come back for are the Japanese dishes. Negi Ma, a teriyaki-marinated beef rolled with onions, and Yaki Gyoza (pot stickers) are both amazing starters. For the main course, try Zarusoba (cold Japanese buckwheat noodles), beef and chicken teriyaki, or Tatsuta Age (marinated chicken). They have plenty of sushi specials, including yellowtail, shrimp, and calamari, but there are other sushi places in town that do it better, admittedly in some cases for a higher price.

Komol. 953 E. Sahara, in the Commercial Center. ☎ **702/731-6542.** Reservations accepted. Main courses $5.60–$11. AE, DISC, MC, V. Daily 11am–10pm. THAI.

Locals feel this is the best Thai restaurant in town. It certainly is a hole-in-the-wall dive, like all good ethnic places. The menu is pretty large, divided into different sections for poultry, beef, and pork, plus a separate section for vegetarian dishes, plus many rice and noodle selections. They will spice to your specifications. Unless you know your spicy Asian food, it might be best to play it on the safe side. While we don't want things bland, too much heat can overwhelm all other flavors. The mild to medium packs enough of a kick for most people.

Among the items tried during a recent visit was a vegetarian green curry and the *Pud-kee-mao* (flat rice noodles stir-fried with ground chicken, mint, garlic, and hot peppers). *Nam Sod* is ground pork with a hot-and-sour sauce, ginger, and peanuts, all of which you wrap up in lettuce leaves—sort of an Asian burrito. Sort of. The Thai iced tea was particularly good—just the right amount of sweetness and tea taste for a drink that is often overly sweet.

Worth noting, the Commercial Center also has any number of other ethnic (mostly Asian) restaurants, including Korean barbecue.

Papamios Italian Kitchen. Sam's Town, 5111 Boulder Hwy., at Flamingo Rd. ☎ **702/454-8041.** Reservations recommended. Main courses $6.25–$14; pizzas $7.45–$9. Weekend brunch $14. AE, CB, DC, DISC, MC, V. Sun 4:30–10:30pm, Mon–Thurs 5–10pm, Fri–Sat 5–11pm; Sun brunch 9am–2pm. ITALIAN.

Make dinner or brunch here an occasion to visit Sam's Town, and, if possible, snag a table on the festive veranda overlooking verdant Mystic Falls Park, the enclosed atrium with fern gullies, babbling brooks, and gushing waterfalls. You don't have to worry about the weather; in this vast climate-controlled park, it's always 70°F. The veranda is a great venue for viewing nightly laser shows. And Papamios's interior is also appealing—casually elegant, with dining areas defined by Corinthian-colonnaded archways, checker-clothed tables lit by oil lamps, and strings of colored lights suspended overhead.

An appetizer of roasted mushrooms and fried polenta topped with buffalo mozzarella makes a great beginning. Entrees, served with salad, include shrimp scampi on a bed of angel-hair pasta; veal marsala with spinach and tiger-striped mushroom ravioli; and linguine tossed with shrimp, mussels, and lobster in lemon/champagne Alfredo sauce with fresh tomato garnish. Tiramisù is the house specialty dessert. More than a dozen wines are offered by the glass.

Weekend brunches here are also lovely. They feature bountiful buffets (with shrimp and crab, salads, fruits, and breakfast pastries), a glass of champagne, and a choice of entrees ranging from grilled baby lamb chops with pineapple relish to huevos rancheros.

Ricardo's. 2380 Tropicana Ave., at Eastern Ave. (northwest corner). ☎ **702/798-4515.** Reservations recommended. Main courses $7.50–$13; lunch buffet $7.25; children's plates $3–$4, including milk or soft drink with complimentary refills. AE, CB, DC, DISC, MC, V. Sun–Thurs 11am–10pm, Fri–Sat 11am–11pm. MEXICAN.

This hacienda-style restaurant is a great favorite with locals. It has several stucco-walled dining rooms separated by arched doorways—all of them lovely, with candlelit oak tables and booths upholstered in Aztec prints. One room is a plant-filled greenhouse, another a garden room under a lofty pine-beamed ceiling. Yet a third dining area has a ceramic-tiled fireplace (ablaze in winter) and a dark wood coffered ceiling. Strolling Mexican musicians entertain at night.

Start off with an appetizer of deep-fried battered chicken wings served with melted Cheddar (ask for jalapeños if you like your cheese sauce hotter). Nachos smothered with cheese and guacamole are also very good here. For an entree, you can't go wrong with chicken, beef, or pork fajitas served sizzling on a hot skillet atop sautéed onions, mushrooms, and peppers; they come with rice and beans, tortillas, a selection of salsas, guacamole, and tomato wedges with cilantro. All the usual taco/enchilada/tamale combinations are also listed. A delicious dessert is *helado* Las Vegas: ice cream rolled in corn flakes and cinnamon, deep-fried, and served with honey and whipped cream. Be sure to order a pitcher of Ricardo's great margaritas. The same menu is available all day, but a buffet is offered at lunch. The kids' menu on a placemat with games and puzzles features both Mexican and American fare.

✪ **Shalimar.** 3900 S. Paradise Rd., in the Citibank Plaza. ☎ **702/796-0302.** Reservations recommended. Lunch buffet $7.50; dinner main courses $10.50–$16. AE, DISC, MC, V. Mon–Fri 11:30am–2:30pm and 5:30–10:30pm; Sat–Sun 5:30–10:30pm. INDIAN.

In a town full of buffet deals, it's hard to get excited about another one, but on the other hand, all those other buffet deals offer pretty much the identical food: carving stations, various cafeteria hot dishes, and so forth. Here at Shalimar, a lunch buffet means about two dozen different North Indian–style dishes. All for about $7.50. It's not as colorful or huge (in fact, it's just a table covered with steam trays) as those buffets up the street, but it is far more interesting and different. It's also a great deal and one of the first places to run to if you are sick of Strip food. Just ask the locals, who voted it their favorite ethnic restaurant in the *Las Vegas Review Journal*'s annual poll.

The buffet usually includes *tandoori* (chicken marinated in spiced yogurt cooked in a clay oven), *marsala* (tandoori in a curry sauce), *naan* (the flat Indian bread), and various vegetable dishes. (Vegetarians will find plenty to eat here—they offer special veggie dishes daily.) One stand-out at a recent visit was the *Bengan Bharta* (eggplant diced fine and cooked with onions, tomatoes, and spices). There was also a yellow squash curry that was outrageously good. The tandoori chicken was perfect, tender, and moist. (Tandoori, by the way, is a very low-fat way of preparing chicken.) In the evening, a full Indian menu, with *vindaloo* (an especially hot curry where the meat is marinated in vinegar), flavored naans (try the garlic or onion), and other Indian specialties are offered à la carte. They will spice to order: mild, medium, hot, or very hot. If you make a mistake, you can always order *raita* (yogurt mixed with mild spices and cucumber); it cools your mouth nicely.

The restaurant has managed to spruce up its strip mall corner nicely, thanks to some Indian-style metal hanging lamps and peaked archways.

Z Tejas Grill. 3824 Paradise Rd., between Twain Ave. and Corporate Dr. ☎ **702/732-1660.**
Reservations recommended. Main courses $7.25–$12 lunch, $8.75–$17 dinner. AE, CB, DC,
DISC, JCB, MC, V. Daily 11am–11pm. TEX-MEX.

This Austin, Texas–based restaurant's rather odd name came about because its original chef, a Frenchman, kept referring to it as "zee" Tejas Grill. Featuring self-proclaimed "South by Southwestern" cuisine, it recently got a handsome makeover, lining the interior with stream-lined warm woods and black accents. There is a vine-covered patio for outdoor dining, rare for Vegas, with misters for summer and a fireplace and heaters for winter. For some reason, traffic noise does not permeate from the nearby street. You might also consider downing some large and excellent margaritas at the newly enlarged, very lively bar, particularly on weeknights, when happy hour (4–7pm) finds all starters half price. Given the size of said starters, this would be a very cheap meal option. In particular, we like the generously portioned grilled fish tacos, which come wrapped in fresh tortillas, stuffed with all kinds of veggies and served with a spicy Japanese sauce. Not your usual drippy, fattening tacos. Less of a bargain but mighty tasty is the tender and piquant black sesame tuna, with a black peppercorn vinaigrette and a soy mustard sauce. There is a larger version of this found under the entrees, called "Voodoo Tuna"—it's not quite as good. A better choice would be the spicy grilled Jamaican jerk chicken, nuanced with lime and served with peanut sauce and rum-spiked coconut-banana ketchup; it comes with two side dishes—when we were there, garlic mashed potatoes and a corn casserole soufflé.

INEXPENSIVE

Celebrity Deli. 4055 S. Maryland Pkwy., at Flamingo Rd. ☎ **702/733-7827.** Reservations
not accepted. Main courses $7–$12. Mon–Sat 9am–8pm, Sun 9am–4pm. AE, MC, V.
DELI.

A basic, solid New York deli, lacking the mammoth portions of the Stage Deli (though perhaps that's a good thing) but lacking also the occasionally mammoth prices of same. It also does not require navigating the Strip and the Caesars Forum Shops (which means it's more convenient for those staying at accommodations east of the Strip)—and, in many ways, it's more authentic, from its revolving pastry case to the middle-aged waitresses with thick foundation and thicker ankles who shout your order back to the kitchen. The clientele are classic Vegas characters, of an age to have been fans of the youthful Paul Anka. If you are lucky, you might sit next to a table full of dealers swapping war stories about their pit bosses.

As mentioned, these are not the monster portions of modern-day chain delis, but you won't go hungry. Don't look for anything vegetarian here; instead, you got your pastrami on rye, your matzo ball soup, chopped liver, tongue, meat loaf, lox and bagel, etc. Desserts are a bit sparse for a deli, but you can't go wrong with the black-and-white cookies. Go ahead—have a nosh.

Einstein Bros. Bagels. 4624 S. Maryland Pkwy., between Harmon and Tropicana aves., in
the University Gardens Shopping Center. ☎ **702/795-7800.** All items under $6. MC, V.
Mon–Sat 6am–8pm (until 5pm in summer), Sun 7am–5pm. BAGELS.

You may not like digging into an enormous buffet first thing in the morning, and continental breakfast in a hotel is usually a rip-off. A welcome alternative is a fresh-baked bagel, of which there are 15 varieties here—everything from onion to wild blueberry. Cream cheeses also come in many flavors, anything from sun-dried tomato to vegetable and jalapeño. Einstein's is a pleasant place for the morning meal, with both indoor seating and outdoor tables cooled by misters. Service is friendly, and four special-blend coffees are available each day.

Note: Bagel buffs might also want to check out the nearby **Bagelmania** at 855 Twain Ave. (☎ 702/369-3322). It has the advantage (or disadvantage, depending on your point of view) of not being a chain like Einstein, but the bagels are sometimes chilled for freshness, which is heresy. Avoid this problem by catching them early in the morning, when their extensive selection is hot and fresh.

✪ **Mediterranean Café & Market.** 4147 S. Maryland Pkwy., at Flamingo Rd., in the Tiffany Square strip mall. ☎ **702/731-6030.** Reservations not accepted. Main courses $4–$13 (all sandwiches under $5). AE, DISC, MC, V. Mon–Sat 11am–9pm. MEDITERRANEAN.

It is an immeasurable thrill to find this totally authentic, mom-and-pop Middle Eastern restaurant in Las Vegas, where high-quality ethnic eateries are scarce. When the weather's cool, it's pleasant to sit out front under the umbrellas. Inside, tables are covered with fruit-motif plastic cloths, walls adorned with Mediterranean landscapes (paintings and photographs) and Persian miniatures; a plastic grape arbor girds the room, and shelves are cluttered with inlaid ivory boxes, hookahs, and brassware. Background music is Greek, Turkish, and Arabic.

Everything here is homemade and delicious. You might order up a gyro (slivers of rotisseried beef and lamb enfolded into a pita with lettuce and tomato). Other good choices are a filo pie layered with spinach and feta cheese, served with hummus; skewers of grilled chicken and vegetable kabobs with lavash bread and hummus; and a combination platter of hummus, tabbouleh, stuffed grape leaves, and falafel. All entrees come with pita bread and salad. Try a side order of *bourrani* (creamy yogurt dip mixed with steamed spinach, sautéed garlic, and slivered almonds). Finish up with baklava and rich Turkish coffee. Wine and beer are available. You can also come by in the morning for Middle Eastern breakfasts. A Mediterranean market adjoins.

Sadie's Soul Kitchen. 505 E. Twain and Paradise Rd. ☎ **702/796-4177.** Reservations recommended. Main courses $7–$12. MC, V. Mon–Thurs 11am–9pm, Fri–Sat 11am–9:30pm, Sun noon–5:30pm. SOUL FOOD.

Yes, there is a Sadie and you can find her cooking in the kitchen of this authentic soul-food establishment. Its uninspired, mall Chinese restaurant decor doesn't look like much, and may make you think the food will match. That would be a mistake. Sadie has cooked all over the world and has been making Las Vegas happy for 7 years now. Beef, pork, and chicken come fried, smothered, or barbecued and you can't go wrong with any. Smothered means the lovely fried stuff is covered in a thick, delicious brown gravy—a half chicken portion of same adds up to a lot of food. Sadie's BBQ sauce is sweet with a mild spicy kick. Rib meat isn't falling off the bone, but it is crisp and meaty. Entrees come with your choice of side orders—try the just-right coleslaw—and too small portions of corn muffins. It can be slow at lunch (unless something is happening at the Convention Center), but dinner usually finds the place bustling, so call ahead.

Toto's. 2055 E. Tropicana Ave. ☎ **702/895-7923.** Reservations not required. Main courses $6.25–$14.25. AE, DISC, MC, V. Mon–Thurs 11am–2pm, Fri–Sat 11am–11pm, Sun 9am–10pm. MEXICAN.

A family-style Mexican restaurant favored by locals, with enormous portions and quick service, this is good value for your money. Perhaps even more so; with all that food, you could probably split portions and still be satisfied. There are no surprises on the menu, though there are quite a few seafood dishes. Everything is quite tasty and they don't skimp on the cheese. The nongreasy chips come with fresh salsa, and the nachos are terrific. Chicken tamales got a thumbs-up, while the veggie burrito was happily received by non–meat eaters; though not especially healthy, all the ingredients were fresh, with huge slices of zucchini and roasted bell peppers. The operative word here is *huge;* the burritos are almost the size of your arm. The generous portions continue with dessert—a piece of flan was practically pie-sized. The Sunday margarita brunch is quite fun, and the drinks are large (naturally) and yummy.

7 West Las Vegas

EXPENSIVE

Cafe Nicolle. 4760 W. Sahara Blvd. at Decatur, in the Sahara Pavilion. ☎ **702/870-7675.** Reservations recommended for large parties. Main courses $7–$15 lunch, $16–$25 dinner. AE, DC, MC, V. Mon–Sat 11am–10:30pm. CONTINENTAL.

Cafe Nicolle is a local favorite, a place to go for either a special occasion (we noted at least one preprom couple) or just to hang out on the lovely patio, which features a cooling mist on hot summer nights. (Patio dining is particularly unique for Vegas, and the space is just charming.) Even the wait staff will eat here on their off nights, which is a mighty fine recommendation. Inside, it's airy, though unimaginatively decorated ('80s black lacquer), with tables set far enough apart for a pleasant buzz but not enough for your neighbor to eavesdrop.

There are no surprises on the menu—pastas, crêpes, chicken, veal—but everything is prepared beautifully and served attractively with generous portions. They have extremely good, fresh fish, presented very simply, but so the fish's own flavor is able to shine, as opposed to overwhelming it with a sauce or two. The Florentine crêpe is made with lots of fresh spinach and not too much cheese in the sauce. Be sure to dip your fresh bread in the excellent garlic-and-rosemary olive oil found on the table.

Cafe Nicolle is not all that different from restaurants found on the Strip, but if you need a break from the hubbub and the sometimes suffocating crush of people there or just want a chance to dine in a restaurant with windows and breathe some fresh air, this is worth the short drive.

Garlic Cafe. 3650 S. Decatur Blvd., at Spring Mountain Rd. ☎ **702/221-0266.** Reservations recommended. Main courses $9.25–$28. AE, DC, MC, V. Daily 5–10pm. INTERNATIONAL.

If you don't like garlic, there is no reason to read further. If you do like garlic, head toward the Garlic Cafe right now. Garlic is the food of the gods, and Warren, the owner/chef/creator of this cafe, understands that. Unlike similar ventures (the Stinking Rose in San Francisco, for example) this is a more international menu. Warren found that garlic was a unifying theme around the world, so here are dishes from Thailand, Jamaica, Japan, Hungary, and so on. You can decide on the level of garlic in your dish. Their garlic scale usually runs from 1 to 5 (each level is one head of garlic, so a "5" equals five whole heads), and they will go as high as you want. The current record holder is up to 60. The waiters will help you decide what level is best for any given dish; certain ones (like the duck) would get overwhelmed by too much of our favorite seasoning.

Everyone gets a roast *skordalia* (partly puréed garlic) and bagel-chip appetizer, but you can order still others; the choices differ nightly but will always include a perfectly roasted head of garlic. The entree portions are huge (which makes up for the somewhat high prices), and they are very nicely presented. Not to mention imaginatively—okay, incredibly eccentrically—named. Like the Salmon in Garfunkel Crust (a fillet of salmon in a garlic-basil cracker crust with béarnaise sauce) or Grandpa Murray in a Hurry "Don't Worry!" Chicken Curry. If you are nice, maybe

Sweet Sensations

Plenty of opportunities exist in Vegas for satisfying your sweet tooth, but for the discriminating, here are four that you might have to make a detour for. We think they are worth it.

Not that there aren't lots of donut places around town—actually, there aren't that many. But still, the ones you find are the chain variety, fine if you have a yen on the spot, but in reality, you might as well be eating frosted foam rubber. If you are a connoisseur with a car or happen to be checking out the restaurants in the Chinatown area on Spring Mountain Road, go to **Ronald's Donuts,** 4600 Spring Mountain, at Decatur (☎ **702/873-1032**). Hours are Monday through Saturday 5am–5pm, Sunday 5am–2pm. Some have called them celestial. You decide. Or you can do a comparison taste test with **Krispy Kreme Donuts,** just a few more minutes down the road at 7010 Spring Mountain, at Rainbow (☎ **702/222-2320**). At this writing, this is the only branch of the legendary glazed donut mecca west of the Mississippi. If the sign is flashing "Hot Donuts," you're in luck. (And it probably will be.) Dine-in 5:30am–11pm, drive-through 24 hours.

Two of our other favorites are:

- **Freed's Bakery.** 4780 S. Eastern Ave., at Tropicana Blvd. ☎ **702/456-7762.** Monday through Saturday 7am–6pm. If you've got a serious sugar craving, this is worth making the 15-minute drive from the Strip. Despite the minimall setting, it's like walking into Grandma's kitchen, provided you had an old-fashioned granny who felt pastries should not be fancy but should definitely be gooey, chocolatey, and buttery. The chocolate coffee cake is especially good. They also have fresh bread, napoleons, strawberry cheesecake, creme puffs, hamatasan, sweet rolls, danishes, and donuts. Some may find the goodies too heavy and rich, but for those of us with a powerful sweet tooth this place hits the spot.

- **Luv-It Frozen Custard.** 505 E. Oakey, at the Strip. ☎ **702/384-6554.** Monday through Thursday 11am–10pm, Friday 11am–11pm, Saturday noon–11pm, Sunday 1–10pm. Hot Vegas days call for cool desserts, and frozen custard (softer than regular ice cream, but harder than soft serve) is a fine way to go. With less fat and sugar than premium ice cream, from which it also differs slightly in taste and texture, you can even fool yourself into thinking this is somewhat healthy. Made every few hours using fresh cream and eggs, Luv-It frozen custard has basic flavors available for cup or cone, but more exotic ones (maple walnut, apple spice) in tubs.

they will let you take the menu home so that you don't have to try to remember what you ate. Finish it off with some garlic ice cream. It's not as weird as it sounds—a very good vanilla with just a hint of garlic that somehow works in a sweet-and-sour kind of way. The real fun comes with the chocolate-covered (roasted) garlic clove.

The food is not the most utterly memorable ever, but it is competently made and the garlic works as well as you would like. Plus, it's all just a lot of fun, as is imagining the poor soul next to you later at the blackjack tables. No, they don't hand out Breath Assure when you leave. Strangely enough, this restaurant has not yet caught on too much with the tourists, despite having a theme.

Dining West of the Strip

Lorenzi Park

95

Canyon Dr. · Lantern Ln.

Rancho Cir. · Alta Dr.

Palomino Ln.

Campbell Dr.

Lacy Ln.

Rancho Ln.

Martin Luther King Blvd.

15

3rd Pl.

3rd St.

California St.

4th St.

Colorado Ave.

Main St.

604

Westwood

Silver Ave.

2

New York Ave.
Chicago Ave.
Philadelphia Ave.
St. Louis Ave.
Boston Ave.
Baltimore Ave.
Cleveland Ave.
Cincinnati Ave.

Charleston Blvd.

Ashby Ave.

Cragin Park

Decatur Blvd.

Oakey Blvd.

Rancho Dr.

Highland Dr.

Industrial Rd.

Las Vegas Blvd. (The Strip)

3

Sahara Ave.

Valley View Blvd.

Meade Ave.

Penwood Ave.

Rancho Dr.

Westwood Dr.

15

Circus Circus Dr.

Stardust Rd.

Fashion Show Dr.

Fashion Show Mall

Sirius Ave.

Decatur Blvd.

Desert Inn Rd.

4

Spring Mountain Rd.

Fashion Show Dr.

604

Twain Ave.

Viking Rd.

6

5

7

Flamingo Rd.

15

Jones Blvd.

Harmon Ave.

Naples Dr.

Polaris Ave.

Saddle Ave.

8

NA-0303

Cafe Nicolle **3**	The Garlic Cafe **6**
Cathay House **7**	Poppa Gar's **2**
Dragon Sushi **4**	Thai Spice **5**
Enigma Cafe **1**	Viva Mercados **8**

0 .75 mi. 1.2 km

N

147

MODERATE

Cathay House. 5300 W. Spring Mountain Rd., in Spring Valley. ☎ **702/876-3838.** Reservations recommended. Main courses $6.75–$19. AE, CB, DC, DISC, JCB, MC, V. Daily 11am–10:30pm. CHINESE.

Las Vegas actually has a Chinatown—a very large strip mall (naturally) on Spring Mountain Road near Wynn. There are several Asian restaurants there, including the average **Plum Tree Inn** and **Pho Vietnam,** a Vietnamese place. The Plum Tree Inn serves dim sum, but ask locals who look like they know, and they will send you instead farther up Spring Mountain Road to the Cathay House (on the opposite side of the street). This only looks far from the Strip on a map; it's really about a 7-minute drive from Treasure Island.

Ordering dim sum, if you haven't experienced it, is sort of like being at a Chinese sushi bar, in that you order many individual, tasty little dishes. Of course, dim sum itself is nothing like sushi. Rather, it's a range of pot stickers, pan-fried dumplings, *baos* (soft, doughy buns filled with meat like barbecued pork), translucent rice noodles wrapped around shrimp, sticky rice in lotus leaves, chicken feet, and so forth. Some of it's steamed, some is fried—for that extra good grease! You can make your own dipping sauce by combining soy sauce, vinegar, and hot pepper oil. The Chinese eat this for breakfast; the rest of us probably can't handle it until a bit later in the day. The wait staff pushes steam carts filled with little dishes; point, and they will attempt to tell you what each one is. Better, just blindly order a bunch and dig in. Each dish ranges from approximately $1 to $3; each server makes a note of what you just received, and the total is tallied at the end. (For some reason, it almost always works out to about $9 a person.) Dim sum is usually available only until mid-afternoon.

The stand-out at the Cathay House was a vegetable bao that included Chinese glass noodles. Lightly browned and not overly doughy like many baos, it was slightly sweet and utterly delicious. The shrimp wrapped in rice noodles were big and plump, while anything that was fried was so good we decided to ignore our arteries for a while. Cathay House (which features quite a good view through the windows on one side) also has a full dinner menu, which includes the strawberry chicken invented by Chin's; it's considerably cheaper here.

Thai Spice. 4433 W. Flamingo, at I-15. ☎ **702/362-5308.** Reservations not required. Main courses $6 lunch, $7–$15 dinner. AE, DISC, MC, V. Mon–Sat 11am–10pm. THAI.

Just off the Strip, and just across from the Rio Hotel, this modern-looking nonglitzy Thai restaurant offers decent food and reasonable prices. The subdued ambience (okay, it's a little boring, but not everything can be flashy, even in Vegas), quick service, and good food make it a favorite for locals. The menu is extensive and offers an array of Thai dishes and Chinese fare. For appetizers, the tom kha kai soup and pork or chicken satay are excellent. Skip the terrible moo goo gai pan in favor of terrific pad Thai and tasty lemon chicken. Lunch specials are $5.50 and include spring rolls, salad, soup, and steamed rice. Make sure you tell the waitress how spicy you want your food.

Viva Mercados. 6182 W. Flamingo, at Jones. ☎ **702/871-8826.** Reservations for large parties only. Main courses $8–$17. AE, DISC, MC, V. Sun–Thurs 11am–10pm, Fri–Sat 11am–11pm. MEXICAN.

Ask any local about Mexican food in Vegas and almost certainly they will point to Viva Mercados as the best in town. That recommendation, plus the restaurant's health-conscious attitude, makes this worth the roughly 10-minute drive from the Strip.

A Classic Vegas Restaurant

In a world gone mad—and that's the way Vegas seems sometimes—it's good to know some things never change. The following restaurant doesn't serve the best food in town, but it's been around forever. And that should be rewarded. Besides, it's classically Las Vegas, a rapidly vanishing species. Go for the experience.

Green Shack, 2504 E. Fremont, 1 block south of Charleston Blvd. (☎ 702/383-0007), is just a little dive, but more importantly, it's the oldest continuously operating restaurant in Las Vegas. That should count for something. Its menu hasn't changed a bit over the years. Try the fried chicken. They open at 4pm in the bar and 5pm in the dining room and close when they feel like it. Closed Mondays.

Given all those warnings lately about Mexican food and its heart attack–inducing properties, Viva Mercados's approach to food is nothing to be sniffed at. No dish is prepared with or cooked in any kind of animal fat. Nope, the lard so dear to Mexican cooking is not found here. The oil used is an artery-friendly canola. Additionally, this makes the place particularly appealing to vegetarians, who will also be pleased by the regular veggie specials. Everything is quite fresh, and they do particularly amazing things with seafood. Try the Maresco Vallarta, which is orange roughy, shrimp, and scallops cooked in a coconut tomato sauce, with capers and olives. They have all sorts of noteworthy shrimp dishes, and 11 different salsas, ranked 1 to 10 for degree of spice. (Ask for advice, first.) The staff is friendly (try to chat with owner Bobby Mercado) and the portions hearty.

INEXPENSIVE

Dragon Sushi. 4115 Spring Mountain Rd., at Valley View. ☎ **702/368-4336.** Reservations not required. Sushi $3.50–$5.50 per portion. Main courses all under $10. AE, MC, V. Sun–Thurs 10:30am–10:30pm, Fri–Sat 10:30am–midnight. SUSHI.

Those used to really extraordinary sushi won't find this place particularly special, but then again, this is Las Vegas and it's not like you can eat fish that was swimming in the ocean just hours before. Under the circumstances, though, Dragon Sushi does a more than adequate job. The *Unagi* (eel) is particularly good. But a big attraction is the VIP tatami rooms. For $10 for a small room (seats 6 or less) and $20 for a large (up to 22 people), you have your own private room, with paper sliding doors, a small bonsai tree, and a table just off the floor, surrounded by tatami mats. No show here—they are delightfully plain, simply Japanese. This is a fine choice for a romantic dinner, as you feed each other with fingers and chopsticks, away from prying eyes, but perhaps not from the very attentive staff.

✪ **Enigma Cafe.** 918½ S. Fourth St., at Charleston Blvd. ☎ **702/386-0999.** Reservations not accepted. No items over $6. Mon 7am–3pm, Tues–Fri 7am–midnight, Sat–Sun 9am–midnight. No credit cards. CALIFORNIA/MEDITERRANEAN.

Finding the Enigma Cafe is almost as good as finding a breeze on a really hot Vegas day. Or maybe it's more like suddenly finding yourself transported out of Vegas and into California. Owners Julie and Len have taken two 1930s-era cottages and turned them into a cafe/coffeehouse/art space that, during the day, is a restful, garden patio setting (orders are taken inside one house; inside the other is the art gallery, with more seating) with folk and classical music playing. At night the space blooms with candles, live music, and poetry readings.

The menu is a huge relief: healthful, interesting sandwiches ("Mossy Melt" is tuna salad "revved up with" horseradish and havarti, toasted open-face) and familiar ones (ham and Swiss, but well garnished), salads (again with a range from the ordinary green variety to "Dr. Bombay's" curried chicken breast with veggies) to hummus burritos and the "Tippy Elvis Supreme" (named after a local polka band/art project), which is peanut butter and bananas (what else?). You can get a side platter of hummus, feta cheese, veggies, and pita, or have a thick fruit smoothie. And that doesn't even begin to cover their wide range of coffee drinks. Best of all, it's cheap. Considering the soothing effect it has on your mind, spirit, wallet, and stomach, Enigma is like a vacation from your vacation. This is actually very close to both the Strip and Downtown, particularly the latter, where good (and healthful) food is hard to find.

8 Downtown

VERY EXPENSIVE

Andre's. 401 S. 6th St., at Lewis Ave., a few blocks south of Fremont St. ☎ **702/385-5016.** Reservations required. Main courses $20–$33. AE, CB, DC, MC, V. Daily from 6pm; closing hours vary. FRENCH.

Owner-chef Andre Rochat has created a rustic country-French setting in a converted 1930s house in Downtown Las Vegas. Low ceilings are crossed with rough-hewn beams, and wainscoted stucco walls (embedded with straw) are hung with provincial pottery and copperware. Soft lighting emanates from candles on sconces. In addition to a catacomb of cozy interior rooms, there's a lovely, ivy-walled garden patio under the shade of a mulberry tree. This is a major celebrity haunt where you're likely to see Strip headliners. One night, Tom Hanks, Steven Spielberg, and James Spader were all spotted joining some pals for a bachelor party.

The menu changes seasonally. On a recent visit, appetizers included jumbo sea scallops rolled in a crunchy macadamia nut crust with citrus beurre blanc and red beet coulis. And among the entrees, a fan of pink, juicy slices of sautéed duck came with a confit of port wine and onions. A medley of vegetables—perhaps pommes lyonnaise, asparagus, broccoli hollandaise, and baby carrots—accompanies each entree, and sorbets are served between courses. For dessert, there is Andre's classic fruit tarts, flaky butter crusts layered with Grand Marnier custard and topped with fresh, plump berries. An extensive wine list (more than 900 labels) is international in scope and includes many rare vintages; consult the sommelier.

Hugo's Cellar. Four Queens, 202 Fremont St., at Casino Center Blvd. ☎ **702/385-4011.** Reservations required. Main courses $24–$35. AE, DC, DISC, MC, V. Daily 5:30–10:30pm. INTERNATIONAL.

Hugo's Cellar is indeed in a cellar, or at least below street level in the Four Queens Hotel. No, they aren't ashamed of it—quite the opposite. This is their gourmet restaurant, and it is highly regarded by the locals. You pass through a small, dark (romantic, not creepy) bar with a few tables and a friendly bartender, perfect for a little quiet tête-à-tête between hands at the poker tables. Each female guest is given a red rose when she enters the restaurant—the beginning of a series of nice touches. The restaurant proper is dimly lit, lined with dark wood and brick. It's fairly

Note

An additional branch of Andre's has opened in the **Monte Carlo Hotel & Casino,** 3775 Las Vegas Blvd. S. (☎ **702/798-7151**).

Dining Downtown

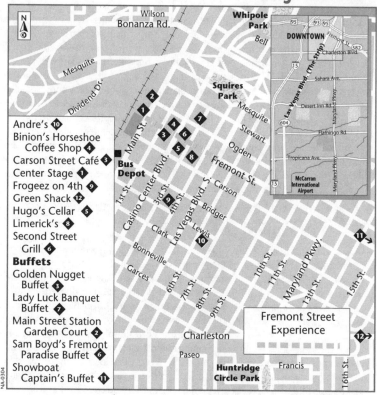

Andre's **10**
Binion's Horseshoe
    Coffee Shop **4**
Carson Street Café **3**
Center Stage **1**
Frogeez on 4th **9**
Green Shack **12**
Hugo's Cellar **5**
Limerick's **8**
Second Street
    Grill **6**
Buffets
Golden Nugget
    Buffet **3**
Lady Luck Banquet
    Buffet **7**
Main Street Station
    Garden Court **2**
Sam Boyd's Fremont
    Paradise Buffet **6**
Showboat
    Captain's Buffet **11**

intimate, but if you really want to be cozy ask for one of the curtained booths against the wall.

The meal is full of ceremony, perfectly delivered by a well-trained and cordial wait staff. Salads, included in the price, are prepared at your table, from a cart full of choices. (In Vegas style, though, most choices are on the calorie-intensive side.) A tiny cup with palate-cleansing sorbet prepares you for the main course. Unfortunately, despite the high regard, the main courses are not all that novel (various cuts of meat, seafood, chicken prepared different ways) and can be disappointing. Promising choices include the Chicken "Hugo" (with basil and pine nuts prepared in a cream sauce), or the Rack of Lamb Indonesian with Indonesian spices. Vegetables are included, as is a finish of chocolate-dipped fruits with cream.

The service is impeccable (you have little to no wait between courses), and it really makes you feel pampered. That salad, the small dessert, and so forth are included, making an initially hefty-seeming price tag appear a bit more reasonable, especially when compared to Strip establishments that aren't much better and can cost nearly twice as much. While the main food is not spectacular, the salads and desserts are fine. It is not worth going out of your way for the food, but perhaps it is for the whole package.

EXPENSIVE

Limerick's. Fitzgerald's Casino Holiday Inn, 301 Fremont St., at 3rd St. ☎ **702/388-2400.** Reservations recommended. Main courses $14–$21. AE, DISC, MC, V. Daily 5:30–10:30pm. STEAK/SEAFOOD.

An extensive renovation in 1996 turned a down-at-the-heels eatery into a posh steak house. Decorated in the classic Olde English gentlemen's club style, Limerick's is meant to be an oasis of gracious dining away from hectic casino life, and the overall effect is comforting and moderately womblike, particularly in the cozy booths at the back. Unfortunately, casino "ca-chings" still creep in, but it's not overly bothersome. The menu is classic, upscale steak house: beef, chops, some lobster, and chicken. The portions are Vegas-sized (the small prime rib was 14 ounces), so bring an appetite (and a love of red meat), or take your leftovers back to the room to feed the kids for a couple days. The filet mignon was tender enough to cut with a fork, while the lamb chops came with a pecan mustard glaze. Patrons who don't eat red meat might want to try the apricot chicken. Appetizers are mostly seafood, though there is a fine-sounding baked brie with strawberry preserves. "Chef's choice" desserts change nightly, and the wine list is good and extensive.

✪ **Second Street Grill.** Fremont Hotel, 200 E. Fremont St. ☎ **702/385-3232.** Main courses $17–$23. Reservations recommended. AE, DC, DISC, MC, V. Sun–Thurs 5–11pm, Fri–Sat 5am–midnight. INTERNATIONAL.

One of the better-kept secrets of Las Vegas, this is a Downtown jewel. A lovely bit of romantic, cozy class tucked away inside the Fremont Hotel, with excellent food to boot. There is hardly a misstep on the menu, from taste to beautiful presentation. To call this Hawaiian-influenced would be accurate, but don't think of the "Polynesian" craze of the '60s and '70s (in other words, forget flaming whatevers, and sickly sweet-and-sour sauce). This is more what might be found at a top-flight restaurant on the Big Island. You begin with warm sourdough bread accompanied by a garlic, eggplant, and olive oil dipping sauce. For starters, try the unusual lemon chicken pot stickers and the duck comfit. Entrees include lobster, ahi tuna, and filet mignon, but the whole fish (opaka paka on a recent visit), served in a bowl with a giant tea leaf lid, is the best bet. It comes with sautéed mushrooms that will melt in your mouth. Other notable side dishes include some fabulous pesto mashed potatoes. Tiramisù fans should be pleased with the Grill's version of that ubiquitous dessert; it's light on the alcohol and more like an airy tiramisù cheesecake. But don't skip the Chocolate Explosion: a piece of chocolate cake topped with chocolate mousse, covered with a rich chocolate shell.

INEXPENSIVE

✪ **Binion's Horseshoe Coffee Shop.** Binion's Horseshoe, 128 E. Fremont St., at Casino Center Blvd. ☎ **702/382-1600.** Reservations not accepted. Main courses $4.25–$15 (most under $8). AE, CB, DC, DISC, MC, V. Daily 24 hours. AMERICAN.

Down a flight of steps from the casino floor, this is no humble hotel coffee shop. It's heralded by a gorgeous stained-glass dome and entered via doors embellished with antique beveled glass panels. The interior is equally impressive, with a magnificent, pressed copper ceiling, rich oak paneling, walls hung with original oil paintings you'll wish you owned, and displays of antiques, turn-of-the-century magazine covers, and black-and-white photographs of the Old West. Notice, too, an exhibit of vintage playing cards that depict real kings and queens (Henry VIII and Anne Boleyn).

The menu lists all the traditional Las Vegas coffee-shop items: sandwiches, burgers, southern-fried chicken, steak and seafood entrees, along with breakfast fare. And you can't beat Binion's specials: two eggs with an immense slab of grilled ham, home fries, toast, and tea or coffee ($3 from 6am to 2pm); a 10-ounce New York steak dinner with baked potato, salad, and roll and butter ($4 from 10pm to 5:45am); a 7-ounce New York steak with eggs, home fries, and toast ($3 from 10pm to 5:45am); a 10-ounce prime-rib dinner, including soup or salad, potato, and vegetables ($5.25 from 5 to 9:45pm)—$6.25 for a 16-ounce T-bone steak instead of prime rib. All bar drinks are available, and there's peanut butter cream pie for dessert.

Carson Street Café. Golden Nugget, 129 E. Fremont St., between 1st St. and Casino Center Blvd. ☎ **702/385-7111.** Reservations not accepted. Main courses $6–$15. AE, CB, DC, DISC, MC, V. Daily 24 hours. AMERICAN.

Las Vegas has many delightful 24-hour hotel restaurants. The Golden Nugget's is reminiscent of an elegant street cafe on the Champs-Elysées, albeit one overlooking a gorgeous hotel lobby instead of a Paris street. Its jewel-toned interior, under a white-fringed green awning, has murals of park scenes and topiary, white latticing, and seating amid potted orange trees and planters of greenery—it couldn't be lovelier.

And the food is notably excellent. A wide-ranging menu offers terrific salads (such as Oriental chicken), overstuffed deli sandwiches, burgers, Mexican fare (chicken burritos, fajita sandwiches), numerous breakfast items, and entrees running the gamut from filet mignon to country fried steak with mashed potatoes and vegetables. From 4 to 11pm, a 10-ounce prime-rib dinner (with baked potato and a vegetable) is $10. And from 11pm to 7am, an 8-ounce grilled ham steak with eggs, hash browns, and toast costs $4. There's a full bar. Dessert options include fresh-baked eclairs, strawberry shortcake, and hot fudge or butterscotch sundaes.

Center Stage. Jackie Gaughan's Plaza Hotel Casino, 1 Main St., at Fremont St. ☎ **702/386-2110.** Reservations necessary. Main courses $6–$16 (many under $10). AE, DISC, MC, V. Daily 5–11pm. STEAK/SEAFOOD.

The aptly named Center Stage offers a dramatic vantage point, the best in town for viewing the Fremont Street Experience. The restaurant occupies a second-story glass dome, with a windowed wall directly facing Fremont Street. Seating is in semicircular booths, all of which provide good to excellent views of Downtown's nightly laser-light show, the music for which is piped into the restaurant. This is both a comfortable and attractive dining room, done up in aesthetically pleasing shades of green with planters of lush faux foliage.

It's a thrilling place to be. What's less than thrilling—though the menu is extremely low-priced—is the lackluster performance in the kitchen. Best bet is to stick to the most basic menu items. Order the prime rib au jus, served with onion soup or salad (take the salad), warm sourdough bread and butter, a vegetable, and baked potato, rice, or fettuccine Alfredo (take the potato). It's just $8, and you get to see the show. Be sure to make reservations and arrive early to snag one of the best seats.

9 Buffets & Sunday Brunches

Lavish, low-priced buffets are a Las Vegas tradition, designed to lure you to the gaming tables and make you feel like you got such a bargain for your meal you can afford to drop more money. They're a gimmick, and we love them. Something about filling up on too much prime rib and shrimp just says "Vegas" to us. Of course, there is quite a range, from some perfunctory steam table displays and salad bars heavy on iceberg lettuce, to unbelievably opulent spreads with caviar and free-flowing champagne. Some are quite beautifully presented, as well. Some of the food is awful, some of it merely works as fuel, and some of it is memorable.

No trip to Las Vegas is complete without trying one or two buffets. Of the dozens, the most noteworthy are described below. Mind you, almost all buffets have some things in common. Unless otherwise noted, every one listed below will have a carving station, a salad bar (quality differs), and hot main courses and side dishes. We will try only to point out when a buffet has something original or notable.

Note: Buffet meals are extremely popular, and reservations are usually not taken (we've indicated when they are accepted, and in all those cases, they are highly recommended). Arrive early (before opening) or late to avoid a long line, especially on weekends.

SOUTH STRIP
MODERATE

Tropicana Island Buffet. 3801 Las Vegas Blvd. S. ☎ **702/739-2222.** Sat/Sun brunch $10, dinner $12. AE, CB, DC, DISC, MC, V. Daily 7am–1pm and 5–10pm.

This buffet is served in a large and delightful dining room, lushly planted with tropical flowers and foliage. There are coral-reef aquariums at the entrance, and the appealing interior keeps to the island theme. Big semicircular booths backed by mirrored walls are separated by bead curtains, and, on the lower level, floor-to-ceiling windows overlook the Trop's stunning palm-fringed pool. Dinners here feature an extensive salad bar and peel-and-eat shrimp.

INEXPENSIVE

✪ **Excalibur's Round Table Buffet.** 3850 Las Vegas Blvd. S. ☎ **702/597-7777.** Breakfast $5, lunch $6, dinner $8. AE, CB, DC, DISC, MC, V. Daily 7–11am, 11am–4pm, and 4–10pm.

This strikes the perfect balance of cheap prices, mandatory, tacky decor, and adequate food. This is what you want in a cheap Vegas buffet. But on a recent trip they didn't have mashed potatoes or macaroni salad, which are essential for an archetypal buffet. The plates are large, so you don't have to make as many trips to the buffet tables.

✪ **Luxor Pharaoh's Pheast Buffet.** 3900 Las Vegas Blvd. S. ☎ **702/262-4000.** Breakfast $6, lunch $7.50, dinner $10. AE, CB, DC, DISC, MC, V. Daily 6:30am–11:30am, 11:30am–4pm, and 4–11pm.

Located on the lower level, where the Luxor showroom used to be, this huge new buffet looks like it was set in the middle of an archaeological dig, complete with wood braces holding up the ceiling, pot shards, papyrus, and servers dressed in khaki dig outfits. It's a unique and fun decor—be sure to avoid tripping on the mummies and their sarcophagi sticking half up out of the ground. The food is better than most cheap buffets, including a Mexican station with some genuinely spicy food, Chinese stir-fry, and different Italian pastas. Desserts were disappointing. A beer and wine cart makes the rounds. Word has probably gotten out, unfortunately, because the lines are always enormous.

MGM Grand Buffet. 3799 Las Vegas Blvd. S. ☎ **702/891-7777.** Brunch $6, dinner $8; reduced prices for children under 10, free for children under 4. AE, DC, DISC, MC, V. Daily 7am–2:30pm and 4–10pm.

This rather average buffet does feature a fresh Belgian waffle station at breakfast. Dinner also has all-you-can-eat shrimp and an all-you-can-eat shrimp and prime-rib option. Also available: low-fat, sugar-free desserts! And at all meals you get a full pot of coffee on your table.

Monte Carlo Buffet. 3770 Las Vegas Blvd. S. ☎ **702/730-7777.** Breakfast $6.50, lunch $7, dinner $9.50. AE, CB, DC, DISC, MC, V. Daily 7–11am, 11am–4pm, and 4–10pm.

A "courtyard" under a painted sky, the Monte Carlo's buffet room has a Moroccan market theme, with murals of Arab scenes, Moorish archways, Oriental carpets, and walls hung with photographs of, and artifacts from, Morocco. Dinner includes a rotisserie (for chicken and pork loin or London broil), a Chinese food station, a taco/fajita bar, a baked potato bar, numerous salads, and more than a dozen desserts plus frozen yogurt and ice-cream machines. Lunches are similar. At breakfast, the expected fare is supplemented by an omelet station, and choices include crêpes, blintzes, and corned beef hash. Fresh-baked New York–style bagels are a plus.

MID-STRIP
VERY EXPENSIVE

✪ **Bally's Sterling Sunday Brunch.** 3645 Las Vegas Blvd. S. ☎ **702/739-4111.** Reservations recommended. Brunch $40. AE, CB, DC, JCB, MC, V. Sunday 9:30am–2:30pm.

This brunch is served in the clubby elegant precincts of Bally's Steakhouse. Flower arrangements and ice sculptures grace lavish buffet spreads tended by white-hatted chefs. There's a waffle and omelet station, a sushi and sashimi bar, and a brimming dessert table. You might choose smoked fish with bagels and cream cheese or help yourself from a mound of fresh shrimp. Entrees vary weekly. On a recent visit the possibilities included rolled chicken stuffed with pistachios and porcini mushrooms, beef tenderloin, steak Diane, seared salmon with beet butter sauce and fried leeks, roast duckling with black currant and blueberry sauce, penne Florentine with pine nuts, and smoked chicken in vodka sauce. Of course, there are deli and breakfast meats, vegetables and scrumptious salads, cheeses, raw bar offerings, seasonal fruits and berries, and side dishes such as stuffed potatoes with caviar and sour cream. Champagne flows freely.

MODERATE

✪ **Bally's Big Kitchen Buffet.** 3645 Las Vegas Blvd. S. ☎ **702/739-4111.** Breakfast $9, brunch $10, dinner $14. AE, CB, DC, JCB, MC, V. Daily 7am–11am, 11am–2:30pm, and 4–10pm.

This gorgeous spread is served in a carpeted and crystal-chandeliered dining room with comfortably upholstered armchair seating. Everything is extremely fresh and of the highest quality. There's always a bountiful salad bar, a good choice of fruits and vegetables, entrees (perhaps seafood casserole in a creamy dill sauce, baked red snapper, pork chops sautéed in Cajun spices, barbecued chicken, and broiled steak in peppercorn sauce), pastas, rice and potato dishes, cold cuts, and a vast array of fresh-baked desserts. The brunch buffet includes breakfast fare and all-you-can-eat shrimp, while the dinner buffet adds Chinese selections.

✪ **Caesars Palace Palatium Buffet.** 3570 Las Vegas Blvd. S. ☎ **702/731-7110.** Breakfast $8, lunch $10, dinner $15; Sat/Sun brunch $14 adults (includes unlimited champagne), $7 children 4 to 12, free for children under 3. AE, CB, DC, DISC, MC, V. Mon–Fri 7:30am–11:30am, 11:30am–3:30pm, and 4:30–10pm; Sat–Sun 8:30am–3:30pm and 4:30–10pm.

Named for the 2nd-century meeting place of Rome's academy of chefs, this elegant dining room is adorned with murals of ancient Rome and fronted by an imposing colonnaded pediment. Selections at lunch and dinner include elaborate salad bars, fresh-baked breads, and much, much more. The evening meal includes a cold seafood station. Especially lavish are weekend brunches with omelet stations (in addition to egg dishes), breakfast meats, fresh-squeezed juices, potatoes prepared in various ways, pastas, rice casseroles, carved meats, cold shrimp, smoked salmon, and a waffle and ice-cream sundae bar in addition to two dessert islands spotlighting cakes and pastries. That's not the half of it.

Harrah's Fresh Market Buffet. 3475 Las Vegas Blvd. S. ☎ **702/369-5000.** Breakfast $7, lunch $9, dinner $12. AE, CB, DC, DISC, MC, V. Daily 7–11am, 11am–3:30pm, and 4–10pm.

The theme here is Farmer's Market, which means lots of big sculptures of fresh fruits and vegetables, if not the actual fresh fruits and vegetables. Following the new trend of various feeding stations, as opposed to one long buffet, you will find seafood, pasta, Mexican, Asian, and American specialties ranging from meat loaf to Cajun entrees. Above average food combined with an extremely friendly staff makes this a better buffet choice.

✪ **Mirage Buffet.** 3400 Las Vegas Blvd. S. ☎ **702/791-7111.** Breakfast $7.50, lunch $9, dinner $13; Sun brunch $14; reduced prices for children 4 to 10, free for children under 4. AE, CB, DC, DISC, MC, V. Mon–Sat 7–10:45am, 11am–2:45pm, and 3–10pm; Sun 8am–9:30pm.

The Mirage offers lavish spreads in a lovely garden-themed setting with palm trees, a plant-filled stone fountain, and seating under verdigris eaves and domes embellished with flowers. You pay somewhat more here than at other buffets, but you certainly get what you pay for. The salad bars alone are enormous, filled with at least 25 different choices such as Thai beef, seafood, salad Niçoise, tabbouleh, Chinese chicken, Creole rice, and tortellini. At brunch champagne flows freely, and a scrumptious array of smoked fish is added to the board, along with such items as fruit-filled crêpes and blintzes. And every meal features a spectacular dessert table (the bread pudding in bourbon sauce is noteworthy). For healthful eating there are many light items to choose from, including sugar- and fat-free puddings. And on Sunday a nonalcoholic sparkling cider is a possible champagne alternative.

INEXPENSIVE

Flamingo Hilton Paradise Garden Buffet. 3555 Las Vegas Blvd. S. ☎ **702/733-3111.** Breakfast $6.75, lunch $8, dinner $10. AE, CB, DC, DISC, JCB, MC, V. Daily 6am–noon, noon–2pm, and 4:30–10pm.

The buffet here occupies a vast room, with floor-to-ceiling windows overlooking a verdant tropical landscape of cascading waterfalls and a pond filled with ducks, swans, and flamingos. The interior, one of the most pleasant in Las Vegas, is equally lush, though its palm trees and tropical foliage are faux. At dinner, there is an extensive international food station (which changes monthly) presenting French, Chinese, Mexican, German, or Italian specialties. A large salad bar, fresh fruits, pastas, vegetables, potato dishes, and a vast dessert display round out the offerings. Lunch is similar, featuring a mix of international cuisines as well as a stir-fry station and a soup/salad/pasta bar. At breakfast, you'll find all the expected fare, including a made-to-order omelet station and fresh-baked breads.

✪ **Rio's Carnival World Buffet.** 3700 W. Flamingo Rd. ☎ **702/252-7777.** Breakfast $7, lunch $9, dinner $11. AE, CB, DC, MC, V. Daily 8:30am–10:30am, 11am–3:30pm, and 3:30–11pm.

The buffet here is located in a festively decorated room with variegated wide, sequined ribbons looped overhead and seating amid planters of lush, faux tropical blooms. Chairs and booths are upholstered in bright hues—green, purple, red, orange, and turquoise. This is an excellent buffet with cheerfully decorative food booths set up like stations in an upscale food court. A barbecued chicken and ribs station offers side dishes of baked beans and mashed potatoes. Other stations offer stir-fry (chicken, beef, pork, and vegetables), Mexican taco fixings and accompaniments, Chinese fare, a Japanese sushi and teppanyaki grill, a Brazilian mixed grill, Italian pasta and antipasto, and fish-and-chips. There's even a diner setup for hot dogs, burgers, fries, and milk shakes. All this is in addition to the usual offerings of most Las Vegas buffets. A stunning array of oven-fresh cakes, pies, and pastries (including sugar-free and low-fat desserts) are arranged in a palm-fringed circular display area, and there's also a make-your-own sundae bar. A full cash bar is another Rio plus. Everything is fresh and beautifully prepared and presented.

Treasure Island Buffet. 3300 Las Vegas Blvd. S. ☎ **702/894-7111.** Breakfast $6, lunch $7, dinner $9; Sun brunch $9. AE, DC, DISC, JCB, MC, V. Mon–Sat 7–10:45am and 11am–3:45pm; daily 4–10:30pm; Sun 7:30am–3:30pm.

The buffet is served in two internationally themed rooms. The American room, under a central rough-hewn beamed canopy hung with the flags of the 13 colonies, re-creates New Orleans during the era of Jean Lafitte. And the Italian room, modeled after a Tuscan villa overlooking a bustling piazza, has strings of festival lights overhead and food displays under a striped awning. Both rooms are filled with authentic antiques and artifacts typical of their locales and time periods. And both also serve identical fare, including extensive American breakfasts. Dinners offer a Chinese food station, peel-and-eat shrimp, a salad bar, potato and rice side dishes, cheeses and cold cuts, fresh fruits and vegetables, breads, and a large choice of desserts. Lunch is similar, and Sunday brunch includes unlimited champagne.

NORTH STRIP
INEXPENSIVE

Circus Circus Buffet. 2880 Las Vegas Blvd. S. ☎ **702/734-0410.** Breakfast $3.50, lunch $4.50, dinner $6; Sat/Sun brunch $4.50. AE, CB, DC, DISC, MC, V. Mon–Fri 6–11:30am, noon–4pm, and 4:30–11pm; Sat–Sun 6am–4pm and 4:30–11pm.

Here's a choice: the cheapest buffet on the Strip, versus the worst buffet food in town. Here you'll find 50 items of typical cafeteria fare, and none of them all that good. Kids love it; some adults find it inedible. If food is strictly fuel for you, you can't go wrong here. Otherwise, trundle off to another buffet.

Sahara Oasis Buffet. 2535 Las Vegas Blvd. S. ☎ **702/737-2111.** Breakfast $3, brunch $4, dinner $6. AE, CB, DC, DISC, MC, V. Daily 6–11am, 11:30am–3:30pm, and 4–10pm.

This buffet is a vast spread served in an attractive room with a wall of windows overlooking the pool and brass palm trees shading the food display tables. It's not fancy fare, but it is abundant, fresh, and tasty.

Stardust Warehouse Buffet. 3000 Las Vegas Blvd. S. ☎ **702/732-6111.** Breakfast $6, lunch $7, dinner $9; Sun brunch $8. AE, CB, D, DC, JCB, MC, V. Mon–Sat 7–10:30am, 10:30am–3pm, and 4–10pm; Sun 7am–3:30pm and 4–10pm.

This buffet features, as the name suggests, a raftered warehouse decor, with big restaurant cans of olive oil and chili, sacks of flour, crates of apples, and other provender on display. Tables are covered in laminated burlap potato sacking. It's a pleasant setting for very good buffet meals, featuring a carving station (roast beef, ham, and turkey). You can also pump your own frozen yogurt.

Stratosphere Buffet. 2000 Las Vegas Blvd. S. ☎ **702/380-7711.** Breakfast $5.50, lunch $6.50, dinner $9. AE, CB, DC, DISC, JCB, MC, V. Daily 7am–11am and 11am–4pm; Sun–Thurs 4–9pm, Fri–Sat 4–10pm.

In a cheerful World's Fair–themed buffet room—with a hot-air balloon motif adorning murals, columns, and carpeting—the Stratosphere sets out fresh-looking fare and plenty of it. Breakfast is average at best, disappointing at worst. Lunch and dinner have stations for Mexican, Chinese, and kosher-style fare; daily changing international stations (perhaps Jamaican, Creole, or Italian); and a station for picnic food such as fried chicken and hot dogs. Desserts are supplemented by a make-your-own-sundae frozen-yogurt bar and a flambé dessert station turning out bananas Foster and cherries jubilee.

EAST OF THE STRIP
MODERATE

✪ **Las Vegas Hilton Buffet of Champions.** 3000 Paradise Rd. ☎ **702/732-5111.** Breakfast $8, lunch $9, dinner $13; weekend brunch $12 (includes unlimited champagne); half price for children age 12 and under. CB, DC, DISC, ER, MC, V. Mon–Fri 7–10am, 11am–2:30pm, and 5–10pm; Sat–Sun 8am–2:30pm and 5–10pm.

This buffet is served in a beautiful gardenlike dining room with pristine white trellises, big planters of flowers, and magnificent white wrought-iron chandeliers and sconces. As the name implies, the room, located near the casino entrance to the race and sports SuperBook, is sports-themed. Cream walls are adorned with attractive murals and photographs of hockey, football, boxing, and horse racing, and there are bookshelves stocked with sporting literature. All in all, it's one of the loveliest buffet rooms in town. And the fare is fresh and delicious. Dinner additionally features all-you-can-eat crab and shrimp.

INEXPENSIVE

✪ **Sam's Town, The Great Buffet.** 5111 Boulder Hwy. ☎ **702/456-7777.** Breakfast $5, lunch $7, dinner $9 (Fri seafood buffet $13); Sun brunch $7; all buffets half price for children 6 and under. AE, CB, DC, DISC, MC, V. Mon–Sat 8–11am and 11am–3pm; Sun–Thurs 4–9pm, Fri–Sat 4–10pm; Sun 8am–3pm.

Friendly service and good food have made Sam's Town's buffets extremely popular. About 70% of their clientele consists of local folks, not tourists. The buffet room is as homey as your living room, with fruit-motif carpeting, gaslight-style brass chandeliers, and planters of foliage creating intimate dining niches. Dinners includes a Chinese stir-fry station, a burger grill, and a wide array of side dishes and fresh fruits and vegetables. For dessert, numerous pies and cakes are supplemented by frozen yogurt with homemade fudge, homemade candies, caramel apples, and fruit cobbler. Cajun seafood entrees are featured on Tuesday night. But best of all are the Friday seafood buffets, offering paella, deep-fried oysters, crawfish étouffée, Cajun red snapper, steamed Dungeness crab with drawn butter, shrimp scampi with pasta, raw oysters, peel-and-eat shrimp, and much more. Sunday champagne brunch offers extensive breakfast and lunch fare, including blintzes, Mexican breakfast tortes, a carving station, Southern and Cajun specialties, and unlimited champagne.

DOWNTOWN
MODERATE

✪ **Golden Nugget Buffet.** 129 E. Fremont St. ☎ **702/385-7111.** Breakfast $5.75, lunch $7.50, dinner $10.25; Sun brunch $11. AE, CB, DC, DISC, MC, V. Mon–Sat 7–10:30am, 10:30am–3pm, and 4–10pm; Sun 8am–10pm.

This buffet has often been voted number one in Las Vegas. Not only is the food fresh and delicious, but it's served in an opulent dining room with marble-topped serving tables amid planters of greenery and potted palms. Mirrored columns, beveled mirrors, etched glass, and brass add sparkle to the room, and swagged draperies provide a note of elegance. Most of the seating is in plush booths. The buffet tables are also laden with an extensive salad bar (about 50 items), fresh fruit, and marvelous desserts including Zelma Wynn's (Steve's mother) famous bread pudding. Every night fresh seafood is featured. Most lavish is the all-day Sunday champagne brunch, which adds such dishes as eggs Benedict, blintzes, pancakes, creamed herring, and smoked fish with bagels and cream cheese. *Note:* This stunning buffet room is also the setting for a $3 late-night meal of steak and eggs with home fries and biscuits with gravy; it's served 11pm to 4am.

INEXPENSIVE

Lady Luck Banquet Buffet. 206 N. 3rd St. ☎ **702/477-3000.** Breakfast $5, lunch $5.50, dinner $7.75. AE, CB, DC, DISC, JCB, MC, V. Daily 6–10:30am, 10:30am–2pm, and 4–10pm.

This buffet is served in a pretty garden-themed room. Dinner includes all-you-can-eat prime rib, and, frequently, there are Chinese, Polynesian, and Italian specialties as well. Offerings additionally include an extensive salad bar, a make-your-own-sundae bar, an array of fresh-baked pies and cakes, and beverages.

✪ **Main Street Station Garden Court.** 200 N. Main St. ☎ **702/387-1896.** Breakfast $5, lunch $7, dinner $9; Fri seafood buffet $13; Sat and Sun champagne brunch $8; free for children age 3 and under. AE, CB, DC, DISC, MC, V. Mon–Fri 7am–10:30am, 11am–3pm, and 4–10pm; Sat–Sun 7am–3pm and 4–10pm.

Set in what is truly one of the prettiest buffet spaces in town (and certainly in Downtown), with very high ceilings and tall windows bringing in much-needed, actual natural light, the Main Street Station Garden Court buffet is one of the best in town, much less in Downtown. Featuring nine live-action stations (meaning you can watch your food being prepared), including a wood-fired brick-oven pizza (delicious), many fresh salsas at the Mexican station, a barbecue rotisserie, fresh sausage at the carving station, Chinese, Hawaiian, and Southern specialties (soul food and the like). On Friday night, they have all this plus countless kinds of seafood all the way up to lobster.

✪ **Sam Boyd's Fremont Paradise Buffet.** 200 E. Fremont St. ☎ **702/385-3232.** Breakfast $5, lunch $6, dinner $9 ($14 for Seafood Fantasy); Sun brunch $8. AE, CB, DC, DISC, JCB, MC, V. Mon–Sat 7–10:30am and 11am–3pm; Mon, Wed, and Thurs 4–10pm, Sat 4–11pm; Seafood Fantasy Sun and Tues 4–10pm, Fri 4–11pm; Sun 7am–3pm.

This buffet is served in an attractive, tropically themed room. Diners sit in spacious booths amid lush jungle foliage—birds of paradise, palms, and bright tropical blooms—and the buffet area is surrounded by a "waterfall" of Tivoli lighting under a reflective ceiling. Island music, enhanced by bird calls and the sound of splashing waterfalls, helps set the tone. Meals here are on the lavish side.

Sunday, Tuesday, and Friday nights the buffet is renamed the Seafood Fantasy, and food tables, adorned with beautiful ice sculptures, are laden with lobster claws, crab legs, shrimp, raw oysters, smoked salmon, clams, and entrees such as steamed mussels, shrimp scampi, and scallops Provençale—all in addition to the usual meat carving stations and a few nonseafood entrees. It's great! And finally, the Fremont has a delightful champagne Sunday brunch served by "island girls" in colorful Polynesian garb. It includes not only unlimited champagne but a full carving station, lox with bagels and cream cheese, an omelet station, and desserts.

Showboat Captain's Buffet. 2800 Fremont St. ☎ **702/385-9123.** Lunch $5, dinner $6.45. AE, CB, DC, DISC, MC, V. Mon–Fri 10am–3:30pm; daily 4:30–10pm.

This buffet occupies a cheerful New Orleans garden-themed room. Wednesday is all-you-can-eat New York strip steak night. They have added a taco and a pizza bar. The Showboat initiated Las Vegas hotel buffets.

7

What to See & Do in Las Vegas

You aren't going to lack for things to do in Las Vegas. More than likely, you have come here for the gambling, which should keep you pretty busy (we say with some understatement). But you can't sit at a slot machine forever. (Or maybe you can.) In any event, it shouldn't be too hard to find ways to fill your time between poker hands.

Just walking on the Strip and gazing at the gaudy, garish, absurd wonder of it all can occupy quite a lot of time. This is the number-one activity we recommend in Vegas; at night, it is a mind-boggling sight like no other. And, of course, there are shows and plenty of other nighttime entertainment. But if you need something else to do, or if you are trying to amuse yourself while the rest of your party gambles away, this chapter will guide you. Don't forget to check out the free attractions, such as the Mirage's volcano and white tiger exhibit, Treasure Island's pirate battle, and the new Masquerade Show at the Rio Hotel.

You might also consider using a spa at a major hotel; they are too pricey (as high as $20 a day) to fill in for your daily gym visit, but spending a couple of hours working out, sweating out Vegas toxins in the steam room, and generally pampering yourself will leave you feeling relaxed, refreshed, and ready to go all night again.

There are also plenty of out-of-town sightseeing options, like **Hoover Dam** (a major tourist destination), **Red Rock Canyon,** and nexus-of-all-conspiracy-theories **Area 51,** along with excursions to the Grand Canyon. We've listed the best of these in chapter 11.

SUGGESTED ITINERARIES

The itineraries outlined here are for adults. If you're traveling with kids, incorporate some of the suggestions in "Especially for Kids," listed later in this chapter. The activities mentioned briefly here are described more fully later in this chapter.

If You Have 1 Day

Spend most of the day **casino-hopping.** These are buildings like no other, thank goodness. Each grandiose interior tops the last. Be sure to see the Mirage (including the white tigers), Treasure Island, Caesars Palace (including the Forum Shops and the talking

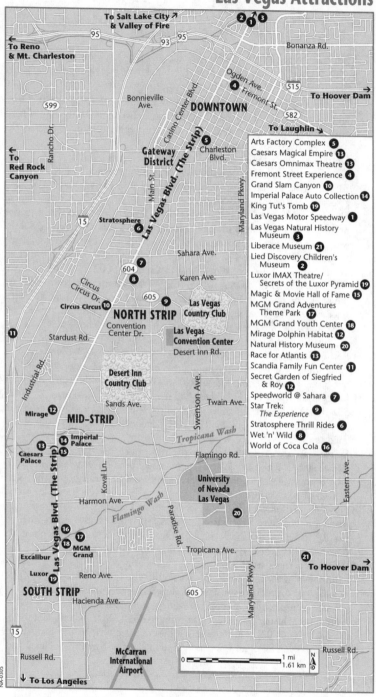

Las Vegas Attractions

To Salt Lake City ↗
& Valley of Fire
❷ ↗ ❸
❶

To Reno
& Mt. Charleston ←

Bonanza Rd.

95
93   95

515

599

Bonnieville
Ave.

Ogden Ave.
❹ Fremont St.

To Hoover Dam →

DOWNTOWN

582

To Laughlin ↘

Casino Center Blvd.

To
Red Rock ←
Canyon

Gateway
District

Charleston
Blvd.

❺

Main St.

Las Vegas Blvd. (The Strip)

Maryland Pkwy.

Rancho Dr.

15

Stratosphere

❻

Sahara Ave.

❼
604

Karen Ave.

❽

Circus
Circus Dr.

605   ❾

Las Vegas
Country Club

Circus Circus ❿

NORTH STRIP

Convention
Center Dr.

Las Vegas
Convention Center

⓫

Stardust Rd.

Desert Inn Rd.

Industrial Rd.

Desert Inn
Country Club

Sands Ave.

Swenson Ave.

Twain Ave.

Mirage ⓬

MID-STRIP

Tropicana Wash

⓭

❶④
Imperial
Palace

❶⑤

Flamingo Rd.

Caesars
Palace

Las Vegas Blvd. (The Strip)

Koval Ln.

Flamingo Wash

Paradise Rd.

University
of Nevada
Las Vegas

Eastern Ave.

Harmon Ave.

❷⓪

⓰

⓱

Tropicana Ave.

⓲
Excalibur

MGM
Grand

Reno Ave.

⓴
To Hoover Dam →

Maryland Pkwy.

⓳
Luxor

605

SOUTH STRIP

Hacienda Ave.

15

Russell Rd.

McCarran
International
Airport

Russell Rd.

0   1 mi
1.61 km

N

NA-0305

↓ To Los Angeles

Arts Factory Complex ❺
Caesars Magical Empire ⓭
Caesars Omnimax Theatre ⓭
Fremont Street Experience ❹
Grand Slam Canyon ❿
Imperial Palace Auto Collection ⓮
King Tut's Tomb ⓳
Las Vegas Motor Speedway ❶
Las Vegas Natural History
   Museum ❸
Liberace Museum ㉑
Lied Discovery Children's
   Museum ❷
Luxor IMAX Theatre/
   Secrets of the Luxor Pyramid ⓳
Magic & Movie Hall of Fame ⓯
MGM Grand Adventures
   Theme Park ⓱
MGM Grand Youth Center ⓲
Mirage Dolphin Habitat ⓬
Natural History Museum ⓴
Race for Atlantis ⓭
Scandia Family Fun Center ⓫
Secret Garden of Siegfried
   & Roy ⓬
Speedworld @ Sahara ❼
Star Trek:
   The Experience ❾
Stratosphere Thrill Rides ❻
Wet 'n' Wild ❽
World of Coca Cola ⓰

Sin City Inverted

If you want to get away from the glitz and kitsch or just go where most of the tourists don't go, here are 10 "un-Vegasey" things to do, kindly supplied by James P. Reza, Geoff Carter, and the editors of *Scope* magazine.

- **Enigma Garden Café** (see also the listings in chapters 6 and 10). Open around the clock, this wonderful garden cafe draws an intriguing mix of local artists, musicians, strippers, lawyers, and many other colorful characters. As close to a true oasis as you'll ever find.
- **Double Down Saloon** (see also the listing in chapter 10). Sin City's coolest bar, hands down. Enjoy cocktails, plug songs into the world's wildest jukebox, admire the bizarre mural work by Vegas artists, or just mingle with local characters and the occasional celebrity.
- **Utopia** (see also the listing in chapter 10). This two-story discotheque is not only the best nightclub in town but may also have a lock on the entire Southwest. Dance to techno, rave, acid jazz, and rare groove while watching people feel each other up.
- **West Sahara Library Fine Arts Museum,** 9002 W. Sahara Ave. (☎ 702/228-1940). Don't laugh. Las Vegas has its very own gala art museum, ensconced in the most impressive new building built in the Valley since Wayne Newton set up residence. Built to Smithsonian specs, the museum is one of the few urban buildings in Vegas that lends a sense of space and quality to the surrounding stucco.
- **Retro Vintage Couture,** 906 S. Valley View (☎ 702/877-8989). Melina Crisostomo's vintage clothing boutique is one of no kind we're aware of. Try out entire wardrobes from the '40s to the '70s, assisted by the wonderful staff.
- **Contemporary Arts Collective,** 103 E. Charleston, No. 102 (☎ 702/382-3886). Las Vegas's premier artist collective maintains a gallery inside the "Arts Factory" art compound. The CAC's unique vision of this town is too good to miss.
- **Jazzed Cafe and Vinoteca** (see also the listing in chapter 10). Run by professional dancers Kirk Offerle and Connie Chambers, this tiny, elegant bistro stays open until the wee hours, lit by candles and the brilliance of the clientele. Great java, terrific wine list.
- **Floyd Lamb State Park,** I-95 North; exit at Durango. This huge former working ranch once served as a forerunner of those trendy "desert spas" so popular in Scottsdale. Today you'll find acres and acres of grassy picnic areas, walking, hiking, biking, and horse trails, huge shade trees, and two lakes. Wanna be a true native? Always call it "Tule Springs."
- **Chinatown Mall,** 4255 Spring Mountain Rd. The Occident meets the Orient in a big way. A prodigious meeting of great restaurants, interesting shops, and unique amenities, all with roots buried deep in the Far East.
- **Huntridge Theater for the Performing Arts,** 1208 E. Charleston Blvd. (☎ 702/477-7703). This 50-year-old theater has played host to the likes of Abbott and Costello, Judy Garland, Nine Inch Nails, Sarah McLachlan, and Beck.

statues), New York New York, the MGM Grand, the Luxor, and the Excalibur. Then at night, take a drive (if you can) down **the Strip.** As amazing as all this is during the day, you can't believe it at night. Aside from just the Strip itself, there is the **pirate battle** at Treasure Island (consider watching it from the Battle Bar) and the **volcano explosion** next door at the Mirage. Eat at a buffet (details in chapter 6), and have a drink at the top of the Stratosphere, goggling at the view from the tallest building west of the Mississippi. Oh, and maybe you should gamble a little, too.

If You Have 2 Days

Do more of the above since you may well have not covered it all. Then do something really Vegasey and visit the **Liberace Museum.** The **Dolphin Habitat** at the Mirage is worth a look. Or you can rest your feet at the Caesars **OMNIMAX Theatre** and their giant-screen films. At night, take in a show. We think *Mystère,* the production from the avant-garde **Cirque du Soleil,** is the finest in Vegas, but there are plenty to choose from. Be sure to leave some time to go Downtown to check out the casinos in the classic Glitter Gulch and the **Fremont Street Experience** light show.

If You Have 3 Days

By now you've spent 2 days gambling and gawking. So take a break and drive out to **Red Rock Canyon.** The panoramic 13-mile Scenic Loop Drive is best seen early in the morning when there's little traffic. If you're so inclined, spend some time hiking here. If you want to spend the whole day out, have lunch at nearby **Bonnie Springs Ranch.** After lunch enjoy a guided trail ride into the desert wilderness or enjoy the silliness at **Old Nevada** (see chapter 11 for details). Return to town to experience dinner and a show at **Caesars Magical Empire,** an interactive theater experience that is thoroughly entertaining (details in this chapter).

If You Have 4 Days or More

Plan a tour to **Hoover Dam.** Leave early in the morning, returning to Las Vegas after lunch via **Valley of Fire State Park,** stopping at the **Lost City Museum** in Overton en route (see chapter 11 for details). Alternatively, you can rest up by spending the day by the hotel pool, or going to the hotel spa and possibly consuming a healthful salad or smoothie at the **Engima Cafe.** At night, presumably refreshed and toxins purged, hit the casinos and/or catch another show. If you aren't tired of magic, **Lance Burton** is a wonderful show for a reasonable price, or there is *EFX* if you feel like splurging, or *Jubliee!* if your trip won't be complete without a topless revue. You can also feast at dinner. **Gatsby's** or **Emeril's,** both in the MGM Grand, are two of the best restaurants, but if you also want a good dinner with a great free show, go to Treasure Island's **Buccaneer Bay Club,** which overlooks the pirate battle.

As you plan any additional days, consider excursions to other nearby attractions such as **Lake Mead,** the **Grand Canyon,** or even **Area 51.** Inquire about interesting tours at your hotel sightseeing desk.

1 Las Vegas Attractions

Arts Factory Complex. 103 E. Charleston Blvd. ☎ **702/382-3886.** Mon–Fri noon–5pm and by appointment.

Believe it or not, Las Vegas has a burgeoning art scene (what some would consider soul crushing is what others consider inspiration) and this complex, located in the Gateway district, is the place to find proof. It features a few galleries and a number of work spaces for local artists. Several of the spaces are closed to the public, but the two that are open are worth a look.

Note

While you're at Caesars, check out the talking statues at the Forum Shops and catch an OMNIMAX movie (the latter described below).

Subversive Souvenirs: This is a uniquely Vegas art gallery featuring the work of local artists. Most of the art has a Vegas theme, from photographs of the Strip to a large neon cactus to surreal circuslike posters. This kind of stuff could only be produced in the city of lights.

Not all of the art is appropriate for the home—or even affordable for the home, with prices ranging from $75 to $4,000. Regardless, it is an entertaining display.

Smallworks Gallery: This gallery is more for collectors than your average tourist. A few of the works had recently been purchased by the San Francisco Museum of Modern Art, which tells you something, and most are priced around $2,800, which tells you even more. With three galleries, they feature three new artists every 6 weeks. The art is definitely unique but not necessarily local. (On a recent visit, one of their featured artists was New York–based Susan Leopold.) The artwork is tastefully displayed in their small warehouse space, which has been jazzed up with polished hardwood floors and feels more like a museum than a gallery.

Best of all, however, is the **gift shop,** which has all the kitsch goodies you expect—and desperately hope—to find in Vegas. Large fuzzy dice, lawn flamingos, dice clocks, and other Vegas memorabilia fill this small shop and provide an entertaining (not to mention affordable) contrast to the high-class art next door.

✪ **Caesars Magical Empire.** Caesars Palace, 3570 Las Vegas Blvd. S. ☎ **800/445-4544** or 702/731-7333. Reservations required. Admission (including a 3-course meal and wine, tax, and gratuities) $75 adults, half price for children. Fri–Tues 4:30–11:30pm. Children must be at least 10 years of age.

Caesars spent a lot of money constructing this facility, and it shows. It's an impressive place of tunnels, grottoes, revolving rooms, theaters, and so forth, with a surprise around every corner. Upon arrival, you are assigned to a group of no more than 24, which is escorted through catacombs by Centurion guards to a private dining room. There you are treated to an intimate magic show by your own private magician. Assisted by some very funny wait staff, there is usually a little story played out as you eat your dinner. Up-close magic is performed between courses. Afterward, you are taken through the rest of the Cavern (beware the Forbidden Crypt of Ramses if you have anything even remotely resembling motion sickness—they ask only if you have "balance problems"); you'll end up in a 7-story dome, with massive Egyptian columns and sculptures, where you can see several other magic shows ranging in size. Here, you can experience **Lumineria,** a 5-minute show combining smoke, dancing fire, and high-tech lighting effects (cover your eyes before the finale—it's nearly blinding), or chat with some skeletons (Habeas and Corpus) on the walls and, best of all, request songs from "Invisibella," the player-piano ghost with a nearly unlimited repertoire and a great sense of humor. All throughout are additional spots with some kind of trick to them; be sure to ask the bartenders for advice. (And look for ghosts in the bathroom mirrors.) The idea for the concept was L.A.'s Magic Castle; Caesars has put its own ancient civilization stamp on it, and the place is truly impressive.

The three-course dinner isn't bad (salad and dessert were pretty good, main course average, though it featured a tasty polenta), and the whole experience is playful and genuinely fun. You can stay as long as you want, even after you have

Fremont Street was the hub of Las Vegas for almost 4 decades before the first casino hotel, El Rancho, opened on the Strip in 1941.

seen all the shows (though that could take a while as they rotate performers in the venues). There are two different bars inside, with video poker in case you are jonesing. You could hang out for hours in the Grotto Bar, making requests to Invisibella. As you are assigned one of the 10 dining rooms by lottery, you could go several nights in a row and see a different show with a different magician (and presumably, story) each time. Remember, this is interactive theater, so if your magician tries to get you involved, play along, as your fun factor will increase if you are a good sport.

Allow yourself at least 3 hours to see everything once. Considering how much show, spectacle, food, and just plain entertainment you get, this is one of the best values in the city.

Caesars OMNIMAX Theatre. Caesars Palace, 3570 Las Vegas Blvd. S. ☎ **800/634-6698** or 702/731-7901. Admission $7 adults; $5 seniors, children 2–12, hotel guests, and military personnel. Show times vary. You must purchase tickets at the box office (open daily 9am–11pm) on the day of the performance.

If you've never seen one of these 3-D-like films, you're in for a treat. The OMNIMAX Theatre here is housed in a geodesic dome, a space-age environment with 368 seats that recline 27°, affording a panoramic view of the curved 57-foot screen. The movies, projected via 70mm film (which is 10 times the frame size of ordinary 35mm film), offer an awesome visual display enhanced by a state-of-the-art sound system (89 speakers engulf the audience in sound). Depending on the film being shown, viewers might soar over the Rocky Mountains, plummet down steep waterfalls, ride the rapids, travel into outer space, or perch at the rim of an erupting volcano. Shows change frequently, but whatever you see will be stupendous.

✪ **Fremont Street Experience.** Fremont St., between Main St. and Las Vegas Blvd. in Downtown Las Vegas. www.vegasexperience.com. Free admission. Shows nightly.

For some years, Downtown Vegas has been losing ground to the Strip. But thanks to a $70 million revitalization project, that is starting to change. Fremont Street, the heart of "Glitter Gulch," has been closed off and turned into a pedestrian mall. The Fremont Street Experience is a 5-block open-air pedestrian mall, a landscaped strip of outdoor cafes, vendor carts, and colorful kiosks purveying food and merchandise. Overhead is a 90-foot-high steel-mesh "celestial vault"; at night, it is the **Sky Parade,** a high-tech light-and-laser show (the canopy is equipped with more than 2.1 million lights) enhanced by a concert hall–quality sound system, which takes place four times nightly. But there's music between shows as well. Not only does the canopy provide shade, it cools the area through a misting system in summer and warms you with radiant heaters in winter. The difference this makes cannot be overemphasized; what was once a ghost town of tacky, rapidly aging buildings, in an area with more undesirables than not, is now a bustling (at least at night), friendly, safe place (they have private security guards who hustle said undesirables away). It's a place where you can stroll, eat, or even dance to the music under the lights. The crowd it attracts is more upscale than in years past, and of course, it's a lot less crowded than the hectic Strip. Some rightly mourn the passing of cruising

---

Insider Tip

A good place to view the Sky Parade light show is from the balcony at Fitzgerald's Hotel.

Glitter Gulch, gawking at the original lights. It does indeed mean the end of classic Las Vegas, but on the other hand, classic Las Vegas was dead and nearly buried anyway. This has given a second life to a deserving neighborhood.

And in a further effort to retain as much of classic Las Vegas as possible, the **Neon Museum** is installing vintage hotel and casino signs along the promenade. The first installation is the horse and rider from the old Hacienda, which presently rides the sky over the intersection of Fremont and Las Vegas Boulevard. (Eventually, the Neon Museum hopes to have an indoor installation on the Fremont Street Experience, to showcase some of the smaller signs they have collected.)

Imperial Palace Auto Collection. Imperial Palace Hotel, 3535 Las Vegas Blvd. S. ☎ **702/731-3311.** Admission $7 adults, $3 seniors and children under 12, free for children under 5 and AAA members. Daily 9:30am–11:30pm.

If you're not a "car person," don't assume you won't be interested in this premier collection of antique, classic, and special-interest vehicles. There's more here than just cars and trucks. Check out the graceful lines and handsome sculpture of one of the 43 Model J Dusenbergs (the largest collection in the world valued at over $50 million). The craftsmanship and attention to detail make these cars, and others here, true works of art.

There's also a great deal of history. Take a walk down President's Row where you can see JFK's 1962 "bubbletop" Lincoln Continental, Lyndon Johnson's 1964 Cadillac, Eisenhower's 1952 Chrysler Imperial 20-foot-long parade car, Truman's 1950 Lincoln Cosmopolitan with gold-plated interior, FDR's unrestored 1936 V-16 Cadillac, and Herbert Hoover's 1929 Cadillac. Directly opposite this tribute to democracy, in both location and political theory, is the dictator section. Here you will see Adolf Hitler's armored, bulletproof, and mineproof 1936 Mercedes-Benz 770K, Emperor Hirohito's 1935 Packard, Czar Nicholas II's 1914 Rolls-Royce, former Mexican president Lazaro Cardena's black 1939 V-12 Packard (armor-plated to resist 50-caliber machine gun bullets), and Argentinean strongman Juan Peron's 1939 straight-8 Packard (no pictures of Evita anywhere). The Imperial Palace owner, who came under fire some years ago for throwing a birthday party for Hitler, claims he is not a Fascist, just a buff, but you do have to wonder.

Commercial vehicles of bygone days include antique buses, military transports, taxis (among them, the 1908 French model that appeared in the movie version of *My Fair Lady*), gasoline trucks, fire engines, delivery trucks and vans, dump trucks, and pickup trucks. Other highlights are Al Capone's 1930 V-16 Cadillac, Elvis Presley's powder-blue 1976 Cadillac Eldorado, Liberace's pale-cream 1981 Zimmer (complete with candelabra), W. C. Fields's black 1938 Cadillac V-16 touring sedan with built-in bar, Caruso's 1920 green-and-black Hudson, Howard Hughes's 1954 Chrysler (because of his phobia about germs, Hughes installed a special air-purification system that cost more than the car itself!), and a 1947 Tucker (one of only 51 manufactured before the company went out of business).

King Tut's Tomb & Museum. Luxor Las Vegas, 3900 Las Vegas Blvd. S. ☎ **702/262-4000.** Admission $4. Sun–Thurs 9am–11pm, Fri–Sat 9am–11:30pm.

This full-scale reproduction of King Tutankhamen's Tomb includes the antechamber, annex, burial chamber, and treasury housing replicas (all handcrafted in Egypt by artisans using historically correct gold leaf and linens, pigments, tools, and ancient methods) of the glittering inventory discovered by archaeologists Howard Carter and Lord Carnarvon in the Valley of Kings at Luxor in 1922. All items have been meticulously positioned according to Carter's records. It's hardly like seeing the real thing, but if you aren't going to Egypt any time soon, perhaps checking out reproductions isn't a bad idea. A 20-minute audio tour (available in English, French, Spanish, and Japanese) is preceded by a 4-minute introductory film.

Las Vegas Motor Speedway. 7000 Las Vegas Blvd. N., directly across from Nellis Air Force base (take I-15 north to Speedway exit 54). ☎ **702/644-4443** for ticket information. Tickets $10–$75 (higher prices for major events).

This 107,000-seat facility, the first new superspeedway to be built in the Southwest in over 2 decades, opened with a 500K Indy Racing League event. A $100 million state-of-the-art motor-sports entertainment complex, it includes a 1.5-mile super-speedway, a 2.5-mile FIA-approved road course, paved and dirt short-track ovals, and a 4,000-foot drag strip. Also on the property are facilities for Go-Kart, Legends Car, Sand Drag, and Motorcross competition. The new speedway is accessible via shuttle buses to and from the Imperial Palace hotel, though some of the other major hotels have their own shuttles to the Speedway.

✪ **Liberace Museum.** 1775 E. Tropicana Ave., at Spencer St. ☎ **702/798-5595.** Admission $7 adults, $4.50 seniors over 60, $3.50 students, $2 children 6–12, free for children under 6. Mon–Sat 10am–5pm, Sun 1–5pm.

You can keep your Louvres and Vaticans and Smithsonians; *this* is a museum. Housed, like everything else in Vegas, in a strip mall, this is a shrine to the glory and excess that was the art project known as Liberace. You've got your costumes (bejeweled), your many cars (bejeweled), your many pianos (bejeweled), and many jewels (also bejeweled). It just shows what can be bought with lots of money and no taste. The thing is, Liberace was in on the joke (we think). The people who come here largely aren't. Many of these guests would not have liked him living next door to them if his name was, say, Bruce Smith, but they idolize the man-the-myth. Not found here is any reference to AIDS or chauffeurs who had plastic surgery to look more like him. But you will find a Czar Nicholas uniform with 22-karat-gold braiding and a blue velvet cape styled after the coronation robes of King George V and covered with $60,000 worth of rare chinchilla. Not to mention a 50.6-pound rhinestone costing $50,000, the world's largest, presented to him by the grateful (I'll bet they were) Austrian firm that supplied all his costume stones. The gift shop has plenty of rhinestone-covered objects plus countless Liberace knickknacks of increasing tackiness. This is a one-of-a-kind place. Unless you have a severely underdeveloped appreciation for camp or take your museum-going very seriously, you shouldn't miss it. The museum is 2½ miles east of the Strip on your right.

Luxor IMAX Theater/Secrets of the Luxor Pyramid. Luxor Las Vegas, 3900 Las Vegas Blvd. S. ☎ **702/262-4000.** Admission $7 for IMAX 2-D, $8.50 for 3-D; for "Secrets" Episode One $4, Episode Two $5. A combined ticket, including both episodes of *Secrets of the Luxor Pyramid* (described below), is $9. Sun–Thurs 10am–11pm, Fri–Sat 10am–11:30pm. Show times vary depending on the length of the film.

This is a state-of-the-art theater that projects films on a 7-story screen. There are two different films running: one in standard two dimensions, the other 3-D. The glasses for the latter are really cool headsets that include built-in speakers, bringing certain sounds right into your head. The movies change periodically but always include some extraordinary special effects. If you have a fear of heights, make sure to ask for a seat on one of the lower levels.

Secrets of the Luxor Pyramid is a two-part adventure. In Episode One, you become part of the audience for a live broadcast that begins a tabloid TV talk show. The topic is the mysterious happenings below the pyramid. The guests are a militaristic government agent, Colonel Calggert, and Mac MacPherson (the good guy). Parts of this are in 3-D, and it sets up the story for Episode Two.

Episode Two is a motion-simulator ride in which technology is used to create an action adventure involving a chase sequence inside a pyramid. In a rapidly plummeting elevator (the cable has broken!) you'll descend to an ancient temple 2 miles beneath the Luxor pyramid. Against the orders of Colonel Claggert, you'll accompany MacPherson and Carina Wolinski (the love interest) in their search for a mysterious crystal obelisk containing the secrets of the universe. In a thrill ride through the temple's maze, you'll experience an explosive battle with evil forces, rescue Carina from the clutches of Dr. Osiris, and narrowly escape death before returning to the surface. You have an option to take a different route if you have motion sickness, which means you won't get the best special effects. Otherwise, it's a standard thrill ride with interesting touches.

✪ **Magic and Movie Hall of Fame.** O'Shea's Casino, 3555 Las Vegas Blvd. S., between Sands Ave. and Flamingo Rd. ☎ **702/737-1343.** Admission $10 adults, $3 children under 12 accompanied by an adult. ($5 discount coupons available outside.) Tues–Sat 10am–6pm. Magic shows at 1 and 4:30pm.

Given its location in the cheesy and just a tad sleazy O'Sheas, one might be tempted to skip over this Hall of Fame as a cheap tourist trap—or, at least, something appealing only to kiddies. That would be a mistake. This well-produced and informative tribute to magicians, ventriloquists, and past movie stars has all the fun of old curiosity shows.

The tour begins with a chronological history of late 19th-century and 20th-century magicians. Harry Kellar's perfection of levitation, Thurston's dice cases and spike cabinet, Harry Blackstone Jr., who used a buzz saw to cut a woman in two, Mephistophelean Dante as the original "Abracadabra" and "Hocus Pocus," and of course Houdini—all have eerie, darkened displays that give you the feeling that you are looking at something truly supernatural. Black-and-white videos show actual footage of their acts along with a description of their contribution to magic. There are also exhibits on contemporary magicians such as Doug Henning and Siegfried and Roy, but they emphasize more the illusion than the unknown. The whole thing is carnival creepy and reminds you of the days when magicians were mysterious and maybe just a little bit in touch with forces from the Great Beyond.

Surprisingly, there is also an extensive exhibit of the history of ventriloquism from Ancient Greece, to King Saul and the Witch at Endor, to Shari Lewis and Lamb Chop. Best of all, you can even try ventriloquism yourself with the help of a dummy, a mirror, and audio and written help. (It's not easy!) There are also contributions by modern-day ventriloquists such as Jeff Dunham and Ronn Lucas. By the end, you come away with a new appreciation for the skills involved in this rather forgotten and underappreciated vaudeville act.

The "Movie" part is manifested in a large display of costumes from classic movies. It's anticlimatic after what you've seen before, but you can ogle Clark Gable's suit coat from *Gone with the Wind*, Charlie Chaplin's military uniform from *The Great Dictator*, Errol Flynn's "Robin Hood" tights, and Marilyn Monroe's dress from *River of No Return*. (You should see how tiny her waist was—are people made like that anymore?).

Either before or after the tour you can pick up a show by Vivian Fox, a magician and ventriloquist. Alas, though he seems like a nice enough guy, his show is less than impressive, and you can safely give it a miss.

Natural History Museum. 4505 Maryland Pkwy., on UNLV campus. ☎ **702/895-3381.** Free admission. Mon–Fri 8am–4:45pm, Sat 10am–2pm.

This is a cool place to beat the heat and noise of Vegas, while examining some attractive, if not overly imaginative, displays on Native American craftwork and Las Vegas history. Crafts include 19th-century Mexican religious folk art, a variety of colorful dance masks of Mexico, and Native American pottery. The first part of the hall is often the highlight, with impressive traveling art exhibits. Children won't find much that is entertaining outside of some glass cases containing examples of local, usually poisonous reptiles (which, if you are lucky, or unlucky, depending on your view, will be dining on mice when you drop by). Outside is a pretty garden demonstrating how attractive more desert-appropriate plants (in other words, those requiring little water) can be. One wishes the local casinos, with their lush, and wasteful, lawns would take notice.

Race for Atlantis Ride IMAX 3-D Ride. 3500 Las Vegas Blvd. S., in the Forum Shops at Caesar's Palace. Admission $9.50 adults, $6.75 children under 12. Sun–Thurs 10am–11pm, Fri–Sat 10am–midnight.

Following the trend in virtual reality theme-park rides, Caesar's Palace joined forces with IMAX to create the Race for Atlantis. If you've never been on a virtual reality ride, you will enjoy it, but the production values pale compared to *Star Trek: The Experience* (but then again, that's also twice as expensive). This experience begins as you walk past a giant statue of Neptune and his chariot drawn by wild-looking Sea Serpents. The stone hallway appears to lead into an underwater palace. As the line twists around, a sci-fi fantasy world unfolds with mists clouding the multicolored lights of the legendary city of Atlantis. Once in the ride you are treated to a 3-D visor and a silly safety rap sung by Neptune's cowardly secretary. The ride itself is a 3-D motion simulator, which uses computer animation to create the lost city and the racecourse. The goal is to get to the ring before the evil demon god gets there first. If you like a bumpy ride, be sure to sit in the very front or very back. During the 4-minute race, your chariot is impeded by flying shrapnel, the evil god, and even by Neptune's own inept secretary. With the 3-D glasses all of these sharp objects flying at you can get pretty intense. Eventually, the ring is saved and the famed city of Atlantis survives. Not for the weak of stomach.

Secret Garden of Siegfried and Roy & ✪ Mirage Dolphin Habitat. Mirage Hotel, 3400 Las Vegas Blvd. S. ☎ **702/791-7111.** Admission $10, free for children under 10. Mon–Fri 11am–5:30pm, Sat–Sun 10am–5:30pm. Dolphin exhibit only on Wed, when the Secret Garden is closed; admission $5. Hours subject to change.

Siegfried and Roy's famous white tigers have long had a free exhibit in the Mirage. They still do, but now they have an additional space, a gorgeous area behind the dolphin exhibit. Here, the white tigers are joined by white lions, Bengal tigers, an Asian elephant, a panther, and a snow leopard. (Many of these are bred by Siegfried & Roy and are also in their nightly show.) It's really just a glorified zoo, featuring only the big-ticket animals; however, it is a very pretty place, with plenty of foliage and some bits of Indian- and Asian-themed architecture. Zoo purists will be horrified at the smallish spaces the animals occupy, but all are rotated between here and their more lavish digs at the illusionist team's home. What this does allow you to do is get very up close with a tiger, which is quite a thrill—those paws are massive indeed. Visitors are given little portable phonelike objects on which they can play a

Siegfried & Roy's House

When they aren't on stage, they are just plain (okay, nothing is plain with them) Siegfried Fischbacher and Roy Horn. And they live in a house at 1639 Valley on the corner of Vegas Drive (right across from the golf course). We aren't giving much away; if you want to be anonymous, you don't put a big gold "SR" on all your gates, which by the way are huge and gilt. White lions top the massive white stucco wall that lines the property. You can't see any of the fabulous wonders inside (there is a book on sale at the Mirage, complete with many photos of their house, overdecorated, stuffed-within-an-inch-of-its-life with objects from around the world, tigers roaming freely), but you can see the bits of the vaguely Spanish mission-style dwelling peeking over the top of the walls. Across the street are much smaller houses, also sporting the gold "SR" on their gates. These have been purchased by the Austrian magicians, as guesthouses, turning the whole block into a sort of compound. Drive by with the windows down and maybe you can hear lions and tigers (and bears) roar.

series of programs, listening to Roy and Mirage owner Steve Wynn discuss conservation or the attributes of each animal and deliver anecdotes.

The Dolphin habitat is more satisfying. It was designed to provide a healthy and nurturing environment and to educate the public about marine mammals and their role in the ecosystem. Specialists worldwide were consulted in creating the habitat, which was designed to serve as a model of a quality, secured environment. The pool is more than eight times larger than government regulations require, and its 2.5 million gallons of man-made seawater are cycled and cleaned once every 2 hours. It must be working, as the adult dolphins here are breeding regularly. The Mirage displays only dolphins already in captivity—no dolphins will be taken from the wild. You can watch the dolphins frolic both above and below ground through viewing windows, in three different pools. (There is nothing quite like the kick you get from seeing a baby dolphin play.) The knowledgeable staff, who surely have the best job in Vegas, will answer questions. If they aren't already, ask them to play ball with the dolphins; they toss large beach balls into the pools, and the dolphins hit them out with their noses, leaping out of the water cackling with dolphin glee. You catch the ball, getting nicely wet, and toss it back to them. If you have never played ball with a dolphin, shove that happy child next to you out of the way and go for it. There is also a video of a resident dolphin (Duchess) giving birth (to Squirt) underwater. You can stay as long as you like, which might just be hours.

Speedworld at Sahara. 2535 Las Vegas Blvd. S., in the Sahara Hotel. ☎ **702/737-2111.** Indy-car simulator $8 (you must be at least 48 in. tall to ride), 3-D simulator $5. Mon–Thurs 10am–10pm, Fri–Sun 10am–midnight.

As auto racing is the fastest-growing spectator sport in America, Speedworld is sure to be a popular stop. Consisting of two parts, the first is an 8-minute virtual-reality ride featuring a three-quarter-sized replica of an Indianapolis race car. Hop aboard for an animated, simulated ride—either the Indy itself or a race around the streets of Las Vegas (start with the Strip, with all the hotels flashing by, and then through the Forum Shops—whoops! there goes Versace!—and so forth). Press the gas and you lean back and feel the rush of speed; hit a bump and you go flying. Should your car get in a crash, off you go to a pit stop. At the end, a computer-generated report tells you your average speed, how many laps you made, how you did racing against the others next to you, and so forth. It's a pretty remarkable experience.

A separate 3-D motion theater sets you up, complete with goggles, to view a film that puts you right inside another race car, for yet another stomach-churning (more so than the virtual-reality portion) ride. Speed junkies and race-car buffs will be in heaven here, though those with tender stomachs should consider shopping at the well-stocked theme gift shop instead.

Star Trek: The Experience. Las Vegas Hilton, 3000 Paradise Rd. ☎ **702/732-5111.** www.startrekexp.com. Admission $13. Daily 11am–11pm.

It goes without saying that Trekkers (note use of correct term) will be delighted with this. On the other hand, normal, sensible fans, and those who couldn't care less about *Star Trek,* may find themselves saying, "I spent $13 and 2 hours in line for this?"

A fancy entry in the latest Vegas attractions fad, the motion-simulator ride, you can't fault the setup and interior design; after a walk through a space-themed casino (check out those light-beam-activated slot machines!), your long wait in line will be somewhat entertaining, thanks to memorabilia (displayed as if this were the stuff of fact, not fiction) and TVs showing various *Trek* clips. As you make your way to the ride proper, you encounter actors dressed in Trek-gear, who let you know that you've crossed the line into the Trek future. There is a story line, but we won't spoil it for you; suffice to say it involves evil doings by the Borgs, time travel, and if all doesn't work out, the very history of *Star Trek* could be affected. Do expect to be beamed aboard the *Enterprise* (that's really kind of cool), and know that if you have a sensitive stomach, you can skip the actual motion-simulator part, a wild, and sometimes headache-inducing, chase through space. In addition to the expected lengthy wait (on average, 20 minutes; best shot at a slight lull would be between noon and 1pm on weekdays), the quality of your experience can vary depending on the quality of those Trek-garbed actors, whose line delivery can be awfully stilted. On the way out, through the shops selling everything Trek and space-oriented, don't miss the TV showing a "news report" about some of the very things you just experienced.

Stratosphere Thrill Rides. Stratosphere, 2000 Las Vegas Blvd. S. ☎ **702/380-7777.** Admission for either ride $5; $3 per re-ride, plus $5 to ascend the tower (if you dine in the buffet room or Top of the World, there's no charge to go up to the tower). Sun–Thurs 10am–midnight, Fri–Sat 10am–2am. Minimum height requirement for both rides is 48 in.

Atop the 1,149-foot Stratosphere Tower are two marvelous thrill rides. The **Let It Ride High Roller** (the world's highest roller coaster) was recently revamped to go at even faster speeds as it zooms around a hilly track that is seemingly suspended in midair. Even more fun is the **Big Shot,** a breathtaking free-fall ride that thrusts you 160 feet in the air along a 228-foot spire at the top of the tower, then plummets back down again. Sitting in an open car, you seem to be dangling in space over Las Vegas. We have one relative, a thrill-ride enthusiast, who said he never felt more scared than when he rode the Big Shot. After surviving, he promptly put his kids on it, who loved it.

World of Coca-Cola. 3785 Las Vegas Blvd. S., just north of Tropicana Ave. in Showcase Mall. ☎ **800/720-COKE.** Admission $2, free for children under 6. Sun–Thurs 10am–11pm, Fri–Sat 10am–midnight.

The world's most popular cola (sorry, Pepsi) now has a "museum" devoted to the wonders of Coke. What are the wonders of Coke? Well, if you can overlook that this attraction is one giant advertisement, there are actually a few. Did you know that when Coke was first produced, it was touted as a medicinal remedy? Learn about it on the first part of the self-guided tour (that is, after an elevator takes you up through the world's largest Coke bottle), which leads you through the history of

Coca-Cola. Admire a tray with Hilda Clark, first actress to be a spokesperson for the cola, now worth $83,000, view all-time favorite Coke commercials (fun for nostalgia's sake), admire an art gallery showing various artistic portrayals of Coke, and finish up at a water-ballet fountain that with precision timing will shoot Coke into your strategically placed cup. You can also sample fountain drinks of every Coke product known to man—do your own blind taste tests on the spot. Finally, there are two floors devoted to a gift shop that seems to have an unlimited amount of overpriced objects emblazoned with the Coke logo. Don't buy anything, just to annoy them.

2 Getting Married

This is one of the most popular things to do in Las Vegas. Why? It's very easy to get married here. Too easy. See that total stranger standing next to you? Grab him or her, head down to the **Clark Country Marriage License Bureau,** 200 S. 3rd at Briger Avenue (☎ **702/455-3156;** open Monday to Sunday from 8am to midnight, 24 hours legal holidays), to get your license, find a wedding chapel (not hard since they line the north end of the Strip—Las Vegas Boulevard South), and tie the knot. Just like that. No blood test, no waiting period—heck, not even an awkward dating period.

But even if you have actually known your intended for some time, Las Vegas is a great place to get married. The ease is the primary attraction, but there are a number of other appealing reasons. You can have any kind of wedding you want, from a big, traditional production number, to a small, intimate affair, to a spur-of-the-moment "just the happy couple in blue jeans" kind of thing, to Elvis in a pink Cadillac at a drive-up window. (Oh, yes. More on that later.) The wedding chapels take care of everything; usually they will even provide a limo to take you to the license bureau and back. Most offer all the accessories, from rings to flowers to a videotape memory of the event.

We personally know several very happy couples who opted for the Vegas route. Motivations differed, with the ease factor heading the list (though the Vegas-ness of the whole thing came in a close second), but one and all reported having great fun. Really, what more romantic way to start off your life together than in gales of laughter?

In any event, the more than 100,000 couples who take advantage of all this can't be wrong. If you want to follow in the footsteps of Elvis and Priscilla (at the recently imploded Aladdin Hotel), Michael Jordan, Joan Collins, Bruce Willis and Demi Moore, the following is a list of the most notable wedding chapels on or near the Strip. There are many more in town, and almost all the major hotels offer a chapel as well; though the latter are cleaner and less tacky than some of the Strip chapels, they do tend to be without any personality at all. (One exception might be the chapel at the Excalibur Hotel, where you can dress in medieval costumes.)

With regard to decor, there isn't a radical difference between the major places, though some are decidedly more spiffy and less sad than others. Attitude certainly makes a difference with several. (In passing, standing outside a wedding chapel for a couple of hours makes for interesting people-watching, as you see brides in full white gowns accompanied by a whole retinue, pregnant brides in ordinary dresses, or happy couples wearing sweats, all ready to march down that aisle.)

You can also call **Las Vegas Weddings and Rooms** (☎ **800/488-MATE**), a one-stop shop for wedding services. They'll find a chapel or outdoor garden that suits your taste (not to mention such only-in-Vegas venues as the former mansions of

An Elvis Impersonator's Top 10 Reasons to Get Married in Las Vegas

Jesse Garon has appeared in numerous Las Vegas productions as "Young Elvis." He arrives at any special event in a 1955 pink, neon-lit Cadillac. Jesse Garon is available for weddings, receptions, birthdays, conventions, grand openings, and so on. Video and print support also available. For all your Elvis impersonator needs, call ☎ **702/474-9227.**

1. The only place in the world where Elvis will marry you, at a drive-up window, in a pink Cadillac—24 hours a day.

2. Chances are you'll never forget your anniversary.

3. Where else can you treat all your guests to a wedding buffet for only 99¢ a head?

4. Four words: One helluva bachelor party.

5. On wedding night, show spouse that new "watch me disappear" act you learned from Siegfried and Roy.

6. Show your parents who's boss—have your wedding your way.

7. Wedding bells ring for you everywhere you go. They just sound like slot machines.

8. You can throw dice instead of rice.

9. Easy to lie about age on the marriage certificate—just like Joan Collins did!

10. With all the money you save, it's dice clocks for everyone!

Elvis Presley and Liberace), book you into a hotel for the honeymoon, arrange the ceremony, and provide flowers, a photographer (or videographer), wedding cake, limo, car rental, music, champagne, balloons, and a garter for the bride. Basically they can arrange anything you like. Theme weddings are a specialty. They even have a New Age minister on call who can perform a Native American ceremony. And yes, you can get married by an Elvis impersonator. Let Las Vegas Weddings arrange your honeymoon stay—sightseeing tours, show tickets, and meals, as well.

Be aware that Valentine's Day is a very popular day to get married in Vegas. Some of the chapels perform as many as 80 services.

But remember, you also don't have to plan ahead. Just show up, get your paperwork, close your eyes, and pick a chapel. And above all, have fun. Good luck and best wishes to you both.

ABOUT THE PRICES   Weddings can be very cheap in Vegas: A license is about $35, and a basic service not much more. Even a full-blown shebang package—photos, music, some flowers, video, cake, other doodads—will run only about $500 total. We haven't quoted any prices here since the ultimate cost depends entirely on how much you want to spend. Go cheap, and the whole thing will put you back maybe $100, including the license (maybe even somewhat less); go elaborate, and the price is still reasonable by today's wedding price standards. Be sure to remember that there are often "hidden" charges, such as expected gratuities for the minister, and so forth. If you're penny-pinching, you'll want to keep those in mind.

Chapel of the Bells. 2233 Las Vegas Blvd. S. ☎ **800/233-2391** or 702/735-6803. Mon–Thurs 9am–9pm, Fri–Sat 9am–midnight. They stay open as late as they need to on holidays.

Sporting perhaps the largest and gaudiest sign on the Strip, this chapel also shares a parking lot with the bright pink Fun City Motel. We won't make any jokes. The chapel has wood paneling, sage carpeting, and gilt trim up by the pulpit. Electric candles light the walls. It only seats about 25. They prefer advance booking but can do same-day ceremonies if called for.

Chapel of Love. 1430 Las Vegas Blvd. S. ☎ **800/922-5683** or 702/387-0155. Mon–Thurs 8am–10pm, Fri–Sat 8am–midnight, Sun 9am–9pm.

A friendly place largely run by women (men take the photos and are the limo drivers), featuring four different chapels. None are very big; the Lavender and Peach Chapels hold only 16. (And yes, the difference would be in the modest floral themes on the wallpaper and at the pulpit and the stained-glass windows.) The Rose Chapel holds 50, and the Rainbow Chapel (no, it's not done in rainbows, thank heavens, though there is one on the window under the kissing doves) holds 35. Obviously, some of these rooms are downright tiny and the decor not the most memorable (though the wallpaper adds a touch of individuality; so many of the other chapels just have white walls with wood paneling). But this is a pretty place and very affordable. There is a also a reception room for a cold buffet or hot hors d'oeuvres. Their packages are quite reasonable, and they put all the "hidden" charges (such as suggested gratuities for the minister and so forth) right in their brochure, so there are no surprises.

⭐ **Cupid's Wedding Chapel.** 827 Las Vegas Blvd. S. ☎ **800/543-2933** or 702/598-4444. Sun–Thurs 10am–10pm, Fri–Sat 10am–1am.

"The little chapel with the big heart." Well, they just might be. The manager explains that, unlike other chapels on the Strip, they schedule weddings an hour apart. This gives them time for the full production number; they pride themselves on offering "a traditional church wedding at a chapel price." This includes a bridal processional, dimmed lights as the minister introduces the happy couple, and then a tape of the couple's favorite song, so they can have their first dance right there at the pulpit after their "first" kiss. They also offer family weddings for those couples blending preexisting ones; the children become a part of the service, and as their parents exchange rings with each other, the kids are given their own small token, to let them know the parents are marrying them as well. "I am a diehard romantic," said the manager, "I want huggin', kissin', and I don't care if they faint—a wedding is a place for romance." You just know she cries at each and every service they perform. The chapel is pleasantly low-frills and down to earth, with white walls and pews, and modern stained glass with doves and roses. (Kitsch-phobes will be pleased to know the cupids are only in the lobby.) It seats 60 to 70. And, yes, if they don't have something already scheduled, they will take walk-ups. There is a restaurant (Thai) right next door that was closed as of this writing, but if it has reopened, there's your reception!

Graceland Wedding Chapel. 619 Las Vegas Blvd. S. ☎ **800/824-5732** or 702/474-6655. Sun–Thurs 9am–9pm, Fri–Sat 9am–midnight.

Housed in a landmark building that is one of the oldest wedding chapels in Vegas, the Graceland bills itself as "the proverbial Mom and Pop outfit. We offer friendly, courteous service, and are willing to go that extra step." No, there is no Elvis connection; one of the owners was friends with Elvis and asked his permission to use the name. This is a tiny New England church building with a small bridge and white picket fence out front. Inside is a 33-seat chapel; burgundy and white walls with a large, modern stained-glass window of doves and roses behind the pulpit.

The pews are dark blond wood. It is not the nicest of the chapels. Jon Bon Jovi and Lorenzo Lamas got married here, though not to each other.

Little Chapel of the Flowers. 1717 Las Vegas Blvd. S. ☎ **800/843-2410** or 702/735-4331. www.littlechapel.com. Mon–Sun 8am–10pm.

This is another miniature old-fashioned church building with a very tiny garden and gazebo. They have two chapels off their pretty and comfortable lobby (mock-antique look). The Victorian chapel, which holds only 30, has white walls and dark-wood pews and doesn't look very Victorian at all. The Heritage Chapel holds 70 and adds rose-colored drapes and electric candle chandeliers. They also offer a medium-size reception room and live organ music upon request. It's a pretty, friendly place, but not particularly special in terms of look (though it is not shabby as some chapels are). They do not allow rice or confetti throwing.

Little White Chapel. 1301 Las Vegas Blvd. S. ☎ **800/545-8111** or 702/382-5943. Open 24 hours.

This is arguably the most famous of the chapels on the Strip, maybe because they have the big sign saying Michael Jordan and Joan Collins were married there (again, not to each other), maybe because they were the first to do the drive-up window. It is indeed little and white. However, they feel like a factory line, processing wedding after wedding after wedding, 24 hours a day. Move 'em in and move 'em out. (No wonder they put in that drive-up window!) The staff, dressed in hot pink smocks, was brusque, hasty, and had a bit of an attitude (though we know one couple who got married here and had no complaints). They do offer full wedding ceremonies, complete with candlelight service and traditional music. There are two chapels, the smaller of which has a large photo of a forest stream. They also have a gazebo for outdoor services, but since that is right on the Strip, it's not as nice as it sounds. If you want something special, there are probably better choices, but for a true Vegas wedding experience this is Kitsch Wedding Central.

Mission of the Bells. 1205 Las Vegas Blvd. S. ☎ **888/627-7961** or 702/366-0646. Mon–Fri 9am–6pm, Sat noon–8pm, Sun 10am–6pm.

This is the largest wedding chapel on the Strip; the chapel holds 125. The outside is like an adobe mission (hence the name) topped by a large bell, and so the inside carries through on the Southwestern theme, with wood benches, fake adobe wall at the altar, Native American design stained-glass windows, a very tall cathedral ceiling, and Western Indian–style chandeliers. It is large and warm, not claustrophobic. However, the management always seems to be suspicious and just a tad strange. Across the street is Slightly Sinful, "a romantic boutique," in case you need a trousseau or to otherwise stock up for the wedding night.

San Francisco Sally's Victorian Chapel. 1304 Las Vegas Blvd. S. ☎ **800/658-8677** or 702/385-7777. Sun–Thurs 10am–4pm, Fri–Sat 10am–8pm.

An extremely tiny wedding chapel bursting at the seams with Victorian frills (fringed lamps, swags of lace curtains). They basically offer "an Olde Tyme Parlor Wedding." This is perfect if you want a very intimate wedding—like you, your intended, and someone to officiate. It literally can't hold more than six people. (And the space at the back of the room opens for an even tinier reception area—it can barely fit the cake!) But if you love Victoriana, or you want to play dress-up at your wedding, this is the place. The shop rents out dresses and costumes, so you can wear a Scarlett O'Hara antebellum outfit or some other period number for your big day. (It's all fantasy anyway, so why not go whole hog?) They specialize in extras without extra charges like altering and whatnot. The women who run it refer to themselves as "a bunch of mother hens"; they're delightful and will pamper you to within an inch of your life. (One couple drops in every year just to say hi.) Some may find it a bit cutesy, but it really is quite charming and has its own distinct personality, unlike most of the other chapels in the area (where the interiors all start to blur together after a while). This is decidedly a special place that might be just right depending on your wedding desires and fantasies.

Silver Bell Chapel. 607 Las Vegas Blvd. S. ☎ **800/221-8492** or 702/382-3727. www. tricks.corn/silverbell. Sun–Thurs 8am–midnight, Fri–Sat 24 hours.

Let's call this the Little Chapel Lined in Neon, at least at night. It's slightly chapel-shaped on the outside, with a small garden including a very little stream and bridge out front. Only 35 people can fit in the small, white-walled chapel, seated on white-wood pews. They are opening an outside wedding and reception garden and should have a drive-through window by 1998.

⭐ **A Special Memory Wedding Chapel.** 800 S. Fourth St., at Gass. ☎ **800/9-MARRYU** or 702/384-2211. www.aspecialmemory.com. Sun–Thurs 8am–10pm, Fri–Sat 8am–midnight.

This is a terrific new wedding chapel, particularly when compared to the rather tired facades of the classics on the Strip. This is absolutely the place to go if you want a traditional, big-production wedding; you won't feel in the least bit tacky or in any other way like you got married in Vegas. It's a New England church-style building, complete with steeple. The interior looks like a proper church (well, a plain one—don't think ornate gothic cathedral) with a peaked roof, pews with padded red seats, modern stained-glass windows of doves and flowers, and lots of dark wood. It is all very clean and new and seats about 87 comfortably. There is a short staircase leading to an actual bride's room; she can make an entrance coming down it or through the double doors at the back. The area outside the chapel is like a minimall of bridal paraphernalia stores. Should all this just be too darn nice and proper for you, they also offer a drive-up window (where they do about 300 weddings a month!). It costs you $25—just ring the buzzer for service. They have a photo studio on site and will do a small cake, cold cuts, and champagne receptions. There is a gazebo for outside weddings, and they sell T-shirts!

Wee Kirk O' the Heather. 231 Las Vegas Blvd. S. ☎ **702/382-9830.** Mon–Sun 10am–midnight.

This is the oldest wedding chapel in Las Vegas (it's been here since 1940) and the one at the very end of the Strip, right before Downtown (and thus even closer to the license bureau). It would be declared a historic landmark, except some renovations in the past moved just enough interior walls to alter it sufficiently to keep it from being official. It had been closed for 2 years and is in the middle of some remodeling, so it was unclear at press time how it would look. The planned changes should still keep the look simple, and they plan to have fresh flowers (unlike the artificial ones everywhere else) to match the season. They have an organ as well.

3 Attractions in Nearby Henderson

About 6 miles from the Strip in the town of Henderson are four factories in fairly close proximity to each other. All offer free tours to the public. Quite honestly, none of these are particularly special or informative (with one possible exception), but since all are virtually next door to each other, if you go out for one, you might as well do all the rest. It's best to see them on a weekday when they're fully operative.

Henderson Attractions

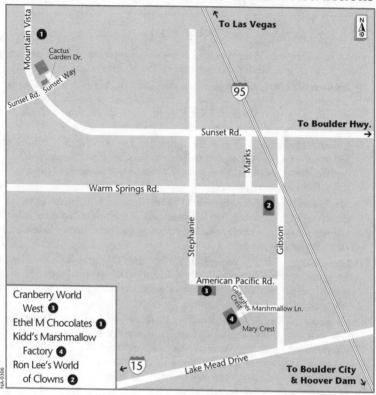

To get to Henderson, drive east on Tropicana Avenue, make a right on Mountain Vista, then go 2 miles to Sunset Way; turn left into Green Valley Business Park. You will soon see Ethel M Chocolates, a good place to begin. Use the map in this section to find your way to the other three facilities.

Cranberry World West. 1301 American Pacific Dr., Henderson. ☎ **800/289-0917** or 702/566-7160. Free admission. Daily 9am–5pm.

By far the best produced and most informative of the tours. If you are interested in cranberries or the history of Ocean Spray marketing, this is the place to go. There is a well-produced 7-minute film about cranberry history, harvesting, and the manufacturing processes and then a well-laid-out self-guided tour with interactive video displays (push a button and a TV comes on) plus some cheap Animatronic farmers talking about their jobs. The tour ends with all the juice you can drink, plus some small samples of other products.

Ethel M Chocolates. 2 Cactus Garden Dr., just off Mountain Vista and Sunset Way in the Green Valley Business Park. ☎ **702/433-2500** for recorded information, or 702/458-8864. www.ethelm.com. Free admission. Daily 8:30am–7pm. Closed Dec 25.

This tourist attraction draws about 2,000 visitors a day. Ethel Mars began making fine chocolates in a little candy kitchen around the turn of the century and her small enterprise evolved to produce not only dozens of varieties of superb boxed chocolates but some of the world's most famous candies: M&Ms, Milky Way, 3 Musketeers, Snickers, and Mars bars.

Going Vegas

If you're looking for a quintessential Las Vegas experience, try these suggestions from James P. Reza, Geoff Carter, and the editors of *Scope* magazine.

- **Peppermill's Fireside Lounge** (see also the listing in chapter 10). This lounge is so evocative of the Me Decade, it's impossible not to love it. Dark, cozy, sexy, and somewhat kitschy, a great place for romantic encounters. Try to sit by the year-round fire pit, if you can stand the heat.
- **Binion's Horseshoe** (see also the listing in chapter 5). This Downtown hotel/casino proffers the greatest souvenir in Sin City, if not the entire US of A: a free picture of you taken in front of a million dollars worth of paper currency. Did we mention it was free?
- **Magic and Movie Hall of Fame at O'Shea's** (see also the listing earlier in this chapter). Curator Valentine Vox has assembled an amazing collection of magic and ventriloquism memorabilia, representing everyone from Houdini to Edgar Bergen.
- **GameWorks,** 3769 Las Vegas Blvd. S. (☎ 702/432-4263). This multilevel entertainment center gives visitors a chance to wreak digitized havoc on the latest video-game creations. A few brave souls try the 75-foot climbing wall; most just hang in the lounge and shoot pool.
- **Cheetah's** (see also the listing in chapter 10). How could you possibly visit Sin City and not sample the ubiquitous lap dance? Couples are welcome at Cheetah's, the site of Paul Verhoven's laughably overdone film *Showgirls.* More quality, less silicone, and a VIP lounge that has hosted lap dances for Wilt Chamberlain, Sting, and Drew Barrymore.
- **Forum Shops at Caesars Palace** (see the listing in chapter 9). The most unique shopping experience in the world. Take Rodeo Drive, marry it to Rome, douse the whole thing in Spielberg, and you're still nowhere near this elegant retail space.
- **The Sky Lounge at the Polo Towers** (see the listing in chapter 10). Hidden on the 19th floor of a time-share condominium complex, this lounge offers a far more engaging view than the Stratosphere Tower, absolutely free of charge. Watch out for kamikaze tour groups.
- **Hard Rock Hotel & Casino** (see also the listing in chapter 5). Everything about this hotel/casino—the bars, the Joint showroom, Mr. Lucky's 24/7—manages to evoke classic Vegas, a city that was built for young hipsters, not fanny-pack–wielding families.
- **Love Shack** (various locations, check local listings). Our vote for Sin City's best lounge act. Covering the music of the '70s and '80s with tenacious fervor, Love Shack is nothing short of a funky riot in 6-inch heels and mascara.
- **Red Rock Canyon** (see chapter 11 for complete details). Providing needed respite from the neon jungle, Red Rock is as beautiful as the desert gets. This haven for hikers and rock-climbers gets a bit overrun at times, but it is still worth the trip. *Note:* Don't feed the wild burros. Unlike the entertainers at Cheetah's, they bite.

Alas, the tour lasts only about 10 minutes and consists entirely of viewing stations with an audiotape explaining the chocolate baking process. You learn very little. But the place does look like a bakery, rather than a factory, which is nice, as no one wants to see their chocolates handled without love. Even more sadly, you only get a couple of small chocolates for a sample—delicious, but hardly satisfying. (Surely, this is by design; now overwhelmingly in the mood for sugar, you are more likely to buy some of their expensive chocolate.)

Interestingly, what is really worth seeing is outside. Also on the premises is a lovely and extensive 2½-acre garden displaying 350 species of rare and exotic cacti with signs provided for self-guided tours. It's best appreciated in spring when the cacti are in full bloom. There is a little gazebo in which to sit and enjoy the garden, which would be quite peaceful were it not for the busloads of tourists in the area. Behind the garden, also with a self-guided tour, is Ethel M's "Living Machine," a natural wastewater treatment and recycling plant that consists of aerated tanks, ecological fluid beds, a constructed wetlands, reed beds, and a storage pond.

Kidd's Marshmallow Factory. 1180 Marshmallow Lane, Henderson. ☎ **800/234-2383** or 702/564-3878. Free admission. Mon–Fri 9am–4:30pm, Sat–Sun 9:30am–4:30pm.

Same idea. Come learn about marshmallows, and get a sample. Sure smells good, though. Kidd and Company was founded in Chicago in the 1880s.

Ron Lee's World of Clowns. 330 Carousel Pkwy., Henderson. ☎ **800/829-3928** or 702/434-3920. Free admission. Daily 8am–5:30pm.

The most easily missed of the group, this factory manufactures clown figurines (and other types, most notably Disney figures). The tour itself consists of simply looking in windows as people mold and paint. The real attraction (outside of a beautiful carousel) is the gift shop, with a nearly limitless amount of high-quality figurines, primarily with a clown motif.

4 Especially for Kids

Like much of the rest of the world, you may be under the impression that Las Vegas has evolved from an adults-only fantasyland into a vacation destination suitable for the entire family. The only explanation for this myth is that Las Vegas was referred to as "Disneyland for adults" by so many and for so long that the town became momentarily confused and decided it actually was Disneyland. Some of the gargantuan hotels then spent small fortunes on redecorating in an attempt to lure families with vast quantities of junk food and a lot of hype. They now vehemently deny that any such notion ever crossed their collective minds, and, no, they don't know how that roller coaster got into the parking lot.

To put things simply, Las Vegas makes money—lots and lots of money—by promoting gambling, drinking, and sex. These are all fine pursuits if you happen to be an adult, but if you haven't reached the magical age of 21, you really don't count in this town. In any case, the casinos and even the Strip itself are simply too stimulating, noisy, and smoky for young kids.

Older progeny may have a tolerance for crowds and the incessant pinging of the slot machines, but they will be thoroughly annoyed with you when casino security chastises them if they so much as stop to tie their shoe laces anywhere near the gaming tables. Since you can't get from your hotel room to the parking lot without ambling through a casino, you can't reasonably expect a teenager to be in a good mood once you stagger outside. And those amusement parks and video halls that haven't yet been purged are expensive places to park your kids for an afternoon or evening, assuming they are old enough to be left unsupervised.

Nevertheless, you may have a perfectly legitimate reason for bringing your children to Las Vegas (like Grandma was busy, or you were just stopping through on your way from somewhere else), so here are some places to take the children both on and off the Strip.

Circus Circus (see p. 85) has ongoing circus acts throughout the day, a vast video game and pinball arcade, and dozens of carnival games on its mezzanine level. Behind the hotel is Grand Slam Canyon, detailed below. **Excalibur** (see p. 55) also offers video and carnival games, plus thrill cinemas and free shows (jugglers, puppets, etc.). At **Caesars Palace,** the Magical Empire (for kids 12 and older only, see p. 164), Race for Atlantis IMAX ride, and OMNIMAX movies (see p. 165) are a thrill for everyone in the family; a video-game arcade adjoins the OMNIMAX Theatre. Animated talking statues in the **Forum Shops** are also a kick, while kids should also be wowed by clamoring around inside the giant moving Trojan horse outside FAO Schwarz, in the shops, and marveling at the Atlantis fountain show. *Star Trek: The Experience* (see p. 171) deserves to draw families to the **Las Vegas Hilton,** but it may be a bit much for younger children. The ship battle in front of **Treasure Island** (see p. 71) is sure to please, as will the erupting volcano and the Secret Garden of Siegfried and Roy and dolphin habitat at the **Mirage** (see p. 169); while you're here, see the tigers and the sharks. Ditto the various attractions at **Luxor Las Vegas** (the IMAX Theater, p. 167; King Tut's Tomb, p. 166; and Secrets of the Luxor Pyramid, p. 167) and Speedworld (p. 170) at the **Sahara.**

Kids will enjoy the **Magic and Movie Hall of Fame** (see p. 168), but they'll want to leave before you do.

Of moderate interest to youngsters are the quartet of **factory tours in Henderson** (see p. 176), especially Ethel M Chocolates and Kidd's Marshmallow Factory, though they will like the free sweets best. The World of Coca-Cola is a big advertisement for soft drinks, but there are some moments, particularly the fountain precise drink killer, that should divert the kids. More educational is the Natural History Museum at UNLV, but only the reptile exhibit will really interest kids.

Appropriate shows for kids include *King Arthur's Tournament* at **Excalibur** (see p. 235), *Siegfried and Roy* at the **Mirage** (see p. 237), *Lance Burton* at the **Monte Carlo** (see p. 236), *EFX* at the **MGM Grand** (see p. 231), and Cirque du Soleil's *Mystère* at **Treasure Island** (see p. 229). As a general rule, early shows are less racy than late-night shows.

Beyond the city limits (see chapter 11 for details on all of these) is **Bonnie Springs Ranch/Old Nevada,** with trail and stagecoach rides, a petting zoo, old-fashioned melodramas, stunt shoot-outs, a Nevada-themed wax museum, crafts demonstrations, and more. **Lake Mead** has great recreational facilities for family vacations. Finally, organized tours (see below) to the Grand Canyon and other interesting sights in southern Nevada and neighboring states can be fun family activities. Check your hotel sightseeing desk.

Specifically kid-pleasing attractions are described below.

Grand Slam Canyon Theme Park. 2880 Las Vegas Blvd. S., behind Circus Circus Hotel. ☎ **702/794-3939.** Free admission; pay per ride. AE, DC, DISC, MC, V. Park hours vary; call ahead.

This isn't a half-bad place to spend a hot afternoon, especially now that Circus Circus, the casino/hotel that built this indoor amusement park, has undergone a face-lift. The glass dome that towers overhead lets in natural light, a solace to those of us who look peaked under the glow of the artificial kind. A double-loop roller coaster careens around the simulated Grand Canyon, and there's the requisite water flume, a laser tag area, and a modest number of other rides for kids of all ages. A dinosaur-bone excavation area will provide a good time for preschoolers and a place to rest for the supervising adults. Video games and an arcade are separate from the attractions, cutting down just a tad on the noise level. Jugglers and magicians provide impromptu entertainment. Our only caveat is don't leave kids here alone. They could easily get lost.

Las Vegas Natural History Museum. 900 Las Vegas Blvd. N., at Washington. ☎ **702/384-3466.** Admission $5 adults, $2.50 children 4–12. Mon–Sun 9am–4pm.

Conveniently located across the street from the Lied Discovery Children's Museum (described below), this humble temple of taxidermy harkens back to elementary school field trips circa 1965, when stuffed elk and brown bears forever protecting their kill were as close as most of us got to exotic animals. Worn around the edges but very sweet and relaxed, the museum is enlivened by a hands-on activity room and two life-size dinosaurs that roar at one another intermittently. A small boy was observed leaping toward his dad upon watching this display, so you might want to warn any sensitive little ones that the big tyrannosaurs aren't going anywhere. Surprisingly, the gift shop here is particularly well stocked with neat items you won't mind too terribly buying for the kids.

Lied Discovery Children's Museum. 833 Las Vegas Blvd. N., a half block south of Washington, across the street from Cashman Field. ☎ **702/382-5437.** Admission $5 adults, $4 children 12–17, $3 children 3–11. DISC, MC, V. Tues–Sat 10am–5pm, Sun noon–5pm.

A hands-on science museum designed for curious kids, the bright, airy, 2-story Lied makes an ideal outing for toddlers and young children. With lots of interactive exhibits to examine, including a miniature grocery store, a bubble tube for encasing oneself inside a soap bubble, a radio station, and music and drawing areas, you'll soon forget your video poker losses. Clever, thought-inducing exhibits are everywhere. Learn how it feels to be handicapped by playing basketball from a wheelchair. Feed a wooden "sandwich" to a cut-out of a snake and to a human cut-out and see how much nutrition each receives. See how much sunscreen their giant stuffed mascot needs to keep from burning. On weekend afternoons from 1 to 3pm, free drop-in art classes are offered, giving you a bit of time to ramble around the gift store or read the fine print on the exhibit placards. The Lied also shares space with a city library branch, so after the kids run around you can calm them back down with a story or two.

MGM Grand Adventures. Behind the MGM Grand Hotel, 3799 Las Vegas Blvd. S. ☎ **702/891-3200.** Admission only (no rides): $2. Admission with unlimited rides: hotel guests $9, everyone else $11. Sky Screamer: 1 person $22.20, 2 people $17.50 each, 3 people $12.50 each. Open daily. Hours and cost vary seasonally.

This theme park, slapped together without a great deal of thought on a former parking lot, looks as if some Hollywood set designers dropped off a variety of hokey movie facades and then, unburdened, cheerfully rode off into the sunset. The attractions, such as a clothes-soaking log flume and kiddie bumper cars, are sparsely scattered among a great many food and T-shirt emporiums. It leaves one with the impression that fun has a lot to do with the contents of one's pocketbook and/or stomach. For some peculiar reason, the park sports three tiny boxing arenas where you and a friend can suit up like samurai and duke it out. This is also home of the Sky Screamer, a combination bungee jump/swing that will thrill kids old enough (and daring enough) to give it a try. (They must be at least 10 years old and 42 inches to ride the Screamer.) There is a separate charge for this ride on top of park admission, although you can pay $2 for park entrance alone, a better deal if you only wish to fly through the air. It's also fun just to sit on a bench and watch people on this contraption.

MGM Grand Youth Center. MGM Grand Hotel, 3799 Las Vegas Blvd. S. ☎ **702/ 892-3200.** For children 3–12 (no diaper wearers). Daily 10am–midnight. Costs vary, depending upon season and whether you are a guest of the hotel (call ahead to get more information).

This is the sole child care center on the Strip, and according to the genial manager, it's booked solid summers and holidays. MGM Grand hotel guests get first priority to leave their youngsters in a warren of brightly decorated and well-supervised, albeit windowless, rooms. Arts and crafts compete with Nintendo and videos for kids' attention, and there are no organized activities (although they do serve meals). You can pay through the nose to have a counselor accompany your child to the theme park (4 hours/$50), but it might be cheaper to bring along a baby-sitter. If we were children and our parents left us here on a family vacation, we'd never let them forget it.

Scandia Family Fun Center. 2900 Sirius Ave., at Rancho Dr. just south of Sahara Ave. ☎ **702/364-0070.** Free admission, but there's a fee for each game or activity. Super Saver Pass $11 (includes 1 round of miniature golf, 2 rides, and 5 game tokens); Unlimited Wristband Package $16 (includes unlimited bumper boat and car rides, unlimited miniature golf, and 10 tokens for batting cages or arcade games). Sept to early June: Sun–Thurs 10am–11pm, Fri–Sat 10am–midnight; mid-June to Aug: Sun–Thurs 10am–midnight, Fri–Sat 10am–1am.

This family amusement center just a few blocks off the Strip offers three 18-hole miniature golf courses ($5.50 per game, free for children under 6), a state-of-the-art video arcade with 225 machines, miniature car racing and bumper boats ($4 per ride, small children ride free with an adult), and automated softball- and baseball-pitching machines for batting practice ($1.25 for 25 pitches). A snack bar is on the premises.

Wet 'n' Wild. 2601 Las Vegas Blvd. S., just south of Sahara Ave. ☎ **702/871-7811.** www.wetnwild.com. Admission $24 adults, $12 seniors over 55, $18 children under 10, free for children under 3. Early May to Sept 30: daily 10am–6 or 8pm (sometimes later). Season and hours vary somewhat from year to year, so call ahead.

When temperatures soar, head for this 26-acre water park right in the heart of the Strip and cool off while jumping waves, careening down steep flumes, and running rapids. Among the highlights: **Royal Flush,** a thrill ride that washes you down a precipitous chute into a saucerlike bowl at 45 miles per hour, then flushes you into a bottomless pool; **Surf Lagoon,** a 500,000-gallon wave pool; **Banzai Banzai,** a roller-coaster–like water ride (aboard a plastic sled, you race down a 45°-angled 150-foot chute and skip porpoiselike across a 120-foot pool); **Der Stuka,** the world's fastest and highest water chute; **Raging Rapids,** a simulated white-water rafting adventure on a 500-foot-long river; **Lazy River,** a leisurely float trip; **Blue Niagara,** a dizzying descent inside intertwined looping tubes from a height of 6 stories; **Willy Willy,** a hydra-hurricane that propels riders on inner tubes around a 90-foot-diameter pool at 10 miles per hour; **Bomb Bay,** a bomblike casing 76 feet in the air that sends you on a speedy vertical flight straight down to a pool target; and the **Black Hole,** an exhilaratingly rapid space-themed flume descent in the dark enhanced by a bombardment of colorful fiber-optic star fields and spinning galaxy patterns en route to splashdown. There are additional flumes, a challenging children's water playground, and a sunbathing area with a cascading waterfall, as well as video and arcade games. Food concessions are located throughout the park, and you can purchase swimwear and accessories at the Beach Trends Shop. Also, be on the lookout for discount coupons. Many Las Vegas packages include a free admission (sometimes partial-day).

5 Organized Tours

Just about every hotel in town has a sightseeing desk offering a seemingly infinite number of tours in and around Las Vegas. You're sure to find a tour company that will take you where you want to go.

Gray Line (☎ **702/384-1234**) offers a rather comprehensive roster, including:

- 8½-hour **city tours,** including visits to Ethel M Chocolates and Cranberry World, the view from the Stratosphere Tower, and the Fremont Street Experience.
- Full-day excursions to **Laughlin, Nevada,** an up-and-coming mini-Vegas 100 miles south with casino hotels on the banks of the Colorado River.
- Half-day excursions to **Hoover Dam** and **Lake Mead** (see chapter 11 for details).
- A full-day excursion to **Red Rock Canyon** and **Mt. Charleston.**
- An 8-hour excursion to the **Valley of Fire** that includes lunch at a Lake Mead resort and a drive by Wayne Newton's Ranch.
- A full-day **river-rafting tour** on the Colorado River from the base of Hoover Dam through majestic Black Canyon.
- A morning or afternoon **air tour** (and you thought they only had buses) of Grand Canyon.
- A 10-hour **Grand Canyon excursion** that includes "flightseeing" and river rafting on the Colorado.

Call for details or inquire at your hotel sightseeing desk, where you'll also find free magazines with coupons for discounts on these tours.

GRAND CANYON TOURS   Generally, tourists visiting Las Vegas don't drive 300 miles to Arizona to see the Grand Canyon, but there are dozens of sightseeing tours departing from the city daily. In addition to the Gray Line tours described above, the major operator, **Scenic Airlines** (☎ **800/634-6801** or 702/638-3200), runs deluxe, full-day guided air-ground tours for $199 per person ($169 for children 2 to 11); the price includes a bus excursion through the national park, a flight over the canyon, and lunch. All scenic tours include "flightseeing." The company also offers both full-day and overnight tours with hiking. And though all Scenic tours include hotel pickup and drop-off, if you take the Premium Deluxe Tour ($239 for adults, $189 for children), you'll be transported by limo.

Scenic also offers tours to other points of interest and national parks, including Yellowstone and Grand Teton. Ask for details when you call.

INDIVIDUALIZED TOURS   A totally different type of tour is offered by Char Cruze of ✪ **Creative Adventures** (☎ **702/361-5565**). Char, a charming fourth-generation Las Vegan (she was at the opening of the Flamingo), spent her childhood riding horseback through the mesquite and cottonwoods of the Mojave Desert, discovering magical places you'd never find on your own or on a commercial tour. Char is a lecturer and storyteller as well as a tour guide. She has extensively studied southern Nevada's geology and desert wildlife, its regional history and Native American cultures. Her personalized tours, enhanced by fascinating stories about everything from miners to mobsters, visit haunted mines, sacred Paiute grounds, ghost towns, canyons, and ancient petroglyphs. Depending on your itinerary, the cost is about $100 a day if you use your own car (more, depending on the number of people, if rental transportation is required). It's a good idea to make arrangements with her prior to leaving home.

6 Playing Golf

There are dozens of local courses, including very challenging ones—the **Sheraton Desert Inn Country** has hosted many PGA tournaments. Beginner and intermediate golfers might prefer the other courses listed.

Angel Park Golf Club. 100 S. Rampart Blvd., between Charleston Blvd. and Westcliff St. ☎ **888/446/5358** or 702/254-4653. $55 weekdays, $65 weekends, $5 twilight.

This 36-hole par-70/71 public course was designed by Arnold Palmer. Players call this a great escape from the casinos, and claiming no matter how many times they play it, they never get tired of it. In addition to the 18-hole Palm and Mountain Courses, which are both very challenging, Angel Park offers a night-lit Cloud 9 course (12 holes for daylight play, 9 at night), where each hole is patterned after a famous par-3.

Yardage: Palm Course 6,438 championship, 5,721 regular, 4,565 ladies; Mountain Course 6,783 championship, 6,272 regular, 5,143 ladies.

Facilities: pro shop, night-lit driving range, 18-hole putting course, restaurant, snack bar, cocktail bar, beverage cart.

Black Mountain Golf & Country Club. 500 Greenway Rd., in nearby Henderson. ☎ **702/565-7933.** $52 before 10am, $30 before 1pm, $20 after 1pm.

Two new greens have recently been added to this 18-hole, par-72 semiprivate course, which requires reservations 4 days in advance. It's considered a great old course, with lots of wildlife, including roadrunners. However, unpredictable winds may blow during your game.

Yardage: 6,541 championship, 6,223 regular, 5,478 ladies.

Facilities: pro shop, putting green, driving range, restaurant, snack bar, cocktail lounge.

Craig Ranch Golf Club. 628 W. Craig Rd., Losee Rd. and Martin Luther King Blvd. ☎ **702/642-9700.** $16 walking, $24 in golf cart.

This is an 18-hole, par-70 public course.

Yardage: 6,001 regular, 5,221 ladies.

Facilities: driving range, pro shop, PGA teaching pro, putting green, snack bar.

Desert Inn Golf Club. 3145 Las Vegas Blvd. S. ☎ **702/733-4290.** $150 for guests, $215 for nonguests.

The Desert Inn course gets the nod from champions. It's an 18-hole, par-72 resort course, the most famous and demanding in Las Vegas. *Golf Digest* calls it one of America's top resort courses and what Las Vegas golf is all about. The very high fees may make it out of your reach. The driving range is open to Desert Inn and Caesars guests only; anyone can play the course, but nonguests pay a higher fee.

Yardage: 7,150 championship, 6,715 regular, 5,800 ladies.

Facilities: driving range, putting green, pro shop, restaurant. You can reserve 90 days in advance for Sunday to Thursday, 2 days in advance for Friday and Saturday.

Desert Rose Golf Club. 5483 Clubhouse Dr., 3 blocks west of Nellis Blvd., off Sahara Ave. ☎ **702/431-4653.** $51 Mon–Fri before 10am, $38 after 10am; $51 Sat–Sun before noon, $38 after noon.

This is an 18-hole, par-71 public course.

Yardage: 6,511 championship, 6,135 regular, 5,458 ladies.

Facilities: driving range, putting and chipping greens, PGA teaching pro, pro shop, restaurant, cocktail lounge.

Las Vegas National Golf Club. 1911 Desert Inn Rd., between Maryland Pkwy. and Eastern Ave. ☎ **702/796-0016.**

This is an 18-hole, par-72 public course, and a classic layout.

Yardage: 6,815 championship, 6,418 regular, 5,741 ladies.

Facilities: pro shop, golf school, driving range, restaurant, cocktail lounge.

Green Fees Monday through Thursday $75, Friday through Sunday $105, discounted tee times available. Reservations up to 60 days in advance; $5 to $7 fee applies.

7 Staying Active

Bring your sports gear to Las Vegas. The city and surrounding areas offer plenty of opportunities for active sports. In addition to many highly rated golf courses (described above), just about every hotel has a large swimming pool and health club, and tennis courts abound. All types of water sports are offered at Lake Mead National Recreation Area, there's rafting on the Colorado, horseback riding at Mount Charleston and Bonnie Springs, great hiking in the canyons, and much, much more. Do plan to get out of those smoke-filled casinos and into the fresh air once in a while. It's good for your health and your finances.

Note: When choosing a hotel, check out its recreational facilities, all listed in chapter 5.

BICYCLING Escape the City Streets, 8221 W. Charleston Blvd. (☎ **702/ 596-2953**) rents 21-speed mountain bikes and offers delivery (for an extra charge) to all Downtown and Strip hotels. Rates are $26 for the first day, $20 for a half day or consecutive days, $108 for a full week. You must show a major credit card (American Express, MasterCard, or Visa). Inquire about bike trips to Red Rock Canyon and other good biking areas.

BOWLING The **Showboat Hotel & Casino,** 2800 E. Fremont St. (☎ **702/385-9153**), is famous for housing the largest bowling center in North America—106 lanes—and for being the oldest stop on the Professional Bowlers Tour. A major renovation a few years back made its premises bright and spiffy. Open 24 hours.

BUNGEE JUMPING At **A. J. Hackett Bungy,** 810 Circus Circus Dr., between Las Vegas Boulevard South and Industrial Road (☎ **702/385-4321**). If you want to take a *real* gamble, this is the place to do it, where the odds are stacked in your favor but the thrill is nearly immeasurable. A. J. Hackett Bungy is a worldwide chain—over 1 million jumps and they haven't lost anyone yet. The instructors are enthusiastic and do much to make you feel comfortable. Expect about an hour wait (there is a bar with a TV and pool table to keep you occupied), but given how meticulous and careful they are with each jumper, you'll be glad they aren't rushing people through. An elevator in the shape of a rocket takes you to the top of a 175-foot tower, the base for an exhilarating plunge toward a large swimming pool below. During the ride up, you will receive your instructions; basically, stick your toes over the edge, arms out in front, and dive. Unless you are like our guinea pig, who needed a gentle shove. The whole jump lasts perhaps 3 minutes, but you will have enough adrenaline pumping through your veins to keep you up all night. (And then go gamble!) Dive at night, and you sail right into the lights of Vegas. The price is $61 for your first jump, including a membership and T-shirt ($81 with a videotape or $50 without any frills), $25 for the second and third jumps; the fourth is free. Students and military with ID should inquire about discounts. If you're under 18, you must be accompanied by a parent. Call for hours.

FISHING   One doesn't usually think of fishing in the desert, but there are lakes and large ponds. Closest to Las Vegas are the ponds in **Floyd R. Lamb State Park,** 9200 Tule Springs Rd. (☎ **702/486-5413**). The park is about 15 miles from the Strip. To get there take I-15 to U.S. 95 north, get off at the Durango exit, and follow the signs. You can fish here for catfish, trout, bluegill, sunfish, and large-mouth bass. You will need your own gear, bait, and tackle, as well as a Nevada fishing license, which is available at any sporting goods store (check the Las Vegas yellow pages). There's also fishing at Lake Mead (see listing in chapter 11 for details).

HEALTH CLUBS   Almost every hotel in Las Vegas has an on-premises health club. The facilities, of course, vary enormously. Descriptions are given of each club in hotel facilities listings in chapter 5.

But none offers the amazing range of facilities you'll find at the **Las Vegas Sporting House,** 3025 Industrial Rd., right behind the Stardust Hotel (☎ **702/733-8999**). Opened in 1978, this 65,000-square-foot club is ultraluxurious. UNLV teams and many athletes and Strip headliners (including Siegfried and Roy) work out here. Facilities include 10 racquetball/handball courts, two squash courts, two outdoor tennis courts (lit for night play), a full gymnasium for basketball and volleyball, an outdoor pool and sunbathing area, a 25-meter indoor pool for lap swimming, indoor and outdoor jogging tracks, treadmills, Lifecycles, Virtual Reality bikes, stair machines, and free weights. In addition, there are full lines of Cybex, Universal, and Paramount machines, along with some Nautilus equipment; sauna, steam, and Jacuzzi; a pro shop; men's and women's skin-care and hair salons; massage; free baby-sitting service while you work out; restaurant, bar, and lounge. Aerobics classes are given at frequent intervals throughout the day, and you can try "spinning," a new workout technique that burns 800 calories in 40 minutes! Cost for a single visit is $15 to $20 (depending on the club's arrangement with your hotel); reduced weekly rates are available. Open daily 24 hours.

A cheaper alternative would be **Gold's Gym,** 3758 E. Flamingo (☎ **702/ 451-4222**), or **24 Hour Fitness,** 3053 Valley View, corner of Sirius (☎ **702/ 368-1111**)—about 1 mile from the Strip; both of which offer full gym facilities for $7 a day (free if you are member from another city).

HIKING   Except in summer, when the temperature can reach 120°F in the shade, the Las Vegas area is great for hiking. The best hiking season is November to March. Great locales include the incredibly scenic Red Rock Canyon and Valley of Fire State Park (see individual headings in chapter 11 for details).

HORSEBACK RIDING   The **Mt. Charleston Horse Back Riding** (☎ **800/955-1314** or 702/872-5408), under the auspices of the Mount Charleston Lodge, offers glorious scenic trail rides to the edge of the wilderness. The 1½-hour trail rides depart from stables on Kyle Canyon Road and cost $30. Since the schedule varies, it's best to call in advance for details. The stables also offer sleigh rides in winter and hayrides in summer. Riding stables at **Bonnie Springs Ranch** (☎ **702/875-4191**) also offer guided trail rides daily. Rates are $20 per hour.

JET-SKIING   Las Vegas Adventure Tours (LVAT) (☎ **800/553-5452** or 702/564-5452) offers jet-ski rides on Lake Mead. Call LVAT, too, about horseback

Desert Hiking Tips

Hiking in the desert is exceptionally rewarding, but it can be dangerous. Some safety tips:

1. Do not hike alone.

2. Carry plenty of water and drink it often. Don't assume spring waters are safe to drink. A gallon of water per person per day is recommended for hikers.

3. Be alert for signs of heat exhaustion (headache, nausea, dizziness, fatigue, and cool, damp, pale, or red skin).

4. Gauge your fitness accurately. Desert hiking may involve rough or steep terrain. Don't take on more than you can handle.

5. Check weather forecasts before starting out. Thunderstorms can turn into raging flash floods, which are extremely hazardous to hikers.

6. Dress properly. Wear sturdy walking shoes for rock scrambling, long pants (to protect yourself from rocks and cacti), a hat, sunscreen, and sunglasses.

7. Carry a small first-aid kit.

8. Be careful when climbing on sandstone, which can be surprisingly soft and crumbly.

9. Don't feed or play with animals, such as wild burros in Red Rock Canyon.

10. Be alert for snakes and insects. Though they're rarely encountered, you'll want to look into a crevice before putting your hand into it.

11. Visit park or other information offices before you start out and acquaint yourself with rules and regulations and any possible hazards. It's also a good idea to tell them where you are going, when you will return, how many are in your party, and so on. Some park offices offer hiker-registration programs.

12. Follow the hiker's rule of thumb: Take only photographs, and leave only footprints.

riding, hot-air ballooning, Grand Canyon flightseeing, and all-terrain-vehicle desert tours.

RACQUETBALL   There are courts in several locations around town. The **Las Vegas Athletic Club East,** 1070 E. Sahara Ave., at Maryland Parkway (☎ 702/733-1919), has seven courts open 24 hours a day, 7 days a week. Rates are $10 per person per day; $25 per week. Call to reserve a court.

The **Las Vegas Athletic Club West,** 3315 Spring Mountain Rd., between I-15 and Valley View Boulevard (☎ 702/362-3720), has eight courts open weekdays 5am to 11pm; weekends 8am to 8pm. Rates are $10 per person per visit; $25 per week.

The **Las Vegas Sporting House,** 3025 Industrial Rd., right behind the Stardust Hotel (☎ 702/733-8999), has 10 racquetball/handball courts open 24 hours a day, 7 days a week. Rates are $15 per visit if you're staying at a local hotel.

The **University of Nevada, Las Vegas (UNLV),** 4505 Maryland Pkwy., just off Swenson Street (☎ 702/895-3150), has eight racquetball courts open weekdays 6am to 9:45pm, Saturday 8am to 5:30pm, Sunday 10am to 5:30pm. Hours may vary somewhat each semester. Rates are $2 per person per hour. Call before you go to find out if a court is available. You must pick up a guest pass in the Physical Education Building.

RIVER RAFTING Black Canyon Raft Tours (☎ 800/696-RAFT or 702/ 293-3776) offers daily raft trips on the Colorado River from February to the end of November. As an authorized concessionaire, Black Canyon can get into otherwise restricted areas at the base of the dam. Trips include 3 hours of scenic rafting and lunch. You'll see waterfalls gush from majestic canyon walls, pass tranquil coves, spy bighorn sheep on sheer cliffs, and spot blue herons, cormorants, and falcons. Knowledgeable guides provide a lot of fascinating area history and geology. Each raft is piloted by an experienced navigator. Rates, including Las Vegas hotel pickup and return, are $80 per person, $65 if you drive to and from the expedition depot.

ROCK CLIMBING Red Rock Canyon, just 19 miles west of Las Vegas, is one of the world's most popular rock-climbing areas. In addition to awe-inspiring natural beauty, it offers everything from boulders to big walls. If you'd like to join the bighorn sheep, Red Rock has more than 1,000 routes to inaugurate beginners and challenge accomplished climbers. Experienced climbers can contact the **visitor center** (☎ 702/363-1921) for information.

If you're interested in learning or improving your skills, an excellent rock-climbing school and guide service called **Sky's the Limit** (☎ 800/733-7597 or 702/363-4533) offers programs for beginning, intermediate, and advanced climbers. No experience is needed. The school is accredited by the American Mountain Guides Association.

TENNIS Tennis buffs should choose one of the many hotels in town that have tennis courts.

Bally's (☎ 702/739-4598) has eight night-lit hard courts. Fees per hour range from $10 to $15 for guests, $15 to $20 for nonguests. Facilities include a pro shop. Hours vary seasonally. Reservations are advised.

The **Flamingo Hilton** (☎ 702/733-3444) has four outdoor hard courts (all lit for night play) and a pro shop. It is open to the public Monday to Friday 7am to 8pm, Saturday and Sunday 7am to 6pm. Rates are $20 per hour for nonguests, $12 for guests. Lessons are available. Reservations are required.

The **Riviera** (☎ 702/734-5110) has two outdoor hard courts (both lit for night play) that are open to the public, subject to availability; hotel guests have priority. It is open 24 hours. There is no charge for guests; nonguests pay $10 per hour. Reservations are required.

The **Desert Inn** (☎ 702/733-4557) has five outdoor hard courts (all lit for night play) and a pro shop. They are open to the public. Hours are daybreak to 10pm. Rates are $10 per person for a daily pass (you book for an hour but can stay longer if no one is waiting); they are free for guests. Reservations are necessary.

In addition to hotels, the **University of Nevada, Las Vegas (UNLV),** Harmon Avenue just east of Swenson Street (☎ 702/895-0844), has a dozen courts (all lit for night play) that are open weekdays 6am to 9:45pm, weekends 8am to 9pm. Rates are $5 per person per day on weekdays; $10 weekends. You should call before going to find out if a court is available.

8 Spectator Sports

Las Vegas isn't known for its sports teams. Except for minor-league baseball and hockey, the only consistent spectator sports are those at UNLV. The **Las Vegas Motor Speedway** (described in "Las Vegas Attractions," above) is a major new venue for car racing and should draw major events to Las Vegas.

But since the city has several top-notch sporting arenas, there are important annual events that take place in Las Vegas, details for which can be found in the

"Las Vegas Calendar of Events" in chapter 2. The **PBA Invitational Bowling Tournament** is held in the Showboat's massive bowling center each January. The **PGA Tour Las Vegas Senior Classic** is held each April in nearby Summerlin, and **Las Vegas Invitational** in Las Vegas each October. The **National Finals Rodeo** is held in UNLV's Thomas and Mack Center each December. From time to time, you'll find NBA exhibition games, professional ice-skating tournaments, or gymnastics exhibitions. Then there are the only-in-Vegas spectaculars, such as Evel Knievel's ill-fated attempt to jump the fountains in front of Caesars.

Finally, Las Vegas is well known as a major location for boxing matches. These are held in several Strip hotels, most often at Caesars or the MGM Grand, but sometimes at the Mirage. Tickets are hard to come by and quite expensive.

BASEBALL

The **Las Vegas Stars,** a AAA baseball team, play from April to August at the 10,000-seat **Cashman Field Center,** 850 Las Vegas Blvd. N. (☎ **702/386-7200** for tickets and information). Tickets are priced at $4 to $7.

BASKETBALL

The **Thomas and Mack Center,** also on the UNLV campus at Tropicana Avenue and Swenson Street (☎ **702/895-3900**), is an 18,500-seat facility used for a variety of sporting events. It is home to the **UNLV's Runnin' Rebels,** who play 16 to 20 games during a November-to-March season. Other events here include major boxing tournaments, NBA exhibition games, and rodeos. For information and to charge tickets, call the stadium number or Ticketmaster (☎ **702/474-4000**).

FOOTBALL

The **Sam Boyd Stadium** at the University of Nevada, Las Vegas (UNLV), Boulder Highway and Russell Road (☎ **702/895-3900**), is a 32,000-seat outdoor stadium. The **UNLV Rebels** play about six football games here each year between September and November. And the stadium is also used for motor sports and supercross events, truck and tractor pulls, high school football games, and the Las Vegas Bowl in December. For information and to charge tickets, call the above number or Ticketmaster (☎ **702/474-4000**).

HOCKEY

Las Vegas Thunder (International Hockey League) plays about 40 games at UNLV's Thomas and Mack Center (Tropicana Avenue and Swenson Street) between October and early April (call ☎ **702/798-PUCK** for information).

MAJOR SPORTS VENUES IN HOTELS

Caesars Palace (☎ **800/634-6698** or 702/731-7110) has a long tradition of sporting events, from Evel Knievel's attempted motorcycle jump over its fountains in 1967 to Grand Prix auto races. Mary Lou Retton has tumbled in gymnastic events at Caesars, and Olympians Brian Boitano and Katarina Witt have taken to the ice, as has Wayne Gretzky. And well over 100 world-championship boxing contests have taken place here since the hotel opened. In the spirit of ancient Rome, Caesars awards riches and honors to the "gladiators" who compete in its arenas.

The **MGM Grand's Garden Events Arena** (☎ **800/929-1111** or 702/891-7777) is a major venue for sporting events: professional boxing matches, rodeos, tennis, ice-skating shows, World Figure Skating Championships, and more.

The **Mirage** (☎ **800/627-6667** or 702/791-7111) also features occasional championship boxing matches.

8 About Casino Gambling

What? You didn't come to Las Vegas for the Liberace Museum? We are shocked. *Shocked.*

Yes, there are gambling opportunities in Vegas. We've noticed this. You will, too. The tip-off will be the slot machines in the airport as soon as you step off the plane. Or the slot machines in the convenience stores as soon as you drive across the state line. Let's not kid ourselves, gambling is what Vegas is about. The bright lights, the shows, the showgirls, the food—it's all there just to lure you in and make you open your wallet. (The free drinks certainly help ease the latter as well.)

You can disappoint them if you want, but what would be the point? *This is Las Vegas.* You don't have to be a high roller. You would not believe how much fun you can have with a nickel slot machine. You won't get rich, but neither will most of those guys playing the $5 slots, either. Of course, that's not going to stop anyone from trying. Almost everyone plays in Vegas with the hopes of winning The Big One. That only a few ever do doesn't stop them from trying again and again and again. That's how the casinos make their money, by the way.

It's not that the odds are stacked so incredibly high in their favor—though the odds are in their favor, and don't ever think otherwise. Rather, it's that if there is one constant in this world, it's human greed. Look around in any casino, and you'll see countless souls who, having doubled their winnings, are now trying to quadruple them, and are losing it all back again. And then trying to recoup their initial bankroll and losing still more in the process. See that chandelier up there? Enjoy it—you paid for it.

Which is not meant to dissuade you from gambling. Just be sure to look at it as recreation and entertainment, *not* as an investment or money-making opportunity. Spend only as much as you can afford to lose and not a penny more. It doesn't matter if that's $10 or $100,000. You can have just as good a time with either. (Though if you can afford to lose $100,000, we would like to meet you.)

Remember also that there is no system that is sure to help you win. We all have our own system and our own ideas. Reading books and listening to others at the tables will help you pick up some tips, but if there were a surefire way to win, the casinos would have taken care of it (and we will leave you to imagine just what that might

Impressions

Stilled forever is the click of the roulette wheel, the rattle of dice, and the swish of cards.

—Shortsighted editorial in the *Nevada State Journal*
after gambling was outlawed in 1910

entail). Try to have the courage to walk away when your bankroll is up, not down. Remember, your children's college fund is just that, and not a gambling budget supplement.

The first part of this chapter is a contribution from James Randi, a master magician, who looks at the four major fallacies people bring with them to the gaming tables in Las Vegas; it's fascinating, and we thank him for this contribution. The second part tells you the basics of betting. Knowing how to play the games not only improves your odds but makes playing more enjoyable. In addition to the instructions below, you'll find dozens of books on how to gamble at all casino hotel gift shops, and many casinos offer free gaming lessons on the premises. The third part of this chapter describes all the major casinos in town. Remember that gambling is supposed to be entertainment; picking a gaming table where the other players are laughing, slapping each other on the back, and generally enjoying themselves tends to make for considerable more fun than a table where everyone is sitting around in stony silence, morosely staring at their cards. Unless you really need to concentrate, pick a table where everyone seems to be enjoying themselves, and you will too, even if you don't win. Maybe.

1 The Four Most Pervasive Myths About Gambling

by James Randi

> *James Randi is a world-class magician (as the Amazing Randi), now involved in examining supernatural, paranormal, and occult claims. He is the author of 11 books on these subjects, and the president of the James Randi Educational Foundation in Fort Lauderdale, Florida. The JREF offers a prize of $1,100,000 to any person who can produce a demonstration of any paranormal activity. His Web site is www.randi.org, where details of the offer can be found.*

Most of us know little, if anything, about statistics. It's a never-never land we can live without, something for those guys in white coats and thick glasses to mumble over. And because we don't bother to learn the basics of this rather interesting field of study, we sometimes find ourselves unable to deal with the realities that the gambling process produces.

I often present my audiences with a puzzle. Suppose that a mathematician, a gambler, and a magician are walking together on Broadway, and come upon a small cluster of people who are observing a chap standing at a small table set up on the sidewalk. They are told that this fellow has just tossed a quarter into the air and allowed it to fall onto the table, nine times. And that has produced nine "tails" in a row. Now the crowd is being asked to bet on what the next toss of the coin will bring. The question: How will each of these three observers place their bets?

The mathematician will reason that each toss of the coin is independent of the last toss, so the chances are still exactly 50/50 for heads or tails. He'll say that either bet is okay, and that it doesn't make any difference which decision is made.

The gambler will go one of two ways; either he'll reason that there's a "run" taking place here—and that a bet on another tail will be the better choice—or he'll opine that it's time for the head to come up—and he'll put his wager on that likelihood.

The magician? He has the best chance of winning, because he knows that there is only one chance in 512 that a coin will come up tails nine times in a row—*unless there's something wrong with that coin!* He'll bet tails, and he'll win!

The reasoning of the mathematician is quite correct, that of the gambler is quite wrong (in either one of his scenarios), but just as long as that isn't a double-tailed coin. The point of view taken by the magician is highly specialized, but human nature being what it is, that view is probably the correct one.

In professional gambling centers like Las Vegas, great care is taken to ensure that there are no two-tailed quarters or other purposeful anomalies that enable cheating to take place. The casinos make their percentages on the built-in mathematical advantage, clearly stated and available to any who ask, and though that is a very tiny "edge," it's enough to pay for the razzle-dazzle that is offered the customers. It's volume that supports the business. The scrutiny that is applied to each and every procedure in Vegas is everywhere evident.

So, **Fallacy Number One** is: Cheating of some sort is necessary for an operation to prosper. It isn't.

Fallacy Number Two: Some people just have "hunches" and "visions" that enable them to win at the slots and tables. Sorry folks, it just ain't so. The science of parapsychology, which has studied such claims for many decades now, has never come up with evidence that any form of clairvoyance ("clear-seeing," the supposed ability to know hidden data, such as the next card to come up in a deal or the next face on the dice) or telepathy ("mind-reading") actually exists. It's remarkably easy for us to imagine that we have a hot streak going, or that the cards are falling our way, but the inexorable laws of chance prevail and always will.

Fallacy Number Three: There are folks who can give us systems for winning. Now, judicious bet-placing is possible, and there are mathematical methods of minimizing losses, it's true. But the investment and base capital needed to follow through with these methods makes them a rather poor investment. The return percentage can be earned much more easily by almost any other form of endeavor, at less risk and less expenditure of boring hours following complicated charts and equations. The best observation we can make on the "systems" is: Why do the inventors sell something that they themselves could use to get rich, which is what they say you can do with it? Think about that!

Of course, the simplest of all the systems is bet-doubling. It sounds great, in theory, but an hour spent tossing coins in your hotel room, or at the gaming tables, will convince you that theory and practice are quite different matters. Bet-doubling, as applied to heads-or-tails (on a fair coin!), consists of placing a unit bet on the first coin toss, then pocketing the proceeds if you win, but doubling your bet on the next toss if you lose. If you get a lose, lose, win sequence, that means you will have lost three units (one plus two) and won four. You're up one unit. You start again. If you get a lose, lose, lose, win sequence, you've put out 15 units, and brought in 16. Again, you're only up one unit. And no matter how long your sequences go, you'll *always* be up only one unit at the end of a sequence. It requires you to make that "unit" somewhat sizable if you want to have any significant winnings at all, and that may mean going bankrupt by simply running out of capital before a sequence ends—and if you hang on, you'll only have been able to end up *one* unit ahead, in any case. Not a good investment, at all.

Fallacy Number Four: Studying the results of the roulette wheels will provide the bettor with useful data. We're peculiar animals in that we constantly search for meaning in all sets of observations. That's how subjects of Rorschach tests find weird faces, figures, and creatures in ink blots that are actually random patterns with single symmetry. Similarly, any set of roulette results are, essentially, random numbers; there are no patterns to be found there that can give indications of probable future spins of the wheels. Bearing in mind that those wheels are carefully monitored to detect any biases or defects, we should conclude that finding clues in past performances is futile.

I recall that when I worked in Wiesbaden, Germany, just after World War II, I stuck around late one night after closing at the "Spielbank" and watched as an elderly gentleman removed all the rotors of the 12 wheels they had in operation, wrote out the numbers 1 to 12 on separate scraps of paper, and reassembled the wheels according to the random order in which he drew each slip of paper from a bowl. He was ensuring that any inconsistencies in the wheels would be essentially nullified. Yet, as he told me, the front desk at the casino continued to sell booklets setting out the results of each of the wheels, because patrons insisted on having them, and persisted in believing that there just had to be a pattern there, if only it could be found.

We're only human. We can't escape certain defects in our thinking mechanism, but we can resist reacting to them. When we see Penn and Teller, Ayala, Siegfried and Roy, or Lance Burton doing their wonders, we smile smugly and assure ourselves that those miracles are only illusions. But if we haven't solved those illusions, and we haven't, how can we assume that we aren't being fooled by our own self-created delusions? Let's get a grip on reality and enjoy Las Vegas for what it really is: a grand illusion, a fairyland, a let's-pretend project, but not one in which the laws of nature are suspended or can be ignored.

Enjoy!

2 The Games

BACCARAT

The ancient game of baccarat, or *chemin de fer,* is played with eight decks of cards. Firm rules apply, and there is no skill involved other than deciding whether to bet on the bank or the player. Any beginner can play, but check the betting minimum before you sit down as this tends to be a high-stakes game. The cards are shuffled by the croupier and then placed in a box that is called the "shoe."

Players may wager on "bank" or "player" at any time. Two cards are dealt from the shoe and given to the player who has the largest wager against the bank, and two cards are dealt to the croupier acting as banker. If the rule calls for a third card (see rules on chart shown, below), the player or banker, or both, must take the third card. In the event of a tie, the hand is dealt over.

The object of the game is to come as close as possible to the number 9. To score the hands, the cards of each hand are totaled and the *last digit* is used. All cards have face value. For example: 10 plus 5 equals 15 (score is 5); 10 plus 4 plus 9 equals 23 (score is 3); 4 plus 3 plus 3 equals 10 (score is 0); and 4 plus 3 plus 2 equals 9 (score is 9). The closest hand to 9 wins.

Each player has a chance to deal the cards. The shoe passes to the player on the right each time the bank loses. If the player wishes, he or she may pass the shoe at any time.

Baccarat Rules

PLAYER'S HAND

Having

0-1-2-3-4-5	Must draw a third card.
6-7	Must stand.
8-9	Natural. Banker cannot draw.

BANKER'S HAND

Having	**Draws**	**Does Not Draw**
	When giving Player 3rd card of:	When giving Player 3rd card of:
3	1-2-3-4-5-6-7-9-10	8
4	2-3-4-5-6-7	1-8-9-10
5	4-5-6-7	1-2-3-8-9-10
6	6-7	1-2-3-4-5-8-9-10
7	*Must stand.*	
8-9	Natural. Player cannot draw.	

If the player takes no third card, the banker must stand on 6. No one draws against a natural 8 or 9.

Note: When you bet on the bank and the bank wins, you are charged a 5% commission. This must be paid at the start of a new game or when you leave the table.

BIG SIX

Big Six provides pleasant recreation and involves no study or effort. The wheel has 56 positions on it, 54 of them marked by bills from $1 to $20 denominations. The other two spots are jokers, and each pays 40 to 1 if the wheel stops in that position.

All other stops pay at face value. Those marked with $20 bills pay 20 to 1; the $5 bills pay 5 to 1; and so forth.

BLACKJACK

The dealer starts the game by dealing each player two cards. In some casinos they're dealt to the player faceup, in others facedown, but the dealer always gets one card up and one card down. Everybody plays against the dealer. The object is to get a total that is higher than that of the dealer without exceeding 21. All face cards count as 10; all other number cards except aces count as their number value. An ace may be counted as 1 or 11, whichever you choose it to be.

Starting at his or her left, the dealer gives additional cards to the players who wish to draw (be "hit") or none to a player who wishes to "stand" or "hold." If your count is nearer to 21 than the dealer's, you win. If it's under the dealer's, you lose. Ties are a push and nobody wins. After all the players are satisfied with their counts, the dealer exposes his or her facedown card. If his or her two cards total 16 or less, the dealer must "hit" (draw an additional card) until reaching 17 or over. If the dealer's total goes over 21, he or she must pay all the players whose hands have not gone "bust." It is important to note here that the blackjack dealer has no choice as to whether he or she should stay or draw. A dealer's decisions are predetermined and known to all the players at the table.

HOW TO PLAY   Here are eight "rules" for blackjack.

1. Place the amount of chips that you want to bet on the betting space on your table.

2. Look at the first two cards the dealer starts you with. If your hand adds up to the total you prefer, place your cards *under your bet money,* indicating that you don't wish any additional cards. If you elect to draw an additional card, you tell the dealer to "hit" you by making a sweeping motion with your cards, or point to your open hand (watch your fellow players).

3. If your count goes over 21, you go "bust" and lose, even if the dealer also goes "bust" afterward. Unless hands are dealt faceup, *you then turn your hand faceup on the table.*

4. If you make 21 in your first two cards (any picture card or 10 with an ace), you've got blackjack. *You expose your winning hand immediately,* and you collect 1½ times your bet, unless the dealer has blackjack, too, in which case it's a push and nobody wins.

5. If you find a "pair" in your first two cards (say, two 8s or two aces) you may "split" the pair into two hands and treat each card as the first card dealt in separate hands. *Turn the pair faceup on the table,* place the original bet on one of these cards, then place an equal amount on the other card. *Split aces are limited to a one-card draw on each.*

6. You may double your original bet and make a one-card draw after receiving your initial two cards. *Turn your hand faceup* and you'll receive one more card facedown.

7. Anytime the dealer deals himself or herself an ace for the "up" card, you may insure your hand against the possibility that the hole card is a 10 or face card, which would give him or her an automatic blackjack. To insure, you place an amount up to one half of your bet on the "insurance" line. If the dealer does have a blackjack, you do not lose, even though he or she has your hand beat, and you keep your bet and your insurance money. If the dealer does not have a blackjack, he or she takes your insurance money and play continues in the normal fashion.

8. *Remember:* The dealer *must* stand on 17 or more and *must* hit a hand of 16 or less.

PROFESSIONAL TIPS   Advice of the experts in playing blackjack is as follows.

1. *Do not* ask for an extra card if you have a count of 17, 18, 19, 20, or 21 in your cards, no matter what the dealer has showing in his or her "up" card.

2. *Do not* ask for an extra card when you have 12, 13, 14, 15, 16, or more if the dealer has a 2, 3, 4, 5, or 6 showing in his or her "up" card.

3. *Do ask* for an extra card or more when you have a count of 12 through 16 in your hand if the dealer's "up" card is a 7, 8, 9, 10, or ace.

There's a lot more to blackjack-playing strategy than the above, of course. So consider this merely as the bare bones of the game.

A final tip: Avoid insurance bets; they're sucker bait!

CRAPS

The most exciting casino action is always at the craps tables. Betting is frenetic, play fast-paced, and groups quickly bond yelling and screaming in response to the action.

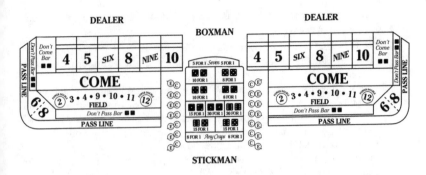

THE TABLE The craps table is divided into marked areas (Pass, Come, Field, Big 6, Big 8, and so on), where you place your chips to bet. The following are a few simple directions.

PASS LINE A "Pass Line" bet pays even money. If the first roll of the dice adds up to 7 or 11, you win your bet; if the first roll adds up to 2, 3, or 12, you lose your bet. If any other number comes up, it's your "point." If you roll your point again, you win, but if a 7 comes up again before your point is rolled, you lose.

DON'T PASS LINE Betting on the "Don't Pass" is the opposite of betting on the Pass Line. This time, you lose if a 7 or an 11 is thrown on the first roll, and you win if a 2 or a 3 is thrown on the first roll.

If the first roll is 12, however, it's a push (standoff), and nobody wins. If none of these numbers are thrown and you have a point instead, in order to win, a 7 will have to be thrown before the point comes up again. A "Don't Pass" bet also pays even money.

COME Betting on "Come" is the same as betting on the Pass Line, but you must bet *after* the first roll or on any following roll. Again, you'll win on 7 or 11 and lose on 2, 3, or 12. Any other number is your point, and you win if your point comes up again before a 7.

DON'T COME This is the opposite of a "Come" bet. Again, you wait until after the first roll to bet. A 7 or an 11 means you lose; a 2 or a 3 means you win; 12 is a push, and nobody wins. You win if 7 comes up before the point. (The point, you'll recall, was the first number rolled if it was none of the above.)

FIELD This is a bet for one roll only. The "Field" consists of seven numbers: 2, 3, 4, 9, 10, 11, and 12. If any of these numbers is thrown on the next roll, you win even money, except on 2 and 12, which pay 2 to 1 (at some casinos 3 to 1).

BIG 6 AND 8 A "Big 6 and 8" bet pays even money. You win if either a 6 or an 8 is rolled before a 7.

ANY 7 An "Any 7" bet pays the winner five for one. If a 7 is thrown on the first roll after you bet, you win.

"HARD WAY" BETS In the middle of a craps table are pictures of several possible dice combinations together with the odds the casino will pay you if you bet and win on any of those combinations being thrown. For example, if 8 is thrown by having a 4 appear on each die, and you bet on it, the bank will pay 10 for 1; if 4 is thrown by having a 2 appear on each die, and you bet on it, the bank will pay 8 for 1; if 3 is thrown, the bank pays 15 for 1. You win at the odds quoted if the *exact* combination of numbers you bet on comes up. But you lose either if a 7 is

Impressions

The most exciting thing in craps is to win. The next most exciting thing is to lose.

—Nick the Greek

rolled or if the number you bet on was rolled any way other than the "Hard Way" shown on the table. In-the-know gamblers tend to avoid "Hard Way" bets as an easy way to lose their money. And note that the odds quoted are *not* 3 to 1, 4 to 1, or 8 to 1; here the key word is *for*—that is, 3 for 1 or 8 for 1.

ANY CRAPS   Here you're lucky if the dice "crap out"—if they show 2, 3, or 12 on the first roll after you bet. If this happens, the bank pays for 8 for 1. Any other number is a loser.

PLACE BETS   You can make a "Place Bet" on any of the following numbers: 4, 5, 6, 8, 9, and 10. You're betting that the number you choose will be thrown before a 7 is thrown. If you win, the payoff is as follows: 4 or 10 pays at the rate of 9 to 5; 5 or 9 pays at the rate of 7 to 5; 6 or 8 pays at the rate of 7 to 6. "Place Bets" can be removed at any time before a roll.

SOME PROBABILITIES   Because each die has six sides numbered from 1 to 6, and craps is played with a pair of dice, the probability of throwing certain numbers has been studied carefully. Professionals have employed complex mathematical formulas in searching for the answers. And computers have data-processed curves of probability.

Suffice it to say that 7 (a crucial number in craps) will be thrown more frequently than any other number over the long run, for there are six possible combinations that make 7 when you break down the 1 to 6 possibilities on each separate die. As to the total possible number of combinations on the dice, there are 36.

Comparing the 36 possible combinations, numbers, or point combinations, run as follows:

> *2 and 12* may be thrown in *1 way* only.
> *3 and 11* may be thrown in *2 ways.*
> *4 and 10* may be thrown in *3 ways.*
> *5 and 9* may be thrown in *4 ways.*
> *6 and 8* may be thrown in *5 ways.*
> *7* may be thrown in *6 ways.*

So 7 has an advantage over all other combinations, which, over the long run, is in favor of the casino. You can't beat the law of averages.

KENO

This is one of the oldest games of chance. Originating in China, the game can be traced back to a time before Christ, when it operated as a national lottery. Legend has it that funds acquired from the game were used to finance construction of the Great Wall of China.

Keno was first introduced into the United States in the 1800s by Chinese railroad construction workers. Easy to play, and offering a chance to sit down and converse between bets, it is one of the most popular games in town—despite the fact that *the house percentage is greater than that of any other casino game!*

To play, you must first obtain a keno form, available at the counter in the keno lounge and in most Las Vegas coffee shops. In the latter, you'll usually find blank keno forms and thick black crayons on your table. Fill yours out, and a miniskirted

	PRICE PER WAY	PRICE PER GAME

$50,000.00 LIMIT TO AGGREGATE PLAYERS EACH GAME

MARK NUMBER OF SPOTS OR WAYS PLAYED	NO. OF GAMES	TOTAL PRICE

WINNING TICKETS MUST BE COLLECTED IMMEDIATELY AFTER EACH KENO GAME IS CALLED.

1	2	3	4	5	6	7	8	9	10
11	12	13	14	15	16	17	18	19	20
21	22	23	24	25	26	27	28	29	30
31	32	33	34	35	36	37	38	39	40

WE PAY ON MACHINE ISSUED TICKETS - TICKETS WITH ERRORS NOT CORRECTED BEFORE START OF GAME WILL BE ACCEPTED AS ISSUED.

41	42	43	44	45	46	47	48	49	50
51	52	53	54	55	56	57	58	59	60
61	62	63	64	65	66	67	68	69	70
71	72	73	74	75	76	77	78	79	80

WE ARE NOT RESPONSIBLE FOR KENO RUNNERS TICKETS NOT VALIDATED BEFORE START OF NEXT GAME.

keno runner will come and collect it. After the game is over, she'll return with your winning or losing ticket. If you've won, it's customary to offer a tip, depending on your winnings.

Looking at your keno ticket and the keno board, you'll see that it is divided horizontally into two rectangles. The upper half (in China the yin area) contains the numbers 1 through 40, the lower (yang) half contains the numbers 41 through 80. You can win a maximum of $50,000, even more on progressive games, though it's highly unlikely (the probability is less than a hundredth of a percent). Mark up to 15 out of the 80 numbers; bets range from about 70¢ on up. A one-number mark is known as a one-spot, a two-number selection is a two-spot, and so on. After you have selected the number of spots you wish to play, write the price of the ticket in the right-hand corner where indicated. The more you bet, the more you can win if your numbers come up. Before the game starts, you have to give the completed form to a keno runner or hand it in at the keno lounge desk, and pay for your bet. You'll get back a duplicate form with the number of the game you're playing on it. Then the game begins. As numbers appear on the keno board, compare them to the numbers you've marked on your ticket. After 20 numbers have appeared on the board, if you've won, turn in your ticket immediately for a payoff before the next game begins. Otherwise, you will forfeit your winnings, a frustrating experience to say the least.

On a straight ticket that is marked with one or two spots, all of your numbers must appear on the board for you to win anything. With a few exceptions, if you mark from 3 to 7 spots, 3 numbers must appear on the board for you to win anything. Similarly, if you mark 8 to 12 spots, usually at least 5 numbers must come up for you to win the minimum amount. And if you mark 13 to 15 spots, usually at least 6 numbers must come up for a winning ticket. To win the maximum amount ($50,000), which requires that all of your numbers come up, you must select at least 8 spots. The more numbers on the board matching the numbers on your ticket, the more you win. If you want to keep playing the same numbers over and over, you can replay a ticket by handing in your duplicate to the keno runner; you don't have to keep rewriting it.

In addition to the straight bets described above, you can split your ticket, betting various amounts on two or more groups of numbers. To do so, circle the groups. The amount you bet is then divided by the number of groups. You could, if you so desired, play as many as 40 two-spots on a single ticket. Another possibility is to play three groups of four numbers each as eight spots (any two of the three groups of four numbers can be considered an eight spot). It does get a little complex, since combination betting options are almost infinite. Helpful casino personnel in the keno lounge can assist you with combination betting.

POKER

Poker is *the* game of the Old West. There's at least one sequence in every western where the hero faces off against the villain over a poker hand. In Las Vegas poker is a tradition, although it isn't played at every casino.

There are lots of variations on the basic game, but one of the most popular is **Hold 'Em.** Five cards are dealt faceup in the center of the table and two are dealt to each player. The player uses the best five of seven, and the best hand wins. The house dealer takes care of the shuffling and the dealing and moves a marker around the table to alternate the start of the deal. The house rakes 1% to 10% (it depends on the casino) from each pot. Most casinos include the usual seven-card stud and a few have hi-lo split.

If you don't know how to play poker, don't attempt to learn at a table. Find a casino that teaches it in free gaming lessons.

Pai gow poker (a variation on poker) has become increasingly popular. The game is played with a traditional deck plus one joker. The joker is a wild card that can be used as an ace or to complete a straight, a flush, a straight flush, or a royal flush. Each player is dealt seven cards to arrange into two hands: a two-card hand and a five-card hand. As in standard poker, the highest two-card hand is two aces, and the highest five-card hand is a royal flush. The five-card hand *must* be higher than the two-card hand (if the two-card hand is a pair of sixes, for example, the five-card hand must be a pair of sevens or better). Any player's hand that is set incorrectly is an automatic lose. The object of the game is for both of the player's hands to rank higher than both of the banker's hands. Should one hand rank exactly the same as the banker's hand, this is a tie (called a "copy"), *and the banker wins all tie hands*. If the player wins one hand but loses the other, this is a "push," and no money changes hands. The house dealer or any player may be the banker. The bank is offered to each player, and each player may accept or pass. Winning hands are paid even money, less a 5% commission.

ROULETTE

Roulette is an extremely easy game to play, and it's really quite colorful and exciting to watch. The wheel spins, and the little ball bounces around, finally dropping into one of the slots, numbered 1 to 36, plus 0 and 00. You can bet on a single number, a combination of numbers, or red or black, odd or even. If you're lucky, you can win as much as 35 to 1 (see the table). The method of placing single-number bets,

Roulette Chart Key	Odds	Type of Bet
		Straight Bets
A	35 to 1	*Straight-up:* All numbers, plus 0 and 00.
B	2 to 1	*Column Bet:* Pays off on any number in that horizontal column
C	2 to 1	*First Dozen:* Pays off on any number 1 through 12. Same for second and third dozen.
D	Even money	**Combination Bets**
E	17 to 1	*Split:* Pays off on 11 or 12.
F	11 to 1	Pays off on 28, 29, or 30.
G	8 to 1	*Corner:* Pays off on 17, 18, 20, or 21.
H	6 to 1	Pays off on 0, 00, 1, 2, or 3.
I	5 to 1	Pays off on 22, 23, 24, 25, 26, or 27.

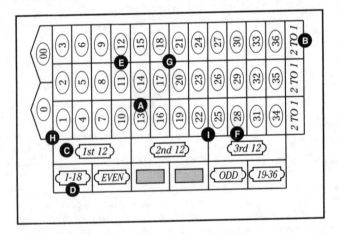

column bets, and others is fairly obvious. The dealer will be happy to show you how to "straddle" two or more numbers and make many other interesting betting combinations. Each player is given different-colored chips so that it's easy to follow the numbers you're on.

Some typical bets are indicated by means of letters on the roulette layout depicted here. The winning odds for each of these sample bets are listed. These bets can be made on any corresponding combinations of numbers.

SLOTS

You put the coin in the slot and pull the handle. What, you thought there was a trick to this?

Actually, there is a bit more to it. But first, some background. Old-timers will tell you slots were invented to give wives something to do while their husbands gambled. Slots used to be stuck at the edges of the casino and could be counted on one hand, maybe two. But now they *are* the casino. The casinos make more from slots than from craps, blackjack, and roulette combined. There are 115,000 slot machines (not including video poker) in the county alone. Some of these are at the airport, steps from you as you deplane. It's a just a matter of time before the planes flying into Vegas feature slots that pop up as soon as you cross the state line.

But in order to keep up with the increasing competition, the plain old machine, where reels just spun, has become nearly obsolete. Now, they are all computerized, and have added buttons to push, so you can avoid carpel tunnel syndrome yanking the handle all night. (The handles are still there on many of them.) The idea is still simple: Get three (sometimes four) cherries (clowns, sevens, dinosaurs, whatever) in a row, and you win something. Each machine has its own combination; some will pay you something with just one symbol showing; on most the more combinations there are, the more opportunities for loot. Some will even pay if you get three blanks. Study each machine to learn what it does.

The **payback** goes up considerably if you bet the limit (from two to as many as 45 coins). But while the payoff can be much bigger, the odds *against* winning also go up when you put in the limit. (So if you hit something on a machine and realize your $25 win would have been $500 had you only put in more money, take a deep breath, stop kicking yourself, and remember you might not actually have hit that winning combination so easily had you bet the limit.)

Progressive slots are groups of machines where the jackpot gets bigger every few moments (just as lottery jackpots build up). Bigger and better games keep showing up; for example, there's Anchor Gaming's much-imitated **Wheel of Gold,** wherein if you get the right symbol, you get to spin a roulette wheel, which guarantees you a win of a serious number of coins. **Totem Pole** is the Godzilla of slot machines, a behemoth that allows you to spin up to three reels at once (provided you put in the limit). And of course, there's our personal favorite, **Piggy Bankin'.** This has a LED display on which a silly tune plays and a pig cavorts (at erratic times, he trots across the screen, oinks, giggles when you lose and imitates Elvis, among other playful actions). It's so much fun to watch you start putting in the coins just to get the pig to move—forget about the money. But meanwhile, money is building up in the piggy bank, an extra bonus you win if you hit the right symbol.

Other gimmick machines include **Clear Winner,** where you can satisfy your curiosity about the inner workings of a slot machine, and **Rockin' Reels,** which looks like a jukebox. And, of course, there are always those **Big Giant Slot** machines, gimmicky devices found in almost every casino. They may not win as often as regular slots (though there is no definite word on it one way or the other), but not only are they just plain fun to spin, they often turn into audience participation gambling, as watchers gather to cheer you on to victory.

Are there surefire ways to win on a slot machine? No. But you can lose more slowly. The slots are on computer timers, and there are times when they are hitting and times when they are not. A bank of empty slots probably (but not certainly) means they aren't hitting. Go find a line where lots of people are sitting around with trays full of money. (Of course, yours will be the one that doesn't hit.) A good rule of thumb is that if your slot doesn't hit something in four or five pulls, leave it and go find another. It's not as though you won't have some choice in the matter. Also, each casino has some bank of slots that they advertise as more loose or with a bigger payback. Try these. It's what they want you to do, but what the heck.

Slot Clubs

If you play slots or video poker, it definitely pays to join a slot club. These so-called clubs are designed to attract and keep customers in a given casino by providing incentives—meals, shows, discounts on rooms, gifts, tournament invitations, discounts at hotel shops, VIP treatment, and (more and more) cash rebates. Of course, your rewards are greater if you play just in one casino, but your mobility is limited.

When you join a slot club (inquire at the casino desk), you're given something that looks like a credit card, which you must insert into an ATM-like device whenever you play. (Don't forget to retrieve your card when you leave the machine, as we sometimes do—though that may work in your favor if someone comes along and plays the machine without removing it.) The device tracks your play and computes bonus points.

Which slot club should you join? Actually, you should join one at any casino where you play, since even the act of joining usually entitles you to some benefits. It's convenient to concentrate play where you're staying; if you play a great deal, a casino hotel's slot-club benefits may be a factor in your accommodations choice. Consider, though, particularly if you aren't a high roller, the slot clubs Downtown. You get more bang for your buck, because you don't have to spend as much to start raking in the goodies.

One way to judge a slot club is by the quality of service when you enroll. Personnel should politely answer all your questions (for instance, is nickel play included? or is there a time limit for earning required points?) and be able to tell you exactly how many points you need for various bonuses.

To maximize your slot-club profits and choose the club that's best for you is a complex business. If you want to get into it in depth, order a copy of Jeffrey Compton's *The Las Vegas Advisor Guide to Slot Clubs* ($9.95 plus shipping), which examines just about every facet of the situation (☎ **800/244-2224**). Compton gives high ratings to the clubs at Caesars Palace, the Desert Inn, the Mirage, Treasure Island, the Flamingo Hilton, the Rio, the Sahara, Sam's Town, the Four Queens, the Golden Nugget, and Lady Luck.

SPORTS BOOKS

Most of the larger hotels in Las Vegas have sports book operations—they look a lot like commodities-futures trading boards. In some, almost as large as theaters, you can sit comfortably, occasionally in recliners and sometimes with your own video screen, and watch ball games, fights, and, at some casinos, horse races on huge TV screens. To add to your enjoyment, there's usually a deli/bar nearby that serves sandwiches, hot dogs, soft drinks, and beer. As a matter of fact, some of the best sandwiches in Las Vegas are served next to the sports books. Sports books take bets on virtually every sport. They are best during important playoff games or big horse races, when everyone in the place is watching the same event, shrieking, shouting, and moaning sometimes in unison. Joining in with a cheap bet (so you feel like you, too, have a personal stake in the matter) makes for bargain entertainment.

VIDEO POKER

Rapidly coming up on slots in popularity, video poker works the same way as regular poker, except you play against the machine. You are dealt a hand, you pick which cards to keep and which to discard, and then get your new hand. And, it is

If you aim to leave Las Vegas with a small fortune, go there with a large one.
—Anonymous American saying

hoped, collect your winnings. Somewhat more of a challenge and more active than slots because you have some control (or at least illusion of control) over your fate, and they are easier than playing actual poker with a table full of folks who probably take it very seriously.

There are a number of varieties of this machine, with **Jacks Are Better, Deuces Wild,** and so forth. Be sure to study your machine before you sit down. (The best returns are offered on the **Jacks Are Wild** machines, when the payback for a pair of Jacks or better is two times your bet, and three times for three of a kind.) Some machines offer **Double Down:** After you have won, you get a chance to draw cards against the machine, with the higher card the winner. If you win, your money is doubled and you are offered a chance to go again. Your money can increase nicely during this time, and you can also lose it all very fast, which is most annoying. Technology is catching up with Video Poker, too. Now they even have touch screens, which offer a variety of different poker games, blackjack, and video slots—just touch your screen and choose your poison.

3 The Casinos

Casino choice is a personal thing. Some like to find their lucky place and stick with it, while others love to take advantage of the nearly endless choices Vegas offers. Everyone should casino-hop at least once to marvel (or get dizzy) at the decor/spectacle and the sheer excess of it all. But beyond decoration, there isn't too much difference. You've got your slot machines, gaming tables, big chandeliers.

Virtually all casinos make sure they have no clocks or windows—they do not want you to interrupt your losing streak by realizing how much time has passed. Of course, we've all heard the legend that Vegas casinos pump in fresh oxygen to keep the players from getting tired and wanting to pack it in. The veracity of this is hard to confirm, but we can only hope it's true, especially when we think of that time we looked up after a long stretch of gambling and discovered it was Thursday.

Don't be a snob, and don't be overly dazzled by the fancy casinos. Sometimes you can have a better time at one of the older places Downtown, where stakes are lower, pretensions are nonexistent, and the clientele are often friendlier.

What follows is a description of most of the major casinos in Vegas, including a claustrophobia rating, whether they have a Big Giant Slot Machine (it's a sucker bet, but we love them), and a completely arbitrary assessment based on whether we won there.

SOUTH STRIP

Excalibur. 3850 Las Vegas Blvd. S. ☎ **702/597-7777.**

As you might expect, the Excalibur casino is replete with suits of armor, stained-glass panels, knights, dragons, and velvet and satin heraldic banners, with gaming action taking place beneath vast iron-and-gold chandeliers fit for a medieval castle fortress. This all makes it fine for kitsch-seekers, but anyone hating crowds or sensitive to noise will hate it. The overall effect is less like a castle and more like a dungeon. A popular feature here is Circus Bucks, a progressive slot machine that builds from a jackpot base of $500,000; players can win on a $3 pull. Excalibur's

100,000-plus square feet of gaming facilities also include a race and sports book, a keno lounge, a poker room, blackjack, minibaccarat, Caribbean stud, Let-It-Ride, casino war (like the game you played as a kid), craps, roulette, pai gow poker, Big Six, and slot/video poker machines. A nonsmoking area is a plus. One of us won a lot of money here and refused to share it with the other, so our final judgment about the casino is, well, mixed.

Luxor Las Vegas. 3900 Las Vegas Blvd. S. ☎ **702/262-4000.**

More accessible than ever thanks to the addition of the air-conditioned people-mover from Excalibur, Luxor has been completely remodeled and, in our opinion, improved immeasurably. You enter through a giant temple gateway flanked by massive statues of Ramses. Gone is the space-wasting center area that used to contain the bathrooms, cashiers, and casino offices. This additional space gives the casino a much more airy feel, which gives it a low claustrophobia level—in parts you can see all the way up the inside of the pyramid. King Tut heads and sphinxes adorn slot areas. There's a nonsmoking slot area. The Gold Chamber Club offers rewards of cash, merchandise, meals, and special services to slot and table players. And sports action unfolds on 17 large-screen TVs and 128 personalized monitors in Luxor's race and sports book. Additional gaming facilities include a keno lounge, blackjack, craps, roulette, poker, baccarat, minibaccarat, pai gow, Big Six, Caribbean stud, and slot/video poker machines. We already felt inclined to like this casino thanks to a good run at blackjack, but the redesign has made it even more inviting.

MGM Grand. 3799 Las Vegas Blvd. S. ☎ **702/891-7777.**

The world's largest casino—at 171,500 square feet, we've been to countries that were smaller!—is divided into four themed areas, in a futile attempt to make it seem smaller. Many of the Wizard of Oz decorations have been removed, but spend an hour in here and you might well feel like Dorothy after she got hit by the twister. One section features a high-roller slot area with machines that operate on coins valued at $100 and $500! The sports casino houses a big poker room, a state-of-the-art race and sports book, and the Turf Club Lounge. And the French Riviera–themed Monte Carlo casino has a luxurious marble-columned and gold-draped private high-end gaming area. Carousels of progressive slots unique to the MGM Grand include the very popular Majestic Lions high-frequency $1 slot machines that pay out more than $1 million daily and Lion's Share $1 slots capable of jackpots exceeding $1 million each at any time. And since Chrysler is a resort sponsor, there are several win-a-car slots. The MGM Grand Director's Club offers guests prizes ranging from comps and gifts to cash rebates. Additional gaming facilities include a keno lounge, blackjack, craps, roulette, baccarat, minibaccarat, pai gow, pai gow poker, Caribbean stud, Let-It-Ride, Casino War, Big Six, and slot/video poker machines.

Monte Carlo. 3770 Las Vegas Blvd. S. ☎ **702/730-7777.**

All huge ceilings and white-light interiors: Obviously, they are trying to evoke gambling in Monaco. While the decor shows lots of attention, it perhaps had too much attention. Bulbs line the ceiling, and everywhere you look is some detail or other. It's busy on both your eyes and your ears. So despite the effort put in, it's not a pleasant place to gamble. There's a large and comfortable race and sports book area, with its own cocktail lounge. And you can win a BMW sports car at a bank of 25¢ "Rich and Famous" slots. The Club Monte Carlo offers slot players cash rebates, merchandise, rooms, and meals for accumulated points. Other gaming facilities include a keno lounge, bingo room, poker room, blackjack, craps, roulette, baccarat, minibaccarat, Let-It-Ride, Caribbean stud, pai gow, pai gow poker, Big Six, and slot and video poker machines.

⭐ **New York New York.** 3790 Las Vegas Blvd. S. ☎ **702/740-6969.**

Another theme-run-wild place: tuxes on the backs of gaming chairs, change carts that look like yellow cabs, and so forth, all set in a miniature New York City. It's all fabulous fun, but despite a low claustrophobia level (thanks to an unusually high ceiling), it is a major case of sensory overload akin to the reaction elicited by a first-time look at the Strip. This may prove distracting. On the other hand, we won there, so we love it. And it is, if one can say this about anything in Vegas with a straight face, in spots quite beautiful. Serious gamblers understandably may sniff at it all and prefer to take their business to a more seemly casino, but everyone else should have about the most Vegasey time they can. Additional gaming facilities include a keno lounge, blackjack, craps, roulette, baccarat, minibaccarat, pai gow, pai gow poker, Caribbean stud, Let-It-Ride, Casino War, Big Six, and slot/video poker machines.

Orleans. 4500 W. Tropicana Ave. ☎ **702/365-7111.**

This is not a particularly special gambling space, though it has a low claustrophobia level, but over the sound system they play Cajun and Zydeco music, so you can two-step while you gamble, which can make losing somewhat less painful. It has all the needed tables—blackjack, craps, and so forth—plus plenty of slots, including a Wheel of Fortune machine that works like those other roulette wheel slots, but in this case, actually plays the theme song from the TV show. It will even applaud for you if you win.

Tropicana. 3801 Las Vegas Blvd. S. ☎ **702/739-2222.**

The Trop casino is quite good-looking, and, yes, highly tropical, with gaming tables situated beneath a massive, stained-glass archway and art nouveau lighting fixtures. In summer it offers something totally unique: swim-up blackjack tables located in the hotel's stunning 5-acre tropical garden and pool area. Slot and table game players can earn bonus points toward rooms, shows, and meals by obtaining an Island Winners Club card in the casino. A luxurious high-end slot area has machines that take up to $100 on a single pull. Numerous tournaments take place here, and free gaming lessons are offered weekdays. Facilities include a sports book, keno lounge, poker room, blackjack, craps, roulette, baccarat, pai gow poker, Let-It-Ride, Caribbean stud, minibaccarat, pai gow, and slot and video poker machines.

MID-STRIP

⭐ **Bally's Las Vegas.** 3645 Las Vegas Blvd. S. ☎ **702/739-4111.**

Bally's casino is one of the cleanest and best lit and definitely has that high-rent appeal. It's large (the size of a football field) with lots of colorful signage. The big ceiling makes for a low claustrophobia level. There's a Most Valuable Player Slot Club, offering members cash rebates, room discounts, free meals and show tickets, and invitations to special events, among other perks. The casino hosts frequent slot tournaments, and free gaming lessons are offered. Gaming facilities include a keno lounge, a state-of-the-art race and sports book, blackjack tables, craps, roulette, baccarat, minibaccarat, Caribbean stud (Bally's innovated this now popular Las Vegas game), pai gow, a Big Six wheel, Let-It-Ride tables, and slot/video poker machines. There are also blackjack tables and slot/video poker machines in Bally's Avenue Shoppes. There is not, however, a Big Giant Slot machine. For shame.

Memories of a Longtime Dealer

Lou has been a part of the gaming industry for 40 years, the first 20 of which he spent as a dealer in Las Vegas.

"My favorite places were the Flamingo, the Sands, and the Desert Inn. That's when the corporations weren't there. That's when the other folks were in. The mob guys—I never knew it, but that's what they were. I was just a kid. Bugsy had just gotten killed when I went to work at the Flamingo. The Sands was my very first favorite. That was the hotel of all hotels. They had the very best management team. They took care of their help. Their benefits were better than any union. It was the place.

"Years ago you had great entertainment. You could go to a lounge and catch better acts than in the showroom. Major stars were in the lounges, or they would come in and sit in with the acts after the showroom closed. Don Rickles: Sinatra would get up with him once in awhile. Sinatra gave me my first $100 tip. He was playing blackjack. Then he said, 'Do you want to play it or keep it?' I wanted to be polite, so I said, 'Bet it.' And he lost. In those days when the stars would appear on stage, between shows they would come out into the casinos. Sinatra and Sammy would deal. They would blow money, but the casinos didn't care. It was a fun, fun place.

"The casinos were run the way they were supposed to be run—for the customer, not so corporate-minded. In those days, you could go to Vegas, get your room very reasonable, your food was practically free, your shows were practically free, you would spend $500 in the casino, but you would come back and be happy because gaming was a form of entertainment. When they ran the casinos you would have a ball, come home, and be happy. They were very happy if the restaurants and shows lost money—you still lost that $500. Now it would cost

Barbary Coast. 3595 Las Vegas Blvd. S. ☎ **702/737-7111.**

The Barbary Coast has a cheerful 1890s-style casino ornately decorated with $2 million worth of gorgeous stained-glass skylights and signs, as well as immense crystal-dangling globe chandeliers over the gaming tables. It's worth stopping in just to take a look around when you're in the central "four corners" area of the Strip. The casino has a free Fun Club for slot players; participants earn points toward cash and prizes. Gaming facilities include a race and sports book, keno, blackjack tables, craps, roulette, minibaccarat, Let-It-Ride, pai gow poker, and slot/video poker machines.

✪ **Caesars Palace.** 3570 Las Vegas Blvd. S. ☎ **702/731-7110.**

Caesars casino is simultaneously the ultimate in gambling luxury and the ultimate in Vegas kitsch. Cocktail waitresses in togas parade about, as you gamble under the watchful gaze of faux marble Roman statues. The very high ceiling makes for a very low claustrophobia level, especially thanks to the recent face-lift, which has lightened up the paint and made the whole casino much brighter. A notable facility in the latter is the state-of-the-art **Race and Sports Book,** with huge electronic display boards and giant video screens. (Caesars pioneered computer-generated wagering data that can be communicated in less than half a second and sophisticated satellite equipment that can pick up virtually any broadcast sporting event in the world.) The domed VIP slot arena of the Forum Casino (minimum bet is $5, you $100 to stay at a hotel, and food is much more expensive, and to get a ticket to one of these shows is ridiculous. Now you gamble only $150 and you aren't as happy when you come home, because you don't feel like you've been treated to anything. It all goes into the same pocket—what difference does it make? It gives the customer the same hours and more fun. They don't understand that. It's not the same industry as when they ran it. And it shows."

LOU THE DEALER'S GAMING TIPS   If you are a **craps** shooter, just look around at the tables where they have the most chips. Find the guy with the most chips, and do what he does. Follow him along.

For **blackjack,** everybody will tell you in all your books to try to play single and double decks. I don't agree with that and I never will. The average player goes in to enjoy himself and to win a few dollars. So he is not a professional card counter. Play a shoe. If that shoe is going bad and you catch a run, you will make a lot more money than with a single deck.

Look at gaming as a form of entertainment. Look at that $100 that you might have spent on dinner or a club, where we laughed and had a few drinks and had a good time. Think of it that way.

If you double your money, quit. Not quit gambling, but quit that table. Go have a sandwich or watch a show. And *then* come back. The odds aren't that tremendously in favor of the casinos. How they make their money is through greed; gamblers doubling their money then trying to quadruple it and losing it all, and more.

Try to survive. Don't try to win the hotel. Just to win a few dollars. Then stop and enjoy it.

but you can wager up to $1,500 on a single pull!) is a plush, crystal-chandeliered precinct with seating in roomy, adjustable chairs. Slot players can accumulate bonus points toward cash back, gifts, gratis show tickets, meals, and rooms by joining the Emperors Club. Club membership also lets you in on grand-prize drawings, tournaments, and parties.

Most upscale of Caesars's gaming rooms is the intimate, European-style casino adjoining the **Palace Court** restaurant. Total facilities in all three casinos contain craps tables, blackjack, roulette, baccarat, minibaccarat, Let-It-Ride, Caribbean stud, pai gow poker, two Big Six wheels, slot/video poker machines, and a keno lounge. It's a gorgeous and elegant place to gamble, but we've never won there, so we hate it.

Flamingo Hilton. 3555 Las Vegas Blvd. S. ☎ **702/733-3111.**

If you've seen the movie *Bugsy*, you won't recognize this as Mr. Siegel's baby. The Flamingo is in the middle of redoing its casino area, which is just as well, because right now, it feels overly crowded, thanks to overall tight confines. It sprawls across a large space, meandering around corners, so it is very difficult to get out of. Actual daylight does stream in from windows and glass doorways on the Strip, however. There are slots here offering Cadillacs and Continentals as jackpots. Players Club slot bettors qualify for free meals, shows, rooms, and other play-based incentives. Free gaming lessons are offered weekdays. Gaming facilities include a keno lounge, a state-of-the-art race and sports book, poker room, Caribbean stud, blackjack,

Let-It-Ride, "double down" poker, craps, roulette, minibaccarat, pai gow poker, *sic bo*, Big Six, and slot/video poker machines. One of our favorite slot machines is here, but we won't tell you which one to save it for ourselves. Sorry.

Gold Coast. 4000 W. Flamingo Rd. ☎ **702/367-7111.**

Adjacent to the Rio, this casino is not only well lit but totally unique in Vegas: It has windows! It's a little thing, but it made us really excited. They also had a higher ratio of video poker machines to slot machines, rather than the other way around.

Harrah's. 3475 Las Vegas Blvd. S. ☎ **702/369-5000.**

Confetti carpeting and fiber-optic fireworks overhead combine with murals and an overall Mardi Gras theme to make a festive environment. Does it help you win more? Who knows. But the different, better energy that has resulted from this recent, costly face-lift certainly couldn't hurt. Don't miss the "party pits," gaming-table areas where dealers are encouraged to wear funny hats, celebrate wins, and otherwise break the usual stern dealer facade. Singing, dancing, and the handing out of party favors have all been known to break out. Gambling is supposed to be fun, so enjoy it. Slot and table game players can earn bonus points toward complimentary rooms, meals, and show tickets by acquiring a Harrah's Gold Card in the casino. Facilities include a sports book, keno lounge, poker room, blackjack, craps, roulette, minibaccarat, pai gow poker, red dog, casino war (in the party pit), Let-It-Ride, Big Six, and slot and video poker machines. There are nonsmoking areas, and free gaming lessons are offered weekdays.

Imperial Palace. 3535 Las Vegas Blvd. S. ☎ **702/731-3311.**

The 75,000-square-foot casino here reflects the hotel's pagoda-roofed Asian exterior with a dragon-motif ceiling and giant wind-chime chandeliers. There is a non-smoking slot machine area separate from the main casino (as opposed to just another part of the room, at best, in other casinos), and a Breathalyzer for voluntary alcohol limit checks on your way to the parking lot (useful since there are nine bars on the casino premises). Visitors can get free Scratch Slotto cards for prizes up to $5,000 in cash (cards and free passes to the auto collection are distributed on the sidewalk out front). A gaming school offers lessons in craps and blackjack, and slots tournaments take place daily. The Imperial Palace boasts a 230-seat race and sports book, attractively decorated with oil murals of sporting events; the room is tiered like a grandstand, and every seat has its own color monitor. Other gaming facilities include a keno lounge, blackjack, craps, roulette, minibaccarat, pai gow poker, Caribbean stud, Big Six, and slot/video poker machines. One Big Giant Slot machine is red, white, and blue; try singing the National Anthem to it, and see if you win more money.

Maxim. 160 E. Flamingo Rd. ☎ **702/731-4300.**

This friendly but dimly lit facility (with some of the '70s frills) is the neighborhood bar of casinos. They have a racetrack game where you can place bets on little mechanical horses and jockeys—kind of a kid's toy for adults. Pick up a fun book here for a free $1,000 slot pull. Gaming facilities include a keno lounge, sports book, blackjack, craps, roulette, Caribbean stud, Let-It-Ride, pai gow poker, and slot/video poker machines.

✪ Mirage. 3400 Las Vegas Blvd. S. ☎ **702/791-7111.**

Gamble in a Polynesian village in one of the prettiest casinos in town. It has a meandering layout, and the low ceiling makes for a medium claustrophobia level, but neither of these things is overwhelming. This remains one of our favorite places to gamble. Facilities include a separate poker room and a plush European-style *salon privé* for high rollers at baccarat, blackjack, and roulette; an elegant dining room serves catered meals to gamblers there. Slot players can join the Club Mirage and work toward bonus points for cash rebates, special room rates, complimentary meals and/or show tickets, and other benefits. The elaborate race and sports book offers theater stereo sound and a movie theater–size screen. Other gaming facilities here: a keno lounge, 75 blackjack tables, craps, roulette, baccarat, minibaccarat, pai gow, pai gow poker, Big Six, and slot and video poker machines. It's one of the most pleasant, and popular, casinos in town, so it more often than not is crowded.

The Rio. 3700 W. Flamingo Rd. ☎ **702/252-7777.**

This Brazilian-themed resort's 85,000-square-foot casino is, despite the presence of plenty of glitter and neon, very dark. It has about the highest claustrophobia rating of the major casinos. Its sports book feels a little grimy. The waitresses wear scanty costumes (particularly in the back), probably in an effort to distract you and throw your game off. Do not let them. The part of the casino in the new Masquerade Village is considerably more pleasant (the very high ceilings help) though still crowded, plus the loud live show adds still more noise. In an area called Jackpot Jungle, slot machines come equipped with TV monitors that present old movies and in-house information while you play. And in the high-end slot area ($5 to $100 a pull), guests enjoy a private lounge and gratis champagne. There are nonsmoking slot and gaming table areas. Facilities include a keno lounge, race and sports book, blackjack, craps, roulette, baccarat, minibaccarat, pai gow, Caribbean stud, survival dice, Let-It-Ride, Big Six, and slot and video poker machines.

Treasure Island. 3300 Las Vegas Blvd. S. ☎ **702/894-7111.**

Treasure Island's huge casino is highly themed. If you have ever gone to Disneyland's Pirates of the Caribbean and thought, "Gee, if only this were a casino," this is the place for you. Kids seem to be everywhere, because they are dazzled by the pirate stuff. Many people complain they don't like the atmosphere here, possibly because that very theme backfires. Especially luxurious are a high-limit baccarat/blackjack area (where players enjoy a buffet of hot hors d'oeuvres) and a high-limit slot area. Slot club members can earn meals, services, show tickets, and cash rebates. Throughout the casino there is something called Slot 2000. Hit a button, and a video screen pops up showing a (female) casino worker, to whom you can talk. She will answer questions, send someone over with drinks, make reservations, and otherwise help make your time there better. If you win a jackpot, she will come on and congratulate you. No, she can't see you, so don't try to flirt. There are nonsmoking gaming tables in each pit. A race and sports book boasts state-of-the-art electronic information boards and TV monitors at every seat as well as numerous large-screen monitors. Other facilities include a keno lounge, over 50 blackjack tables, craps, roulette, poker, minibaccarat, pai gow, pai gow poker, Caribbean stud, Let-It-Ride, Big Six, and slot and video poker machines.

NORTH STRIP

Circus Circus. 2880 Las Vegas Blvd. S. ☎ **702/734-0410.**

This vast property has three full-size casinos that, combined, comprise one of the largest gaming operations in Nevada (more than 100,000 square feet). More importantly, they have an entire circus midway set up throughout, so you are literally gambling with trapeze stunts going on over your head. The other great gimmick is the slot machine carousel—yep, it turns while you spin the reels. The Ringmaster Players Club offers slot/video poker and table players the opportunity to earn points redeemable for cash, discounted rooms and meals, and other benefits. Circus Bucks progressive slot machines here build from a jackpot base of $500,000, which players can win on a $2 pull. Gaming facilities include a 10,000-square-foot race and sports book with 30 video monitors ranging from 13 to 52 inches, 40-seat and 89-seat keno lounges, poker tables, blackjack, craps, roulette, a Big Six wheel, Let-It-Ride, pai gow poker, dice, Caribbean stud poker, and slot and video poker machines. Unfortunately, it is crowded, noisy, and there are lots of children passing through. That, plus some low ceilings (not in the Big Top, obviously), make for a very high claustrophobia rating, though the new Commedia del'Arte clown motif (as opposed to the old garish circus motif) has upgraded its appearance.

✪ **Desert Inn.** 3145 Las Vegas Blvd. S. ☎ **702/733-4444.**

Possibly the most genuinely elegant casino in Vegas, it's also one of the smallest for a major hotel. They don't care—they are looking for one good James Bond figure, rather than the masses. Crystal chandeliers here replace the usual neon glitz, and gaming tables are comfortably spaced. The ambience is reminiscent of intimate European gaming houses and is downright quiet. Some might find this almost creepy. Others may find it a huge relief. Since there are fewer slot machines here than at most major casinos, there's less noise in ringing bells and clinking coins. Most table games have a $5 minimum. Facilities include a race and sports book, poker, blackjack, Spanish 21 (like blackjack, but there are no 10s in the deck), craps, pai gow, pai gow poker, Let-It-Ride, Caribbean stud, minibaccarat, baccarat, roulette, and slot/video poker machines. A sophisticated casino lounge is a plus. The very high ceiling gives it a nonexistent claustrophobia rating.

The Riviera. 2901 Las Vegas Blvd. S. ☎ **702/734-5110.**

The Riviera's 100,000-square-foot casino, one of the largest in the world, means that there are plenty of opportunities to get lost and cranky. A wall of windows lets daylight stream in (most unusual), and the gaming tables are situated beneath gleaming brass arches lit by recessed, pink neon tubing. The casino's Slot and Gold (seniors) clubs allow slot players to earn bonus points toward free meals, rooms, and show tickets. Nickeltown is just that—nothin' but nickel slots and video poker. The race and sports book here offers individual monitors at each of its 250 seats, and this is one of the few places in town where you can play the ancient Chinese game of *sic bo* (a fast-paced dice game resembling craps). Additional facilities include a large keno parlor, blackjack, craps, roulette, baccarat, pai gow poker, Caribbean stud, Let-It-Ride, Big Six, and slot/video poker machines.

The Sahara. 2535 Las Vegas Blvd. S. ☎ **702/737-2111.**

The Sahara is in the process of changing its casino's look and adding a large new area, so it might be worth checking out. This is one place where there seem to be more tables than slots and video poker machines, but that might change with the new addition. When we were last there, they had a whole row of Piggy Bankin' machines that were all paying off, so we were happy. The Sahara runs frequent slot tournaments and other events, and its slot club, Club Sahara, offers cash rebates and other perks. Gaming facilities include a race and sports book, keno lounge, blackjack, craps, roulette, poker, Let-It-Ride, pai gow poker, Caribbean stud, a Big Six wheel, and slot/video poker machines. *Note:* This is the only Strip casino that offers pan, a card game.

The Stardust. 3000 Las Vegas Blvd. S. ☎ **702/732-6111.**

Always mobbed, this popular casino features 90,000 square feet of lively gaming action, including a 250-seat race and sports book with a sophisticated satellite system and more than 50 TV monitors airing sporting events and horse-racing results around the clock. Adjacent to it is a sports handicapper's library offering comprehensive statistical information on current sporting events. Stardust Slot Club members win cash rebates, with credit piling up even on nickel machines; free rooms, shows, meals, and invitations to special events are also possible bonuses. Other gaming facilities include a large, well-lit keno lounge, a poker room, an elegant baccarat lounge, blackjack, craps, roulette, minibaccarat, pai gow poker, Caribbean stud, Let-It-Ride, Big Six, and slot and video poker machines. If you're a novice, avail yourself of gratis gaming lessons. We usually do well there, so even though it's a little loud, we like it. Check out those $1 slots just inside the front door—they've been very good to us.

The Stratosphere. 2000 Las Vegas Blvd. S. ☎ **702/380-7777.**

Originally set up to evoke a world's fair but ending up more like a circus, the Stratosphere redid the whole area in order to make it more appealing for the many adults who were staying away in droves. The newly redone facility aims for class but doesn't necessarily achieve it. It's not that it fails, it just no longer has any identity at all. They heavily advertise their high payback on certain slots and video poker: 98% payback on dollar slots and 100% payback on quarter video poker (if you bet the maximum on each). We can't say we noticed a difference, but other people around us were winning like crazy. There's a test area for new slot games, a Harley slot area with motorcycle-seat stools, and a high-roller slot room ($5 minimum bet) where chairs move up and down and can vibrate to give you a back massage while you play. The Stratosphere Players Club sponsors frequent tournaments, and its members can earn points toward gifts, VIP perks, discounted room rates, meals, and cash rebates. Other facilities include a keno lounge, a sports book, bingo, blackjack (with new rules that allow for more wins, supposedly), craps, roulette, poker, minibaccarat, pai gow, pai gow poker, Caribbean stud, Let-It-Ride, Big Six, and slot and video poker machines.

Westward Ho Hotel & Casino. 2900 Las Vegas Blvd. S. ☎ **702/731-2900.**

This small but centrally located strip casino hosts many slot tournaments, and slot players who obtain Preferred Customer cards can amass credits toward complimentary rooms, meals, and shows, among other benefits. Gaming facilities include blackjack, craps, roulette, Big Six, and slot/video poker machines.

EAST OF THE STRIP

✪ **Hard Rock Hotel & Casino.** 4455 Paradise Rd. ☎ **702/693-5000.**

Where Gen X goes to gamble. The Hard Rock has certainly taken casino decor to a whole new level. The attention to detail and the resulting playfulness is admirable, if not incredible. Gaming tables have piano keyboards at one end; some slots have Fender guitar fret boards as arms; gaming chips have band names and/or pictures on them; slot machines are similarly rock-themed (check out the Jimi Hendrix machine!); and so it goes. The whole thing is set in the middle of a circular room, around the outskirts of which is various rock memorabilia in glass cases. Rock blares over the sound system, allowing boomers to boogie while they gamble. A bank of slots makes gambling an act of charity: Environmentally committed owner Peter

Morton (the Hard Rock's motto is "Save the Planet") donates profits from specified slots to organizations dedicated to saving the rain forests. A Back Stage Pass allows patrons to rack up discounts on meals, lodging, and gift-shop items while playing slots and table games. The race and sports book here provides comfortable seating in leather-upholstered reclining armchairs. Gaming facilities (with selected non-smoking tables) include blackjack, roulette, craps, Caribbean stud, minibaccarat, Let-It-Ride, pai gow poker, and slot/video poker machines. All this is genuinely amazing, but the noise level is above even that of a normal casino and we just hated it. It's worth looking at anyway.

✪ **Las Vegas Hilton.** 3000 Paradise Rd. ☎ **702/732-7111.**

The casino has two parts, thanks to the space-themed portion adjacent to the Star Trek Experience. In an area designed to look like a space port, you find space-themed slot machines, many of which have no handles—just pass your hand through a light beam to activate. Other gimmicks are throughout (though already some have been dropped since the recent opening), including urinals that give you an instant "urinalysis"—usually suggesting this is your lucky day to gamble. We do like a well-designed space in which to lose our money. Over in the original casino section, Austrian crystal chandeliers add a strong touch of class. It's actually medium size, but it does have an enormous sports book—at 30,500 square feet, the world's largest race and sports book facility. It, too, is a luxurious precinct equipped with the most advanced audio, video, and computer technology available, including 46 TV monitors, some as large as 15 feet across. In fact, its video wall is second in size only to NASA's. The casino is adjacent to the lobby, but neither are especially loud nor frantic. Especially plush are the vast 6,900-square-foot baccarat room—with gorgeous crystal chandeliers, silk-covered walls, and velvet-upholstered furnishings—and the VIP slot area where personnel are attired in tuxedos. Both areas offer gracious service to players. Because so many conventioneers stay here, the crowd is more changeable than at most casinos. By joining Club Magic, a slot club, you can amass bonus points toward cash prizes, gifts, and complimentary rooms, meals, and show tickets. In addition to the above, gaming facilities include a keno lounge, blackjack, craps, roulette, baccarat, pai gow, pai gow poker, Caribbean stud, Big Six, and slot/video poker machines.

Sam's Town. 5111 Boulder Hwy., at Flamingo Rd. ☎ **702/456-7777.**

In its three immense floors of gaming action (153,083 square feet, second only to the MGM Grand in size), Sam's Town maintains the friendly, just-folks ambience that characterizes the entire property. The casino is adorned with Old West para-phernalia (horseshoes, Winchester rifles, holsters, and saddlebags), and country music plays nonstop. If you don't like country music, don't go here. Sam's Town claims its friendliness extends to looser slots. The casino gives away a house (with a car and $10,000 in cash) every 3 months and offers 10-times odds on craps and single-deck blackjack. Join the Sam's Town Slot Club to earn points toward rooms, meals, and cash rebates. Free gaming lessons are offered weekdays from 11am to 4pm, poker lessons at other times. Gaming facilities include a race and sports book with more than 60 monitors, two keno lounges, a 590-seat bingo parlor, blackjack, craps, roulette, poker, pai gow poker, Caribbean stud, and slot/video poker machines (including a nonsmoking slot area).

DOWNTOWN

Binion's Horseshoe. 128 E. Fremont St., between Casino Center Blvd. and First St. ☎ **702/382-1600.**

The World's Series, Las Vegas Style

Binion's Horseshoe is internationally known as the home of the World Series of Poker. It was "Nick the Greek" Dondolos who first approached Benny Binion in 1949 with the idea for a high-stakes poker marathon between top players. Binion agreed, with the stipulation that the game be open to public viewing. The competition, between Dondolos and the legendary Johnny Moss, lasted 5 months with breaks only for sleep. Moss ultimately won about $2 million. As Dondolos lost his last pot, he rose from his chair, bowed politely, and said, "Mr. Moss, I have to let you go."

In 1970, Binion decided to re-create the battle of poker giants, which evolved into the annual World Series of Poker. Johnny Moss won the first year, and went on to snag the championship again in 1971 and 1974. Thomas "Amarillo Slim" Preston won the event in 1972 and popularized it on the talk-show circuit. Last year, there were more than 4,000 entrants from 22 countries, each ponying up the $10,000 entrance fee, and total winnings were in excess of $11 million (more than $93 million in prize money has been distributed since the tournament began). There were also a couple of celebrities, actors Matt Damon and Edward Norton, fresh from a movie where they played a couple of card sharks. They decided to try out their newly acquired moves against the pros, who were unhappy that these kids were barging in on their action, and so, rumor has it, offered a separate, large bounty to whatever player took them out. Both actors got knocked out on the first day but took it with good grace and apparently had a blast.

Professionals who know say that "for the serious player, the Binions *are* this town." Benny Binion could neither read nor write, but boy, did he know how to run a casino. His venerable establishment has been eclipsed over the years, but it claims the highest betting limits in Las Vegas on all games (probably in the entire world, according to a spokesperson). It offers single-deck blackjack and $2 minimums, 10-times odds on craps, and high progressive jackpots. We especially like the older part of the casino here, which—with its flocked wallpaper, gorgeous lighting fixtures, and gold-tasseled burgundy velvet drapes—looks like a turn-of-the-century Old West bordello. Unfortunately, all this adds up to a very high claustrophobia level. Gaming facilities include a keno lounge, race and sports book, a 500-seat bingo parlor, blackjack, craps, roulette, baccarat, minibaccarat, pai gow poker, Let-It-Ride, Caribbean stud, Big Six, and slot and video poker machines. They have two Big Giant Slot machines, at least one of which has been very, very good to us.

While you're visiting Binion's casino, be sure to see the display of $1 million (comprised of 100 $10,000 bills) encased in a gold horseshoe-shaped vault. If you'd like a photograph of yourself with all that moolah, you can get one taken free from 4pm to midnight daily.

California Hotel/Casino. 12 Ogden Ave., at 1st St. ☎ **702/385-1222.**

The California is a festive place filled with Hawaiian shirts and balloons. This friendly facility actually provides sofas and armchairs in the casino area—an unheard-of luxury in this town. Players can join the Cal Slot Club and amass points toward gifts and cash prizes or participate in daily slot tournaments. Gaming facilities include a keno lounge, sports book, blackjack tables, craps, roulette, minibaccarat, pai gow poker, Let-It-Ride, Caribbean stud, and slot and video

---

Impressions

I am, after all, the best hold 'em player alive. I'm forced to play this tournament, you understand, to demonstrate this fact.

— Once and future casino owner Bob Stupak on why he
entered Binion's Horseshoe World Series of Poker

---

poker machines. This is the first place we found our favorite Piggy Bankin' machines.

El Cortez. 600 Fremont St., between 6th and 7th sts. ☎ **702/385-5200.**

This friendly casino features frequent big-prize drawings (up to $50,000) based on your Social Security number. It's also popular for low limits (10¢ roulette and 25¢ craps). Gaming facilities include a race and sports book, keno, blackjack, craps, roulette, minibaccarat, and slot/video poker machines.

Fitzgeralds. 301 Fremont St., at 3rd St. ☎ **702/388-2400.**

They recently redid their casino in greens and golds, and the overall effect is not quite as tacky as you might expect. In fact, it's rather friendly, and with a medium to low claustrophobia level. The casino is actually two levels: From the upstairs part you can access a balcony from which you get an up-close view of the Fremont Street Experience. Their mascot, Mr. O'Lucky (a costumed leprechaun), roams the casino. You don't have to be nice to him. Blackjack, craps, and keno tournaments are frequent events here. Slot machines that paid back over 100% the previous week are marked with a Mr. Lucky sign. The Fitzgerald Card offers slot players gifts, meals, and other perks for accumulated points. Several slot machines have cars as prizes, fun books provide two-for-one gaming coupons, and there are $1 minimum blackjack tables. Facilities include a sports book, a keno lounge, blackjack, craps, Let-It-Ride, roulette, Spanish 21 (see the Desert Inn above), "21" Superbucks, Caribbean stud, and slot and video poker machines. They have dollar Piggy Bankin' machines.

Four Queens. 202 Fremont St., at Casino Center Blvd. ☎ **702/385-4011.**

The Four Queens is New Orleans–themed, with turn-of-the-century-style globe chandeliers, which make for good lighting and a low claustrophobia level. It's small, but the dealers are helpful, which is one of the pluses of gambling in the more manageably sized casinos. The facility boasts the world's largest slot machine: More than 9 feet high and almost 20 feet long, six people can play it at one time! It's the Mother of all Big Giant Slot machines, and frankly, it intimidates even us. Here is also the world's largest blackjack table (it seats 12 players). The Reel Winners Club offers slot players bonus points toward cash rebates. Slot, blackjack, and craps tournaments are frequent events, and there are major poker tournaments every January and September. The casino also offers exciting multiple-action blackjack (it's like playing three hands at once with separate wagers on each). Gaming facilities include a keno lounge, sports book, blackjack, craps, roulette, pai gow poker, Caribbean stud, Let-It-Ride, and slot/video poker machines.

Golden Gate. 1 Fremont St. ☎ **702/382-3510.**

This is one of the oldest casinos Downtown, and though its age is showing, it's still fun to go there. As you might expect from the name, old San Francisco (think earthquake time) artifacts and decor abound. At one end of the narrow casino is the

Impressions

What I like most about gambling is that it does not make sense. The hobby of gambling, even at my wimpy betting level, allows me to believe things that I know are not true. It gives me a chance to apply the most Byzantine rules and structures to my most ordinary actions, all in search of that compelling fiction known as luck.

—Edward Allen, *Penny Ante*

bar, where a piano player performs ragtime jazz, which is better than the homogenized pap offered in most casino lounges. Unfortunately, the low ceiling, dark period wallpaper, and small dimensions give this a high claustrophobia level.

Golden Nugget. 129 E. Fremont St., at Casino Center Blvd. ☎ **702/385-7111.**

Frankly, this is not the standout that other casino properties owned by Steve Wynn are. It goes for luxury, of course, but so much is crammed into so little space that the only feeling that emerges is one of overcrowding. That's not to say we didn't like it, because we won a lot of money here. And compared to most other Downtown properties, this is the most like the Strip. It is much cleaner and fresher feeling, in an area filled with dingy, time-forgotten spaces. Slot players can earn bonus points toward complimentary rooms, meals, shows, and gifts by joining the 24 Karat Club. Gaming facilities include an attractive and comfortable keno lounge, a race and sports book, blackjack ($1 minimum bet), craps, roulette, baccarat, pai gow, pai gow poker, red dog, Big Six, and slot/video poker machines.

✪ **Gold Spike.** 400 Ogden Ave., at Las Vegas Blvd. ☎ **702/384-8444.**

Okay, we just criticized dingy, time-forgotten spaces (see above) in Downtown, and the Gold Spike certainly lands in that category. So what? Here, everyone is equal, and everyone is having a good time, or at least they can sincerely join you in your misery. Think 1970s shag carpeting, faux wood paneling, and a best-not-thought-too-hard-about 49¢ shrimp cocktail. Best of all, they have penny slots! (Not very many, to be sure, and getting a seat at one can require patience.) Hey tightwads, take a buck, and spend a few hours.

Jackie Gaughan's Plaza Hotel/Casino. 1 Main St., at Fremont St. ☎ **702/386-2110.**

This is old Vegas, with an attempt at '60s glamour (think women in white go-go boots). Now it's a little worn. Gaming facilities include a keno lounge (featuring double keno), race and sports book, blackjack, craps, roulette, baccarat, Caribbean stud, pai gow poker, poker, pan, Let-It-Ride, and slot/video poker machines. Cautious bettors will appreciate the $1 blackjack tables and penny slots here.

Lady Luck. 206 N. 3rd St., at Ogden Ave. ☎ **702/477-3000.**

Even though Lady Luck is an older casino with the anticipated drop in glamour, it's surprisingly cheerful and with a low to medium claustrophobia level. Decorations give it a festive quality, and cocktail waitresses push drink carts, to mix you up something right on the spot. The Mad Money Slot Club offers scrip, cash, meals, accommodations, and prizes as incentives. Liberal game rules are attractive to gamblers. You can play "fast action hold 'em" here—a combination of 21, poker, and pai gow poker. Other gaming facilities include a keno lounge, blackjack, craps, roulette, minibaccarat, pai gow poker, and slot/video poker machines.

✪ **Main Street Station.** 200 N. Main St., between Fremont St. and I-95. ☎ **702/387-1896.**

Part of a long-closed old hotel that has been recently renovated and reopened to great success, this is the best of the Downtown casinos, at least in terms of comfort and pleasant environment. Even the Golden Nugget, nice as it is, has more noise and distractions. The decor here is, again, classic Vegas/old-timey (Victorian-era) San Francisco, but with extra touches (check out the old-fashioned fans above the truly beautiful bar) that make it work much better than other attempts at the same. Strangely, it seems just about smoke-free, perhaps thanks in part to a very high ceiling. The claustrophobia level is zero. Gaming facilities include a keno lounge, blackjack, craps, roulette, Caribbean stud, Let-It-Ride, pai gow poker, and slot/video poker machines.

Sam Boyd's Fremont Hotel & Casino. 200 E. Fremont St., between Casino Center Blvd. and 3rd St. ☎ **702/385-3232.**

This 32,000-square-foot casino offers a relaxed atmosphere and low gambling limits ($2 blackjack, 25¢ roulette). It's also surprisingly open and bright for a Downtown casino. Just 50¢ could win you a Cadillac or Ford Mustang here, plus a progressive cash jackpot. Casino guests can accumulate bonus points redeemable toward cash by joining the Five Star Slot Club, and take part in frequent slot and keno tournaments. Gaming facilities include two keno lounges, a race and sports book, blackjack, craps, roulette, Caribbean stud, Let-It-Ride, pai gow poker, and slot/video poker machines. No Big Giant Slot machine, though.

Showboat. 2800 Fremont St., between Charleston Blvd. and Mojave Rd. ☎ **702/ 385-9123.**

The Showboat's casino, recently renovated, has a Mardi Gras/Bourbon Street theme. It's not the most elaborate in town, but it is certainly clean, friendly, and comfortable. At night, a jazz band plays from an open pavilion. The Showboat's enormous 24-hour bingo parlor is a facility also noted for high payouts. Slot players can join a club to accumulate bonus points toward free meals, rooms, gifts, and cash prizes. And if you're traveling with kids ages 2 to 7, you can leave them at an in-house baby-sitting facility free for 3 hours while you gamble. Older kids can be dropped at the Showboat's 106-lane bowling center. In addition to bingo, gaming facilities include a keno lounge, race and sports book, blackjack (including single-deck "21"), craps, roulette, Let-It-Ride, pai gow, Caribbean stud, and slot and video poker machines.

Unless you're looking for souvenir decks of cards, Styrofoam dice, and miniature slot machines, Las Vegas is not exactly a shopping mecca. It does, however, have several noteworthy malls that can amply supply the basics. And many hotels also offer comprehensive, and sometimes highly themed, shopping arcades, most notably Caesars Palace (details below). You might consider driving **Maryland Parkway,** which runs parallel to the Strip on the east and has just about one of everything: Target, Toys R Us, several major department stores, Tower Records, major drug stores (in case you forgot your shampoo and don't want to spend $8 on a new one in your hotel sundry shop), some alternative-culture stores (tattoo parlors and hip clothing stores), and so forth. It goes on for blocks.

1 The Malls

Boulevard Mall. 3528 S. Maryland Pkwy., between Twain Ave. and Desert Inn Rd. ☎ **702/732-8949.** Mon–Fri 10am–9pm, Sat 10am–8pm, Sun 11am–6pm.

The Boulevard is the largest mall in Las Vegas. Its 144-plus stores and restaurants are arranged in arcade fashion on a single floor occupying 1.2 million square feet. Geared to the average consumer (not the carriage trade), it has anchors like Sears, JC Penney, Macy's, Dillard's, and Marshalls. Other notables include The Disney Store, The Nature Company, a 23,000-square-foot Good Guys (electronics), The Gap, Gap Kids, The Limited, Victoria's Secret, Colorado (for outdoor clothing and gear), Howard and Phil's Western Wear, and African and World Imports. There's a wide variety of shops offering moderately priced shoes and clothing for the entire family, books and gifts, jewelry, and home furnishings, plus more than a dozen fast-food eateries. In short, you can find just about anything you need here. There's free valet parking.

Fashion Show Mall. 3200 Las Vegas Blvd. S., at the corner of Spring Mountain Rd. ☎ **702/369-8382.** Mon–Fri 10am–9pm, Sat 10am–7pm, Sun noon–6pm.

This luxurious and centrally located mall, one of the city's largest, opened in 1981 to great hoopla. Designers Adolfo, Geoffrey Beene, Bill Blass, Bob Mackie, and Pauline Trigere were all on hand to display their fashion interpretations of the "Las Vegas look."

The mall comprises more than 130 shops, restaurants, and services. It is anchored by Neiman-Marcus, Saks Fifth Avenue, Macy's, Robinsons-May, and Dillard's. Other notable tenants: Abercrombie and Fitch, The Disney Store, The Walt Disney Gallery, The Discovery Channel Store, Lillie Rubin (upscale women's clothing), The Gap, Benetton, Uomo, Banana Republic, Victoria's Secret, Caché, Williams-Sonoma Grand Cuisine, The Body Shop, Mondi (upscale women's clothing), Waldenbooks, Louis Vuitton, and Sharper Image. There are several card and book shops, a wide selection of apparel stores for the whole family (including large sizes and petites), 9 jewelers, 21 shoe stores, and gift and specialty shops. There are dozens of eating places (see chapter 6 for specifics). Valet parking is available, and you can even arrange to have your car hand washed while you shop.

Galleria at Sunset. 1300 W. Sunset Rd., at Stephanie St., just off I-515 in nearby Henderson. ☎ **702/434-0202.** Mon–Sat 10am–9pm, Sun 11am–6pm.

This upscale 1 million-square-foot shopping center, 9 miles southeast of Downtown Las Vegas, opened in 1996, with performing Disney characters on hand to welcome shoppers and a nighttime display of fireworks. The mall has a Southwestern motif, evidenced in the use of terra-cotta stone, interior landscaping, cascading fountains, and skylights; eight 20-foot hand-carved pillars flank the main entrance. Anchored by four department stores—Dillard's, JC Penney, Mervyn's California, and Robinsons-May—the Galleria's 110 emporia include branches of The Disney Store, The Gap/Gap Kids/Baby Gap, The Limited and The Limited Too, Eddie Bauer, Miller's Outpost, Ann Taylor, bebe, Caché, Compagnie International, Lane Bryant, Lerner New York, Victoria's Secret, The Body Shop, B. Dalton, and Sam Goody. In addition to shoes and clothing for the entire family, you'll find electronics, eyewear, gifts, books, home furnishings, jewelry, and luggage here. Dining facilities include an extensive food court and two restaurants.

The Meadows. 4300 Meadows Lane, at the intersection of Valley View and U.S. 95. ☎ **702/878-4849.** Mon–Fri 10am–9pm, Sat–Sun 10am–7pm.

Another immense mall, The Meadows comprises 144 shops, services, and eateries, anchored by four department stores: Macy's, Dillard's, Sears, and JC Penney. In addition, there are 15 shoe stores, a full array of apparel for the entire family (including maternity wear, petites, and large sizes), an extensive food court, and shops purveying toys, books, CDs and tapes, luggage, gifts, jewelry, home furnishings (The Bombay Company, among others), accessories, and so on. Fountains and trees enhance the Meadows's ultramodern, high-ceilinged interior, and a 1995 renovation added comfortable conversation/seating areas and made the mall lighter and brighter. It is divided into five courts, one centered on a turn-of-the-century carousel (a plus for kids). A natural history–themed court has a "desert fossil" floor, and an entertainment court is the setting for occasional live musical and dramatic performances. You can rent strollers at the Customer Service Center.

2 Factory Outlets

Las Vegas has two big factory outlets just a few miles past the southern end of the Strip. If you don't have a car, you can take a no. 301 CAT bus from anywhere on the Strip and change at Vacation Village to a no. 303.

Belz Factory Outlet World. 7400 Las Vegas Blvd. S., at Warm Springs Rd. ☎ **702/896-5599.** Mon–Sat 10am–9pm, Sun 10am–6pm.

Belz houses 145 air-conditioned outlets, including a few dozen clothing stores and shoe stores. It offers an immense range of merchandise at savings up to 75% off

Impressions

Tip Number 3: Win a bunch of money. I can't recommend this too highly. If it hasn't occurred to you, win $1,200 and see for yourself. It's very energizing and really adds to your Vegas fun.

—Merrill Markoe, *Viva Las Wine Goddesses!*

retail prices. Among other emporia, you'll find Adolfo II, Casual Corner, Levi's, Nike, Dress Barn, Oshkosh B'Gosh, Leggs/Hanes/Bali, Esprit, Aileen, Bugle Boy, Carters, Reebok, Spiegel, Guess Classics, Oneida, Springmaid, We're Entertainment (Disney and Warner Bros.), Bose (electronics), Danskin, Van Heusen, Burlington, Royal Doulton, Lennox (china), Waterford (crystal), and Geoffrey Beene here. There is also a carousel.

Factory Stores of America. 9155 Las Vegas Blvd., at Serene St. ☎ **702/897-9090.** Mon–Sat 10am–8pm, Sun 10am–6pm.

A 30-acre open-air mall with Spanish-style architecture, this is the only outlet center in the country with a casino bar/lounge on its premises. Its 41 stores include Corning/Revere, Izod, Mikasa, American Tourister, Van Heusen, B.U.M. Equipment, Spiegel, London Fog, VF (sportswear), Book Warehouse, Geoffrey Beene, and Adolfo II. Come here for clothing, housewares, shoes, china, and much, much more.

3 Hotel Shopping Arcades

Just about every Las Vegas hotel offers some shopping opportunities. The following have the most extensive arcades. The physical spaces of these shopping arcades are always open, but individual stores keep unpredictable hours. *Note:* The Forum Shops at Caesars—as much a sightseeing attraction as a shopping arcade—are in the must-see category.

Bally's   Bally's **Avenue Shoppes** number around 20 emporia offering pro team sports apparel, toys, clothing (men's, women's, and children's), logo items, gourmet chocolates, liquor, jewelry, nuts and dried fruit, flowers, handbags, and T-shirts. In addition, there are several gift shops, three restaurants, art galleries, and a pool-wear shop. There are blackjack tables and slot and video poker machines right in the mall, as well as a race and sports book. You can dispatch the kids to a video arcade here while you shop.

Caesars Palace   Since 1978, Caesars has had an impressive arcade of shops called the **Appian Way.** Highlighted by an immense white Carrara-marble replica of Michelangelo's *David* standing more than 18 feet high, its shops include the aptly named Galerie Michelangelo (original and limited-edition artworks), jewelers (including branches of Ciro and Cartier), a logo merchandise shop, and several shops for upscale men's and women's clothing. All in all, a respectable grouping of hotel shops, and an expansion is in the works.

But in the hotel's tradition of constantly surpassing itself, in 1992 Caesars inaugurated the fabulous ✪ **Forum Shops,** an independently operated 250,000-square-foot Rodeo-Drive-meets-the-Roman-Empire affair complete with a 48-foot triumphal arch entranceway, a painted Mediterranean sky that changes as the day progresses from rosy-tinted dawn to twinkling evening stars, acres of marble, lofty scagliola Corinthian columns with gold capitals, and a welcoming goddess of fortune under a central dome. Its architecture and sculpture span a period from

300 B.C. to A.D. 1700. Storefront facades, some topped with statues of Roman senators, resemble a classical Italian streetscape, with archways, piazzas, ornate fountains, and a barrel-vaulted ceiling. The "center of town" is the magnificent domed Fountain of the Gods, where Jupiter rules from his mountaintop surrounded by Pegasus, Mars, Venus, Neptune, and Diana. And at the Festival Fountain, seemingly immovable "marble" Animatronic statues of Bacchus (slightly in his cups), a lyre-playing Apollo, Plutus, and Venus come to life for a 7-minute revel with dancing waters and high-tech laser-light effects. The shows take place every hour on the hour. The whole thing is pretty incredible, but also very Vegas, particularly the Bacchus show, which is truly frightening and bizarre. Even if you don't like shopping, it's worth the stroll just to giggle.

More than 70 prestigious emporia here include Louis Vuitton, Plaza Escada, Bernini, Christian Dior, A/X Armani Exchange, bebe, Caché, Gucci, Ann Taylor, and Gianni Versace, along with many other clothing, shoe, and accessory shops. Other notables include a Warner Brothers Studio Store (a sign at the exit reads THATIUS FINITUS FOLKUS), The Disney Store, Kids Kastle (beautiful children's clothing and toys), Rose of Sharon (classy styles for large-size women), Sports Logo (buy a basketball signed by Michael Jordan for $695!), Field of Dreams (more autographed sports memorabilia), Museum Company (reproductions ranging from 16th-century hand-painted Turkish boxes to ancient Egyptian scarab necklaces), West of Santa Fe (western wear and Native American jewelry and crafts), Antiquities (neon Shell gas signs, 1950s malt machines, Americana; sometimes "Elvis" is on hand), Endangered Species Store (ecology-themed merchandise), Brookstone (one-of-a-kind items from garden tools to sports paraphernalia), and Victoria's Secret. There's much more, including jewelry shops and art galleries.

And as if that weren't enough, in 1998 the Forum Shops added an extension. The centerpiece is a giant **Roman Hall,** featuring a 50,000-gallon circular aquarium and another fountain that also comes to life with a show of fire (don't stand too close—it gets really hot), dancing waters, and Animatronic figures as the mythical continent of Atlantis rises and falls every 90 minutes. The production values are much higher than the Bacchus extravaganza, but it takes itself more seriously, so the giggle factor remains. The hall is also the entrance to the Race for Atlantis IMAX 3-D ride.

In this shopping area, you will find a number of significant stores, including a DKNY, Emporio Armani, Niketown, Fendi, Polo for Ralph Lauren, Guess, Virgin Megastore, and FAO Schwarz. Do go see the latter, as it is fronted by a gigantic Trojan horse, in which you can clamber around, while its head moves and smoke comes out its nostrils. We love it. Also in the shops is Wolfgang Puck's Chinois, a Cheesecake Factory, and a Caviartorium, where you can sample all varieties of the high-priced fish eggs.

The shops are open Sunday to Thursday 10am to 11pm, Friday and Saturday 10am to midnight. An automated walkway transports people from the Strip to the shopping complex. Heralded by a marble temple housing four golden horses and a charioteer, it is flanked by flaming torchiers and fronted by a waterfall cascading over a bas-relief of the god Neptune—you can't miss it! Often a gladiator with sword and shield is there to greet you at the other end. Valet parking is available.

Circus Circus   There are about 15 shops between the casino and Grand Slam Canyon, offering a wide selection of gifts and sundries, logo items, toys and games, jewelry, liquor, resort apparel for the entire family, T-shirts, homemade fudge/candy/soft ice cream, and, fittingly, clown dolls and puppets. At Amazing Pictures you can have your photo taken as a pinup girl, muscle man, or whatever else your fantasy dictates. Adjacent to Grand Slam Canyon, there is a new shopping arcade themed along a European village, with cobblestone walkways and fake woods and so forth, decorated with replicas of vintage circus posters. It's much nicer than what the tacky Circus Circus has had before. Among the stores are Marshall Russo, Headliners, The Sweet Tooth, and Carousel Classics.

Excalibur   The shops of **"The Realm"** for the most part reflect the hotel's medieval theme. Dragon's Lair, for example, features items ranging from pewter swords and shields to full suits of armor, and Merlin's Mystic Shop carries crystals, luck charms, and gargoyles. Other shops carry more conventional wares—gifts, candy, jewelry, women's clothing, and Excalibur logo items. A child pleaser is Kids of the Kingdom, which displays licensed character merchandise from Disney, Looney Tunes, Garfield, and Snoopy. Wild Bill's carries western wear and Native American jewelry and crafts. And at Fantasy Faire you can have your photo taken in Renaissance attire.

Flamingo Hilton   The **Crystal Court** shopping promenade here accommodates men's and women's clothing/accessories stores, gift shops, and a variety of other emporia selling jewelry, beachwear, Southwestern crafts, fresh-baked goods, logo items, children's gifts, toys, and games.

Harrah's   Harrah's has finished up a massive new renovation that includes a new shopping center called **Carnivale Court.** It's entirely outdoors and features live entertainment strolling around, plus a show at night with fireworks and circus-type acts. Among the store highlights is a Ghirardelli Chocolate store, a branch of the famous San Francisco–based chocolate company. This store is remarkably like a smaller version of the one in SF (alas, without the vats of liquid chocolate being mixed up), and in addition to candy, you can get a variety of delicious sundaes and other ice-cream treats. Other stores include On Stage (a CD and video store) and Carnival Corner (gourmet foods and cigars). You might also swing into the hotel and examine the artwork found in **The Art of Gaming**—all gambling-related artwork.

Luxor Hotel/Casino   Gaza Gallerie is a new 20,000-square-foot shopping arcade with eight full shops. Most of the stores emphasize clothing. Adjacent is the Cairo Bazaar, a trinket shop.

MGM Grand   The hotel's **Star Lane Shops** include more than a dozen upscale emporia lining the corridors en route from the monorail entrance. The Knot Shop carries designer ties by Calvin Klein, Gianni Versace, and others. El Portal features luggage and handbags—Coach, Dior, Fendi, Polo Ralph Lauren, and other exclusive lines. Grand 50's carries *Route 66* jackets, Elvis T-shirts, photos of James Dean, and other mementos of the 1950s. MGM Grand Sports sells signed athletic uniforms, baseballs autographed by Michael Jordan, and the like; it is the scene of occasional appearances by sports stars such as Floyd Patterson and Stan Musial. You can choose an oyster and have its pearl set in jewelry at The Pearl Factory. Other Star Lane Shops specialize in movie memorabilia, Betty Boop merchandise, *EFX* wares, children's clothing, decorative magnets, MGM Grand logo items and Las Vegas souvenirs, seashells and coral, candy, and sunglasses. Refreshments are available at a Häagen-Dazs ice-cream counter and Yummy's Coffees and Desserts. In other parts of the hotel, retail shops include a *Wizard of Oz* gift shop, Front Page (for newspapers, books, magazines, and sundries), a spa shop selling everything from beachwear to top-of-the-line European skin care products, a liquor store, a candy store, Kenneth J. Lane jewelry, and Marshall Rousso (men's and women's clothing).

In addition, theme-park emporia sell Hollywood memorabilia, cameras and photographic supplies, MGM Grand and theme-park-logo products, toys, fine china and crystal, animation cels, collectibles (limited-edition dolls, plates, figurines), Hollywood-themed clothing and accessories, and western wear. At Arts and Crafts you can watch artisans working in leather, glass, wood, pottery, and other materials, and at Photoplay Gallery you can have your picture taken as *Time* magazine's man or woman of the year.

Monte Carlo   An arcade of retail shops here includes Bon Vivant (resort wear for the whole family, dress wear for men), Crown Jewels (jewelry, leather bags, crystal, Fabergé eggs, gift items), a florist, logo shop, jeweler, food market, dessert store, and Lance Burton magic paraphernalia shop.

The Rio   The new 60,000-square-foot **Masquerade Village** is a nicely done addition to the Rio. It's done as a European village, and is 2 stories, featuring a wide variety of shops including the nation's largest Nicole Miller, Speedo, and the N'awlins store, which includes "authentic" voodoo items, Mardi Gras masks, and so forth. It's attached to a cafe that sells beignets (from Cafe Du Monde mix) and chicory coffee.

The Riviera   The Riviera has a fairly extensive shopping arcade comprising art galleries, jewelers, a creative photographer, and shops specializing in women's shoes and handbags, clothing for the entire family, furs, gifts, logo items, toys, phones and electronic gadgets, and chocolates.

Sam's Town   Though Sam's Town does not contain a notably significant shopping arcade, it does house the huge **Western Emporium** (almost department-store size), selling western clothing for men and women, boots (an enormous selection), jeans, belts, silver and turquoise jewelry, Stetson hats, Native American crafts, gift items, and old-fashioned candy. You can have your picture taken here in period western costume. Open daily at 9am; closing hours vary.

Stratosphere   Shopping is no afterthought here. The internationally themed second-floor **Tower Shops** promenade, which will soon house 40 stores, is entered via an escalator from the casino. Some shops are in "Paris," along the Rue Lafayette and Avenue de l'Opéra (there are replicas of the Eiffel Tower and Arc de Triomphe in this section). Others occupy Hong Kong and New York City streetscapes. Already-extant emporia include The Money Company (money-motif items from T-shirts to golf balls), a T-shirt store, a magic shop, Key West (body lotions and more), Victoria's Secret, a magnet shop, Norma Kaplan (for glitzy/sexy women's footwear), an electronics boutique, a logo shop, and several gift shops. There are branches of Jitters (a coffeehouse) and Häagen-Dazs, and stores are supplemented by cart vendors.

Treasure Island   Treasure Island's shopping promenade—doubling as a portrait gallery of famed buccaneers (Blackbeard, Jean Lafitte, Calico Jack, Barbarosa)—has wooden ship figureheads and battling pirates suspended from its ceiling. Emporia here include the Treasure Island Store (your basic hotel gift/sundry shop, also offering much pirate-themed merchandise, plus a section devoted to Calvin Klein clothing), Loot 'n' Booty, Candy Reef, Captain Kid's (children's clothing), and Damsels in Dis'Dress (women's sportswear and accessories). The Mutiny Bay Shop, in the video-game arcade, carries logo items and stuffed animals. In the casino are the Buccaneer Bay Shoppe (logo merchandise) and the Treasure Chest (a jewelry store; spend those winnings right on the spot). And the Crow's Nest, en route to the Mirage monorail, carries Cirque du Soleil logo items. Cirque du Soleil and *Mystère* logo wares are also sold in a shop near the ticket office.

4 Vintage Clothing

The Attic. 1018 S. Main St. ☎ **702/388-4088.** Mon–Sat 10am–7pm, Sun 11am–5pm. MC, V.

Sharing a large space with **Cafe Neon,** a coffeehouse that also serves Greek-influenced cafe food (so you can raise your blood sugar again after a long stretch of shopping), and a comedy club stage, and upstairs from an attempt at a weekly club (as of this writing, the Saturday night Underworld), The Attic (the current star of a Visa commercial) has plenty of clothing choices on many racks. During a recent visit, a man came in asking for a poodle skirt for his 8-year-old. They had one.

Buffalo Exchange. 4110 S. Maryland Pkwy., at Flamingo, near Tower Records. ☎ **702/791-3960.** Mon–Sat 11am–7pm, Sun noon–6pm. MC, V.

This is actually part of a chain of such stores spread out across the western United States. If the chain part worries you, don't let it—this merchandise doesn't feel processed. Staffed by plenty of incredibly hip alt-culture kids (ask them for what's happening in town during your visit), it is stuffed with dresses, shirts, pants, and so forth. Like any vintage shop, the contents are hit and miss; you can easily go in one day and come out with 12 fabulous new outfits, but you can just as easily go in and come up dry. It is probably the most reliable of the local vintage shops.

The Haight. 1647 E. Charleston Blvd. ☎ **702/387-7818.** Mon–Sat 11am–6pm, Sun noon–5pm. MC, V.

Upstairs from an antique store, this is in a small old house, and so not only is the stock in various rooms, they've turned the retro-tiled bathroom into the dressing room. They have a large selection of used Levis and otherwise specialize in '60s and '70s vintage clothing.

Our House. 1639 E. Charleston Blvd. ☎ **702/384-4748.** Mon–Sat 11am–5pm, Sun noon–5pm.

A tiny store filled with the most happening in new and vintage clothing (think club kid wear) and some new jewelry designs. Not a huge selection, but very kinda now, kinda wow. They are right next door to The Haight and the start of the Charleston antique row.

5 Reading Material: Used Books, Comics & a Notable Newsstand

USED BOOKS

Dead Poet Books. 3858 W. Sahara, corner of Valley View, near Albertson's. ☎ **702/227-4070.** Mon–Sat 10am–6pm, Sun noon–5pm. AE, DISC, MC, V.

Eliot? Byron? Tennyson? None of the above. Actually, the dead poet in question was a man from whose estate the owners bought their start-up stock. He had such good taste in books, they "fell in love with him" and wanted to name the store in his memory. Just one problem—they never did get his name. So they just called him "the dead poet." He wasn't a poet, but surely anyone with such fine taste in books must have been one in his soul. His legacy continues in this book-lover's haven.

A LAS VEGAS SPECIALTY STORE

Gambler's Book Shop. 630 S. 11th St., just off Charleston Blvd. ☎ **800/522-1777** or 702/382-7555. Mon–Sat 9am–5pm.

Here you can buy a book on any system ever devised to beat casino odds. Owner Edna Luckman carries more than 4,000 gambling-related titles, including many out-of-print books, computer software, and videotapes. She describes her store as a place where "gamblers, writers, researchers, statisticians, and computer specialists can meet and exchange information." On request, knowledgeable clerks provide on-the-spot expert advice on handicapping the ponies and other aspects of sports betting. The store's motto is "knowledge is protection."

COMIC BOOKS

Alternative Reality Comics. 4800 S. Maryland Pkwy. ☎ **702/736-3673.** Mon–Sat 11am–7pm, Sun noon–6pm.

The place in Vegas for all your comic-book needs. They have a nearly comprehensive selection, with a heavy emphasis on the underground comics. But don't worry, the superheroes are here, too.

A NOTABLE NEWSSTAND

International Newsstand. 3900 Paradise Rd., in Citibank Plaza. ☎ **702/796-9901.** Daily 8:30am–9pm. AE, MC, V.

Homesick for local news? No matter where you are from, come here. It's crammed full of seemingly every city newspaper in the land, plus a large selection of foreign cities. They surely don't have everything, but it seems like they do. Okay, the actual count is every major U.S. city, plus 10 other countries. One impressed shopper said this would put many a formerly worthy newsstand in any cosmopolitan city to shame. There is also a wide array of magazines, both foreign and domestic, though they get less space than at other newsstands thanks to the newspapers.

6 Antiques

Antiques in Vegas? You mean really old slot machines, or the people playing the really old slot machines?

Actually, Vegas has quite a few antique stores—nearly two dozen, of consistent quality and price, nearly all located within a few blocks of each other. We have one friend, someone who takes interior design *very* seriously, who comes straight to Vegas for most of her best finds (you should see her antique chandelier collection!).

To get there, start in the middle of the 1600 block of East Charleston Boulevard and keep driving east. The little stores, nearly all in old houses dating from the '30s, line each side of the street. Or you can stop in at **Silver Horse Antiques,** (☎ **702/385-2700**), 1651 E. Charleston Blvd., and pick up a map to almost all the locations, with phone numbers and hours of operation.

For everything under one roof, try **Sampler Shops Antique Mall,** (☎ **702/368-1170**), 6115 W. Tropicana Ave. Open Monday to Saturday noon to 6pm, Sunday noon to 5pm. Over 200 small antique shops sell their wares in this mall, which offers a diversity of antiques ranging from exquisite Indian bird cages to Star

Wars memorabilia (let's not call those sorts of items "antiques" but rather "nostalgia"). Changing selections of course mean you can never guarantee what will be available, but you can probably count on antique clothing and shoes, lamps, silver, decorative plates and china, old sewing machines, antique furniture, and '50s prom dresses. The displays are well labeled and well laid out, making it easy to take in all the antiques. The oldest antiques are from the mid-1800s and range in price from $100 to $4,000.

7 Wigs

Serge's Showgirl Wigs. 953 E. Sahara Ave. #A-2. ☎ **702/732-1015.** Mon–Sat 10am–5:30pm.

Oh, you probably thought all those showgirls just naturally had bountiful thick manes. Sorry to burst your bubble. Actually, we aren't—if you don't know it's all illusion, you ought to. Meanwhile, if you have a desire to look like a showgirl yourself (and why not?), come to Serge's, which for 23 years has been supplying Vegas wiggy needs, with over 2,000 wigs to chose from. Wigs range in price from $130 to over $1,500, depending on quality and realness, and you can pick from Dolly Parton's wig line or get something custom-made. They also make hairpieces and toupees, and carry hair-care products. If these prices are too rich to bring your fantasy alive, right across the way is **Serge's Showgirl Wigs outlet,** with prices running from a more reasonable $60 to $70.

10 Las Vegas After Dark

You will not lack for things to do at night in Vegas. It is a town that truly comes alive only at night. Don't believe us? Just look at the difference between the Strip during the day, when it's kind of dingy and nothing special, and at night when the lights hit and the place glows in all its glory. Night is when it's happening in this 24-hour town. In fact, most bars and clubs don't even get going until close to midnight. That's because it's only around then that all the many restaurant workers and people connected with the shows get off the clock and can go out and play themselves. It's extraordinary. Just sit down in a bar at 11pm; it's empty. You might well conclude it's dead. Return in 2 hours and find it completely full and jumping.

But you also won't lack for things to do before 11pm. There are shows all over town, ranging from traditional magic to cutting-edge acts like *Mystère*. The showgirls remain, topless and otherwise; Las Vegas revues are what happened to vaudeville, by the way, as chorus girls do their thing in between jugglers, comics, magicians, singers, and specialty acts of dubious category. Even the topless ones are tame; all that changes is the already scantily clad showgirls are even more so.

Every hotel has at least one lounge, usually offering live music. The days of fabulous Vegas lounge entertainment, where sometimes the acts were of better quality than the headliners (and headliners like Sinatra would join the lounge acts onstage between their own sets), are gone. Most of what remains are homogeneous and bland, and serve best as a brief respite or background noise. On the other hand, finding the most awful lounge act in town can be rewarding on its own.

Vegas still does attract the best in headliner entertainment in its showrooms and arenas. Bette Midler did an HBO special from the MGM Grand in early 1997, and U2 started its PopArt tour at UNLV's stadium. Liza Minnelli, Harry Belafonte, Penn and Teller, Melissa Manchester, Wayne Newton, Chaka Khan, Johnny Mathis, Barbara Mandrell, Englebert Humperdinck, and Wynnona have all played Vegas recently. (And up until just a few years ago, the legendary Sinatra still did regular stints here.) It is still a badge of honor for comedians to play Vegas, and there is almost always someone of marquee value playing one showroom or the other.

Of course, if you prefer alternative or real rock music, your choices are more limited. More rock bands are coming through town, attracted to either the Hard Rock Hotel's venue or the

Huntridge Theater, so that means you can actually see folks like Marilyn Manson and Beck in Vegas. But otherwise, the alternative club scene in town is severely limited. Check out the listings below for bars and coffeehouses, several of which offer live alternative or blues music.

If you want to know what is playing here during your stay, consult the local free alternative papers: the *Scope* (biweekly, with great club and bar descriptions in their listings) and *City Life* (weekly, with no descriptions but comprehensive listings of what's playing where all over town). Both can be picked up at restaurants, bars, record and music stores, and hep retail stores. Or you can call *Scope* directly; act nice, and they might just give you a tip on the spot. If you are looking for good alt-culture tips, try asking the cool staff at the **Buffalo Exchange** vintage clothing store (☎ **702/791-3960**); they have their fingers right on the pulse of the underground.

Admission to shows runs the gamut, from about $19 for *An Evening at La Cage* (a female impersonator show at the Riviera) to $80 and more for top headliners or *Siegfried and Roy.* Prices usually include two drinks or, in rare instances, dinner.

To find out who will be performing during your stay, and for up-to-date listings of shows (prices change, shows close), you can call the various hotels featuring headliner entertainment, using toll-free numbers. Or call the **Las Vegas Convention and Visitors Authority** (☎ **702/892-0711**) and ask them to send you a free copy of *Showguide* or *What's On in Las Vegas* (one or both of which will probably be in your hotel room.)

Every hotel entertainment option is described below with information on ticket prices, what is included in the price (drinks, dinner, taxes, and/or gratuities), showroom policies (as to preassigned or maître d' seating and smoking), and how to make reservations. Whenever possible, reserve in advance, especially on weekends and holidays. If the showroom has **maître d' seating** (as opposed to assigned seats), you may want to tip him to upgrade your seat. A tip of $15 to $20 per couple will usually do the trick at a major show, less at a small showroom. An alternative to tipping the maître d' is to wait until the captain shows you to your seat. Perhaps it will be adequate, in which case you've saved some money. If not, you can offer the captain a tip for a better seat. If you do plan to tip, have the money ready; maître d's and captains tend to get annoyed if you fumble around for it. They have other people to seat. You can also tip with casino chips (from the hotel casino where the show is taking place only) in lieu of cash. Whatever you tip, the proper etiquette is to do it rather subtly—a kind of palm-to-palm action. There's really no reason for this, since everyone knows what's going on, but being blatant is in poor taste. Arrive early at maître d' shows to get the best choice of seats.

If you buy tickets for an assigned-seat show in person, you can look over a seating chart. Avoid sitting right up by the stage if possible, especially for big production shows. Dance numbers are better viewed from the middle of the theater. With headliners, you might like to sit up close.

Note: All of these caveats and instructions aside, most casino-hotel showrooms offer good visibility from just about every seat in the house.

In addition to the below listed, consider the **Fremont Street Experience,** described in chapter 7.

1 What's Playing Where

It used to be that a show was an essential part of the Vegas experience. Back in those days, a show was pretty simple: A bunch of scantily clad (and we mean scantily— topless shows were part of the fun) showgirls paraded around while a comedian engaged in some raunchy patter. The showgirls are still here, and still scantily clad

---

Lounge Lizard Supreme

All those faux hipster artists doing woeful lounge act characters in Hollywood and New York only wish they could be Mr. Cook E. Jarr, whose sincerity and obvious drive to entertain puts mere performance art to shame. With George Hamilton's tan, Cher's first shag haircut (it's certainly not his factory original coif), and a bottomless, borderless catalog of rock, pop, soul, swing, and standard favorites, he's more Vegas than Wayne Newton. With a cult following of blue-collar casino denizens and the youthful cocktail set, Cook's recently been given his own small room at the **Continental Hotel**, 4100 Paradise Rd., at Flamingo (☎ **702/737-5555**). There he holds court, playing human jukebox with karaoke-style backing recordings, terrible jokes, an array of disco-era lights, and (his favorite) a smoke machine. He's actually a solid, throaty singer, with a gift for vocal mimicry as he moves from Ben E. King to Bee Gees to Tony Bennett turf. And his tribute the night Sinatra died—a version of "My Way" in which he voiced, alternatively, Sammy, Dino, and Elvis welcoming Ol' Blue Eyes to Heaven—was priceless. Cook E. Jarr plays Friday and Saturday nights at 11pm.

(though not as often topless; guess cable TV has taken some of that thrill away), but the productions around them have gotten impossibly elaborate. And they have to be; they have to compete with a free pirate-battle stunt show held several times nightly right on the Strip. Not to mention a volcano, a Mardi Gras parade in the sky, lounge acts galore, and the occasional imploding building. All for free. The big resort hotels, in keeping with their general over-the-top tendencies, are pouring mountains of money into high-spectacle extravaganzas, luring big-name acts into decades-long residencies and surrounding them with special effects that would put some Hollywood movies to shame.

Unfortunately, along with big budgets come big-ticket prices. Sure, you can still take the family to a show for under $100, but you're not going to see the same production values for the same $100 that might almost get you two tickets to *EFX*. Which is not to say you always get what you pay for: There are some reasonably priced shows that are considerably better values than their more expensive counterparts.

OUR FAVORITES   The **Best Show** is definitely *Mystère* at Treasure Island. The best **magic show**, and one of the most reasonably priced productions (and thus overall best value for the money), is Lance Burton at Monte Carlo. Best **classic Vegas topless revue** is *Jubilee!* at Bally's. Best **modern-day Vegas production** is *EFX* at MGM Grand.

The following section will describe, by name, each of the major production shows currently playing in Las Vegas. But we begin by listing each major hotel and the production show(s) playing there in the event you want to catch a show in a particular location.

- **Bally's:** ✪ *Jubilee!* (Las Vegas–style review)
- **Excalibur:** *An Evening in Vienna* (afternoon show featuring the Lippizaner Stallions) and *King Arthur's Tournament* (medieval-themed review)
- **Flamingo Hilton:** *Forever Plaid* (off-Broadway review featuring '60s music) and *The Great Radio City Spectacular* (Las Vegas–style review featuring the Radio City Music Hall Rockettes)
- **Harrah's:** *Spellbound* (magic review)

- **Imperial Palace:** *Legends in Concert* (musical impersonators)
- **Jackie Gaughan's Plaza:** *The Xtreme Scene* (sexy Las Vegas–style review)
- **MGM Grand:** ✪ *EFX* (special-effects review featuring David Cassidy)
- **The Mirage:** ✪ *Siegfried and Roy* (magical extravaganza)
- **Monte Carlo:** ✪ *Lance Burton: Master Magician* (magic show and review)
- **Rio Suite Hotel:** *Danny Gans* (impressions)
- **Riviera Hotel:** *An Evening at La Cage* (female impersonators), *Crazy Girls* (sexy Las Vegas–style review), and *Splash* (aquatic review)
- **Stardust:** *Enter the Night* (Las Vegas–style review)
- **Stratosphere Tower:** *American Superstars* (an impression-filled production show) and *Viva Las Vegas* (Las Vegas–style review)
- **Treasure Island:** ✪ Cirque du Soleil's *Mystère* (unique circus performance)
- **Tropicana:** *Folies Bergère* (Las Vegas–style review)

2 The Major Production Shows

This category covers production shows major and minor, including country music shows, magic shows, female impersonator shows, and racy revues like *Teeze* and *Xposed*.

American Superstars. Stratosphere, 2000 Las Vegas Blvd. S. ☎ **800/99-TOWER** or 702/380-7777.

One of the increasing number of celebrity impersonator shows (cheaper than getting the real headliners), *American Superstars* is one of the few where said impersonators actually sing live. Five performers do their thing; celebs impersonated vary depending on the evening. A typical Friday night featured Gloria Estefan, Charlie Daniels, Madonna, Michael Jackson, and Diana Ross and the Supremes. (And recently they added the Spice Girls—the catty among us will notice the impersonators have better figures than the real Girls.) The performers won't be putting the originals out of work anytime soon, but they aren't bad. Actually, they are closer in voice than in looks to the celeb in question (half the black performers were played by white actors), which is an unusual switch for Vegas impersonators. The "Charlie Daniels" actually proved to be a fine fiddler in his own right and was the hands-down crowd favorite. The live band actually had a look-alike of their own: Kato Kaelin on drums (it's good that he's getting work). The youngish crowd (by Vegas standards) included a healthy smattering of children and seemed to find no faults with the production. The action is also shown on two large, and completely unnecessary, video screens flanking the stage, so you don't have to miss a moment.

- **Showroom Policies:** Smoking not permitted; maître d' seating.
- **Price:** Admission $25.25 includes tax.
- **Show Times:** Fri–Wed at 7 and 10pm. Dark Thurs.
- **Reservations:** Up to 3 days in advance.

✪ **Cirque du Soleil's *Mystère*.** Treasure Island, 3300 Las Vegas Blvd. S. ☎ **800/392-1999** or 702/894-7722.

The in-house ads for *Mystère* (say miss-*tair*) say "Words don't do it justice," and for once, that's not just hype. The show is so visual that trying to describe it is a losing proposition. And simply calling it a circus is like calling the Hope Diamond a gem, or the Taj Mahal a building. It's accurate, but something seems a little left out of the description.

Impressions

I've built my own world here. Wayne's world.
—Las Vegas superstar Wayne Newton talking about his 52-acre estate, Casa de Shenandoah, 5 miles out of town

Cirque du Soleil began in Montréal as a unique circus experience, not only shunning the traditional animal acts in favor of gorgeous feats of human strength and agility, but also adding elements of the surreal and the absurd. The result seems like a collaboration between Salvador Dalí and Luis Buñuel, with a few touches by Magritte and choreography by Twyla Tharp. Mirage Resorts has built them their own theater, an incredible space with an enormous dome and superhydraulics that allow for the Cirque performers to fly in space. Or so it seems.

While part of the fun of the early Cirque was seeing what amazing stuff they could do on a shoestring, seeing what they can do with virtually unlimited funds is spectacular. Unlike, arguably, other artistic ventures, Cirque took full advantage of their new largesse, and their art only rose with their budget. The show features one simply unbelievable act after another (seemingly boneless contortionists and acrobats, breathtakingly beautiful aerial maneuvers), interspersed with Dada-ist, Commedia Dell'Arte clowns, and everyone clad in costumes like nothing you've ever seen before. All this and a giant snail. The show is dreamlike, suspenseful, funny, erotic, mesmerizing, and just lovely. At times, you might even find yourself moved to tears. However, for some children, it might be a bit too sophisticated and arty. Even if you've seen Cirque before, it's worth coming to check out, thanks to the large production values. It's a world-class show, no matter where it's playing. That this is playing in Vegas is astonishing.

- **Showroom Policies:** Nonsmoking with preassigned seating.
- **Price:** $70 adults, $35 for children under 11 (drinks and tax extra).
- **Show Times:** Wed–Sun at 7:30 and 10:30pm. Dark Mon–Tues.
- **Reservations:** You can reserve by phone via credit card up to 7 days in advance (do reserve early since it often sells out).

Crazy Girls. Riviera Hotel, 2901 Las Vegas Blvd. S. ☎ **800/634-3420** or 702/734-9301.

Crazy Girls, presented in an intimate theater, is probably the raciest revue on the Strip. It features sexy showgirls with perfect bodies in erotic song-and-dance numbers enhanced by innovative lighting effects. Think of *Penthouse* poses coming to life. Perhaps it's best summed up by one older man from Kentucky: "It's okay if you like boobs and butt. But most of the girls can't even dance."

- **Showroom Policies:** Nonsmoking with maître d' seating.
- **Price:** General admission $23.36, VIP admission $31.60 (includes two drinks; gratuity extra).
- **Show Times:** Tues–Sun at 8:30 and 10:30pm, with an extra midnight show Sat. Dark Mon.
- **Reservations:** Tickets can be purchased at the box office and over the phone, in advance if you wish.

Impressions

Welcome to Dreamland.
—A. Alvarez, *The Biggest Game in Town*

① Family-Friendly Shows

Appropriate show for kids, all described in this chapter, include the following:
- **King Arthur's Tournament** at Excalibur (*see* p. *235*)
- **Siegfried and Roy** at the Mirage (*see* p. *237*)
- **Lance Burton** at the Monte Carlo (*see* p. *236*)
- **Starlight Express** at the Hilton (*see* p. *241*)
- **EFX** at the MGM Grand (*see* p. *231*)
- **Cirque du Soleil's** *Mystère* at Treasure Island (*see* p. *229*)

♦ **Danny Gans: The Man of Many Voices.** Rio Suites, 3700 W. Flamingo Rd. ☎ **800/PLAY-RIO** or 702/252-7777.

Danny Gans has taken over the newly refurbished Copacabana Showroom for an indefinite run. If he's still on when you visit, don't miss him. Gans, who has starred on Broadway, is an impressionist extraordinaire. Natalie Cole, who heard him perform her father's famous song, "Unforgettable," exclaimed, "No one has ever done a better impression of my dad." His show is also unforgettable. In addition to startlingly realistic impressions of dozens of singers (everyone from Sinatra to Springsteen), he does movie scenes (such as Fonda and Hepburn in *On Golden Pond*), Bill Clinton, weird duets (Michael Bolton and Dr. Ruth, or Stevie Wonder singing to Shirley MacLaine "I Just Called to Say I Was You"), and, of course, a first-rate Elvis. A mind-boggling highlight is Gans's rendition of "The Twelve Days of Christmas" in 12 different voices, which necessitates rapidly switching back and forth from such diverse impressions as Paul Lynde, Clint Eastwood, Peter Falk, and Woody Allen, among others. This show gets a standing ovation every night.

- **Showroom Policies:** Nonsmoking with maître d' seating.
- **Price:** $60 (including two drinks, tax, and gratuities).
- **Show Times:** Wed–Sun at 7:30pm. Dark Mon–Tues.
- **Reservations:** Tickets can be ordered up to 30 days in advance.

✪ **EFX.** MGM Grand, 3799 Las Vegas Blvd. S. ☎ **800/929-1111** or 702/891-7777.

Essentially the first major show of the post–Cirque du Soleil era, *EFX*'s $40 million makeover (thanks to new star David Cassidy) has used its money wisely, updating the classic Vegas revue into essentially a live-action version of the modern over-the-top Strip hotels. It's not so much cheese anymore, as expensive and occasionally jaw-dropping cheese. Which is not to say it's bad—quite the opposite. The nominal story line, about a man who has lost his imagination, allows the very likable Cassidy, playing on his regular guy image, to assume the personas of King Arthur, P. T. Barnum, Houdini, and H. G. Wells, in order to deliver set pieces of better-than-usual dancing, magic, singing, acrobatics, and illusion. And, of course, special effects ("EFX" is the movie industry term for same). The sets are lavish beyond belief; the costumes and some of the acting show the Cirque influence (faintly Grand Guignol); and the choreography is considerably more imaginative and fresh than any other such show in town. The songs are somewhat bland, but sung almost totally live, and some prove surprisingly hummable. And the effects (flying saucers and cast members, fire-breathing dragons, 3-D time travel, lots of explosions) show where the money is. Cranks may occasionally spot wires, and sometimes said effects are a little painful on the eyes and ears (and they overdo it on the fog machine). The ticket price isn't cheap, so it might be worth taking the less-expensive seats in the mezzanine, as the view is just as good from there.

- **Showroom Policies:** Nonsmoking with preassigned seating.
- **Price:** $49.50–$70.
- **Show Times:** Tues–Sat at 7:30 and 10:30pm. Dark Sun–Mon.
- **Reservations:** You can reserve by phone any time in advance.

Enter the Night. The Stardust, 3000 Las Vegas Blvd. S. ☎ **800/824-6033** or 702/ 732-6111.

It's kind of cute how the Stardust has tried to stage a full-size topless revue on a small- to medium-size stage. Okay, maybe not *cute,* but the production does seem to be busting at its seams, and it never quite reconciles its aspirations with its reality. There is no plot or point to this; the theme is "enter the night" (of course) and about the passion and mystery that will then ensue, but the songs and actions are vague as to how this is supposed to come about. Instead, what you get is one of those "why is that girl parading around in her underwear?" sort of shows. It's a question that can be quite relevant, depending on your seats, since a circular catwalk extends into the audience; some seats are perched right on the rail edge of this, virtually squashing the occupant's face into a showgirl's midriff. In fact, some of those topless breasts could put out an eye. (Besides, it spoils the illusion when you are close enough to see all that pancake makeup.) Your seat placement is worth noting for this reason, if you don't want to be that up close and personal with a virtually naked total stranger. Others might pay extra.

Anyway, it's a revue, featuring songs about listening to your heart, dancing (the Space Age Viking dance number was a camp highlight), and one blonde (presumably Aki, "Showgirl for the 21st Century") in a flesh-colored G-string performing nearly nude *en pointe* ballet. All this is delivered with a Mickey Mouse Club enthusiasm, which is a bit disconcerting when half the performers are partially naked. There is also nearly naked ice skating, which was actually better than you might think; the skaters are very good and make use of the world's tiniest patch of ice in dramatic and resourceful ways. They were also a huge crowd pleaser, as was the delightful Argentinean gaucho act.

- **Showroom Policies:** Nonsmoking with preassigned seating.
- **Price:** Most seats $30, booths $35–$45 (includes two drinks, tax, and gratuity).
- **Show Times:** Tues, Wed, Thurs, Sat at 7:30 and 10:30pm; Sun–Mon at 8pm only. Dark Fri.
- **Reservations:** You can reserve up to a month in advance by phone.

An Evening at La Cage. Riviera Hotel and Casino, 2901 Las Vegas Blvd. S. ☎ **800/ 634-6753** or 702/734-9301.

No, not inspired by the French movie or the recent American remake, or even the Broadway musical. Actually, it's more the stage show from *Priscilla, Queen of the Desert.* Female impersonators dress up as various entertainers (with varying degrees of success) to lip-synch to said performers' greatest hits (with varying degrees of success). Celebs lampooned can include Cher, Bette Midler, Judy Garland, Whitney Houston, Dionne Warwick, and, intriguingly, Michael Jackson. A Joan Rivers impersonator, looking not unlike the original but sounding (even with the aid of, oddly, a constant echo) not at all like her, is the hostess, delivering scatological phrases and stale jokes. They do make the most of a tiny stage with some pretty stunning lighting, though the choreography is bland. Still, it's a crowd pleaser—one couple was back for their fourth (all comped) visit.

- **Showroom Policies:** Nonsmoking with maître d' seating.
- **Price:** $26.66–$35 (includes two drinks; gratuity extra).
- **Show Times:** Wed–Mon at 7:30 and 9:30pm, with an extra show at 11:15pm Wed and Sat. Dark Tues.
- **Reservations:** Tickets can be purchased at the box office only, in advance if you wish.

Folies Bergère. Tropicana, 3801 Las Vegas Blvd. S. ☎ **800/468-9494** or 702/739-2411.

The longest-running production show in town has recently undergone a "sexier than ever" face-lift, but the result is far from that, more like tamed-down burlesque, as done by a college drama department. Bare breasts pop up (sorry) at odd moments: not during the can-can line, but rather during a fashion show and an en-pointe ballet sequence. The effect is not erotic or titillating, suggesting only that absent-minded dancers simply forgot to put their shirts on. The dance sequences, more acrobatics than true dance, range from the aforementioned ballet and can-can to jazz and hoedown, and only occasionally well costumed. A coyly cute '50s striptease number on a "Hollywood Squares"–type set is more successful, as is a clever and funny juggling act (don't miss his finale with the vest and hat).

- **Showroom Policies:** Nonsmoking with preassigned seating.
- **Price:** $45 for a table seat, $55 for a booth seat (includes coupon for buffet discount).
- **Show Times:** Fri–Wed at 8 and 10:30pm. Dark Thurs.
- **Reservations:** You can charge tickets in advance via credit card.

Forever Plaid. Flamingo Hilton, 3555 Las Vegas Blvd. S. ☎ **800/221-7299** or 702/733-3333.

The Flamingo Hilton presents the off-Broadway hit *Forever Plaid* in its Bugsy's Celebrity Theatre. The plot line is bizarre, to say the least. The Plaids, an early 1960s harmony quartet on the order of The Four Freshmen, are killed on their way to their first big gig (at an Airport Hilton) when their car is broadsided by a busload of parochial-school girls en route to see the Beatles' U.S. television debut on *The Ed Sullivan Show*. After 30 years, they've mysteriously returned to Earth (it has to do with the power of harmony and expanding holes in the ozone layer) to finally perform the show they never got to do in life. This totally weird context is just an excuse for a zany musical stroll down memory lane consisting of 29 oldies—songs like "Rags to Riches," "Sixteen Tons," "Love Is a Many-Splendored Thing," "Three Coins in the Fountain," and "No, Not Much." If you're sentimental about that era, you'll love it.

- **Showroom Policies:** Nonsmoking with maître d' seating.
- **Price:** $22 (includes tax).

Insider Tip

If you'd like to take a backstage tour of the *Folies* set, they are scheduled Sunday to Thursday at 12:30, 1:30, and 2:30pm. Tickets cost $2; call the above phone number for details.

- **Show Times:** Tues–Sun 7:30 and 10:30pm.
- **Reservations:** Tickets can be reserved a week in advance.

The Great Radio City Spectacular. Flamingo Hilton, 3555 Las Vegas Blvd. S. ☎ **800/ 221-7299** or 702/733-3333.

This is the wholesome showgirls show. If you aren't familiar with the venerable Rockettes tradition, the short black-and-white film on their history that opens the production will get you up to date. It also sets the stage for the big entrance by the ladies, arguably the world's best-known chorus line. There is a headliner who accompanies them—this star changes frequently. As of this writing, it was Paige O'Hara, the voice of Belle from Disney's *Beauty and the Beast.* Regardless of who it is, the star's musical numbers are interspersed with a variety of dance productions by the Rockettes that serve as a veritable history of dance, ranging from tap to '40s swing, waltzes, March of the Wooden Soldiers, and the like. Of course, the signature Rockettes' high-kicking line is worked into at least half the numbers. That's their greatest hit—if O'Hara remains with the show, you can count on seeing her do hers, from the aforementioned *Beauty and the Beast.* The variety acts are standard Vegas: a juggler who keeps up a disturbing, David Helfgott–like banter under his breath and a magician who tries too hard. The stand-out here was the trained dogs act, which reduced even cynical viewers to goo. These are all pound-rescued mutts with plenty of star quality, and they work the crowd like pros.

- **Showroom Policies:** Nonsmoking with maître d' seating.
- **Price:** Dinner show based on main-course price ($48 and up includes tax and gratuity). Cocktail show $40 (includes two drinks, tax, and gratuity).
- **Show Times:** Nightly dinner show at 7:45pm, cocktail show at 10:30pm.
- **Reservations:** You can reserve by phone 2 weeks in advance.

Imagine: A Theatrical Odyssey. Luxor, 3900 Las Vegas Blvd. S. ☎ **800/288-1000** or 702/ 262-4000.

Probably the most stunning showroom in Las Vegas, entirely Egyptian-themed, and though the insides of pyramids surely didn't look like this, it's mighty impressive anyway. The plush seats are sharply raked, so there isn't a bad view in the house. Unfortunately, what is presented only occasionally lives up to the standards of the setting. Expect another mixed-bag Vegas revue; a jungle-themed tiki torch opening number leads to some high-drama magic, then more music and dancing, some Chinese jugglers, and an underwater-themed production number, plus a look into the future, which seems to consist of Day-Glo costumes and twinkle lights, with a '60s-mod James Bond soundtrack. Far better was the Cirque du Soleil–inspired bungee jump acrobatic act over the audience and the spectacular concluding Chinese aerialists.

- **Showroom Policies:** Nonsmoking with preassigned seating.
- **Price:** $40 (includes tax).
- **Show Times:** Wed–Mon 7:30 and 10:30pm.
- **Reservations:** By phone up to 7 days in advance.

✪ *Jubilee!* Bally's, 3645 Las Vegas Blvd. S. ☎ **800/237-7469** or 702/739-4567.

A classic Vegas spectacular, crammed with singing, dancing, magic, acrobats, elaborate costumes and sets and, of course, bare breasts. It's a basic review, with production numbers featuring homogenized versions of standards (Gershwin, Cole Porter, some Fred Astaire numbers) sometimes sung live, sometimes lip-synched, and always accompanied by lavishly costumed and frequently topless showgirls.

12 Inaccuracies in the Movie *Showgirls*

By the showgirls in *Jubilee!*

1. Nomi Malone wouldn't be in a Las Vegas production because she can't sing (or act).
2. Showgirls do not live in trailers.
3. Showgirls aren't discovered in strip bars.
4. Showgirls do not pimp themselves at conventions or trade shows.
5. Hotel owners do not throw lavish cast parties.
6. A lead dancer does not become a celebrity.
7. No one learns a show in a day.
8. Pushing someone down the stairs doesn't get you a lead role—it gets you fired.
9. Ice is used backstage to treat injuries, not to erect nipples.
10. Leaving rehearsal to go to Spago to drink champagne is generally frowned upon.
11. Showgirls are not coke-sniffing, champagne-drinking lesbians.
12. Anyway, showgirls do not drink champagne backstage—we prefer Jack Daniels!

Humorous set pieces about Samson and Delilah and the sinking of the *Titanic* (!) show off some pretty awesome sets (and they were doing the *Titanic* long before a certain movie), while the finale features aerodynamically impossible feathered and bejeweled costumes and headpieces designed by Bob Mackie. So what if the dancers are occasionally out of step and the action sometimes veers into the dubious (a Vegas-style revue about a disaster that took more than 1,000 lives?) or even the inexplicable (a finale praising beautiful and bare-breasted girls suddenly stops for three lines of "Somewhere Over the Rainbow")? With plenty of rhinestones and nipples on display, this is archetypal Vegas entertainment and the best of those presently offered.

- **Showroom Policies:** Nonsmoking with preassigned seating.
- **Price:** $49.50 and up (tax included, drinks extra).
- **Show Times:** Sun–Wed at 8pm, Thurs and Sat at 8 and 11pm. Dark Fri.
- **Reservations:** You can reserve up to 6 weeks in advance.

King Arthur's Tournament. Excalibur, 3850 Las Vegas Blvd. S. ☎ **800/933-1334** or 702/597-7600.

If you've seen the Jim Carrey movie *The Cable Guy*, you probably laughed at the scene in which the two protagonists went to a medieval dinner and tournament. Perhaps you thought it was satire, created just for the movie. You would be wrong. It's actually part of a chain, and something very like it can be found right here in Vegas. For a price, you get a modest dinner, which you eat with your hands (in keeping with the theme), and watch a "tournament" of knights (jousting and whatnot) that is every bit as unrehearsed and spontaneous as a professional wrestling match. The story is about the battle between an evil black knight and a heroic white knight for a princess's hand in marriage. Each section of the arena is given a knight to cheer, and the audience is encouraged to hoot, holler, and pound on the tables, which kids love, but many adults will find it tiresome, particularly when they insist you shout "huzzah!" and other period slang. In addition to the knightly battles, there are dances, equestrian acrobatics, tumblers, jugglers, and stunt riders. It's all incredibly camp, and only big Renaissance Faire buffs, kids, and Jim Carrey fans will really enjoy it. Dinner includes a pot of creamy chicken soup, Cornish game hen, stuffed baked potato, vegetable, biscuits, apple tart, and beverage.

- **Showroom Policies:** Nonsmoking with preassigned seating.
- **Price:** $33.54 (including dinner, beverage, tax, and gratuity).
- **Show Times:** "Knightly" at 6 and 8:30pm.
- **Reservations:** You can reserve up to 6 days in advance by phone.

✪ *Lance Burton: Master Magician.* Monte Carlo, 3770 Las Vegas Blvd. S. ☎ **800/ 311-8999** or 702/730-7000.

Magic acts are a dime a dozen in Vegas of late. Along with impersonator acts, they seem to have largely replaced the topless showgirls of yore. Most seem more than a little influenced by the immeasurable success of Siegfried and Roy. So when someone pops up who is original—not to mention charming and, yes, actually good at his job—it comes as a relief.

Monte Carlo dumped a lot of money into building the lush Victorian music hall–style Lance Burton Theater for the star, and it was worth it. Handsome and folksy (he hails from Lexington, Kentucky), Burton is talented and engaging, for the most part shunning the big-ticket special effects that seem to have swamped most other shows in town. Instead, he offers an extremely appealing production that starts small, with "close-up" magic. These rather lovely tricks, he tells us, are what won him a number of prestigious magic competitions. They are truly extraordinary. (We swear that he tossed a bird up in the air, and the darn thing turned into confetti in front of our eyes. Really.) Burton doesn't have patter, per se, but his dry, laconic, low-key delivery is plenty amusing and in contrast to other performers in town who seem as if they have been spending way too much time at Starbucks. He does eventually move to bigger illusions, but his manner follows him—he knows the stuff is good, but he also knows the whole thing is a bit silly, so why not have fun with it? Accompanying him are some perky showgirls, who border on the wholesome, and talented comic juggler Michael Goudeau. The latter is a likable goofball who instantly wins you over (or should) when he juggles three beanbag chairs. All this and extremely comfortable movie theater–style plush seats with cup holders. And for a most reasonable price.

- **Showroom Policies:** Nonsmoking with preassigned seating.
- **Price:** $35 and $40 (includes tax, drinks extra).
- **Show Times:** Tues–Sat at 7:30 and 10:30pm. Dark Sun–Mon.
- **Reservations:** Tickets can be purchased 60 days in advance.

Legends in Concert. Imperial Palace, 3535 Las Vegas Blvd. S. ☎ **702/794-3261.**

A crowd pleaser, which is probably why it's been running since May 1983. Arguably the best of the Vegas impersonator shows (though it's hard to quantify such things), *Legends* does feature performers live, rather than lip-synching. Acts vary from night to night (in a showroom that could use a face-lift) on a nice, large stage with modern hydraulics but twinkle lighting that is stuck in a *Flip Wilson Show* time warp. The personal touches here include scantily clad (but well-choreographed) male and female dancers, and an utterly useless green laser. When we went, the performers included Neil Diamond (whose "America" was accompanied by red-, white-, and blue–clad showgirls covered in flags of all nations), an actual piano-playing

Elton John, the Blues Brothers (a reasonable John Belushi, but a not-even-close Dan Ackroyd), and the inevitable Diana Ross, Four Tops, and the young, thin Elvis (who performs hits from the fat, old Elvis years). The latter, by the way, was preceded by a reverent multimedia presentation (the stage also has video screens that show not only the live action but clips by the real celebs). Best of all, Wayne Newton was there. Yes, the *real* one. During the Blues Brothers bit, the band showed a rare display of spontaneity. When one audience member called out a request for "country," they actually broke into the theme from *Rawhide*. Maybe it was a planned moment, but we were impressed that it didn't seem that way.

- **Showroom Policies:** Nonsmoking, with maître d' seating.
- **Price:** $29.50 (includes two drinks or one Polynesian cocktail such as a mai tai or zombie; tax and gratuity extra).
- **Show Times:** Mon–Sat at 7:30 and 10:30pm. Dark Sun.
- **Reservations:** You can make reservations by phone up to 2 weeks in advance.

MADhattan. New York New York Hotel & Casino, 3790 Las Vegas Blvd. S. ☎ **800/693-6763** or 702/740-6815.

New York New York deserves some praise for delivering a show that attempts to rise out of the rut of the usual Vegas showgirl/magician/juggler variety revue act. In its stead is something more like *Showtime at the Apollo* meets *Stomp* meets *Bring in 'Da Noise, Bring in 'Da Funk*. After a wait in a NYC subway tunnel-like area (complete with a graffiti artist who passes out marking pens and encourages you to act out your own vandalism fantasies), you enter a theater with a stage set meant to invoke urban decay, or at least, the junkyard from *Cats*. A variety of "street scene"–type performers appear (you can just hear the producers asking for acts that were "gritty" and "urban" but not threateningly so), from a postmodern percussionist to girl groups to "Noise/Funk"–style tap dancing. While this lineup does bring more people of color to the stage than is regularly found in Vegas, older audiences may be turned off by the noise and lack of a story line, while younger audiences might well notice they can get similar but better entertainment in Chicago and New York, for a lot cheaper, and, ironically, may opt instead for something more traditionally Vegas.

- **Showroom Policies:** Nonsmoking with preassigned seating.
- **Price:** $40 (tax extra).
- **Show Times:** Tues–Sat 7:30 and 10pm.
- **Reservations:** By phone up to 7 days in advance.

⭐ **Siegfried & Roy.** The Mirage, 3400 Las Vegas Blvd. S. ☎ **800/627-6667** or 702/792-7777.

A Vegas institution for more than 2 decades, illusionists Siegfried and Roy started as an opening act, became headliners at the Frontier, and finally were given their own $30 million show and $25 million theater in the Mirage. They (and their extensive exotic animal menagerie) have amply repaid this enormous investment by selling out every show since. No wonder the Mirage has them booked "until the end of time."

But while the spectacle is undeniable (and the money right on the stage), the result is overproduced. From the get go, there is so much light, sound, smoke, and fire; so many dancing girls, fire-breathing dragons, robots, and other often completely superfluous effects; not to mention an original (and forgettable) Michael Jackson song, that it overwhelms the point of the whole thing. Or maybe it's *become* the point of the whole thing. The magic, which was the Austrian duo's original act, after all, seems to have gotten lost. Sometimes literally. The tricks are at a minimum, allowing the flash pots, lasers, and whatnot to fill out the nearly 2-hour show. More often than not, when a trick is actually being performed, our attention was elsewhere, gawking at an effect, a showgirl, or something. Only the gasps from the audience members who actually happened to be looking in the right place let us know we missed something really neat.

Tellingly, the best part of the show is when all that stuff is switched off, and Siegfried and Roy take the stage to perform smaller magic and chat with the audience. The charm that helped get them so far shines through, and spontaneity is allowed to sneak in. The white tigers are certainly magnificent, but they don't do much other than get cuddled (charmingly) by Roy and badly lip-synch to pretaped roars. The duo is clearly doing something right, judging from the heartfelt standing ovations they receive night after night. But more than one couple was heard to say it was not the best show they had seen, and also to express a feeling that it was overpriced. At these ticket costs (essentially $90 *per person!*) almost anything is. Go if you can't live without seeing a true, modern Vegas legend, but one can find better entertainment values in town.

- **Showroom Policies:** Nonsmoking with preassigned seating.
- **Price:** $89 (includes two drinks, souvenir brochure, tax, and gratuity).
- **Show Times:** Fri–Tues at 7:30 and 11pm, except during occasional dark periods.
- **Reservations:** Tickets can be purchased 3 days in advance.

Spellbound. Harrah's, 3475 Las Vegas Blvd. S. ☎ **800/392-9002** or 702/369-5111.

Now, a warning. *Be prepared:* Out of nowhere, this magic show revue opens with a deafening explosion and blinding lights. Unfortunately, the magic that follows doesn't live up to this grandiose (and irritating) opening. The variety acts in between come as a relief, because frankly, the magic isn't very good. The ostensible headliner (at this writing, it was Jouquin Ayala) delivered high-drama, big-spectacle magic that was strangely disappointing. Further, unless you aren't watching all that closely, you could see the wires, so to speak. Perhaps his tendency to overdramatize every tiny feat he did was an attempt to distract you from the clumsy execution. But if the magic isn't on par with other such shows in Vegas, the dancing and choreography are among the best for the major shows. The routines are fun and infectious, precise but not formal. The dancers execute everything from terrific tap to a trash can and stick rhythm routine clearly influenced by *Stomp* (it was probably only a matter of time before Vegas jumped on that one). Another respite comes in the form of an amazing contortionist act and the "comedy juggler," who juggled two bowling balls and an M&M (peanut).

- **Showroom Policies:** Nonsmoking with preassigned seating.
- **Price:** $35.
- **Show Times:** Mon–Sat at 7:30 and 10pm. Dark Sun.
- **Reservations:** You can charge tickets up to 30 days in advance via credit card.

Splash. Riviera Hotel, 2901 Las Vegas Blvd. S. ☎ **800/634-6753** or 702/734-9301.

Many Vegas shows teeter on the edge of the inexplicable, but this one topples over into the truly bizarre. Set in a showroom badly in need of a face-lift, it begins promisingly (from a camp perspective) as mermaids and synchronized swimmers cavort in a 20,000-gallon tank. Surrounding this are waterfalls and fountains, as dancers in highly silly, aquatic-themed costumes (shells and seaweed) prance and pose. The indication is that we are in for the sort of goofy stage spectacular that used to characterize Vegas. But after this, things go badly awry. The water theme all but vanishes, replaced by some unfortunate production numbers. In one, the lead singer and dancing girls come out in leather biker outfits (albeit ones that show off more skin than leather), riding motorcycles, and sing a medley of songs, most of which have nothing to do with motorcycles. There is a series of celebrity impersonators—Michael Jackson, the artist formerly known as Prince, Madonna—lip-synching to several of said celebs greatest hits. The best moment is when the Madonna tribute turns into live-action highlights from the movie *Evita*, which raised certain questions in our minds: Is having girls dance in their underwear really a fitting tribute to Eva Perón? Why turn the fountains back on at this particular moment? A high point of sorts is hit with a likable bird act and an equally likable juggler, but the absolute nadir of any show in Vegas comes with the "comic antics" of some guy whose "talent" is truly mystifying: He prances, lip-synchs to lines from movies, and waves props in the air. He was insulting, awful, and pointless. Meanwhile, there were glitches in the sound system, and the water spigots occasionally dripped on the performers. *Seating warnings:* Patrons in the front row get raincoats, while seats on the sides are so bad that fully three-quarters of the stage might be obscured.

- **Showroom Policies:** Nonsmoking with preassigned seating.
- **Price:** $45.45–$56.45, the latter for best seats in the house (includes tax; drinks and gratuity extra).
- **Show Times:** Nightly at 7:30 and 10:30pm (10:30pm show is topless).
- **Reservations:** You can reserve by phone up to a month in advance.

Viva Las Vegas. Stratosphere, 2000 Las Vegas Blvd. S. ☎ **800/99-TOWER** or 702/380-7777.

An everything-but-the-kitchen-sink Vegas variety show, good only if you really need an hour's respite in the afternoon from the slots. Which isn't a bad idea, since the preshow warm-up comic's "funny" gaming tips actually prove useful, though not actually all that funny. A lead singer and a small troupe of dancers perform numbers ranging from "Les Miz" to "Viva Las Vegas" (oh, was that a surprise?). A comedian delivered some very adult humor (fat jokes, gay jokes, breast jokes) given the time of day and the number of kids in the audience. The inevitable magician had some adequate close-up magic and an all-too-obvious mind-reading act. One bright point was when the white female dancers donned Jackson Five outfits and lip-synched "ABC," fully aware of the giggles this sight engendered (unlike, unfortunately, the Elvis impersonator who closed the show).

Note: Discount coupons are often found in those free magazines in your hotel room. Sometimes the discount gets you in free, with just the price of a drink.

- **Showroom Policies:** Nonsmoking with maître d' seating.
- **Price:** $11.
- **Show Times:** Mon–Sat 2 and 4pm. Dark Sun.
- **Reservations:** Not accepted.

The Xtreme Scene. Jackie Gaughan's Plaza, 1 Main St. ☎ **800/634-6575** or 702/386-2444.

An all-new revue that has replaced *Xposed*. A standard, racy production show that includes totally naked dancers (yep, topless and bottomless), singers, magicians, and comedians. *Xposed* featured a production number that had dancers clad in black cloaks suggesting figures of Death. Since *Xtreme* should be more extreme, one can only imagine what replaced that little number.

- **Showroom Policies:** Smoking permitted, maître d' seating.
- **Price:** $22 (includes one drink from the bar).

- **Show Times:** Sat–Thurs at 8 and 10pm. Dark Fri.
- **Reservations:** You can reserve up to a week in advance by phone.

3 Headliner Showrooms

Bally's Celebrity Room. Bally's, 3645 Las Vegas Blvd. S. ☎ **800/237-7469** or 702/739-4567.

Superstar headliners play the 1,400-seat Celebrity Room. Dean Martin inaugurated the facility. Today, frequent performers include Barbara Mandrell, Engelbert Humperdinck, Bernadette Peters, Liza Minnelli, Jeff Foxworthy, Hall and Oates, Steve Lawrence and Eydie Gorme, George Carlin, Andrew Dice Clay, Paul Anka, Anne Murray, Louie Anderson, and Penn and Teller.

- **Showroom Policies:** Nonsmoking and preassigned seating.
- **Price:** $25–$45, depending on the performer (tax included, drinks extra).
- **Show Times:** There are one or two shows a night at varying times (this also depends on the performer).
- **Reservations:** You can reserve up to 6 weeks in advance.

Caesars Circus Maximus Showroom. Caesars Palace, 3570 Las Vegas Blvd. S. ☎ **800/445-4544** or 702/731-7333.

From its opening in 1966, Caesars's 1,200-seat Circus Maximus Showroom has presented superstar entertainment—everyone from Judy Garland to Frank Sinatra. Many current headliners started out here as opening acts for established performers, among them Richard Pryor for singer Bobbie Gentry, Jay Leno for Tom Jones, and the Pointer Sisters for Paul Anka. The current lineup of luminaries includes Julio Iglesias, David Copperfield, Howie Mandel, Clint Black, Jerry Seinfeld, Natalie Cole, Diana Ross, Chicago, The Moody Blues, Wynonna, and Johnny Mathis. The luxurious showroom keeps to the Roman theme. Illuminated shields along the wall are replicas of those used by the legions of Caesar, and plush, royal purple booths are patterned after Roman chariots.

- **Showroom Policies:** Nonsmoking with preassigned seating.
- **Price:** $45–$75, depending on the performer (including tax, drinks optional).
- **Show Times:** One or two shows nightly; times depend on performer.
- **Reservations:** You can reserve any time in advance (as soon as a show is confirmed) via credit card.

Desert Inn Crystal Room. 3145 Las Vegas Blvd. S. ☎ **800/634-6906** or 702/733-4444.

The Desert Inn has a long history of superstar entertainment. Frank Sinatra's Las Vegas debut took place in the hotel's Painted Desert Room in 1951, and other early performers included Maurice Chevalier, Noël Coward, Buster Keaton, and Marlene Dietrich. Jimmy Durante once broke the piano board on a new spinet and yelled to the audience, "Mr. Hughes, it was broke when I got it!" And on one memorable night the entire Rat Pack (Dean Martin, Frank Sinatra, Joey Bishop, Sammy Davis

Impressions

If I stand still while I'm singing, I'm a dead man. I might as well go back to driving a truck.

—Legendary Las Vegas headliner Elvis Presley

Jr., and Peter Lawford) invaded the stage when Eddie Fisher was performing! Today this historic showroom has been renamed the Crystal Room. Currently among its major headliners are Smokey Robinson, The Temptations, The Golden Boys (Frankie Avalon, Fabian, and Bobby Rydell), Dennis Miller, Neil Sedaka, and Rita Rudner.

- **Showroom Policies:** Nonsmoking with maître d' seating.
- **Price:** $35–$50, depending on the performer (including two drinks; tax and gratuity extra).
- **Show Times:** Days vary; shows are usually at 9pm.
- **Reservations:** You can reserve up to three engagements in advance.

Hard Rock Hotel's The Joint. Hard Rock Hotel, 4455 Paradise Rd. ☎ **800/693-7625** or 702/693-5000.

When the Hard Rock Hotel opened in 1995, The Eagles were the first act to play its 1,400-seat state-of-the-art, live-concert venue, The Joint. Other performers during the hotel's opening festivities were Melissa Etheridge (with Al Green), B. B. King, Iggy Pop, Duran Duran, and Sheryl Crow. Since then the facility has presented Bob Dylan, Ziggy Marley, Marilyn Manson, Hootie and the Blowfish, the Black Crowes, Donna Summer, Stephen Stills, Jimmy Cliff, Tears for Fears, Johnny Cash, Lyle Lovett, and James Brown. It's rapidly becoming the place in town for rock acts to play.

- **Showroom Policies:** Smoking permitted; seating preassigned or general, depending on the performer.
- **Price:** $20–$100, depending on the performer (drinks and tax extra).
- **Show Times:** 8:30pm (nights of performance vary).
- **Reservations:** You can reserve up to 30 days in advance.

Las Vegas Hilton: Fabulous Fridays. 3000 Paradise Rd. ☎ **800/222-5361** or 702/732-5755.

Before it became the venue for Andrew Lloyd Webber's *Starlight Express,* the Hilton showroom presented superstar headliners for more than 2 decades. Barbra Streisand was the first in 1969, Gladys Knight the last in 1993, and in between Elvis played 837 sold-out shows over a 10-year period. On Friday, when *Starlight Express* is dark, the Hilton has begun presenting headliners once again. Among those who've appeared so far are Creedence Clearwater, political comedian Bill Maher, Nancy Wilson (on a double bill with Ramsey Lewis), Lou Rawls, The Monkees, Johnny Cash and the June Carter Family, Al Jarreau, K.C. and The Sunshine Band, and Peaches and Herb.

- **Showroom Policies:** Nonsmoking with preassigned seating.
- **Price:** $29–$59, depending on the performer (drinks and tax extra).
- **Show Times:** Usually 9pm.
- **Reservations:** You can reserve up to 60 days in advance.

MGM Grand Garden Events Arena. MGM Grand, 3799 Las Vegas Blvd. S. ☎ **800/929-1111** or 702/891-7777.

The 15,222-seat MGM Grand Garden Events Arena is a major venue for sporting events. It also hosts big-name concerts. Barbra Streisand returned to the stage here after an absence of 25 years on New Year's Eve 1993. Others who have played the Arena include Neil Diamond, Sting, Jimmy Buffett, Luther Vandross, Janet Jackson, The Rolling Stones, Bette Midler, Billy Joel, Elton John, and Whitney

Headliner Stadiums

Three arenas are worth a special mention since they often feature major entertainers. **Sam Boyd Stadium,** the outdoor stadium at the University of Nevada, Las Vegas (UNLV), has been host to such major acts as Paul McCartney, U2, the Eagles, and Metallica. **Thomas and Mack Center,** the university's indoor arena, has a more comprehensive concert schedule, including such names as Van Halen, Michael Bolton, and Celine Dion, as well as shows like *Disney on Ice* and Ringling Bros. Circus. Both are located on the **UNLV campus** at Boulder Highway and Russell Road (☎ **702/895-3900**). **Ticketmaster** (☎ **702/474-4000**) handles ticketing for both arenas. The **Huntridge** is a local theater venue where big alternative acts are likely to show up (Beck, Slash's Snakepit, Jim Rose Sideshow Circus, and so forth), though irregularly. It's located at 1208 E. Charleston Blvd. (☎ **702/477-0242**).

Houston. Grand Garden Events tickets are generally also available at **Ticketmaster** (☎ **702/474-4000**).

- **Showroom Policies:** Nonsmoking with preassigned seating.
- **Price:** Varies with event or performer.
- **Show Times:** Vary with event or performer.
- **Reservations:** Advance-reservations policy varies with event or performer.

MGM Grand Hollywood Theatre. MGM Grand, 3799 Las Vegas Blvd. S. ☎ **800/929-1111** or 702/891-7777.

The 650-seat Hollywood Theatre hosts headliners such as Wayne Newton, Tom Jones, The Righteous Brothers, Jeff Foxworthy, Dennis Miller, Rita Rudner, and Randy Travis. It has also featured occasional live telecasts of *The Tonight Show* with Jay Leno.

- **Showroom Policies:** Nonsmoking with preassigned seating.
- **Price:** Usually $44–$55, varies with performer (tax and drinks extra).
- **Show Times:** Vary with performer; there's usually a show at 9pm.
- **Reservations:** Tickets can be ordered any time in advance as soon as they become available.

Orleans Showroom. Orleans Hotel, 4500 W. Tropicana Ave. ☎ **800/ORLEANS.**

A pleasant, medium-size showroom with theater seating and cup holders. Performers booked there so far have included Chuck Berry, the Pointer Sisters, the Everly Brothers, and the Oakridge Boys.

- **Showroom Policies:** Nonsmoking with preassigned seating.
- **Price:** Varies with performer.
- **Show Times:** Varies with performer.
- **Reservations:** Tickets can be ordered any time in advance as soon as they become available.

Sahara Hotel Showroom. 2535 Las Vegas Blvd. S. ☎ **702/737-2878.**

Since the Sahara was just completing a major renovation at press time, few details were available about its showroom. It will present headliner performers. Call for details or check local show listings when you're in town.

- **Showroom Policies:** Nonsmoking with preassigned seating.
- **Price:** Usually $22–$36, varies with performer (tax and drinks extra).

Ladies and Gentleman, Mr. Tom Jones

A little Vegas secret: After one of Mr. Tom Jones's shows at the MGM Grand (he does up to five 2-week stints a year), it's not unusual (sorry, had to) to find him at the piano bar. There, he can drink, visit with the piano player, and, if the bar isn't too full, indulge himself by singing the sorts of songs denied to him by his regular show. Where in the MGM is the piano bar? Ah, that's the problem . . . if we tell you, you might go. And if enough of you do, then there will be too many people, and he won't sing. We will tell you this; there are piano bars in the Brown Derby and Gatsby's restaurants. If you do go, and he is there, just blend in with the wall-paper, okay?

- **Show Times:** Vary with performer; there's usually a show at 9pm.
- **Reservations:** Tickets can be ordered any time in advance as soon as they become available.

4 Comedy Clubs

Catch a Rising Star. MGM Grand, 3799 Las Vegas Blvd. S. ☎ **800/929-1111** or 702/891-7777.

Like The Improv, Catch a Rising Star presents nationally known talent from the comedy circuit. Three comedians perform each night.

- **Showroom Policies:** Nonsmoking with maître d' seating.
- **Price:** $12.50 (tax and drinks extra).
- **Show Times:** Nightly at 8 and 10:30pm.
- **Reservations:** You can charge tickets up to 30 days in advance via credit card.

Comedy Club. Riviera Hotel, 2901 Las Vegas Blvd. S. ☎ **800/634-6753** or 702/734-9301.

The Riviera's comedy club, on the second floor of the Mardi Gras Plaza, showcases four comedians nightly. Once a month, usually on the last weekend, the club hosts a late-night *XXXTREME Comedy Showcase* for shock and X-rated comedians. Other special events include the *All Gay Comedy Revue* and R-rated hypnotist Frank Santos.

- **Showroom Policies:** Nonsmoking with maître d' seating.
- **Price:** $19–$25 (includes two drinks and tax).
- **Show Times:** Nightly at 8 and 10pm, with an extra show Fri and Sat at 11:45pm.
- **Reservations:** Tickets can be purchased at the box office only, in advance if you wish.

Comedy Max. Maxim, 160 E. Flamingo Rd. ☎ **800/634-6987** or 702/731-4423.

The Maxim's very attractive nightclub features three comics nightly, and every seat is good.

- **Showroom Policies:** Nonsmoking with maître d' seating.
- **Price:** $16.25 (includes two drinks, tax, and gratuity). For $19.95 you can enjoy a buffet dinner as well.
- **Show Times:** Nightly at 7, 9, and 10:30pm.
- **Reservations:** You can reserve up to a week in advance by phone.

Comedy Stop. Tropicana, 3801 Las Vegas Blvd. S. ☎ **800/468-9494** or 702/739-2411.

Wayne Newton's Top-10 Favorite Lounge Songs

Wayne Newton is the consummate entertainer. He has performed more than 25,000 concerts in Las Vegas alone, and in front of more than 25 million people worldwide. Wayne has received more standing ovations than any other entertainer in history. Along with his singing credits, his acting credits are soaring—one of his more recent credits is *Vegas Vacation*. Make sure you catch him playing at the MGM Grand. No trip to Vegas is complete without seeing the "King of Las Vegas."

1. "You're Nobody, Til Somebody Loves You" *(You don't have a body unless somebody loves you!)*
2. "Up a Lazy River" *(or "Up Your Lazy River!")*
3. "Don't Go Changin' (Just the Way You Are)" *(The clothes will last another week!)*
4. "Having My Baby" *(Oh God!)*
5. "The Windmills of My Mind" *(A mind is a terrible thing to waste!)*
6. "The Wind Beneath My Wings" *(Soft and Dry usually helps!)*
7. "Copacabana"
8. "When the Saints Go Marching In"
9. "I Am, I Said" *(Huh?!)*
10. "The Theme from the Love Boat" *(or "Would a Dingy Do?")*

Similar to clubs described above, the Comedy Stop here features three nationally known comedy headliners nightly.

- **Showroom Policies:** Smoking permitted with maître d' seating.
- **Price:** $14.30 (includes two drinks; tax and gratuity extra).
- **Show Times:** Nightly at 8 and 10:30pm.
- **Reservations:** You can charge tickets in advance via credit card.

The Improv. Harrah's, 3475 Las Vegas Blvd. S. ☎ **800/392-9002** or 702/369-5111.

This offshoot of Budd Friedman's famed comedy club (the first one opened in 1963 in New York City) presents about four comedians per show in a 400-seat showroom. These are talented performers—the top comics on the circuit who you're likely to see on Leno and Letterman. You can be sure of an entertaining evening.

- **Showroom Policies:** Nonsmoking with preassigned seating.
- **Price:** $15 (tax and drinks extra).
- **Show Times:** Tues–Sun at 8 and 10:30pm. Dark Mon.
- **Reservations:** You can charge tickets up to 30 days in advance via credit card.

The Unknown Comic. Holiday Inn Boardwalk, 3750 Las Vegas Blvd. S. ☎ **702/735-2400.**

The Unknown Comic is Murray Langston, so called because he performs a large part of his act with a bag over his head. Come early to see preshow video clips of his numerous TV appearances on everything from *The Tonight Show* to *Oprah*. Langston is zany (some might say insane) and very manic, a king of one-liners such as, "What's the most successful pick-up line in the South?" "Nice tooth." He also does a bit of ventriloquism with a little bag face called Sad Sack for a dummy. It's weird, but fun.

- **Showroom Policies:** Smoking permitted; seating is first come, first served.
- **Price:** $6 (drinks and tax extra).
- **Show Times:** Tues–Sun at 9pm. Dark Mon.
- **Reservations:** You can make reservations by phone up to 7 days in advance.

5   Coffeehouses

Coffeehouses are both a day and nighttime activity; so far, not too many stay open past midnight. They can either be pretentious or the center of youth culture, depending on your demographic group. They can also be an oasis for those seeking alternative culture or just a respite from the usual Vegas hangouts. We've listed a range here, from ordinary rooms in strip malls to two very nice cafes. Many also offer live music and/or poetry readings; check the listings in *Scope* and *City Life* for details (or just call the place in question).

✪ **Cafe Copioh.** 4550 S. Maryland Pkwy., near Harmon. ☎ **702/739-0305.**

This is a typical Gen X alt-rock coffeehouse with clientele to match. The low-tech decor includes mixed thrift store furniture and a collection of books to borrow. They have a large assortment of specialty coffee drinks, smoothies, and a few sand- wich/bagel/pastry items if you get hungry. A crowded, bustling, smoky hangout at 11:30 on a Saturday night makes one wonder why it closes at midnight. The Goth crowd in Vegas makes this a vampire hangout on certain nights after 10pm (then they wander over to the Wet Stop bar just down the street)—catch them if you can. Open Monday to Thursday 3pm to midnight, Friday and Saturday until 3am, and Sunday 6pm to midnight.

Cafe Espresso Roma. 4440 S. Maryland Pkwy., near Harmon. ☎ **702/369-1540.**

Despite the vintage sofa look, the truth is told by the clean tile counter—this is an artificially manufactured attempt at the coffeehouse scene and, arguably, a suc- cessful one. Most of the patrons are University of Nevada students. They do have poetry and live music on certain nights, but they close too early. Open Monday to Friday 7am to 10pm, Saturday 8am to 9pm, and Sunday 8am to 10pm.

Cafe Neon. 1018 S. Main St., near Charleston Blvd. ☎ **702/388-4088.**

Located on the second floor of the Attic vintage clothing shop, this cafe provides you a place to sit and rest your shopped-till-you-dropped aching feet. Basic, mis- matched coffeehouse furniture sits in a space carved out behind the clothes (some large triangle-shaped aquariums separate it from the racks). It even has a small stage where live comedy (presented by "Guppy Stop Theater") is performed. They have a small but adequate range of cold sandwiches and Greek-influenced salads and desserts. Open Monday to Saturday 10am to 7pm, Sunday 11am to 5pm (some- times later).

✪ **Enigma Cafe.** 918½ S. Fourth St. and Charleston Blvd. ☎ **702/386-0999.**

Though they have fine food here (see chapter 6 for a restaurant review), the menu is more than two-thirds beverages, a seemingly endless variety of coffee drinks, smoothies, and the like. You can sit in the garden patio or in the 1930s house- turned-art-gallery and listen to whatever music they are playing (classical in the morning, Liz Phair in the afternoon), or come back at night when it turns into a real candlelit scene, with poetry readings, "obscure and interesting movies" (shown by the owner of the antique camera store in the front), and live acoustic and folk music. This is a hangout for the neighborhood artists or anyone seeking an oasis of calm and culture in Vegas. It's very close to both Downtown (in particular) and the Strip. Open Monday 7am to 3pm, Tuesday to Friday 7am to midnight, and Saturday and Sunday 9am to midnight.

✪ **Jazzed Cafe & Vinoteca.** 2055 E. Tropicana Ave., at Eastern. ☎ **702/798-5995.**

This genuine European-style (well, by way of California) cafe is owned and operated by the charming and friendly Kirk, a choreographer who lived in Italy for 10 years. It's tiny but intimate, featuring candlelight and cool jazz, with hot art on the walls. They serve multiple coffee drinks (be sure to try the terrific Illy, a renowned Italian brand) and average wine. There's a small but satisfying food menu featuring inexpensive ($4 to $6.50) authentic Italian specialties—simple pastas, focaccia bread, and so forth, all made by Kirk on the spot. It's a great respite from the maddening crowds (and a cheap place to eat well), though it fills up after the shows let out with the owner's show-and-dance pals. (By the way, this is just a quick drive up from the Strip.) A sign warns you *not* to order lemon peel with your espresso—if you do, be prepared to be sworn at (sweetly) in Italian. Open Tuesday to Sunday 6pm to 3am. Credit cards accepted include American Express, Discover, Master-Card, and Visa.

6 Piano Bars

In addition to the establishments listed below, consider the ultraelegant **Palace Court Terrace Lounge,** adjoining the Palace Court restaurant at Caesars (see chapter 6). This romantic piano bar has a stained-glass skylight that retracts for a view of open starlit sky. Off the lounge is an intimate crystal-chandeliered, European-style casino for high-stakes players only. **Gatsby's** at the MGM Grand (see chapter 6) also has a sophisticated and stunning adjoining piano bar as does the **Brown Derby.** And **Cafe Nicolle** (see chapter 6) has a small but agreeable genuine piano bar.

Alexis Park Resort: Pisces Bistro. 375 E. Harmon Ave. ☎ **702/796-3300.** No cover or minimum.

The very upscale Alexis Park offers live entertainment in a beautiful room under a 30-foot domed ceiling; planters of greenery cascade from tiered balconies. When the weather permits, it's lovely to sit at umbrella tables on a terra-cotta patio overlooking the pool. Live music is featured Tuesday to Saturday nights from 8pm until about midnight; a versatile pianist and vocalist perform everything from show tunes to oldies to Top 40. Light fare is available.

The Bar at Times Square. 3790 Las Vegas Blvd. S., in New York New York. ☎ **702/740-6969.**

If you are looking for a quiet piano bar, this is not the place for you. Smack in the middle of the Central Park part of the New York New York casino, every night two pianos are going strong, and the young hipster, cigar-smoking crowd overflows out the doors. It always seems to be packed with a singing, swaying, drinking throng full of camaraderie and good cheer—or at least, booze. Hugely fun, provided you can get a foot in the door. And yes, every night, right outside, the ball on top drops at midnight, for a little auld lang syne.

The Carriage House: Kiefer's. 105 E. Harmon Ave. ☎ **702/739-8000.** No cover or minimum.

This rooftop restaurant has a plushly furnished adjoining piano bar/lounge. Windowed walls offer great views of the Las Vegas neon skyline, making this a romantic setting for cocktails and hors d'oeuvres. There's piano music Thursday to Saturday from 7 to 11pm.

Club Monaco. 1487 E. Flamingo Rd., between Maryland Pkwy. and Tamarus St. (on your right as you come from the Strip; look for the LA-Z-Boy Furniture Gallery). ☎ **702/737-6212.** No cover or minimum.

This low-key, sophisticated piano bar—its walls lined with oil paintings of icons such as Elvis, Bogart, James Dean, and Marilyn Monroe (not to mention Rodney Dangerfield, finally getting respect)—is a romantic setting for cocktails and classic piano-bar entertainment. There's a small dance floor. Friday and Saturday a talented vocalist is on hand as well. Club Monaco is far from a meat market, but it is a relaxed atmosphere in which to meet people. The crowd is over 30. A menu offers salads, burgers, steak sandwiches, pastas, and gourmet appetizers such as oysters Rockefeller and escargot-stuffed mushrooms. Open 24 hours.

Nicky Blair's. 3925 Paradise Rd., between Flamingo and Twain. ☎ **702/792-9900.** No cover or minimum.

A Los Angeles legend, Nicky Blair closed the doors of his venerable L.A. establishment to open a new version here. Pity the Rat Pack is gone; this would be their hangout in the '90s. A U-shaped bar dominates an elegantly dark space, with hardwood floors and banquettes up against one wall. There are plenty of bartenders and waitresses on hand to serve the middle-aged, upscale (and largely local) clientele. The tables seem well spaced, so a romantic tête-à-tête should be possible. You can order the full menu from the restaurant. The piano goes from 7pm until close, which is midnight Monday to Thursday, 2am Friday and Saturday.

7 Gay Bars

Hip and happening Vegas locals know that some of the best scenes and dance action can actually be found in the city's gay bars. And no, they don't ask for sexuality ID at the door. All are welcome at any of the following establishments—as long as you don't have a problem with the people inside, they aren't going to have a problem with you. For women, this can be a fun way to dance and not get hassled by overeager lotharios. (Lesbians, by the way, are just as welcome at any of the gay bars.) If you want to know what's going on in gay Las Vegas during your visit, pick up a copy of *The Las Vegas Bugle,* a free, gay-oriented newspaper that is available at any of the places described below. Or call ☎ **702/369-6260.**

Angles/Lace. 4633 Paradise Rd., at Naples St. ☎ **702/791-0100.** No cover or minimum.

This 24-hour gay bar (Lace is the lesbian bar attached to it), though among the most upscale in Las Vegas, is a casual neighborhood hangout compared to gay bars in other cities. The clientele is mostly local—about 85% men (including drag queens) in their mid-20s to early 30s. Wednesday night there's a drag show in the front room, while the back room hosts Gothic Night. Weekends, male and female strippers perform from midnight until about 4 or 5am. There's a dance floor (the music's pretty loud), a small outdoor courtyard, and a game room with pool tables, darts, and pinball machines. Right next door, by the way, is the 24-hour **Mariposa Cafe,** which features cheap, tasty food.

The Buffalo. 4640 Paradise Rd., at Naples St. ☎ **702/733-8355.** No cover or minimum.

Close to both Angles and Gipsy, this is a leather/Levi's bar popular with motorcycle clubs. It features beer busts (all the beer you can drink for $5) Friday night from 9pm to midnight. Pool tables, darts, and music videos play in an otherwise not-striking environment. It is very cheap, however, with long necks going for $1.75, and it gets very, very busy very late (3 or 4am). Open 24 hours.

The Eagle/Girls Bar. 3430 E. Tropicana Ave., at Pecos. ☎ **702/458-8662.** No cover.

Off the beaten track in just about every sense of the phrase, The Eagle is the place to go if well-lit bars make you nervous. Open 24 hours, it's dark, slightly seedy, and lacks even video poker machines (they might get in the way of your drink and/or ashtray). All in all, it's a refreshing change from the overprocessed slickness that is Las Vegas. The crowd, tending toward middle age, is mostly male and is of the Levi's/leather group. There is a small dance area (calling it a dance floor would be generous), a pool table, and a nice-size bar. Drinks are inexpensive, and special events make them even more so. For instance, The Eagle is rapidly becoming famous for its twice-weekly underwear parties (if you check your pants, you receive draft beer and well drinks for free). That's right: free. Right next door is the "tropical-themed" Girls Bar, which is open every night but Wednesday from 6pm to 2am. It supposedly caters to lesbians, but we didn't notice too much delineation between the two. The 20-minute drive from the strip makes it a questionable option, but if you've got a sense of adventure go see for yourself.

Gipsy. 4605 Paradise Rd., at Naples St. ☎ **702/731-1919.** Cover $4 (except Wed and Sun).

For years, Gipsy reigned supreme as the best gay dance place in the city, and for good reason: great location (Paradise Road near the Hard Rock), excellent layout (sunken dance floor and two bars), and very little competition. More recently some of its spotlight, along with a good portion of the clientele, has been stolen by fiercer competitors. This is why Gipsy spent $750,000 on a renovation that includes a marble and etched-glass interior, an upgraded sound-and-light system, and a quiet bar area that is glassed-off. With broken columns, vines hanging down, and archaeological-type pits, it all comes off as a gay version of *Indiana Jones and the Temple of Doom.* Really. The separate bar area makes the bigger space actually look smaller. The prices have gone up to pay for it all. Drink specials along with special events, shows, male dancers, and theme nights have always made this place a good party bar. Open daily 10pm to 6am.

Good Times. 1775 E. Tropicana Ave., at Spencer, in the Liberace Plaza. ☎ **702/736-9494.** No cover.

This quiet, 24-hour neighborhood bar is located (for those of you with a taste for subtle irony) in the same complex as the Liberace Museum, a few miles due east of the MGM Grand. There is a small dance floor, but on a recent Friday night nobody was using it, the crowd preferring instead to take advantage of the cozy bar area. A small conversation pit is a perfect spot for intimate conversations. Of course, there are the omnipresent pool and video poker if you're not interested in witty repartee. We remember this place as being a lot more crowded than it was during our most recent visit (but perhaps we were there on an off night). It makes a nice respite after the Liberace Museum (after which you may very well need to go next door for a stiff drink).

✪ **Inferno.** 3340 S. Highland Ave, near Spring Mountain. ☎ **702/734-7336.** members. aol.com/inferno. Cover varies.

This new 24-hour dance club opened in late 1996 and quickly stole the crown from Gipsy as the gay hot spot in Vegas. It's conveniently located less than a mile off the strip near Treasure Island in an industrial-type strip mall. The interior features exposed cinder-block walls and girders plus a few miles of chain-link fencing to create an austere look, but that's balanced by a warm and friendly staff. A huge bar dominates the room, and there's a good-size dance floor and a first-rate light-and-sound system. When you add the pool tables, the inescapable video poker, and plenty of seating, you get a package that is accommodating and designed for fun. There always seems to be a crowd (about a 50/50 mix of locals and tourists), which tends to be younger and male (though not exclusively so). Be prepared for a line and a moderate cover on the weekends. Regular drink prices are average, but rotating specials and theme nights help give more bang for your buck.

8 Other Bars

In addition to the venues listed below, consider hanging out at **Country Star,** the **Hard Rock Cafe,** and **Planet Hollywood,** all described in chapter 6. You might also check out the incredible nighttime view at the bar atop the **Stratosphere Hotel**—nothing beats it. There's also the **Viva Las Vegas Lounge** at the Hard Rock Hotel, where eventually every rock-connected person in Vegas will eventually pass through.

Champagnes Cafe. 3557 S. Maryland Pkwy. ☎ **702/737-1699.**

Wonder where old Vegas went? It ossified right here. Red- and gold-flocked wallpaper and other such trappings of "glamour" never die—in fact, with this ultra-low-key lighting, they will never even fade. A seedy old bar with seedy old scary men leering away. They even serve ice-cream shakes spiked with booze—two indulgences wrapped into one frothy package. And quite a double addiction delight. Some might run screaming from the place, while others will think they've died and gone to heaven. Just remember—this is the kind of place director Quentin Tarantino or this year's alt-cult hit movie will make famous. It can't be long. And then it will be overrun with hipsters. Beat the rush, go there now, and brag that you knew about it back before it was so cool it became passé. Again.

The Dispensary. 2451 E. Tropicana Ave., at Eastern. ☎ **702/458-6343.**

Stuck in a '70s time warp (the waterwheel and the ferns are the tip-off, though the songs on the Muzak confirm it), this is a fine place for a nice, long, quiet drink. One that lasts decades, perhaps. It's very quiet, low-key, and often on the empty side. Things pick up on weekends, but it still isn't the sort of place that attracts raucous drunks. (Of course, if it were on the Strip instead of being tucked away, it probably would.) "We leave you alone if you don't want to be bothered," says the proprietor. (We still worry about what happens if you sit here long enough.) If you are a hepcat, but one on the mild side, you will love it.

✪ **Double Down Saloon.** 4640 Paradise Rd., at Naples. ☎ **702/791-5775.**

"House rule: You puke, you clean." Okay, that about sums up the Double Down. Well, no, it doesn't really do the place justice. This is a big local hangout, with management quoting *Scope* magazine's description of its clientele: "Hipsters, blue collars, the well-heeled lunatic fringe." Rumored to have been spotted there: director Tim Burton and Dr. Timothy Leary. Need to know more? Okay, trippy hallucinogenic graffiti covers the walls, the ceiling, the tables, and possibly you if you sit there long enough. Decor includes Abby Rents–type chairs and thrift-store battered armchairs and sofa, a couple of pool tables, and a jukebox that holds everything from the Germs and Frank Zappa to Link Wray, Dick Dale, and the Rev. Horton Heat. On Wednesday night they have a live blues band, while other nights might find local alternative, punk, or ska groups performing. No cover unless they have some out-of-town band that actually has a label deal.

Gordon Biersch Brewing Company. 3987 Paradise Rd., just north of Flamingo. ☎ **702/312-5247.**

This is part of a chain, and while it does feel like it, it is better than the average such entry. The interior is both contemporary and rustic; warmer than its semi-industrial look might usually deliver. It's roomy, so you don't feel stacked up on top of other customers. The house lager (they specialize in German brews) was tasty and the noise level acceptable. A good place to go hoist a few.

Holy Cow. 2432 Las Vegas Blvd. S., at Sahara Ave. ☎ **702/732-COWS.**

Okay, so maybe you go to serious bars for serious drinking, but anyplace with a giant bovine on the roof and an extensive cow theme on the inside can't be all bad. Cows are everywhere—cow paintings, cow-motif lighting fixtures, a "sidewalk of fame" of cow hoof prints outside, even slot machines called (irresistibly) "Moolah"—so if you are heifer-a-phobe, stay away. The microbrew pub upstairs offers a free tour, or you can taste its four hand-crafted microbrews: pale ale, wheat beer, brown ale, and a monthly changing brewmaster's special, which sometimes contains the word *blueberry* in it. Pub grub is also offered, which they assure us requires only one stomach to consume. Frankly, once you get past giggling at all the cow-related puns around (which can take a while), you notice it's a bit busy on the eyes and aggressive with gambling devices. Indeed, this is more casino than bar.

✪ **Main Street Station: Triple 7 Brew Pub.** 200 Main St. ☎ **702/387-1896.**

Yet another of the many things the new(ish) Main Street Station hotel has done right. Stepping into its microbrew pub feels like stepping out of Vegas. Well, maybe, except for the dueling piano entertainment. Part modern warehouse look (exposed pipes, microbrew fixtures visible through exposed glass at back, very high ceiling), but with a hammered tin ceiling that continues the hotel's Victorian decor, this is a look more appropriate to North Beach in San Francisco. Dare we say it? The result produces an environment that is a bit on the yuppified side, but escapes being pretentious. And frankly, it's a much-needed modern touch for the Downtown area. They have their own brewmaster, a number of microbrews ready to try, and if you are feeling like a quick bite, there is also an oyster and sushi bar, plus fancy burgers and pizzas. It can get noisy during the aforementioned piano duel act, but otherwise casino noise stays out. And Downtown being all too heavy on the old Las Vegas side (which is fine for a time but not *all* the time), this is good for a suitable breather.

✪ **Peppermill's Fireside Lounge.** 2985 Las Vegas Blvd. S. ☎ **702/735-7635.**

Walk through the classic Peppermill's coffee shop (not a bad place to eat, by the way) on the Strip, and you land in its dark, plush, cozy lounge. A fabulously dated view of hip, it has low, circular banquette seats, fake floral foliage, low neon, and electric candles. But best of all is the water and fire pit as the centerpiece—a piece of kitsch thought long vanished from the earth, which attracts nostalgia buffs like moths to flames. It all adds up to a cozy, womblike place. Perfect for crashing down a bit after some time spent on the hectic Strip. The enormous, exotic froufrou tropical drinks (including the signature basketball-size margaritas) will ensure that you sink into that level of comfortable stupor.

Pink E's. 3695 W. Flamingo. ☎ **702/252-4666.**

Sick of the attitude at Club Rio? (And well you should be.) Escape directly across the street to Pink E's, where the theme is pink. You were expecting maybe seafoam? Anyway, at least one regular described this as "the only place to go if you are over

25 and have a brain." And like pink. Because everything here is: the many pool tables, the Ping-Pong tables, the booths, the lighting, the lava lamp on the bar, and even the people. In its own way, it's as gimmick-ridden as The Beach dance club (see below), but surely no one would put out a pink pool table in all seriousness? Yeah, it's a ludicrous heresy, but don't you want to play on one? Anyway, Pink E's offers retro diner food and a deejay on weekends. The dress code basically translates to "no gangsta wannabe wear." Go, but wear all black just to be ornery.

Sand Dollar Blues Lounge. 3355 Spring Mountain at Polaris. ☎ **702/871-6651.**

The kind of funky, no decor (think posters and beer signs), atmosphere-intensive, slightly grimy, friendly bar you either wish your town had or wish it had something other than. Just up the road from Treasure Island, this is a great antidote to artificial Vegas. Attracting a solid mix of locals and tourists (employees claim the former includes everything from bikers to chamber of commerce members), the Sand Dollar features live blues (both electric and acoustic, with a little Cajun and zydeco thrown in) every night. We wondered how Vegas had enough blues bands to fill out a whole weekly bill. The answer? All the musicians play in multiple bands in different configurations. The dance floor is tiny and often full. The minimal cover always goes to the band. Depending on your desires, it's either refreshingly not Las Vegas, or just the kind of place you came to Vegas to escape. Go before someone has the idea to build a theme hotel based on it.

The Sky Lounge (at the Polo Towers). 3745 Las Vegas Blvd. S. ☎ **702/261-1000.**

It may not quite be the view offered by the Stratosphere Hotel's bar, but it's pretty darn good and easier to get to. You see too much of the Holiday Inn Boardwalk directly across the street and not quite enough of the MGM Grand to the left, but otherwise there are no complaints. The decor is too modern (heavy on '80s black and purple), but overall the place is quiet (especially during the day) and civil. A jazz vocal/piano performs at night (when the views are naturally best). The atmosphere produced by all this is classic Vegas in the best sense (with only a slight touch of necessary kitsch). Worth a trip for an escape from the mob, though you won't be the only tourist fighting for window seats.

Tom & Jerry's. 4550 S. Maryland and Harmon. ☎ **702/736-8550.**

The dull exterior belies what is inside: a lively bar with three different rooms, each with its own entirely different feel and atmosphere. Decidedly catering to the UNLV crowd (it's right across the street, after all), it prides itself on being ethnically diverse and holding no pretensions. "Drink cheap, be loose, have fun" is the owner's motto, and the result is a bar more enjoyable than the words "college bar" might make you think. Each room has its own ambience; the first is indeed a basic college bar, with a mural homage to UNLV wrapping its walls. The next room serves as the dance area, where cover bands (Prince, Beastie Boys) and reggae groups play all nights but Sunday and Monday. The back room is a pool hall with 20 tables. Most nights feature $1 drinks; Wednesday is $1 pitcher of beer night and you can expect up to a 3-hour wait to get in. There's a $5 cover Tuesday to Saturday.

Tommy Rocker's. 4275 Industrial Blvd. ☎ **702/261-6688.**

Tommy Rocker is the owner—surely he wasn't born with that name—and he plays his club every Friday and Saturday nights, mixing bar band standards with '80s and '90s hits. It's a one-man show, with Strip musicians dropping by after their own shifts are done. (Occasionally, local bands are permitted to play as well.) Sort of like the inside of a Quonset hut painted black, his vaguely beach-frat-party-themed club has become the home for local and out-of-town Parrot Heads (Jimmy Buffet fans, for those not in the know), with the result that the crowd is 5 to 10 years past their heavy college drinking days. The large bar dominates the middle of the room; there are two pool tables and a grill for ordering food, plus an espresso machine.

The Wet Stop. 4440 S. Maryland Pkwy. ☎ **702/791-0977.**

This is a college bar (it's across the street from UNLV), but the crowd changes radically depending on what live band is happening that night. (The acts are usually pretty good, too, both local groups and out-of-town bands.) Blues happens on Friday and Saturday, while Thursday offers the only live reggae in Vegas. The latter brings out the dreadlocks and the hippies. After Utopia closes Sunday morning at 3am (see listing later in this chapter), they open up an after-hours club until 11am so that the club kids will have a place to hang. Other nights of the week alternative groups pop up. This is also a hangout for the Gothic/vampire crowd; they drift over when Cafe Copiah closes, or when local group Blood Count is playing. The set this changing cast plays against is a basic, dark, friendly, busy bar with zero ambience— but who needs it? The crowd does it for you.

A KARAOKE BAR

Ellis Island Casino—Karaoke. 4178 Koval Lane, off Flamingo, behind Bally's. ☎ **702/733-8901.**

Admit it. You sing in the shower. And when the acoustics are just right, you fancy you could give a Vegas lounge singer a run for their money. Here's your chance to test this theory without the comfort of tile acoustics. In this small, smoky den filled with leather and candles, any number of people from all walks of life get up and act out their lounge singer fantasies. You can join them. With over 6,000 titles, including multiple Englebert Humperdink, Mac Davis, and Tom Jones selections, there are plenty of cheesy numbers perfect for this kind of environment. And if you stay here long enough, you'll hear them all.

The bar is decked out with video poker machines, and if you're planning on singing, there is a two-drink minimum. For $10 you can videotape your moment of glory. All you have to do to strut your stuff is choose a song and walk it up to the host. You may have to wait a while for your tune, but part of the fun is watching other people make fools out of them—er, singing. Karaoke is offered daily 9pm to 3am.

9 Dance Clubs

In addition to the options listed below, country music fans might want to wander on over to **Dylan's,** 4660 Boulder Hwy. (☎ **702/451-4006**), and **Rockabilly's,** 3785 Boulder Hwy. (☎ **702/641-5800**). Not far from each other, both offer country music (live and otherwise) and line dancing, with free dance lessons. Dylan's is more casual and basic, whereas Rockabilly's is a bit more posh—the kind of place where you might squeeze a Manhattan in between your beer and line dancing.

✪ **The Beach.** 365 S. Convention Center Dr., at Paradise Rd. ☎ **702/731-1425.** Cover $10 and up Fri–Sat and special events.

If you are a fan of loud, crowded, 24-hour party bars filled with tons of good-looking fun-seekers, then bow in this direction, for you have found mecca. This huge, tropical-themed (hence the whole "Beach" thing) nightclub is right across the street from the Convention Center and is, according to just about anyone you ask, the "hottest" club in the city. It's a 2-story affair with five separate bars downstairs and another three up. Just in case walking the 20 feet to the closest one is too much of an effort, they also have bikini-clad women serving beer out of steel tubs full of ice (they also roam the floor with shot belts). The drinks are on the pricey side ($3.75 for an 8-ounce domestic beer), but the unfailingly gorgeous, 4% body-fat bartenders (both men and women) are friendly and offer rotating drink specials that might keep you from busting your budget. Also downstairs is the large 2-story dance floor, which dominates the center of the room and is built around a full-service bar at one end. The sound system is top-of-the-line, as is the lighting design (but the wash from the rest of the bar made it a little too bright on the floor to appreciate). Nobody really seemed to care though—there wasn't one square inch of space available on a recent Friday night. Upstairs, there are balconies overlooking the dance floor, pool tables, darts, foosball, pinball, and various other arcade games plus slot machines, video poker, and a sports book. Other neat touches include tarot card readings by the stairs and hot-pizza vendors. And let's not forget those Jell-O shot contests where club-goers try to eat shaky cubes of alcohol-spiked gelatin off each other's partially bared bodies. The crowd is aggressively young and pretty, more men than women (70/30 split), and about 60% tourist, which is probably why the place can get away with charging a $10 cover. Party people look no further. There's free valet parking, and if you've driven here and become intoxicated, they'll drive you back home at no charge.

Cleopatra's Barge Nightclub. Caesars Palace, 3570 Las Vegas Blvd. S. ☎ **702/731-7110.** No cover; 2-drink minimum Fri–Sat.

A small, unique nightclub set in part on a floating barge—you can feel it rocking. The bandstand, a small dance floor, and a few (usually reserved) tables are here, while others are set around the boat on "land." It's a gimmick, but one that makes this far more fun than other, more pedestrian hotel bars. Plenty of dark makes for romance, but blaring volume levels mean you will have to scream those sweet nothings. Check out the bare-breasted figurehead on the ship's prow who juts out over the hallway going past the entrance. She could put someone's eye out.

Club Rio. Rio Suite Hotel, 3700 W. Flamingo Rd. ☎ **702/252-7777.** As advertised: Cover $10 for men, local women free, out-of-state women $5—but frequently when we went by on a weekend night, the cover was $20 for everyone.

This is the hottest night spot in Vegas (along with The Beach) as of this writing, but apparently made so by people who don't mind long lines, restrictive dress codes, attitudinal door people, hefty cover charges, and bland dance music. Waits can be interminable and admittance denied thanks to the wrong footwear or shirt. Once inside, you find a large, circular room, with the spacious dance floor taking up much of the space. Giant video screens line the upper parts of the walls, showing anything from shots of the action down below to catwalk footage. Comfy circular booths fill out the next couple of concentric circles; these seem mostly reserved, and when empty they leave the impression that the place isn't very full—so why the wait? The dress code (no sneakers, shirts must have a collar) is supposed to make the clientele look more sophisticated than grungy; the effect is the opposite, as most of the men end up in combinations of chinos and button-down shirts. Of course, it's so dark you can't tell if someone *is* wearing sneakers. Music on a recent visit included a Madonna medley and the perennial "Celebration," not the most au courant of tunes. The total effect is of a grown-up, not terribly drunken, frat and sorority mixer.

✪ **Drink.** 200 E. Harmon Ave., at Koval Lane. ☎ **702/796-5519.** Cover $5–$10 ($15–$25 when major artists are performing); women are admitted free Tues night. No minimum.

Where Gen X Vegas hangs out. Decor is hip, which in this case means an odd mix of industrial warehouse, peeling plaster, and brick country cottage exterior; somehow, it works. The rooms are all good-looking (all are candle-lit, and at least one rope hammock swings in case you need to relax), though much of the detail is lost in the obligatory dark nightclub lighting. Soundproofing is impressive; you can literally pass from the hard-rock room to the dance room with only a second's worth of the two overlapping into each other. (Of course, getting there can be a problem—the hallways from room to room are narrow and bottlenecks frequent. Be patient.) A recent saunter in the hard-rock room heard a mix of retro and more current rock. (A song by The Cult segued into "Magic Carpet Ride," which went into "Spill the Wine," which went into some anonymous '90s faux metal/hard-rock song.) The different sounds mean different appeals for different rooms; thus something for everyone. So if you are traveling in a group, you don't need to have a consensus on music taste. Despite a young, fashion-conscious crowd, it's friendlier than you would imagine, with virtually no attitude, surprisingly enough. (If you go there after Club Rio, the difference in attitude is almost palpable.) Jay Leno, Matthew Perry, Dennis Rodman, and Charles Barkley have apparently been spotted there, but don't hold that against it. They serve food, too. Of the nightly dance clubs, this is the one to go to, unless a hip quotient frightens you. Open Monday to Thursday until 3am, Friday and Saturday until 5am. Closed Sunday. Self-parking is free, valet parking $3.

Monte Carlo Pub & Brewery. Monte Carlo Resort, 3770 Las Vegas Blvd. S. ☎ **702/730-7777.** No cover or minimum.

After 9pm nightly, this immense warehouselike pub and working microbrewery (see details in chapter 6) turns from a casual restaurant into a rollicking, high-energy dance club that is very popular with Gen-X-to-thirtysomething locals. Rock videos blare forth from a large screen and 40 TV monitors around the room, while, onstage, dueling pianos provide music and audience-participation entertainment. The Pub is cigar-friendly and maintains a humidor. There's a full bar, and, of course, the house microbrews are featured; you can also order pizza. Open until 1am Sunday to Thursday, until 3am Friday and Saturday.

Ra. Luxor Las Vegas, 3900 Las Vegas Blvd. S. ☎ **702/262-4000.** Cover $10 for up to four people.

The futuristic Egyptian-themed Ra is the new hot spot in Vegas. The vibe is that Vegas "we're a show, and an attraction," but is still not overly pretentious and the staff are friendly, which is a rare thing for a hot club. It might be worth it to go just to gawk at the heavy gilt decor. You can also find a major light show, cigar lounges off the disco, draped VIP booths, and plenty of little nooks and crannies. Current dance music (mostly techno) is on the soundtrack. The later you go, the more likely the mid- to upper 20s clientele will be entirely local. Ra is supposed to stay open until 6am, but can close earlier if it's slow—and, surprisingly, on a recent Friday night, it was. (That may be deceptive; on other nights, there was a line to get in.)

Sam's Town Western Dance Hall. Sam's Town, 5111 Boulder Hwy. ☎ **702/456-7777.** No cover or minimum.

Attracting a large local crowd, Sam's Town houses a rustic dance hall, its weathered barnwood walls hung with steer horns, neon beer signs, wagon wheels, and other things western. You can dance here to music provided by a deejay from 9pm to 3am. Come by from 7:30 to 9pm for free lessons in line dancing and West Coast swing. Sunday is karaoke night, with a deejay on hand from 9pm.

Studio 54. MGM Grand Hotel, 3799 Las Vegas Blvd. S. ☎ **702/891-1111.** Cover $10 for men Sun–Thurs, $20 Fri–Sat; free for women.

The legendary Studio 54 has been resurrected here in Las Vegas, but with all the bad elements and none of the good ones. Forget Truman, Halston, and Liza doing illegal (or at least) immoral things in the bathroom stalls; that part of Studio 54 remains but a fond memory. However, the snooty, exclusive door attitude has been retained. Hooray. Red-rope policies are all well and good if you are trying to build a mystique in a regular club, but for a tourist attraction, where guests are likely to be one-time-only (or at best, once a year), it's obnoxious. Oddly, this doesn't lead to a high-class clientele; of all the new clubs, this is the most touristy and trashy. The large dance floor has a balcony to look down on it, the decor is industrial (exposed piping and the like), the music is hip hop and electronic, and there is nothing to do other than dance. If the real Studio 54 were this boring, no one would remember it today.

Utopia. 3765 Las Vegas Blvd. S., in the Epicenter. ☎ **702/736-3105.** Cover varies.

According to *Scope* magazine, Utopia is "less a discotheque and more a revolution"—which is an apt description, considering that in Las Vegas, underground once-a-week nightclubs usually disappear in a matter of weeks. (And for that matter, the underground itself is a shaky, hard-to-find thing.) Utopia is still going strong (as of this writing), despite the death (in a car accident) of its founder, Aaron Britt. The music is progressive house, tribal, trance, techno, and rave. The atmosphere is industrial, foggy, and heavy with lasers and other dazzling visuals. A cool and outrageous crowd fills three rooms with fun, peace, and love, in a heart-pounding, techno way. It's for the tragically hip, but isn't it good to know they are out there in Vegas? Internationally known deejays spin and live rave acts play. It's open Saturday only, from 11pm to 3am (or so); you must be at least 21.

Voodoo Lounge. Rio Suites, 3700 Las Vegas Blvd. S. ☎ **702/252-7777.** No cover. Dress code: "No shorts or shirts without collars, business casual."

Occupying, along with the Voodoo Cafe, two floors in the new addition of the Rio, the Lounge combines Haitian voodoo and New Orleans Creole—almost successfully—in its decor and theme. There are two main rooms: one with a large dance floor and stage for live music, and a disco room, which is filled with large video screens and serious light action. Big club chairs in groups form conversation pits, where you might actually be able to have a conversation. The big seller—the bartenders put on a show, à la Tom Cruise in *Cocktail*. They shake, jiggle, and light stuff on fire. Supposedly, the live music includes Cajun acts, but when it comes down to it, rock seems to rule the day. The mid- to late 20s crowd is more heavily local than you might expect.

10 Strip Clubs

No, not entertainment establishments on Las Vegas Boulevard South. This would be the *other* kind of "strip." Yes, people come to town for the gambling and the wedding chapels, but the lure of Vegas doesn't stop there. Though prostitution is not legal within the city, the sex industry is an active, and obvious, force in town. Every other cab carries a placard for a strip club, and a walk down the Strip at night will have dozens of men thrusting flyers at you for clubs, escort services, phone sex lines, and more. And some of you are going to want to check it out.

And why not? An essential part of the Vegas allure is decadence, and naked flesh would certainly qualify, as does the thrill of trying something new and daring. Of course, by and large, the nicer bars *aren't* particularly daring, and if you go to more than one in an evening, the thrill wears off, and the breasts don't look quite so bare.

In the finest of Vegas traditions, the "something for everyone" mentality extends to the strip clubs. Here is a guide to the most prominent and heavily advertised; there are plenty more, of increasing seediness, out there. You don't have to look too hard. The most crowded and zoolike times are after midnight, especially on Friday and Saturday nights. Should you want a "meaningful" experience, you might wish to avoid the rush and choose an off-hour for a visit.

Cheetah's. 2112 Western Ave. ☎ **702/384-0074.** Cover $10. MC, V (but cash preferred—they have an ATM machine). Topless.

This is the strip club used in the movie *Showgirls,* but thanks to the magic of Hollywood and later renovations by the club, only the main stage will look vaguely familiar to those few looking for Nomi Malone. There is also a smaller stage, plus three tiny "tip stages" so that you can really get close to (and give much money to) the woman of your choice—and it gets them closer to the bar. Eight TVs line the walls; the club does a brisk business during major sporting events. The management believes, "If you treat people right, they will keep coming back," so the atmosphere is friendlier than at other clubs. They "encourage couples—people who want to party—to come here. We get a 21 to 40 aged party kind of crowd," the manager told us. And indeed there is a sporty, frat-bar feel to the place. (Though on a crowded Saturday night some unescorted women were turned away, despite policy.) Check out bikini-clad "beer babe" Kim at the beer bar—she's cute and friendly. $10 table dance, $20 couch dance. Open 24 hours.

Club Paradise. 4416 Paradise Rd. ☎ **702/734-7990.** $10 cover, 2-drink minimum (drinks $4.50 and up). MC, V. Unescorted women allowed. Topless.

Possibly the nicest of the strip clubs (the outside looks a lot like the Golden Nugget), the interior and atmosphere are rather like that of a hot nightclub where most of the women happen to be topless. The glitzy stage looks like something from a miniature showroom: The lights flash and the dance music pounds, there are two big video screens (one featuring soft porn, the other showing sports!), the chairs are plush and comfortable, the place is relatively bright by strip-club standards, and they offer champagne and cigars. Not too surprisingly, they get a very white-collar crowd here. The result is not terribly sleazy, which may please some and turn off others. The girls ("actual centerfolds") are heavy (and we do mean heavy) on the silicone. They don't so much dance as pose and prance, after which they don skimpy evening dresses and come down to solicit lap dances, which eventually fills the place up with writhing girls in thongs. The club says it is "women-friendly," and indeed there were a few couples, including one woman who was receiving a lap dance herself—and didn't seem too uncomfortable. Occasionally the action stops down for a minirevue, which ends up being more like seminaked cheerleading than a show. Lap dances $20. Open Monday to Sunday 6pm to 6am.

Crazy Horse, Two.

We've omitted the address of this place on purpose. Full of so much obnoxious jerk attitude, with overly aggressive girls soliciting lap dances, that even the other clubs in town sneer at them. There are plenty of strip bars—pass this one by.

Glitter Gulch. 20 Fremont St. ☎ **702/385-4774.** No cover, 2-drink minimum (drinks $5.75). Topless.

Right there in the middle of the Fremont Street Experience, Glitter Gulch is either an eyesore or the last bastion of Old Las Vegas, depending on your point of view. The inside is modern enough: black light and bubble fountains, arranged around a runway strip. The shows are basic—the women take off sequined gowns to reveal G-strings. Customers sit in comfortable booths, and the dancers then come around and offer up-close and personal table dances, often chatting merrily away while they expose themselves. As you enter, you are assigned your own (overly clothed) waitress who escorts you to your table. They also offer limo service to the hotels. There is even a line of souvenir clothing. Given such services and its convenient location, this is the perfect place for the merely curious—you can easily pop in, check things out, goggle and ogle, and then hit the road, personal dignity intact. Table dances cost $20. Open Sunday to Thursday noon to 4am, Friday to Saturday noon to 6am.

Little Darlings. 1514 Western Ave. ☎ **702/366-0145.** Cover $10 plus $10 all you can drink (includes souvenir florescent mug). No unescorted women. Totally nude.

They call themselves the "Pornocopia of Sex," and given the number of services they offer, you can see why. In addition to a fully stocked adult store, they have private nude dances in booths (dancers must stay 6 inches from the customer at all times). This is one of the few clubs where the women are not allowed any physical contact with the customers. There are also rooms where you can watch a nude woman take a shower (in theory doing erotic things with soap), and "Fantasy Rooms" where a glass pane separates you from a woman performing still more erotic stunts. The women are all healthy and athletic, including some who do impressive work with the poles on stage (using their legs to climb all the way to the rafters). Despite all the nude offerings, the resultant atmosphere is not especially dirty, just rowdy. (Tellingly, they do promotions with a local radio station.) At least one late-20s customer felt it was all too much like high school and that the cover was prohibitively expensive. $15 totally nude private dance in booth; $15 "shower"; $15 table dance; $15 Fantasy Room. Open Monday to Saturday 11am to 6am, Sunday 2pm to 6am.

Olympic Gardens. 1531 Las Vegas S. Blvd. ☎ **702/385-8987.** Cover $15 (includes 2 drinks). AE, DISC, MC, V (they have an ATM machine). Unescorted women allowed. Topless.

Possibly the largest of the strip clubs, this almost feels like a family operation, thanks to the middle-aged women handling the door. They also have a boutique selling lingerie and naughty outfits. (Since they get a lot of couples coming in, perhaps this is in case someone gets inspired and wants to try out what they learned here at home.) There are two rooms: one with large padded tables for the women to dance on, the other featuring a more classic strip runway. The girls all seemed really cute—perhaps the best-looking of the major clubs. The crowd is a mix of 20s to 30s blue-collar guys and techno geeks. As the place fills up and the chairs are crammed in next to each other, it's hard to see how enjoyable, or intimate, a lap

Two Strippers Give 9 Strip-Bar Etiquette Tips

Brittany and Kitty each have several years' experience working in strip bars, so they know what they're talking about. And they both really are sweet girls, honest.

1. Bathe.
2. Don't lie and say you never go into these places.
3. Don't take off your wedding ring—we can still see the mark it leaves.
4. Don't ask if we take credit cards. Bring cash!
5. Don't fall asleep—just because we are open 24 hours, we aren't a hotel.
6. Don't wear wool pants—they scratch.
7. Don't ask for our phone number.
8. Don't lick us. We're not Popsicles.
9. Don't forget: We *aren't* dumb strippers. We are a lot smarter than you think.

dance can be when the guy next to you is getting one as well. That didn't seem to stop all the guys there who all seemed appropriately blissed out. Table dances $20, more in VIP room. Open Monday to Sunday 2pm to 6am.

Palomino. 1848 Las Vegas Blvd. N. ☎ **702/642-2984.** Cover $10, plus 2-drink minimum (drinks $6). Totally nude.

Once the nicest strip club in town, it now edges into the seedy end of things. It's also a bit out of the way. On the other hand, it does offer total nudity in a classic red-walled setting. It's two levels, with the downstairs consisting of a large stage where featured dancers ("all have appeared in *Playboy* or *Penthouse* or some kind of publication") do themed dances with specific music, costumes, and props (one healthy surfer blonde gal used a big, white bed and satin nightie in her set), which can result in some incongruous sights, like an essentially interpretive dance with pauses for gynecological shots. Upstairs has two or three small stages with dancers doing their thing up close and personal. There is also a large room off to the side where they take you for lap dances, ensuring a small measure of privacy. Topless lap dance $20, totally nude $40. Open Monday to Sunday 1:30pm to 4am.

Side Trips from Las Vegas

Though all of Vegas is designed to make you forget that there is an outside world, it might do you and your pocketbook much good to reacquaint yourself with it. Actually, if you are spending more than 3 days in Vegas, this may become a necessity; 2 days with kids and it absolutely will.

Plus, there is such a stark, startling contrast between the artificial wonders of Sin City and the natural wonders that in some cases lie just feet from it. Few places are as developed and modern as Vegas; few places are as untouched as some of the canyons, desert, and mountains that surround it. For all the electrical and design marvel that is the Strip, it could not be without the extraordinary structural feat that is Hoover Dam. Need some fresh air? (My heavens, don't you!) There are plenty of opportunities for outdoor recreation, from white-water rafting to desert hiking—all in a landscape like none other.

The following excursions, with one exception, will take you from 20 to 60 miles out of town. Every one of them offers a memorable travel experience.

1 Hoover Dam & Lake Mead

30 miles SE of Las Vegas

This is one of the most popular excursions from Las Vegas, visited by 2,000 to 3,000 people daily. Why should you join them? Because it's an engineering and architectural marvel and it changed the Southwest forever. Without it, you wouldn't even be going to Vegas. Kids may be bored, unless they like machinery or just plain big things, but expose them to it anyway, for their own good. (Buy them an ice cream and a Hoover Dam snow globe as a bribe.) Obviously, if you are staying at Lake Mead, it's a must. The tour itself is a bit cursory, but you do get up close and personal with the dam. Wear comfortable shoes; the tour involves quite a bit of walking. Try to take the tour in the morning to beat the desert heat and the really big crowds. You can have lunch out in Boulder City, and then perhaps drive back through the **Valley of Fire State Park,** which is about 60 magnificently scenic miles from Lake Mead (purchase gas before you start!). Or you can spend the afternoon with Lake Mead pursuits, hiking, boating, even scuba diving in season, or perhaps a rafting trip down the Colorado River.

Impressions

Everybody knows Las Vegas is the best town by a dam site.
—Masthead slogan of the *Las Vegas Review Journal*

ESSENTIALS

GETTING THERE   By Car   Go east on Flamingo or Tropicana to U.S. 515 south, which automatically turns into 93 south and takes you right to the Dam. This will involve a rather dramatic drive, as you go through Boulder City, come over a rise, and Lake Mead suddenly appears spread out before you. It's a beautiful sight. At about this point, the road narrows down to two lanes and traffic can slow considerably. On busy tourist days, this means the drive can take an hour or more.

Go past the turnoff to Lake Mead. As you near the dam, you'll see a 5-story parking structure tucked into the canyon wall on your left. Park here ($2 charge) and take the elevators or stairs to the walkway leading to the new Visitor Center.

If you would rather go on an **organized tour, Gray Line** (☎ **702/384-1234**) offers several Hoover Dam packages, all of them including admission and a tour of the dam. When you're in Las Vegas, look for discount coupons in numerous free publications available at hotels. The 4½-hour **Hoover Dam Shuttle Tour** departs daily at 7:45am, 9:45am, and 11:45am and includes pickup and drop-off; the price is $29.50 for adults, $24.50 for seniors over 62, $19.50 for children 10 to 16, and $15.50 for children under 10. Most elaborate is the **Grand Hoover Dam and Lake Mead Cruise Tour,** departing daily at 9:45am, which includes a 90-minute paddlewheeler cruise on Lake Mead with a light lunch available for an extra cost, plus admission to Hoover Dam; $41 for adults, $35 for children under 10. You can inquire at your hotel sightseeing desk about other bus tours.

✪ HOOVER DAM

There would be no Las Vegas as we know it without Hoover Dam. Certainly not the neon and glitz. In fact, the growth of the entire Southwest can be tied directly to the electricity that came from the dam.

Until Hoover Dam was built, much of the southwestern United States was plagued by two natural problems: parched, sandy terrain that lacked irrigation for most of the year and extensive flooding in spring and early summer when the mighty Colorado River, fed by melting snow from its source in the Rocky Mountains, overflowed its banks and destroyed crops, lives, and property. On the positive side, raging unchecked over eons, the river's turbulent, rushing waters carved the Grand Canyon.

In 1928, prodded by the seven states through which the river runs during the course of its 1,400-mile journey to the Gulf of California, Congress authorized construction of a dam at Boulder Canyon (later moved to Black Canyon). The Senate's declaration of intention was that "A mighty river, now a source of destruction, is to be curbed and put to work in the interests of society." Construction began in 1931. Because of its vast scope, and the unprecedented problems posed in its realization, the project generated significant advances in many areas of machinery production, engineering, and construction. An army of more than 5,200 laborers was assembled, and work proceeded 24 hours a day. Completed in 1936, 2 years ahead of schedule and $15 million under budget (let's see James Cameron top that!), the dam stopped the annual floods and conserved water for irrigation, industrial, and domestic use. Equally important, it became one of the world's major electrical generating plants, providing low-cost, pollution-free hydroelectric power to a score

Excursions from Las Vegas

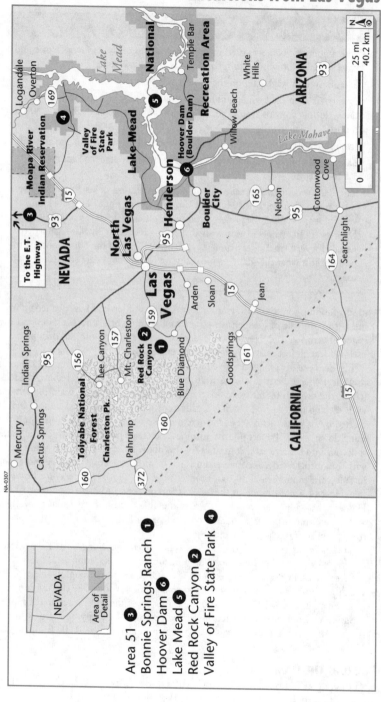

NEVADA

Area of Detail

Area 51 ❸
Bonnie Springs Ranch ❶
Hoover Dam ❻
Lake Mead ❺
Red Rock Canyon ❷
Valley of Fire State Park ❹

261

❓ Did You Know?

- The amount of concrete used in the construction of the Hoover Dam could pave a standard highway from San Francisco to New York.
- The minimum wage paid on the project was $4 a day.
- Ninety-six men died while building, excavating, blasting, and scaling mountains during construction, and on-the-job injuries totaled about 1,500 a month.
- In summer, the canyon rocks are so hot you could literally fry an egg on them.
- Lake Mead contains enough water to cover the entire state of Pennsylvania to a 1-foot depth.
- The dam was originally called Boulder Dam because of its first-designated canyon site, then renamed Hoover Dam in 1930 to honor Herbert Hoover's years of work making the project a reality. Unofficially it was renamed Boulder Dam by FDR, who did not wish to honor Hoover; it finally regained the name Hoover Dam under Truman, who, in 1947, asked the 80th Congress to find out just what the "dam" name really was. Both names are still in popular usage.

---

of surrounding communities. Hoover Dam's $165 million cost has been repaid with interest by the sale of inexpensive power to a number of California cities and the states of Arizona and Nevada. The dam is a government project that paid for itself—a feat almost as awe-inspiring as its engineering.

The dam itself is a massive curved wall, 660 feet thick at the bottom and tapering to 45 feet where the road crosses it at the top. It towers 726.4 feet above bedrock (about the height of a 60-story skyscraper) and acts as a plug between the canyon walls to hold back up to 9.2 trillion gallons of water in Lake Mead—the reservoir created by its construction. Four concrete intake towers on the lake side drop the water down about 600 feet to drive turbines and create power, after which the water spills out into the river and continues south. All the architecture is on a grand scale, with beautiful art deco elements unusual in an engineering project. Note, for instance, the monumental 30-foot bronze sculpture, *Winged Figures of the Republic,* flanking a 142-foot flagpole at the Nevada entrance. According to its creator, Oskar Hansen, the sculpture symbolizes "the immutable calm of intellectual resolution, and the enormous power of trained physical strength, equally enthroned in placid triumph of scientific achievement."

The dam has become a major sightseeing attraction along with Lake Mead, America's largest artificial reservoir and a major Nevada recreation area.

Seven miles northwest of the dam on U.S. 93, you'll pass through **Boulder City,** which was built to house managerial and construction workers. Sweltering summer heat (many days it is 125°F) ruled out a campsite by the dam, whereas the higher elevation of Boulder City offered lower temperatures. The city emerged within a single year, turning a desert waste into a community of 6,000. By 1934 it was Nevada's third largest town.

TOURING THE DAM

The very nice **Hoover Dam Visitor Center,** a vast 3-level circular concrete structure with a rooftop overlook, opened in 1995. You'll enter the Reception Lobby, where you can buy tickets, peruse informational exhibits, photographs, and memorabilia, and view three 12-minute video presentations (respectively, about the importance of water to life, the events leading up to the construction of Hoover Dam, and the construction itself as well as the many benefits it confers). Exhibits on the Plaza Level include interactive displays on the environment, habitation, and development of the Southwest, the people who built the dam, and related topics. Yet another floor up, galleries on the Overlook Level demonstrate, via sculpted bronze panels, the benefits of Hoover Dam and Lake Mead to the states of Arizona, Nevada, and California. The Overlook Level additionally provides an unobstructed view of Lake Mead, the dam, the power plant, the Colorado River, and Black Canyon. (There are multiple photo opportunities throughout this trip.) You can visit an exhibit center across the street where a 10-minute presentation in a small theater focuses on a topographical map of the 1,400-mile Colorado River. It also has a cafeteria. Notice, by the way, how the rest rooms in the Center only have electric dryers, no paper towels. A tribute?

Thirty-minute tours of the dam depart from the Reception Lobby every 15 minutes or so daily, except Christmas. The Visitor Center opens at 8:30am, and the first tour departs soon after. The last tour leaves at 6pm, and the center closes at 6:30pm. Admission is $8 for adults, $7 for senior citizens and $2 for children 6 to 16, free for children under 6. More extensive, and expensive, hard-hat tours are offered every half hour between 9:30am and 3:30pm; "Survive the tour and you keep the hard hat!" Although it's not compulsory, it's not a bad idea to call in advance for the tour (☎ 702/294-3522). Both tours, by the way, are "not recommended for claustrophobics or those persons with defibrillators."

The tour begins with a 561-foot elevator descent into the dam's interior, where an access tunnel leads to the Nevada wing of the power plant. (You only cross to Arizona on the hard-hat tour.) In the three stops on the regular tour, you see the massive turbines that generate the electricity using the water flow, go outside on the downriver side of the dam looking up at the towering structure (which is pretty awesome), and then go into one of the tunnels that contains a steel water diversion pipe that feeds the turbines. (It's one of the largest steel water pipes ever made—its interior could accommodate two lanes of automobile traffic.)

Some fun facts you might hear along the way: It took 6½ years to fill the lake. Though 96 workers were killed during the construction, contrary to popular myth, none were accidentally buried as the concrete was poured (it was poured only at a level of 8 inches at a time). Look for a monument to them outside—"they died to make the desert bloom"—along with one for their doggy mascot who was also killed, although after the dam was completed. Compare their wages of 50¢ an hour to their Depression-era peers, who made 5¢ to 30¢.

LAKE MEAD NATIONAL RECREATION AREA

Under the auspices of the National Park Service, the 1.5-million-acre Lake Mead National Recreation Area was created in 1936 around Lake Mead (the reservoir lake resulted from the construction of Hoover Dam) and later Lake Mohave to the south (formed with the construction of Davis Dam). Before the lakes emerged, this desert region was brutally hot, dry, and rugged—unfit for human habitation. Today it is one of the nation's most popular playgrounds, attracting about nine million visitors annually. The two lakes comprise 290.7 square miles. At an elevation of 1,221.4 feet, Lake Mead itself extends some 110 miles upstream toward the Grand Canyon. Its 550-mile shoreline, backed by spectacular cliff and canyon scenery, forms a perfect setting for a wide variety of water sports and desert hiking.

VISITOR INFORMATION   The **Alan Bible Visitor Center,** 4 miles northeast of Boulder City on U.S. 93 at Nev. 166 (☎ **702/293-8990**), can provide information on all area activities and services. You can pick up trail maps and brochures here, view informative films, and find out about scenic drives, accommodations, ranger-guided hikes, naturalist programs and lectures, bird watching, canoeing, camping, lakeside RV parks, and picnic facilities. The center also sells books and videotapes about the area. It's open daily 8:30am to 4:30pm. For information on accommodations, boat rentals, and fishing, call **Seven Crown Resorts** (☎ **800/752-9669**).

OUTDOOR ACTIVITIES

BOATING & FISHING   A store at **Lake Mead Resort and Marina** under the auspices of Seven Crown Resorts (☎ **800/752-9669** or 702/293-3484) rents fishing boats, ski boats, personal watercraft, and patio boats. It also carries groceries, clothing, marine supplies, sporting goods, water-skiing gear, fishing equipment, and bait and tackle. You can get a fishing license here ($45.50 a year or $17.50 for 3 days; $9 a year for children 12 to 15, under 12 free). The staff is knowledgeable and can apprise you of good fishing spots. Largemouth bass, striped bass, channel catfish, crappie, and bluegill are found in Lake Mead, rainbow trout, largemouth bass, and striped bass in Lake Mohave. You can also arrange here to rent a fully equipped houseboat at **Echo Bay,** 40 miles north.

Other convenient Lake Mead marinas offering similar rentals and equipment are **Las Vegas Bay** (☎ 702/565-9111), which is even closer to Las Vegas, and **Callville Bay** (☎ 702/565-8958), which is the least crowded of the five on the Nevada Shore.

CAMPING   Lake Mead's shoreline is dotted with campsites, all of them equipped with running water, picnic tables, and grills. Available on a first-come, first-served basis, they are administered by the **National Park Service** (☎ 702/293-8990). There's a charge of $10 per night at each campsite.

CANOEING   The **Alan Bible Visitor Center** (see above) can provide a list of outfitters who rent canoes for trips on the Colorado River. There's one catch, however: A canoeing permit ($5 for one; $10 for two to five canoes) is required in advance from the **Bureau of Reclamation.** Call ☎ 702/293-8204 Monday to Thursday for information.

HIKING   The best season for hiking is November to March (it's too hot the rest of the year). Some ranger-guided hikes are offered via the **Alan Bible Visitor Center** (see above), which also stocks detailed trail maps. Three trails, ranging in length from three-quarters of a mile to 6 miles, originate at the Visitor Center. The 6-mile trail goes past remains of the railroad built for the dam project. Be sure to take all necessary desert-hiking precautions (see details in chapter 7).

LAKE CRUISES   A delightful way to enjoy Lake Mead is on a cruise aboard the *Desert Princess* (☎ 702/293-6180), a Mississippi-style paddlewheeler. Cruises depart year-round from a terminal near Lake Mead Lodge (see below) and a dock right at Hoover Dam (inquire at the Visitor Center). It's a relaxing, scenic trip (enjoyed from an open promenade deck or one of two fully enclosed, climate-controlled decks) through Black Canyon and past colorful rock formations known as the "Arizona Paint Pots" en route to Hoover Dam, which is lit at night. Options include buffet breakfast cruises ($21 adults, $10 children under 12), narrated midday cruises ($16 adults, $6 children), cocktail/dinner cruises ($29 adults, $15 children), and sunset dinner/dance cruises with live music ($43 adults, children not allowed). Add $1 to all rates if you depart from Hoover Dam. Dinner is served

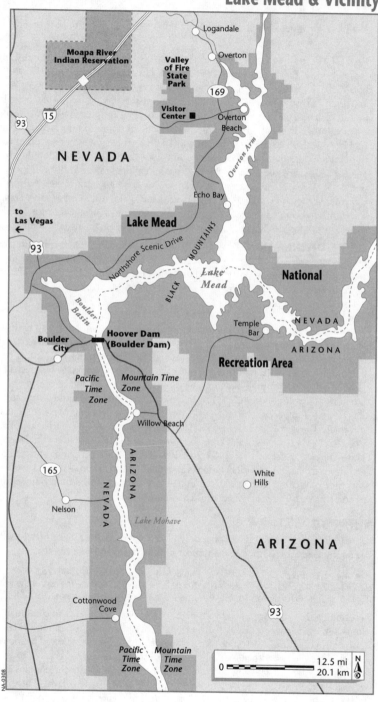

Lake Mead & Vicinity

Logandale

Overton

Moapa River
Indian Reservation

Valley
of Fire
State
Park

169

Visitor
Center ■

Overton
Beach

93

15

N E V A D A

Overton Arm

Echo Bay

to
Las Vegas
←

Lake Mead

Northshore Scenic Drive

BLACK MOUNTAINS

Lake
Mead

National

93

Boulder
Basin

NEVADA

Temple
Bar

ARIZONA

Hoover Dam
(Boulder Dam)

Recreation Area

Boulder
City

Pacific
Time
Zone

Mountain Time
Zone

Willow Beach

White
Hills

165

ARIZONA

NEVADA

Nelson

Lake Mohave

A R I Z O N A

Cottonwood
Cove

93

Pacific
Time
Zone

Mountain
Time
Zone

0   12.5 mi
           20.1 km

N

NA-0308

in a pleasant, windowed, air-conditioned dining room. There's a full bar on board. Call for departure times.

RAFTING   Rafting trips on the Colorado River are offered February to November by **Black Canyon,** 1297 Nevada Hwy. in Boulder City (☎ **800/ 696-7238** or 702/293-3776). Twelve-mile trips begin at the base of Hoover Dam. You'll see canyon waterfalls and wildlife (bighorn sheep, wild burros, chuckwalla lizards, mallards, grebe, and the occasional golden eagle) and stop at a quiet cove for a picnic lunch. There are stunning rock formations en route, and the area is rich in history—southern Paiute rock shelters and 1920s river-gauging stations and cableways. Guides are quite knowledgeable about local lore. Prices (including lunch): $65 for adults, $35 for children 5 to 12, free for children under 5. Bus transportation back to Las Vegas is available. Even if you don't go rafting, stop by Black Canyon's headquarters to see exhibits about the area and a film on Hoover Dam. Their office also functions as an information center and tour operator for a wide array of area activities (Grand Canyon flights, jet-skiing, skydiving, and more).

SCUBA DIVING   October to April, there's good visibility, lessened in summer months when algae flourishes. A list of good dive locations, authorized instructors, and nearby dive shops is available at **Alan Bible Visitor Center** (see above). There's an underwater designated diving area near Lake Mead Marina.

BOULDER CITY

You might want to consider poking around Boulder City on your way back to Vegas. Literally the company town for those building Hoover Dam, it was created by the wives who came with their husbands and turned a temporary site into a real community, since aided by the recreational attractions and attendant businesses of Lake Mead. It doesn't look like much as you first approach it, but once you are in the heart you will discover it is quite charming. There are some antique and curio shops, and a number of family-style restaurants, burger and Mexican joints, including **Totos,** a reasonably priced Mexican restaurant at 806 Buchanan Blvd. (☎ **702/293-1744**); it's in the Von's shopping center. Or you could try the **Happy Days Diner,** 512 Nevada Hwy. (☎ **702/294-2643**), which is right on the road to and from the dam. A '50s diner in looks and menu, it has the usual burgers, shakes, and fries, plus complete breakfasts, is quite inexpensive ($3 for a turkey burger on a recent visit), friendly, and a good place to take the kids.

WHERE TO STAY

In addition to the hotel below (the only place to stay right on Lake Mead itself, aside from campsites), there are a number of little hotels in Boulder City.

Lake Mead Lodge. 322 Lakeshore Rd., Boulder City, NV 89005. ☎ **800/752-9669** or 702/293-2074. 42 units. A/C TV. Early Mar to late Nov $50–$65 double, the rest of the year $35–$50 double. Extra person $6. Children under 5 stay free in parents' room. DISC, MC, V.

If camping isn't your bag, spend your night or nights at this rustic and comfortable bungalow-style lodge. It's an easy drive from Hoover Dam and is right on the lake, but also right on the desert, don't forget, so don't think wooded resort. The rooms are pleasant with wood-paneled ceilings and walls of white-painted brick or rough-hewn pine. All offer full baths and cable TVs. There is a suite with three rooms and a small kitchen, which might be good for families staying a few days. (There are plans to add a second suite in 1999.) The pool is rudimentary, but you might want to relax with a good book in one of the gazebos on the property. About a half mile down the road is the marina, where you can while away a few hours over cocktails on a lakeside patio. The marina is headquarters for boating, fishing, and water sports; it also houses a large shop (see details above under "Boating and Fishing"). And Boulder Beach, also an easy walk from the lodge, has waterfront picnic tables and barbecue grills.

Dining: There's a nautically themed restaurant called **Tale of the Whale** (☎ **702/293-3484**) at the marina (approximately a half mile away), its rough-hewn pine interior embellished with various sea-faring iconography. Open 7am to 9pm Sunday to Thursday, until 10pm Friday and Saturday, it serves hearty breakfasts; sandwiches, salads, and burgers at lunch; and steak-and-seafood dinners, all at moderate prices. Sometimes there's live music Friday and Saturday nights.

2 Valley of Fire State Park

60 miles NE of Las Vegas

Most people visualize the desert as a vast expanse of undulating sands punctuated by the occasional cactus or palm-fringed oasis. The desert of America's Southwest bears little relation to this Lawrence of Arabia image. Stretching for hundreds of miles around Las Vegas in every direction is a seemingly lifeless tundra of vivid reddish earth, shaped by time, climate, and subterranean upheavals into majestic canyons, cliffs, and ridges.

The 36,000-acre Valley of Fire State Park, typifying the mountainous red Mojave Desert, derives its name from the brilliant sandstone formations that were created 150 million years ago by a great shifting of sand and continue to be shaped by the geologic processes of wind and water erosion.

Although it's hard to imagine in the sweltering Nevada heat, for billions of years these rocks were under hundreds of feet of ocean. This ocean floor began to rise some 200 million years ago, and the waters became more shallow. Eventually the sea made a complete retreat, leaving a muddy terrain traversed by ever-diminishing streams. A great sandy desert covered much of the southwestern part of the American continent until about 140 million years ago. Over eons, winds, massive fault action, and water erosion sculpted fantastic formations of sand and limestone. Oxidation of iron in the sands and mud—and the effect of ground water leaching the oxidized iron—turned the rocks the many hues of red, pink, russet, lavender, and white that can be seen today. Logs of ancient forests washed down from faraway highlands and became petrified fossils, which can be seen along two interpretive trails.

Human beings occupied the region, a wetter and cooler one, as far back as 4,000 years ago. They didn't live in the Valley of Fire, but during the Gypsum period (2000 B.C. to 300 B.C.), men hunted bighorn sheep (a source of food, clothing, blankets, and hut coverings) here with a notched stick called an *atlatl* that is depicted in the park's petroglyphs. Women and children caught rabbits, tortoises, and other small game. In the next phase, from 300 B.C. to A.D. 700, the climate became warmer and dryer. Bows and arrows replaced the atlatl and the hunters and gatherers discovered farming. The Anasazi people began cultivating corn, squash, and beans, and communities began replacing small nomadic family groups. These ancient people wove watertight baskets, mats, hunting nets, and clothing. Around A.D. 300 they learned how to make sun-dried ceramic pottery. Other tribes, notably the Paiutes, migrated to the area. By A.D. 1150 they had become the dominant group. Unlike the Anasazis, they were still nomadic and used the Valley of Fire region seasonally. These were the inhabitants who white settlers found when they entered the area in the early to mid-1800s. The newcomers diverted river and spring waters to irrigate their farmlands, destroying the nature-based Paiute way of life. About 300 descendants of those Paiute tribespeople still live on the Moapa Indian Reservation (about 20 miles northwest) that was established along the Muddy River in 1872.

ESSENTIALS

GETTING THERE By Car From Las Vegas take I-15 north to Exit 75 (Valley of Fire turnoff). However, the more scenic route is to take I-15 north, then travel Lake Mead Boulevard east to North Shore Road (Nev. 167), and proceed north to the Valley of Fire exit. The first route takes about an hour, the second 1½ hours.

Numerous **sightseeing tours** go to Valley of Fire. **Gray Line** (☎ 702/384-1234) has a 7-hour tour from Las Vegas, including lunch, that costs $30 for adults, $24.50 for children 17 and under. Inquire at your hotel tour desk.

Valley of Fire can also be visited in conjunction with Lake Mead. From **Lake Mead Lodge,** take Nev. 166 (Lakeshore Scenic Drive) north, make a right turn on Nev. 167 (North Shore Scenic Drive), turn left on Nev. 169 (Moapa Valley Boulevard) west—a spectacularly scenic drive—and follow the signs. Valley of Fire is about 65 miles from Hoover Dam.

WHAT TO SEE & DO

There are no food concessions or gas stations in the park; however, you can obtain meals or gas on Nev. 167 or in nearby **Overton** (15 miles northwest on Nev. 169). Overton is a fertile valley town replete with trees, agricultural crops, horses, and herds of cattle—quite a change in scenery.

At the southern edge of town is the **Lost City Museum,** 721 S. Moapa Valley Blvd. (☎ 702/397-2193), commemorating an ancient Anasazi village that was discovered in the region in 1924. Its population reached one of the highest levels of Native American culture in the United States. Artifacts dating back 12,000 years are on display, as are clay jars, dried corn and beans, arrowheads, seashell necklaces, and willow baskets of the ancient Pueblo culture that inhabited this region between A.D. 300 and 1150. Other exhibits document the Mormon farmers who settled the valley in the 1860s. A large collection of local rocks—petrified wood, fern fossils, iron pyrites, green copper, and red iron oxide—along with manganese blown bottles turned purple by the ultraviolet rays of the sun are also displayed here. The museum is surrounded by reconstructed wattle-and-daub pueblos. Admission is $2, free for children under 18. The museum is open daily 8:30am to 4:30pm. Closed Thanksgiving, December 25, and January 1.

Information headquarters for Valley of Fire is the **Visitor Center** on Nev. 169, 6 miles west of North Shore Road (☎ 702/397-2088). It's open daily 8:30am to 4:30pm. Exhibits on the premises explain the origin and geologic history of the park's colorful sandstone formations, describe the ancient peoples who carved their rock art on canyon walls, and identify the plants and wildlife you're likely to see. Postcards, books, slides, and films are on sale here, and you can pick up hiking maps and brochures. Rangers can answer your park-related questions.

There are hiking trails, shaded picnic sites, and two campgrounds in the park. Most sites are equipped with tables, grills, water, and rest rooms. An $11 per night camping fee is charged for use of the campground; if you're not camping, it costs $4 to enter the park.

Some of the notable formations in the park have been named for the shapes they vaguely resemble—a duck, an elephant, seven sisters, domes, beehives, and so on. Mouse's Tank is a natural basin that collects rainwater, so named for a fugitive

Paiute called Mouse who hid there in the late 1890s. And Native American petroglyphs etched into the rock walls and boulders—some dating from as early as 3,000 years ago—can be observed on self-guided trails. Petroglyphs at Atlatl Rock and Petroglyph Canyon are both easily accessible. In summer, when temperatures are usually over 100°F, you may have to settle for driving through the park in an air-conditioned car.

3 Red Rock Canyon

19 miles W of Las Vegas

If you need a break from the casinos of Vegas, with their windowless, claustrophobic, noise-intensive interiors, Red Rock Canyon is balm for your overstimulated soul. Less than 20 miles away—but in every other respect, worlds apart—this is a magnificent unspoiled vista that should cleanse and refresh you (and if you must, leave you enough time for an afternoon's gambling). You can drive the panoramic 13-mile **Scenic Drive** (open daily 7am until dusk) or explore it in more depth on foot, making it perfect for both athletes and armchair types. There are many interesting sights and trailheads along the drive itself. The wider **National Conservation Area** offers hiking trails and internationally acclaimed rock-climbing opportunities (especially notable is the 7,068-foot Mt. Wilson, the highest sandstone peak among the bluffs). There are picnic areas along the drive and in nearby **Spring Mountain Ranch State Park,** 5 miles south, which also offers plays in an outdoor theater during the summer. Since Bonnie Springs Ranch (see the next section) is just a few miles away, it makes a great base for exploring Red Rock Canyon.

ESSENTIALS
GETTING THERE   By Car   Just drive west on Charleston Boulevard, which becomes Nev. 159. Virtually as soon as you leave the city, the red rocks begin to loom around you. The Visitor Center will appear on your right.

You can also go on an **organized tour. Gray Line** (☎ 702/384-1234), among other companies, runs bus tours to Red Rock Canyon. Inquire at your hotel tour desk.

Finally, you can go **by bike.** Not very far out of town (at Rainbow Boulevard), Charleston Boulevard is flanked by a bike path that continues for about 11 miles to the Visitor Center/scenic drive. The path is hilly but not difficult if you're in reasonable shape. However, exploring Red Rock Canyon by bike should be attempted only by exceptionally fit and experienced bikers. For bike-rental information, see chapter 7.

Just off Nev. 159, you'll see the **Red Rock Canyon Visitor Center** (☎ 702/363-1921), which marks the actual entrance to the park. There, you can pick up information on trails and view history exhibits on the canyon. The center is open daily 8:30am to 4:30pm. Red Rock Canyon can be combined with a visit to Bonnie Springs Ranch.

ABOUT ✪ RED ROCK CANYON
The geological history of these ancient stones goes back some 600 million years. Over eons, the forces of nature have formed Red Rock's sandstone monoliths into arches, natural bridges, and massive sculptures painted in a stunning palette of gray-white limestone and dolomite, black mineral deposits, and oxidized minerals in earth-toned sienna hues ranging from pink to crimson and burgundy. Orange and green lichens add further contrast, as do spring-fed areas of lush foliage. And for-

Wild Weather

Although it can get very hot in Red Rock during the summer, it can also get very cold there during the winter. A recent trip in March to Red Rock and Bonnie Springs found the latter closed—due to snow!

mations like Calico Hill are brilliantly white where ground waters have leached out oxidized iron. Cliffs cut by deep canyons tower 2,000 feet above the valley floor.

During most of its history, Red Rock Canyon was below a warm shallow sea. Massive fault action and volcanic eruptions caused this seabed to begin rising some 225 million years ago. As the waters receded, sea creatures died and the calcium in their bodies combined with sea minerals to form limestone cliffs studded with ancient fossils. Some 45 million years later, the region was buried beneath thousands of feet of windblown sand. The landscape was as arid as the Sahara. As time progressed, iron oxide and calcium carbonate infiltrated the sand, consolidating it into cross-bedded rock. Shallow streams began carving the Red Rock landscape, and logs that washed down from ancient highland forests fossilized, their molecules gradually replaced by quartz and other minerals. These petrified stone logs, which the Paiute Indians believed were weapons of the wolf god, Shinarav, can be viewed in the **Chinle Formation** at the base of the Red Rock Cliffs. About 100 million years ago, massive fault action began dramatically shifting the rock landscape here, forming spectacular limestone and sandstone cliffs and rugged canyons punctuated by waterfalls, shallow streams, and serene oasis pools. Especially notable is the **Keystone Thrust Fault,** dating back about 65 million years when two of the earth's crustal plates collided, forcing older limestone and dolomite plates from the ancient seas over younger red and white sandstones. Over the years, water and wind have been ever creative sculptors, continuing to redefine this strikingly beautiful landscape.

Red Rock's valley is home to more than 45 species of mammals, about 100 species of birds, 30 reptiles and amphibians, and an abundance of plant life. Ascending the slopes from the valley, you'll see cactus and creosote bushes, aromatic purple sage, yellow-flowering blackbrush, yucca and Joshua trees, and, at higher elevations, clusters of forest-green piñon, juniper, and ponderosa pines. In spring, the desert blooms with extraordinary wildflowers.

Archaeological studies of Red Rock have turned up pottery fragments, stone tools, pictographs (rock drawings), and petroglyphs (rock etchings), along with other ancient artifacts. They show that humans have been in this region since about 3000 B.C. (some experts say as early as 10,000 B.C.). You can still see remains of early inhabitants on hiking expeditions in the park. (It's the same Anasazi to Paiutes to white settlers sad progression related in the Valley of the Fire section above.)

In the latter part of the 19th century, Red Rock was a mining site and later a sandstone quarry that provided materials for many buildings in Los Angeles, San Francisco, and early Las Vegas. By the end of World War II, as Las Vegas developed, many people became aware of the importance of preserving the canyon. In 1967 the Secretary of the Interior designated 62,000 acres as Red Rock Canyon Recreation Lands under the auspices of the Bureau of Land Management, and later legislation banned all development except hiking trails and limited recreational facilities. In 1990, Red Rock Canyon became a National Conservation Area, further elevating its protected status; its current acreage is 197,000.

WHAT TO SEE & DO

Begin with a stop at the Visitor Center; not only is there a $5 fee but you can pick up a variety of helpful literature: history, guides, hiking trail maps, and lists of local flora and fauna. You can also view exhibits that tell the history of the canyon and depict its plant and animal life. You'll see a fascinating video here about Nevada's thousands of wild horses and burros, protected by an act of Congress since 1971. Further, you can obtain permits for hiking and backpacking. Call ahead to find out about ranger-guided tours as well as informative guided hikes offered by groups like the Sierra Club and the Audubon Society. And, if you're traveling with children, ask about the free *Junior Ranger Discovery Book* filled with fun family activities. Books and videotapes are on sale here, including a guidebook identifying more than 100 top-rated climbing sites.

The easiest thing to do is to drive the 13-mile scenic loop. It really is a loop and it only goes one way, so once you start you are committed to driving the whole thing. You can stop the car to admire any number of fabulous views and sights along the way, or have a picnic, or to take a walk or hike. As you drive, observe how dramatically the milky white limestone alternates with iron-rich red rocks. Farther along, the mountains become solid limestone, with canyons running between them, which lead to an evergreen forest—a surprising addition to the desert.

However, if you are up to it, we can't stress enough that the way to really see the canyon is by hiking. Every trail is incredible—glance over your options and decide what you might be looking for. You can begin from the Visitor Center or drive into the loop, park, and start from points therein. Hiking trails range from a 0.7-mile-loop stroll to a waterfall (its flow varying seasonally) at Lost Creek to much longer and more strenuous treks. Actually, all the hikes involve a certain amount of effort, as you have to scramble over rocks on even the shorter hikes. Unfit or undexterous people should be aware. Be sure to wear good shoes as the rocks can be slippery. You must have a map; you won't get lost forever (there usually are other hikers around to help you out, eventually), but you can get lost. It is often tough to find a landmark, and once deep into the rocks, everything looks the same, even with the map. Consequently, give yourself extra time for each hike (at least an additional hour), regardless of its billed length, to allow for the lack of paths, getting disoriented, and simply to slow down and admire the scenery.

A popular 2-mile round-trip hike leads to **Pine Creek Canyon** and the creekside ruins of a historic homesite surrounded by ponderosa pine trees. Our hiking trail of choice is the **Calico Basin,** which is accessed along the loop. After an hour walk up the rocks (which is not that well marked), you end up at an oasis surrounded by sheer walls of limestone (which makes the oasis itself inaccessible, alas). In the summer, flowers and deciduous trees grow out of the walls.

As you hike, keep your eyes peeled for lizards, the occasional desert tortoise, flocks of bighorn sheep, birds, and other critters. But the rocks themselves are the most fun, with many minicaves to explore and rock formations to climb on. (Relive childhood with a politically incorrect game of Cowboys and Indians!) On trails along Calico Hills and the escarpment, look for "Indian marbles," a local name for small, rounded sandstone rocks that have eroded off larger sandstone formations. Petroglyphs are also tucked away in various locales.

Biking is another option; riding a bicycle would be a tremendous way to travel the loop. There are also terrific off-road mountain biking trails, with levels from amateur to expert.

After you tour the canyon, drive over to Bonnie Springs Ranch (details in the next section) for lunch or dinner. See chapter 7 for further details on biking and climbing.

4 Bonnie Springs Ranch/Old Nevada

About 24 miles W of Las Vegas, 5 miles past Red Rock Canyon

Bonnie Springs Ranch/Old Nevada is a kind of Wild West theme park with accommodations and a restaurant. If you're traveling with kids, a day or overnight trip to Bonnie Springs is recommended, but it is surprisingly appealing for adults, too. It could even be a romantic getaway, offering horseback riding, gorgeous mountain vistas, proximity to Red Rock Canyon, and temperatures 5° to 10° cooler than on the Strip.

ESSENTIALS

GETTING THERE   If you are traveling **by car,** a trip to Bonnie Springs Ranch can be combined easily with a day trip to Red Rock Canyon; it is about 5 miles further on. But you can also stay overnight.

For those without transportation, there are **Desert Action Jeep Tours** to and from Las Vegas. Call ☎ **702/796-9355** for details.

For additional information, you can call **Bonnie Springs Ranch/Old Nevada** at ☎ **702/875-4191.**

WHAT TO SEE & DO IN OLD NEVADA

Old Nevada (☎ 702/875-4191) is a re-creation of an 1880s frontier town, built on the site of a very old ranch. As tourist sites go, this is a good one; it's a bit cheesy, but knowingly, perhaps even deliberately so. It's terrific for kids up to about the age of 12 or so (before teenage cynicism kicks in) but not all that bad for adults fondly remembering similar places from their own childhood. Many go expecting a tourist trap, only to come away saying that it really was rather cute and charming.

Certainly, Old Nevada looks authentic, with rustic buildings entirely made of weathered wood. And the setting, right in front of beautiful mountains with layered red rock, couldn't be more perfect for a western. You can wander the town (it's only about a block long), taking peeps into well-replicated places of business, such as a blacksmith shop, a working mill, a saloon, and an old-fashioned general store (cum gift shop) and museum that has a potpourri of items from the Old West and Old Las Vegas; antique gaming tables and slot machines, typewriters, and a great display of old shoes including lace-up boots. There is also a rather limp wax museum; the less said about it, the better.

Country music is played in the saloon during the day, except when **stage melodramas** take place (at frequent intervals between 11:30am and 5pm). These are entirely tongue-in-cheek—the actors are goofy and know it, and the plot is hokey and fully intended to be that way. Somehow, it just heightens the fun factor. It's interactive with the audience who, in response to cue cards held up by the players, boos and hisses the mustache-twirling villain, sobs in sympathy with the distressed heroine, laughs, cheers, and applauds. It's hugely silly and hugely fun, provided you all play along. Kids love it, though younger ones might be scared by the occasional gunshot.

Following each melodrama a **western drama** is presented outside the saloon, involving a bank robbery, a shoot-out, and the trial of the bad guy. A judge, prosecuting attorney, and defense attorney are chosen from the audience, the remainder of whom act as jury. The action always culminates in a hanging. None of this is a particularly polished act, but the dialogue is quite funny and the whole thing performed with enthusiasm and affection.

Throughout the area, cowboys continually interact with visiting kids, who, on the weekends, are given badges so that they can join a posse hunting for bad guys. There are also ongoing **stunt shoot-outs** (maybe not the level found at, say, Universal studios) in this wild frontier town, and some rather unsavory characters occasionally languish in the town jail.

In the **Old Nevada Photograph Shoppe** you can have a tin-type picture taken in 1890s Wild West costume (they have a fairly large selection) with a 120-year-old camera. There are replicas of a turn-of-the-century church and stamp mill; the latter, which has original 1902 machinery, was used for crushing rocks to separate gold and silver from the earth. Movies (one about nearby Red Rock Canyon, one a silent film) are shown in the **Old Movie House** throughout the day from 10:30am to 5pm. You can tour the remains of the **old Comstock lode silver mine,** though there isn't much to see there. You can also shop for a variety of "western" souvenirs (though to us, that's when the tourist trap part kicks in). Eateries in Old Nevada are discussed below. There's plenty of parking; weekends and holidays, a free shuttle train takes visitors from the parking lot to the entrance.

Admission to Old Nevada is $6.50 for adults, $5.50 for seniors 62 and over, $4 for children 5 to 11, and free for children under 5. The park is open daily 11:30am to 5pm November to April, and until 6pm the rest of the year.

WHAT TO SEE & DO AT BONNIE SPRINGS RANCH

There are several things to do here free of charge, and it's right next door to Old Nevada. It's quite a pretty place, in a funky, western kind of way, and in season, everywhere there are tons of flowers, including honeysuckle and roses. The main attraction is the small **zoo** on the premises. Now, when we say "zoo," unfortunately we mean in addition to a petting zoo with the usual suspects (deer, sheep, goats, rabbits) and some unusual animals (pot-belly pigs and snooty, beautiful llamas) to caress and feed, there is also a mazelike enclosure of a series of wire mesh pens that contain a variety of livestock, some of whom should not be penned up (though they are well taken care of), including wolves and bobcats. Still, it's more than diverting for kids.

Less politically and ecologically distressing is the aviary, housing peacocks, Polish chickens, peachface and blackmask lovebirds, finches, parakeets, ravens, ducks, pheasants, and geese. Keep your eyes peeled for the peacocks roaming free; with luck, they will spread their tails for a photo-op. With greater luck, some of the angelic, rare white peacocks will do the same. It may be worth dropping by just in the hopes of spotting one in full fan-tailed glory. (And the ranch also sells peacocks, for $25. Now *there's* a souvenir!)

Riding stables offer guided trail rides into the mountain area on a continuous basis throughout the day (from 9am to 3:15pm spring to fall, until 5:45pm in summer). Children must be at least 6 years old to participate. Cost is $18 per hour.

And scenic 20-minute **stagecoach rides** offered weekends and holidays cost $5 for adults, $3 for children under 12.

WHERE TO STAY & DINE

Bonnie Springs Motel. 1 Gunfighter Lane, Old Nevada, NV 89004. ☎ **702/875-4400.** Fax 702/875-4424. 50 units. A/C TV TEL. Sun–Thurs $55–$65 double, Fri–Sat $65–$75 double; Sun–Thurs $100 fantasy suite, Fri–Sat $125 fantasy suite; Sun–Thurs $85 family suite,

Fri–Sat $95 family suite. An optional breakfast trail ride for motel guests is $20 per person; it departs at 9am every morning. Staying at the motel also entitles you to half-price tickets for Old Nevada. AE, MC, V.

This is really a hoot, a funky, friendly little place in the middle of nowhere—except that nowhere is a gorgeous setting. The motel is in two double-story buildings, and offers regular rooms, "western" rooms, "specialty theme" rooms, and kitchen suites. Where to begin? Well, the theme rooms aren't Madonna Inn level; actually, maybe they are, as long as you aren't expecting theme-intensive entries like the Caveman room. Here, the theme is expressed mostly through the use of fabrics, personally decorated by the owner, who did a pretty nice job. The "gay 1890s" room is done in black and pink, with a lace canopy over the bed, an old-fashioned commode, and liberal use of velvet. The politically incorrect American Indian room uses skins, feathers, and has a burl wood chair covered in bearskin. You get the idea. The "western" rooms have more burl wood furniture and electric log fireplaces that blow heat into the room. All special theme rooms have mirrors over the beds and big Jacuzzi tubs in the middle of the room (not in the bathrooms) and come with bottles of champagne (the empties of which you can see littering the road on your way out). All the rooms are quite large, though long and narrow, and have private balconies or patios, and mountain views. There are also large family suites with fully equipped kitchens, bedrooms, living rooms (with convertible sofas), and dressing areas; these are equipped with two phones and two TVs and are available for long-term rentals (many of the people who work at Old Nevada actually rent these as apartments). All rooms have coffeemakers, videos and video players are available for rental, and there is even a tiny train that takes you around the grounds and on a short tour of the desert.

Dining: The **Bonnie Springs Ranch Restaurant** has a lot of character and is a perfect family place. It's heavily rustic (stone floors, log beams, raw wooden chairs made from tree branches, lanterns light the room, a roaring fire goes in winter, plenty of dead animals adorn the walls). A bit touristy, but small-town touristy. The food is basic—steak, ribs, chicken, burgers, potato skins; pancakes and eggs for breakfast—greasy but good. There is a cozy bar attached to the restaurant, its walls covered with thousands of dollar bills with messages on them—a classic neighborhood bar, if it were actually in a neighborhood.

IN OLD NEVADA

The **Miner's Restaurant** is just a snack bar, but quite a large room that looks great thanks to more western motif accessories. Inexpensive fare (sandwiches, decent burgers, pizza, hot dogs) is served, along with fresh-baked desserts. There are tables out on the porch. In summer, you can also get beer and soft drinks in a similarly old-fashioned **Beer Parlor.**

5 A Close Encounter with Area 51

150 miles N of Las Vegas

Want to feel like an extra in the *X Files?* Want to celebrate the 50th anniversary of Roswell? Just want to get an idea of the kind of spots the government picks when it needs a place in which to do secret things? Take the drive from Vegas out to the "E.T. Highway," where folks have been spotting aliens years before it became fashionable. This is about a 150-mile trip one way, so it's probably not something to do on a whim, but even for nonalien buffs, it can be a long, strange—and oddly illuminating—trip indeed.

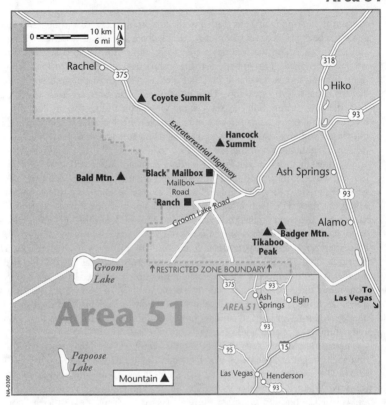

Area 51 is a secret military facility, containing a large air base that the government will not discuss. The site was selected in the mid-1950s for the testing of the U2 spy plane, and is supposedly currently the testing ground for "black budget" aircraft before their public acknowledgment. (Oh, heck, who are we—and they—trying to kid? *Of course* that's where they are testing high-tech gadgets.) But its real fame comes with the stories of aliens, whose bodies and ships were supposedly taken there when they "crashed" at Roswell.

Mind you, the only thing alien you are guaranteed to see is the landscape. Only fans of desert topography will find the scenery attractive. It's a most desolate area, but that's part of the inexplicable charm. There is absolutely a weird vibe in the air; *something* is going on out here. And one thing's for sure: If you need a place for covert, or at least private, activities, there isn't a better location for it. Alien bodies—shoot, you could hide an entire alien fleet.

But don't come looking for monuments, historical markers, or good shopping—with a few exceptions, there's a whole lot of nothing out there. You'd think the tourist possibilities would have led to more development; however, even in Vegas, despite the presence of plenty of alien merchandise in the gift shops and an entire Area 51–themed shopping area at the new airport expansion, there is not as much awareness as you might think. One waitress, when asked if she'd been there, responded, "Not since they remodeled."

All we know for sure is that you turn down one of the most well-maintained dirt roads you will ever encounter, drive a few miles, and come upon a fence with a sign that warns you from going any farther in the utmost of strict terms (though the language has been toned down from "use of deadly force authorized" to threats of fines and jail time). Along the way down that road, notice how there is absolutely no wildlife other than grasshoppers, that the Joshua trees suddenly turn to an enormous size and monstrous shape, and that the few cattle grazing around don't seem like any cattle you've seen before. Then notice those blasted-out craters in the earth, with the core sample holes in the center. When you realize you are looking at nuclear test sites, the desolation and mutations suddenly make sense. Wave hi at the guys in the military vehicles who are making damn sure you don't go through that gate, and hightail it out of there.

The other hot spot is the "town" of **Rachel** (really just a collection of trailer homes), where you can find the **Little A'Le'Inn** diner ("Earthlings Welcome") and gift shop, and in theory, chat with fellow E.T. spotters, who often gather at night to search the skies. The owners don't play along as much as one would like (though they do feel they were "called there for a special purpose"), but their gift shop makes up for it with fine humorous souvenirs (we liked the alien head–shaped guitar pick). Plus, they serve up satisfying diner food. You can also drop in at the **Area 51 Research Center** (just look for the big yellow trailer), which was opened after their founder (Glenn Campbell, who is largely responsible for Area 51's recent cultural icon status, and who wrote the definitive book, *Area 51 Viewer's Guide*) got kicked out of the Little A'Le'Inn. Their headquarters is now in Las Vegas and their store is only open during spring and summer but stocks all manner of Area 51 logo items and a number of related books.

There is no place to stay out here, so unless you want to camp (which could be fun; aliens might even show up better at night), plan this as a lengthy day trip. Be sure to fill your tank before you head out; there are few opportunities to do so once you leave Vegas. If doing this in the heat of the summer, bring water, for your car and yourself. Along the way, keep your eyes peeled for aliens (or weather balloons, jack rabbits, tumbleweeds, broken-down cars . . .) and should you spot one, don't forget to write us all about it.

By the way, word is starting to spread of a *really* mysterious, secret base even farther out in the desert. Just mention Area 58 and watch people go nuts.

To start, you take I-15 north to U.S. 93 north (paying close attention—it's an easy exit to miss; if you do, you can take State Route 168 at Moapa, and take that west back to U.S. 93), and then get off at the E.T. Highway, a 98-mile stretch of State Route 375. The town of Rachel is approximately 43 miles away; the "black mailbox" (it's now white) road, which leads you to Area 51, actually comes first, about 17 miles down the highway. (We strongly suggest going to Rachel first, to get your bearings, chat with knowledgeable locals and other alien spotters, and pick up some literature, including a good local map.) Turn left, and keep driving; any of the dirt roads that lead off of it will get you to the Area 51 fence and gates. Veer right at the fork in the road (not the ranch turnoff, which you come to first) if you want to go to the most commonly talked-about entrance, the one at Groom Lake (though you can't see the lake from where you are forced to stop.)

For more information, call the **Nevada Commission on Tourism** (☎ **800/ NEVADA-8**), and ask them to send you their "Pioneer Territory" brochure and a list of E.T. Highway services (gas stations, chambers of commerce, restaurants, and more). On the Internet, check out **www.ufomind.com** (this is a huge site maintained by the Area 51 Research folks, and contains countless links and all sorts of information) and **www.ufo-hyway.com**.

A Look Back at Vegas: No Tomorrow

by Thomas Lynch

Thomas Lynch is a poet and essayist and a
funeral director in Milford, Michigan. *The
Undertaking—Life Studies from the Dismal Trade*
won the Heartland Prize, the American Book
Award, and was a finalist for the National
Book Award.

Las Vegas is convention central. Orthodontists go there and archi-
tects. Computer geeks and gynecologists, TV preachers and town-
ship clerks, postal workers and pathologists. There's an abundance
of good hotel rooms, cheap eats, agreeable weather. Coming and
going is reasonably painless. There's golf and gambling and ogling
girls—showgirls of unspeakable beauty—and, of course, the mountains and the desert and the sky.

The National Funeral Directors Association advertised its 116th
Annual Convention and International Exposition there in the trade
press as "A Sure Bet." Debbie Reynolds was talking to the Spouse's
Luncheon. Neil Sedaka was singing at the Annual Banquet. There
was a golf outing, a new Web site, the installation of officers. I called
the brother and the brother-in-law and said, "Let's get our funeral
homes covered and go out to Vegas for the convention." Pat and
Mike agreed. All of us are funeral directors. All of us were due for a
break. Here's another coincidence: All of our wives are named Mary.
The Marys all agreed to come along. They'd heard about the showgirls and high-stakes tables and figured Pat and Mike and I would
need looking after. They'd heard about the great malls and the
moving statues and the magic shows.

My publisher paid my airfare and our room at the Hilton. "A
Sure Bet" is what they reckoned too. My book, *The Undertaking—
Life Studies from the Dismal Trade,* was being featured in the Marketplace Booth at the exhibit hall. The association would be selling
and I'd be signing as many copies as we could for a couple of days.
So there I sat, behind a stack of books, glad-handing and auto-
graphing, surrounded by caskets and hearses, cremation urns and
new computer software, flower stands and funeral flags and
embalming supplies. Some things about this enterprise never
change—the basic bias toward the horizontal, the general preference
for black and blue, the arcane lexicons of loss and wonder. And
some are changing every day. Like booksellers and pharmacists and
oncologists, many of the small firms are being overtaken by the large
consolidators and conglomerates. Custom gives way to convenience.
The old becomes old, then new again.

Five thousand undertakers made it to Vegas—the biggest turnout since the last time here, in '74—and 2,300 sales reps and suppliers. It was bigger than Orlando or Kansas City or Chicago, or next year in Boston.

Las Vegas seems perfect for the mortuary crowd—a metaphor for the vexed, late-century American soul which seems these days to run between extremes of fantasy and desolation. Vegas seems just such an oasis: a neon garden of earthly delights amid a moonscape of privations, abundance amid the cacti, indulgence surrounded by thirst and hunger.

Or maybe it's that we undertakers understand these games of chance—the way life is ever asking us to ante up, the way the wager's made before the deal is dealt or dice are tossed, before we pull the lever. Some people play for nickels and dimes, some for dollars, some for keeps. But whatever we play for, we win or lose according to these stakes. We cannot, once winning is certain or losing is sure, change our bet. We cannot play for dollars, then lose in dimes or win in cash when we wager match-sticks. It's much the same with love and grief. They share the same arithmetic and currency. We ante up our hearts in love, we pay our losses off in grief. Baptisms, marriages, funerals—this life's casinos—the games we play for keeps.

Oh we can play the odds, hedge our bets, count the cards, get a system. I think of Blaise Pascal, the 17th-century French mathematician who bet on heaven thus: Better to believe in a God who isn't than not to believe in a God who is. Figure the math of that, the odds. Pascal's Wager is what they called it. All of us play a version of this game.

I came downstairs in the middle of the night and lost two hundred bucks before it occurred to me that this is how they built this city—on folks like me, on what we'd be willing to lose. The next night my Mary won eight hundred on one pull of the lever on the slots. They paid her off in crisp C-notes. We laughed and smiled. She tipped the woman who sold her the tokens. She went shopping the next day for a pair of extravagant shoes and came home as they say with money in her pockets.

We undertakers understand winners and losers. Our daily lives are lessons in the way love hurts, grief heals, and life—always a game of chance—goes on. In Vegas we get to play the game as if there's no tomorrow. And after a long night of winning or losing, its good to have a desert close at hand into which we wander, like holy ones of old, to raise our songs of thanks or curse our luck to whatever God there is, or isn't.

Appendix: Useful Toll-Free Numbers & Web Sites

AIRLINES

Air Canada	800/776-3000	www.aircanada.ca
Alaska Airlines	800/426-0333	www.alaskaair.com
America West Airlines	800/235-9292	www.americawest.com
American Airlines	800/433-7300	www.americanair.com
British Airways	800/247-9297	www.british-airways.com
	0345/222-111	
	in Britain	
Canadian Airlines	800/426-7000	www.cdair.ca
International		
Carnival Airlines	800/824-7386	www.carnivalair.com
Continental Airlines	800/525-0280	www.flycontinental.com
Delta Air Lines	800/221-1212	www.delta-air.com
Hawaiian Airlines	800/367-5320	www.hawaiianair.com
Kiwi International	800/538-5494	www.jetkiwi.com
Air Lines		
Midway Airlines	800/446-4392	
Northwest Airlines	800/225-2525	www.nwa.com
Southwest Airlines	800/435-9792	iflyswa.com
Tower Air	800/34-TOWER	www.towerair.com
	(800/348-6937)	
	outside New York	
	718/553-8500	
	in New York	
Trans World Airlines	800/221-2000	www.twa.com
(TWA)		
United Airlines	800/241-6522	www.ual.com
USAirways	800/428-4322	www.usair.com
Virgin Atlantic	800/862-8621	www.fly.virgin.com
Airways	in Continental U.S.	
	0293/747-747	
	in Britain	

CAR-RENTAL AGENCIES

Advantage	800/777-5500	www.arac.com
Alamo	800/327-9633	www.goalamo.com
Auto Europe	800/223-5555	www.autoeurope.com
Avis	800/331-1212	www.avis.com
	in the continental U.S.	
	800/TRY-AVIS	
	in Canada	

Budget	800/527-0700	www.budgetrentacar.com
Dollar	800/800-4000	www.dollarcar.com
Enterprise	800/325-8007	www.pickenterprise.com
Hertz	800/654-3131	www.hertz.com
Kemwel Holiday Auto	800/678-0678	www.kemwel.com
National	800/CAR-RENT	www.nationalcar.com
Payless	800/PAYLESS	www.paylesscar.com
Rent-A-Wreck	800/535-1391	rent-a-wreck.com
Thrifty	800/367-2277	www.thrifty.com
Value	800/327-2501	www.go-value.com

MAJOR HOTEL & MOTEL CHAINS

Best Western International	800/528-1234	www.bestwestern.com
Clarion Hotels	800/CLARION	www.hotelchoice.com/cgi-bin/ res/webres?clarion.html
Comfort Inns	800/228-5150	www.hotelchoice.com/cgi-bin/ res/webres?comfort.html
Courtyard by Marriott	800/321-2211	www.courtyard.com
Days Inn	800/325-2525	www.daysinn.com
Doubletree Hotels	800/222-TREE	www.doubletreehotels.com
Econo Lodges	800/55-ECONO	www.hotelchoice.com/cgi-bin/ res/webres?econo.html
Fairfield Inn by Marriott	800/228-2800	www.fairfieldinn.com
Hampton Inn	800/HAMPTON	www.hampton-inn.com
Hilton Hotels	800/HILTONS	www.hilton.com
Holiday Inn	800/HOLIDAY	www.holiday-inn.com
Howard Johnson	800/654-2000	www.hojo.com/hojo.html
Hyatt Hotels & Resorts	800/228-9000	www.hyatt.com
ITT Sheraton	800/325-3535	www.sheraton.com
La Quinta Motor Inns	800/531-5900	www.laquinta.com
Marriott Hotels	800/228-9290	www.marriott.com
Motel 6	800/4-MOTEL6 (800/466-8536)	
Quality Inns	800/228-5151	www.hotelchoice.com/cgi-bin/ res/webres?quality.html
Radisson Hotels International	800/333-3333	www.radisson.com
Ramada Inns	800/2-RAMADA	www.ramada.com
Red Carpet Inns	800/251-1962	
Red Lion Hotels & Inns	800/547-8010	www.travelweb.com
Red Roof Inns	800/843-7663	www.redroof.com
Residence Inn by Marriott	800/331-3131	www.residenceinn.com
Rodeway Inns	800/228-2000	www.hotelchoice.com/cgi-bin/ res/webres?rodeway.html
Super 8 Motels	800/800-8000	www.super8motels.com
Travelodge	800/255-3050	
Vagabond Hotels	800/255-3050	www.vagabondinns.com
Wyndham Hotels and Resorts	800/822-4200 in Continental U.S. and Canada	www.wyndham.com

Index

See also separate Accommodations, Restaurants and Buffets indexes below.
Page numbers in italics refer to maps.

FROMMER'S® COMPLETE TRAVEL GUIDES
(Comprehensive guides with selections in all price ranges—from deluxe to budget)

Alaska
Amsterdam
Arizona
Atlanta
Australia
Austria
Bahamas
Barcelona, Madrid & Seville
Belgium, Holland &
  Luxembourg
Bermuda
Boston
Budapest & the Best of
  Hungary
California
Canada
Cancún, Cozumel & the
  Yucatán
Cape Cod, Nantucket &
  Martha's Vineyard
Caribbean
Caribbean Cruises &
  Ports of Call
Caribbean Ports of Call
Carolinas & Georgia
Chicago
China
Colorado
Costa Rica
Denver, Boulder &
  Colorado Springs
England
Europe
Florida

France
Germany
Greece
Hawaii
Hong Kong
Honolulu, Waikiki & Oahu
Ireland
Israel
Italy
Jamaica & Barbados
Japan
Las Vegas
London
Los Angeles
Maryland & Delaware
Maui
Mexico
Miami & the Keys
Montana & Wyoming
Montréal & Québec City
Munich & the Bavarian Alps
Nashville & Memphis
Nepal
New England
New Mexico
New Orleans
New York City
Nova Scotia, New
  Brunswick &
  Prince Edward Island
Oregon
Paris
Philadelphia & the Amish
  Country

Portugal
Prague & the Best of the
  Czech Republic
Provence & the Riviera
Puerto Rico
Rome
San Antonio & Austin
San Diego
San Francisco
Santa Fe, Taos &
  Albuquerque
Scandinavia
Scotland
Seattle & Portland
Singapore & Malaysia
South Pacific
Spain
Switzerland
Thailand
Tokyo
Toronto
Tuscany & Umbria
USA
Utah
Vancouver & Victoria
Vermont, New Hampshire &
  Maine
Vienna & the Danube Valley
Virgin Islands
Virginia
Walt Disney World &
  Orlando
Washington, D.C.
Washington State

FROMMER'S® DOLLAR-A-DAY GUIDES
(The ultimate guides to comfortable low-cost travel)

Australia from $50 a Day
California from $60 a Day
Caribbean from $60 a Day
England from $60 a Day
Europe from $50 a Day
Florida from $60 a Day
Greece from $50 a Day
Hawaii from $60 a Day
Ireland from $50 a Day

Israel from $45 a Day
Italy from $50 a Day
London from $70 a Day
New York from $75 a Day
New Zealand from $50 a Day
Paris from $70 a Day
San Francisco from $60 a Day
Washington, D.C., from
  $60 a Day

FROMMER'S® MEMORABLE WALKS

Chicago
London

New York
Paris

San Francisco

FROMMER'S® PORTABLE GUIDES

Acapulco, Ixtapa/
  Zihuatanejo
Bahamas
California Wine
  Country
Charleston & Savannah
Chicago

Dublin
Las Vegas
London
Maine Coast
New Orleans
New York City
Paris

Puerto Vallarta, Manzanillo
  & Guadalajara
San Francisco
Sydney
Tampa Bay & St. Petersburg
Venice
Washington, D.C.

FROMMER'S® NATIONAL PARK GUIDES

Grand Canyon
National Parks of the American West
Yellowstone & Grand Teton

Yosemite & Sequoia/
  Kings Canyon
Zion & Bryce Canyon

THE COMPLETE IDIOT'S TRAVEL GUIDES
(The ultimate user-friendly trip planners)

Cruise Vacations
Planning Your Trip to Europe
Hawaii

Las Vegas
Mexico's Beach Resorts
New Orleans

New York City
San Francisco
Walt Disney World

SPECIAL-INTEREST TITLES

The Civil War Trust's Official Guide to
  the Civil War Discovery Trail
Frommer's Caribbean Hideaways
Israel Past & Present
New York City with Kids
New York Times Weekends
Outside Magazine's Adventure Guide
  to New England
Outside Magazine's Adventure Guide
  to Northern California

Outside Magazine's Adventure Guide
  to the Pacific Northwest
Outside Magazine's Guide to Family Vacations
Places Rated Almanac
Retirement Places Rated
Washington, D.C., with Kids
Wonderful Weekends from Boston
Wonderful Weekends from New York City
Wonderful Weekends from San Francisco
Wonderful Weekends from Los Angeles

THE UNOFFICIAL GUIDES®
(Get the unbiased truth from these candid, value-conscious guides)

Atlanta
Branson, Missouri
Chicago
Cruises
Disneyland

Florida with Kids
The Great Smoky
  & Blue Ridge
  Mountains
Las Vegas

Miami & the Keys
Mini-Mickey
New Orleans
New York City
San Francisco

Skiing in the West
Walt Disney World
Walt Disney World
  Companion
Washington, D.C.

FROMMER'S® IRREVERENT GUIDES
(Wickedly honest guides for sophisticated travelers)

Amsterdam
Boston
Chicago

London
Manhattan

New Orleans
Paris

San Francisco
Walt Disney World
Washington, D.C.

FROMMER'S® DRIVING TOURS

America
Britain
California

Florida
France
Germany

Ireland
Italy
New England

Scotland
Spain
Western Europe

WHEREVER
YOU TRAVEL,
*H*ELP IS NEVER
FAR AWAY.

From planning your trip to

providing travel assistance along

the way, American Express®

Travel Service Offices are always

there to help you do more.

For the office nearest you in Las Vegas, call
1-800-AXP-3429.

do more

www.americanexpress.com/travel